# AMERICANA NORVEGICA

## I

PUBLICATIONS OF
## THE AMERICAN INSTITUTE
UNIVERSITY OF OSLO

IN CO-OPERATION WITH THE
## DEPARTMENT OF AMERICAN CIVILIZATION
GRADUATE SCHOOL OF ARTS AND SCIENCES
UNIVERSITY OF PENNSYLVANIA

# AMERICANA
# NORVEGICA

*Norwegian Contributions
to American Studies*

VOL. I

EDITORS:

SIGMUND SKARD
OSLO

HENRY H. WASSER
NEW YORK

UNIVERSITY OF PENNSYLVANIA PRESS
PHILADELPHIA, PENNSYLVANIA
1966

Published in Great Britain, India, and Pakistan
by the Oxford University Press
London, Bombay, and Karachi

OSLO: GYLDENDAL NORSK FORLAG

Manufactured in Norway


This publication was in part subsidized by
Norges Almenvitenskapelige Forskningsråd

A.s John Griegs Boktrykkeri, Bergen, Norway

*This volume*
*is gratefully dedicated to*

ERLING D. NAESS,
*Donor of the American Institute,*
*University of Oslo*

# PREFACE

The American Institute of the University of Oslo hereby presents among its *Publications* the first of a series of volumes to be issued under the title *Americana Norvegica*.

The volumes will appear at irregular intervals, and contain shorter contributions to American Studies. The series will welcome articles discussing any subject and applying any method of research within the field of American civilization. Particular attention will be paid to the history of Norwegian-American interrelations.

The Editors of the collection are indebted in various ways to a number of scholars who have assisted in the preparation and publication of the volume. Special mention should be made of Professors L. Åhnebrink (Uppsala), Roger Asselineau (the Sorbonne), Charles Boewe (US Educational Foundation, Karachi), H. H. Clark (Wisconsin), Merle Curti (Wisconsin), Curtis Dahl (Wheaton College), W. B. Dillingham (Emory), H. Galinsky (Mainz), Dietrich Gerhard (Göttingen and Washington University, St. Louis), A. N. J. den Hollander (Amsterdam), H. M. Jones (Harvard), J. J. Kwiat (Minnesota), Leo Marx (Amherst), R. H. Pearce (California, San Diego), Norman Holmes Pearson (Yale), Ingrid Semmingsen (Oslo), David E. Smith (Indiana), Henry Nash Smith (California, Berkeley), Robert E. Spiller (Pennsylvania), Sverre Steen (Oslo), Allen Tate (Minnesota), G. R. Taylor (Amherst), J. W. Ward (Amherst) and Dennis S. R. Welland (Manchester).

Mrs. Ida L. Lange has been extremely helpful in preparing the manuscripts for print. The authors are themselves responsible for translations of Norwegian quotations in the text.

In typography the volume largely adheres to the rules laid down in the *MLA Style Sheet*. In some details of punctuation, however, the authors have been allowed to follow their personal preference.

The Editors and the American Institute express their special gratitude to Mr. Erling D. Naess (New York), to whom the volume is dedicated, and whose generosity made the publication possible.

Oslo and New York, December 1965.

SIGMUND SKARD          HENRY H. WASSER

# TABLE OF CONTENTS

# THE AMERICAN STUDIES MOVEMENT
## PROBLEMS AND PROSPECTS

### By Sigmund Skard

Systematic studies of America have a relatively brief history, covering less than two hundred years. But on both sides of the Atlantic
activity in the field has been immense. And in the literature with some
scholarly pretensions there was almost from the beginning a discernible
effort to go beyond specialized research and build up a connected,
total picture of America and its civilization, emphasizing those fields
which centrally constitute a national culture. In our time such tendencies have received an organized international stimulus through
the American Studies movement.

In this article an attempt is made to give an outline of this movement against its historical background. No single reader could, of
course, have an inclusive knowledge of the literature involved. Many
details still await further investigation, and the present day problems
are highly controversial. Of necessity the present sketch is therefore
preliminary and unpretending.[1]

American Studies did not primarily originate at the academic institutions of learning. They formed a part of the Enlightenment, which
all over Europe had its following among literate readers regardless of
profession. The authors of the early books about the New World,
"philosophers", "ideologists" and men of letters, often displayed a
minimum of pedantic learning. But in their very approach there were
trends that pointed toward a more scholarly treatment of the subject.

The "enlightened" writers lovingly described the society of the
Indians and of the British settlers, to end up with the glory of the
American Republic. And they often wrote with journalistic looseness,
in an almost mythological style. But they were imbued with a deep

sense of the human relevance of the New World and its civilization, — what Crèvecoeur called its "close affinity with our present time". They had a feeling of the uniqueness of the American phenomenon, an historical process that could be studied from its very beginnings in the spirit of Montesquieu and Herder against its background of landscape and climate. And at the same time they felt that it could only be understood in the light of general principles. Distance favored generalization, and so did the lack of bothersome knowledge of details.

More serious and systematic studies of a similar scope were soon to follow. But America itself had little to offer in this respect, at least until the Civil War. Academic education was still quite elementary in the young nation; as late as 1850 there were only eight graduate students in all of the United States. History was not taught at the universities; as late as 1880 there were only eleven professors in the subject. The many home-produced works on the country and its conditions past and present were often sustained by a fervent patriotism. But mostly they were pedestrian collections of facts, or lofty epics, with little grasp of the motive forces in American life.

For more than a century progress toward more penetrating methods was due to Europeans, who gradually created real scholarship in the spirit of Enlightenment. An early and impressive effort was the large work of the Italian Filippo Mazzei (1788), a careful critical survey of many aspects of American culture. And the method was brought into system at the reorganized German universities, in the new inclusive discipline of "Statistics", meaning at that time a combination of Modern History, Geography and Political Science, where detailed research was sometimes combined with a trend toward synthesis, "an intuitive approach, bordering on the mystical".[2] American "Statistics" spread to many European universities, and found its classical expression in the German Christoph Ebeling's immense description of North America, left unfinished after the publication of seven volumes in 1816.

These scholars were much aware of the special character of their subject. But it never occurred to them that the study of America needed any method peculiar to the subject or demanded a place of its own within the hierarchy of learning. Nor did the historians and economists who, at many European universities in the 1840's and 1850's, took up more thorough teaching and research in the field. Notwithstanding, the broad approach remained. It showed in the flood of general works on the United States, from bodiless fantasies to more serious syntheses, and in the early study of the American impact in other parts of the world. This work reached a new climax in the outstanding contribution to American Studies in the first half of the century, Alexis de Tocqueville's *De la démocratie en Amérique* (1835—1840), the most influential work ever written on America by a European. Tocqueville's leading idea was political, as expressed in the title of his book. But his analysis turned out to be a survey of general trends in the growth of American life, seen as a part of world developments.

However, such tendencies were not to dominate the field in the second half of the 19th century and down to the First World War.

This was the period when American Studies began to gain recognition as an academic subject on both sides of the ocean. The immense expansion of the United States in all fields of life after the Civil War and the emergence of its industrialized civilization as a world power created a demand for American Studies in a more systematic form. The new interest was apparent within the traditional disciplines, in virgin fields like American Literature, and in new branches of learning such as Comparative Law, Comparative Economics, Political and Social Sciences which tried to cope with a new and more complicated type of civilization. The first European chair of an American subject existed for a while in the 1870's at the University of Strasbourg, the first American Institute was established in Berlin in 1910. Academic teaching gradually began to develop on a larger scale.

What characterized these new studies, however, was no longer a trend toward synthesis, but an increasing specialization. Both in and outside of the universities all fields of research now tended to be broken down into sharply delineated subjects; and the work was split up among departments and institutes that were largely isolated from each other. Research itself often became myopic and narrow, dominated by a science-inspired faith in the isolated "fact" and the irreproachable "proof", with a deep suspicion of generalization.

This attitude had wide origins. But it developed with special rigor in the German universities, which now set the standards of scholarship in Europe, and perhaps even more in the United States. Everywhere this approach gave a tremendous impetus to American Studies also, placing them on a solid basis of scholarship. But the trend had its drawbacks as well. In some countries research was historical and antiquarian to the point of pushing American material into the background as too modern or too derivative: "America has no language and no history of its own". There was little willingness to see American civilization as an entity, that had its national background and had to be studied from many angles. When in 1866 a radical Liverpool merchant offered to endow the University of Cambridge in England with a readership in "the History, Literature, and Institutions of the United States", the University Senate turned the offer down with a considerable show of irritation, not only because of the generally suspicious character of the subject, but certainly also because of the vague and diffuse definition of it.[3]

The development of more independent research in the American field had to begin in the form of a reaction against such tendencies. But here the United States itself was not yet leading the way. Still the German tradition was solidly entrenched in American universities and specialization was the catchword of the day. There were early indications of a different attitude, isolated efforts to cross the traditional border lines between established subjects. A wider concept of American History appeared even before the First World War, in works by Frederick Jackson Turner, J. B. Mc Master, James H. Robinson, Carl Becker and Charles A. Beard. Thorstein Veblen fearlessly combined Economics and Social Psychology, William James sweepingly analyzed the American religious mind, John Dewey saw education in the context of American society. In the 1880's and 1890's Moses Coit Tyler held a chair of "American History and Literature" at Cornell; at Harvard around 1900 Barrett Wendell under the influence of Hippolyte Taine introduced a parallel study of the Language, Literature and History of any nation, including America. But this was not typical. Most American universities paid no attention to American Literature at all, and the old departments were citadels of independence. Even within the new Social Sciences in America each speciality long tended to isolate itself rigorously from the neighboring disciplines.

Thus it was in Europe that the revolt against excessive specialization gained its first momentum. Great Britain remained a stronghold of conservatism. "Modern" subjects were regarded with suspicion at the universities, James Bryce's magnificent synthesis of the American Commonwealth (1888) was an isolated phenomenon. But in France there were different tendencies, as witnessed for instance by the broad development of French Sociology, and in the Humanities by the foundation of *Revue de synthèse historique* (1900). This expansion also made itself felt in other fields. This period saw the emergence of the typically French *explication de texte*, which takes for granted a certain knowledge of the social and historical background of the literary document. For decades France came to occupy a leading position in the European study of American Literature, and without any philosophical ado the subject of "Littérature et Civilisation Américaines" began penetrating into schools, universities and research.

In contemporary Germany similar ideas were brought into system. The 1880's saw the rise of a synthetic and often speculative *Kulturkunde*, in protest against the atomistic approach of the old historians. The new school emphasized the homogeneous character of social groups and national civilizations, as the classical philologists had always done in *their* field. New studies of periods like the Middle Ages and the Renaissance, and of modern cultures, showed the strength of a more global approach. One German university institute founded in 1912 aimed at an investigation of American religion as part of the entire social, economic, and intellectual life of the United States. At the same time Karl Lamprecht's interdepartmental Institute of World Civilization proclaimed as a part of its program to see America as well as all other nations from the aspects of social mass movements and the morphology of cultures.

Still, these American Studies rarely regarded themselves as a separate discipline. But the First World War brought their Declaration of Independence. The United States emerged from the conflict as a leading power, and the demonstration of its military and economic might was soon equalled in other fields. In all the great nations a serious study of this new factor in world development appeared as "an urgent cultural need". New tendencies in Science and Philosophy softened the rigidity of the traditional systems of thought and strengthened the trend toward synthesis, often in connection with more general efforts to reorganize European life and education. From these stimuli there came a new program of American Studies simultaneously in France and Germany. The originators were educated in the United States, and they may have found some support in similar American trends, particularly at Harvard. But their inspiration seems largely to have been European.

In 1918 Charles Cestre was appointed by the Sorbonne to the first permanent European chair of American "Literature and Civilization", and he presented the program of an independent and integrated discipline. Before anybody else, to my knowledge, he launched the principle that manysidedness should be the distinctive mark of American Studies. After so many scattered efforts, in which American material

had only been accessory to other fields, the time had come for con-
centric investigations, guided by the methods of History, Psychology,
and the Social Sciences, and directed toward American Civilization
as a living whole. "The real thing we have to do, is to study each
single aspect, static or dynamic, of American life as a function of the
entire American Civilization".[4] Cestre's appointment was soon followed
by the establishment of more chairs of "American Literature and
Civilization" in French universities and a full chair of American Civilization at the Collège de France.

The French approach was a practical one; the Germans furnished
the movement with a theoretical superstructure. The new trends were
closely tied to scholarly innovations of the 1920's that made themselves
felt with particular strength in post-war Germany: typology and
structuralism, *Gestalt* psychology and *Geistesgeschichte*, and comparative
research of many kinds, all of them opening up new possibilities for
an inclusive interpretation of "the soul of a nation". And there were
impulses of a more pragmatic nature. The Germans felt they had lost
the World War because of their failure to understand their adversaries.
There was a political demand for a new *Auslandkunde*, which found its
models in books such as Wilhelm Dibelius' sweeping analysis of
British, and E. R. Curtius' and A. Bergstraesser's synthesis of French
civilization (1923 and 1930). American Studies took their place within
this context.

In a manifesto from 1921 Friedrich Schönemann formulated the
program of what he called *Amerikakunde*. The study of America was
not to be a remote corner of Anglistics any longer, but a branch of
a new, integrated and interdisciplinary study of civilization based on
History, Literature and Economics. Similar views were expressed six
years later by the German-American Professor F.-K. Krüger. He
heralded "the methodical sociological integration of Psychology,
History, Political Science, Economics, Geography, etc., actually of all
fields of research, as applied particularly to the USA".[5] The new
approach aroused keen interest. Pedagogical reforms in Weimar
Germany gave the American subject considerable leeway in the schools.
Several universities moved in the same direction, and so did research.
Schönemann's own great work on the United States (1932) parallelled
André Siegfried's synthesis in France (1927), and there were other
similar contributions of importance.

This new departure was not generally accepted, however. The revolutionary subject was met with severe criticism on the part of the

established disciplines ("all *Kulturkunde*, whether German or foreign, runs the risk of dilettantism"). In the widespread German debate of the 1920's scepticism prevailed. What led the movement to catastrophe, however, was not this cold shoulder on the part of "die alten Herren", but the support that from 1933 on was given to the new subject by the Nazi government. The "brown shirt" ideologists picked up the synthetic ideas of the Weimar period and twisted them according to their own needs. Hitler's *Kulturpolitik* with its grotesque generalizations about races and nations, not least about the Americans, was closely tied to the ideas of the new *Auslandkunde*.

German "Americanistics" were developed at a hectic pace during the brief period of Nazi domination. But teaching and research were largely propagandistic, using a "cross faculty" and "global" interpretation in the service of a so-called "National Biology". The very man who was the founder of the new discipline became a fervent Nazi. In one of the nations of their origin "integrated" American Studies thus became thoroughly discredited, and with the collapse of Nazi Germany in 1945 shared the downfall of the Reich itself.

A no more encouraging parallel to this development appeared in the Soviet Union and its satellite states. Under the communist regime no separate American discipline could emerge. It could only form a part of the tightly coherent study of the entire capitalist world, an activity which by definition is all-comprehensive and in all fields of life and society exemplifies the tenets of Marx and Engels. But within this framework the importance of America made such studies a matter of great concern. A picture of the USA, "integrated" in the communist sense, became an obligatory part of knowledge in all the states within the Soviet orbit. In other nations this example could only further emphasize the virtue of caution toward all kinds of rash generalization.

Thus, while these dramatic European experiments in many ways preceded the American growth, their fruits were partly bitter. It was the more gradual and natural developments on America's own soil which, in the long run, were to lead to more lasting gains.

There were a number of factors which, in the United States after the First World War, contributed to this new beginning. In many ways conditions in America and Europe were parallel, but the general position of the United States was different. In swift succession the Americans experienced the triumph in the First World War, the distress and disillusionment in the 1920's, the new national coalesence in the 1930's and the Second World War and its aftermath, when the country suddenly saw itself thrown into the position of international leadership. And these events were accompanied by a transformation of American society that was no less radical and left no field of national life untouched.

This extraordinary experience was also bound to exert its impact on education and scholarship. In a challenging and dangerous world many Americans felt an urge to emphasize the unity of the nation, to redefine its heritage and give a sense of direction to its culture past and present. A new national pride craved for the recognition of indigenous American values, no longer as a mere "extension of Europe", but as an original contribution, and to have them understood at home and abroad, as American literature was now suddenly gaining world renown. These ideas were eagerly adopted by the reform movement for a new synthesis of knowledge, pointing toward a "General Education" that would give the teaching process more meaning, bridge the gap between campus and society, and recreate a feeling of national and social fellowship. The many international contacts within a rapidly shrinking world stressed similar demands.

All these factors gave new strength to the criticism of established teaching and research in the United States that had been growing in the younger generation of American scholars: the traditional emphasis on foreign and past civilizations, particularly British, at the expense of America itself; the academic departmentalism with its formal narrowness; the worship of facts and details; and the fear of large views and value judgments. The time-honored approach to scholarship seemed sadly inadequate in the face of present-day American Civilization with its dynamism and dimensions and its immense range, from broad folksiness to the complexity of modern design, a phenomenon not to be exhausted by a mere enumeration of its parts.

The American Studies movement arose as a natural consequence of this situation. It began as a modest attempt to organize a cross-departmental study of American civilization. Only one such program antedates the First World War. The 1920's added not more than two programs; the forces were still largely engrossed in gaining recognition for the study of American Literature within the traditional framework. The social radicalism of the 1930's increased the awareness of the general powers of society. Ten more programs were organized, among them the postgraduate ones at Yale and Harvard. But only after 1945 did the subject begin to claim recognition as a more or less separate entity.

The intellectual organ of the movement, the *American Quarterly*, was founded in 1949, the American Studies Association in 1951. The latter now has about twenty regional chapters. Research grew impressively; in Literature the tendency toward new synthesis was symbolized by the great joint effort of the *Literary History of the United States* (1950). Since 1954 the results of this scholarly activity have been listed year by year in a bibliography published in the *American Quarterly*.

In the course of a few decades American Studies in America have thus been offered an unusual opportunity of testing their principles in practice. And the opportunity has been used with a boldness of approach and a leeway in practical organization which is rarely equalled in Europe. Everything still seems to be possible within American Studies in the United States. It is typical that hardly two of the established programs are identical.

At the same time the special philosophy championed by the movement is still far from being accepted as a matter of course in its homeland. On the contrary, it remains quite controversial. The American Studies are still fighting a crusade, with everything which that situation implies. The movement has the faith and zeal that have often characterized great reforms in human history. At the same time it is still uncertain of itself, and like some other sects shows a considerable range of opinion. Its programmatic statements may be warmly applauded by some, repudiated with irritation by others, even within the movement itself. This uncertainty is also noticeable when it comes to its basic aims. At times they show an ambiguity that is understandable, but has not always been helpful to objective judgment.

The program was formulated with pragmatic simplicity by the first theorist of the movement, Tremaine McDowell, in his book *American Studies* (1948): "The discipline of American Studies is the intellectual process whereby a student assimilates the complicated and often contradictory details of American civilization which he meets in his courses in social science, history, literature, philosophy, and the fine arts. And it is the intellectual process whereby he fashions out of them a picture of these United States. In so doing he reduces diversity to some degree of unity".

About the operational details McDowell contented himself with saying that the work "must strike a balance between all the relevant humanities and all the relevant social sciences". He was no less terse and uncomplicated about the practical future of organized American Studies. They should regard themselves only as a supplement to the traditional university departments, and attract the relatively few students who showed special interest in "the pattern of American life." The study itself was to remain loose and informal: it was "not an academic discipline" in the traditional sense. "When and if American Studies become departmentalized, they will have lost one of the major reasons for their existence".[6]

As the movement pushed ahead, however, as it deepened its criticism of the tradition of learning and instead pointed optimistically to its own goals of teaching and research, it was unavoidable that the school should define its aims and means with more edge and precision, as did its counterparts in Europe. The movement "needed a rationale", "meanings and methods of its own", adapted to its "single and legitimate field".[7] And these definitions pointed toward more ambitious goals. Many scholars within the movement felt that in order to exist and make a place for itself in the academic struggle for life the American Studies had to assert their scholarly independence by becoming nothing but "a single discipline to which scholars may devote their researches and students their work toward higher degrees". And the reformers did not only think of practical arrangements. They felt that the new subject also needed "a single comprehensive method"; the movement would "remain vulnerable" as long as no dominant method was found. Behind this urge was often the conviction, that in spite of its diversity American Civilization is more than a congeries of separate facts, and that its unique character also calls for special and new means of investigation.[8]

Even within the movement itself the real import of such programs, particularly of the words "discipline" and "method", was from the very beginning a matter for dispute. But the general direction of its work was accepted without discussion. The aim of American Studies was *integration*, that is: the American "area", "culture" or "civilization" should be seen "as a whole rather than from the viewpoint of a single discipline".[9] The organic interplay of its parts should be studied by a cooperation of faculties, subjects and departments across their traditional border lines.

The great variety within the movement is due to the many possible starting points of this co-operation, and the diversified forms it has taken. Originally, the expansion had its center in one single subject, — "one discipline and others", as the saying went.[10] Most frequently there was a rapprochement between History and Literature, the two fields which still represent by far the most common combination. But gradually new disciplines and approaches came to the fore with their special aims and terminologies, and claimed equal rights.

There was an early impact from the History of Ideas, ranging from Vernon L. Parrington and A. O. Lovejoy to Ralph H. Gabriel, Perry Miller and Merle Curti. An increasing part was played by the History of Science and Technology, which claimed to be "at the center" of any synthesis of the new civilization.[11]

From the 1930's onward there was a parallel and growing influence from various forms of structuralist thinking within many branches of learning, such as Linguistics, Esthetics, Philosophy and a number of psychological schools, individual and social. But the strongest impulse came from the behavioral sciences: Sociology, Cultural Anthropology, and Folklore, which saw culture (covert and overt) as a "totality of institutions, adjustments, and values binding a distinctive social group together".[12] The new school tried to study such groups in their internal structures, functional relationships, and media of communication, and applied the method undauntedly to entire civilizations, past and present, primitive and sophisticated, including that of the United States.

The most energetic effort to bring the methods of these divergent fields nearer to each other had its starting point in Literature, which from the very beginning was the dominant field of study within the movement. Basic problems came into focus as literary research and criticism developed in the United States in the interwar and postwar years, within and outside of the American Studies movement. Those tendencies toward scholarly isolation which the movement saw as its main adversary, were not strong in the established disciplines only. They were equally rampant within that New Criticism which reached its maturity in the 1940's, and in the 1950's left its mark on practically all university departments of English and American Literature in the United States. The New Critics certainly showed the influence of structural thinking. But by principle they were ahistorical, and sometimes minimized all connection between creative writing and its social and national milieu. At the opposite extreme the social sciences certainly were "synthetical" enough, with no fear of generalization. But they were so only on the basis of a strictly quantitative method. They showed a similar lack of historical perspective. They saw imaginative writing as a mass phenomenon, and completely disregarded form and value.

To the American Studies movement it became a primary concern to bridge the gap between these two dominant schools. The study of the relation between works of art and their cultural background could even be called "one of the distinctive fields" of the movement. The most promising subject of research was felt to be symbol and image, metaphor and myth, and the entire "figurative language of the culture".[13] Because of the "fusion of concept and emotion" in these phenomena, and their roots simultaneously in individual and social psychology, they were regarded as a common ground of the Humanities and the Social Sciences, where covert and overt tendencies of civilization could be brought into focus and related to each other.

Work along such lines created much enthusiasm and brought important results, but also stirred up a good deal of resistance, which is discussed in the following. Since the American Studies movement is heterogeneous, criticism has sometimes been directed against statements or attitudes that may be of dubious relevance to the movement as a whole. Some of the negative observations have been rejected as unfounded suspicions. Nevertheless, the objections may have their value. They point to real or potential dangers. And they reflect ideas and attitudes within that important sector of American Studies that is *not* part of the movement proper.

Some of this resistance is connected with general contrasts in American intellectual life. In many American universities and colleges, not least in the English Departments, there is still a strong trend of cultural conservatism, which regards the "English and New English" tradition as the core of American development and looks at the motley, incoherent and "pluralistic" civilization of modern USA with aversion and concern. This attitude, while fully understandable, is not always conducive to a fair evaluation of the American Studies movement and its aims. But there is also a more balanced criticism which cannot just be brushed aside as biassed.

The strength of this resistance can partly by measured by the practical results of the new tendencies. Within American scholarly life as a whole American Studies in the restricted sense still play a relatively minor part. The USA now has almost 1900 institutions of higher education, and the overwhelming majority of them teach some field or other of American Civilization. But as late as 1963 only about 120 institutions had "integrated" arrangements for American Studies. And most of those belonged to programs of quite elementary education. Among the more than 170 American universities of top rank little more than twenty had doctoral programs of the new type; at some of the large institutions graduate American Studies are available, but there is no demand for them.[14] Compared to the space granted, for instance, British, French, German, Russian, or even some Oriental studies, the figures are modest.

This situation limits the actual work in many ways. American Studies are highly diversified in their form. But at the graduate level, at least, studies are normally built up as an organized co-operation between various disciplines, headed by committees or small coordinating departments. This means that the specific American Studies programs often represent an additional burden on the staffs. Teaching has to be done largely by professors in traditional departments; and particularly at small institutions, these teachers often have enough to do with their normal duties. They are not always eager to participate in the re-thinking that is essential to any inter-departmental activity, and most of them are not educated for it. This fact helps explain why, so far, relatively few American universities have established graduate departments in American Studies proper, and mostly only the large schools have done so.

The position of the subject also affects recruitment. As yet, relatively few academic teaching posts are opened to specialized "Americanists", and the broad background of their education is not always recognized by appointment to positions in the traditional specialized subjects which still predominate in the departments. As a consequence, there are complaints that American Studies do not always attract the more ambitious type of student, exception being made for the relatively few who take a special interest in the field and enter it in an idealistic spirit.

Behind this cautious attitude on the part of the universities there are a number of basic reservations.

Some scholars and institutions are wary lest an intensive concentration on problems within the relatively brief period of American development may create a provincial narrowness, a "massive overestimation" of American cultural contributions on the part of the teachers, and parochialism on the part of the students: they simply don't know the European roots of things American.[15] The leaders of the movement are much aware of such dangers, and have tried to counter them, among others by introducing in some programs mandatory studies of non-American cultures, or even demanding that all American Studies should by definition be comparative. But it seems doubtful to what extent such plans are realized except on the highest level. Reports from European students about their colleagues in American

Studies programs in the United States, even at top rate universities, indicate that the problem remains a real one.

Equally basic is the fear that the somewhat limitless scope of American Studies may lead to a "flattening out" into intellectual looseness or cheap popularity, allowing the students to "know less and less about more and more".[16] Apparently, such criticism often fails to distinguish between the various types of American Studies within the American system. Much of the teaching in the subject today is undergraduate, or forms part of introductory General Education courses with thousands of students, at an age level which in Europe still belongs in the final grades of secondary school. In such general survey courses of the national culture the American Studies approach seems perfectly logical, and apparently the results are often excellent.[17]

But the same criticism is sometimes also directed against the more scholarly aims of the movement. These critics are afraid that even in graduate work — both in examinations and theses — the crossdepartmental study of widely divergent fields may lead to an amateurish toying with methods and knowledge within disciplines which, each in itself, requires a lifetime of concentrated study. The leaders of the movement are much aware of these dangers, as witnessed by a tightening of requirements in the programs. Some universities insist that their students be trained thoroughly in one discipline before they are allowed to extend into American Studies work. But the younger generation does not always display the same caution.

More extreme recent statements of this kind may be found in the programmatic collection *American Studies in Transition* which was published in 1964. In this volume one young sociologist declares flatly that American Studies (including the literary sector) are closer to the Social Sciences theoretically than to the Humanities, and that in order to fulfill their promise they have to operate as "a specialized branch of cultural anthropology".[18]

Another scholar claims that after too much concentration on the "scribbled" remains and "verbal ingenuities" of civilization the time has now come for the artifacts. American Studies have to realize that "American culture is expressed more adequately in the Brooklyn Bridge than in the poem Hart Crane wrote about it". One reputable university has already based one American Studies course on this "central, differentiating principle". For the understanding of a culture, the program declares, "its material aspects (furniture, buildings, machines) are as important as — not more important than — its nonmaterial ones (law, social patterns, ideas). This means that the historian's primary source material should include all kinds of artifacts including the written text and that the museum should be as familiar to him as the library".[19]

A third scholar in the same volume outlines an American Studies curriculum which makes mass production and mass communication, automation and mechanization "the very warp and woof of our intellectual concern". The results of the study of these new subjects should be published in new ways through photo-journalism, motion pictures, radio and television, and eventually by hourlong documentaries presented as doctoral theses. The time has now come to do away with the "really shocking timidity and time-serving" which still keep such methods from recognition.[20]

It is understandable if programs of this type and scope arouse some doubts within existing departments, and not only among their more arthritic members. Such sweeping claims, if taken seriously, do not only seem to underrate the bulk of actual present day work in American Studies. They obviously underrate the difficulties involved in knowing any scholarly field thoroughly and judging its material in its own context. Some of the newfangled hypotheses praised at the expense of the limited results of traditional scholarship are themselves no less limited, and in addition are often meaningless without the traditional background that is being scoffed at. If Brooklyn Bridge has any symbolic value, it is primarily because of that immense structure of "verbal preconceptions" which gives American culture itself its meaning.

The most penetrating criticism has not been directed against such extravagant statements, however, but against the central idea of integration.

This criticism is partly concerned with the actual operation of some of the present teaching programs. These critics maintain that the proclaimed "integration" often exists on paper only, a "paradoxical mystique" without reality.[21] In some university calendars the list of lectures from many fields of American Civilization actually are a facade, covering no real integration of the subjects. (Even at the highest level the committee of co-operation is often concerned just with one single thesis and its author.) Such teaching programs are ironically called the academic counterpart to those "scissors-and-paste" text books and anthologies with sweeping and "integrated" titles, which bring together between two covers all possible areas of American life, but leave their "organic" interplay to the puzzled reader.[22]

Behind such vagueness lies, in the view of these critics, the complexity of the problem of integration as interpreted by the American Studies movement. The existence of "total", homogeneous cultures is far from being generally recognized. As yet, there are few "shared concepts" about them, as witnessed by the ambiguity of terminology and the motley lists of definitions both of basic ideas and of national characteristics.[23] And certainly it is far from obvious that American Civilization has such inner coherence, let alone a uniqueness that demands an investigation by completely new methods.

Historically speaking, American civilization is "less self-contained than almost any other culture".[24] Its importance in the modern world is to a considerable extent due to its being typical of a general, technical and commercialized form of life. It is possible that the unique feature of American culture is "unprecedented and unmeasured change",[25] even if this trait today certainly is no less pronounced in many other parts of the world. But in any case there is nothing to indicate that a basically different approach is needed in order to understand American social mobility than, for instance, French stability.

Sometimes the claims of a unique "Americanness" of American phenomena also seem to show little awareness of scholarly work on similar questions in other parts of the world. In literary sociology, in particular, the problems of "integration" are being raised in the United States with a seriousness which seems to overlook that such matters were discussed in Europe decades before the American Studies movement got under way.

Sometimes, to a European observer, the pioneering zest of the movement has less connection with the American material itself, than with American academic tradition. A great number of books and articles listed in the annual American Studies bibliography actually seem to present no specific material demanding differentiated rules of operation. At best they show a somewhat wider application of procedures well known from traditional disciplines. If such efforts may appear as in any way revolutionary, departmentalization must have been more rigorous in American universities and in American learned journals than is the case even in Europe.

Decisive to many critics is the question whether any theoretically acceptable integration has proved possible as yet — not only "verbal solutions",[26] but a real fusion of materials and methods. To the present generation of American scholars the test case is the relation of literary criticism to the Social Sciences, since that is the point where the question has been worked on most thoroughly.

To a European, the problem here again seems to have been put too much in specific American terms. The analysts have accepted much too meekly both the New Critics' axiom about the autonomy of the literary text and the sociologists' faith in quantitative criteria. But in any case, the tentative application of these methods to the American material have led to no real meeting of minds so far. In ideas, subjects and interpretation the gap remains, even in the very use of the language, between the figurative, metaphorical concept of the literary scholars and the more literal, declarative understanding of the social scientists. Even the *Literary History of the United States* with its impressive marshalling of forces and its considerable coherence in subject does not pretend to solve those basic problems of theory that have not, so far, been solved anywhere.

And this is only one, and one of the least difficult, areas of possible integration. The international literature, for instance, about the pictorial arts abundantly demonstrates how far research still is from any real method of bridging the abyss between painting, sculpture and architecture on one side and society on the other. Fields such as Music, Religion, or Philosophy are even worse off. When it comes to the far-flung realms of Science — so essential to some theorists of American Studies — integration is even more fragmentary and uncertain. In many fields of cross-departmental cooperation we still have to content ourselves with defining the various degrees of possibility.

Both with regard to its practical organization and its philosophy the American Studies movement in America is thus, after its first decades of hopeful progress, marked by some resignation or a condition of stalemate. This attitude is strikingly apparent in the three cooperative volumes in which members of the movement have recently summarized their leading ideas, or tried them out on various types of material: *Studies in American Culture* (1960), *American Perspectives* (1961), and the above-mentioned *American Studies in Transition* (1964). In these chequered collections there is little concerted approach. And the editors state in so many words: "the hoped-for unity of the book did not materialize"; "the contributors ... have neither expected nor attempted to discover a single position or credo"; even: such intensity and unity were "neither claimed nor sought".[27]

Typical of this sobering attitude is the opinion of two leading scholars within the movement. Robert E. Spiller is one of its founding fathers, the guiding spirit of the *LHUS*, always keenly concerned with the development of a coherent ideology of American Studies. But in his most recent discussion of the problem he generally reverts with fresh arguments to the caution expressed twenty years ago by Tremaine McDowell. Spiller bluntly points to "the failure of the movement to settle on a generally accepted method of dealing with its diversified materials". The task is too manifold: "there is no one research method competent to accomplish it alone". Neither should the movement strive to become a "new discipline"; to do so would rather imply a "defeat, self-inflicted".[28]

Spiller's authoritative paper on "Value and Method in American Studies" exists in two versions, one from 1959 and the other from 1965. If compared in detail, they repeatedly show a qualification of his earlier optimism. In the original paper one passage summed up by saying that the movement "may not be as far from the goal of unified methodology" as some skeptics believe, and that "the unity now exists in the field of American Studies itself". In the final version these hopeful passages are omitted, and replaced by a description of Spiller's own top rate seminar at the University of Pennsylvania, a symposium of literary scholars and social scientists which proved to its leader the present incompatibility of the two fields both in aims and means.[29]

Similar ideas are stated explicitly by another prominent scholar of American Studies of more recent vintage. As early as 1957 Henry Nash Smith expressed his disappointment with the sociologists and cultural anthropologists as collaborators in the effort to create a fusion of methods, as Robert E. Spiller was going to do a few years later. No more than his colleague did Smith visualize an independent American Studies discipline. And he concluded that "no ready-made method for American Studies is in sight. We shall have to develop one for ourselves, and I am afraid that at present we shall have to be content with a very modest program".[30] To both Smith and Spiller the key word is not a homogeneity of methods any more, but a "dualism". And this dualism does no longer reflect American Civilization alone, but "modern man's total view of himself and his world today".[31]

At first glance such statements may seem to abandon central positions of the movement and in the view of some critics to justify their skepticism completely. To quote the most outspoken of them: the movement has put organization first, theories and method after, and that'll never work. "How can we establish programs whose very nature assumes that such a method is not only possible and probable, but immediately at hand — or if not at hand, then, in effect, not needed for genuine disciplined education?"[32] Resignation may sometimes lead to disappointment and defeatism even in devoted scholars within the movement. To quote one of them: "Perhaps the real future of the American Studies movement rests more with the high schools than with the colleges and universities".[33]

But such pessimism is not typical, nor does it seem justified. On the contrary, the main result of the self-scrutiny of the movement during the recent decade is rather a clearing of the ground, and a redefinition of its values and its real task.

Few if any responsible leaders of American Studies today dream any longer — if they ever did — of a future when the galaxy of present studies in the diverse fields of American Civilization will be hitched to the star of "integration", let alone be taken over or replaced by the new school. Now as before the center of teaching and research will remain in the established disciplines, and for good reasons. Even the unique features of the subject are often brought out most strikingly by a traditional approach, against the background of the tightly coherent, "vertical" relationships and value systems within each separate field. The "horizontal" integration can never become more than one sector in the study of American life.

Moreover, even where integration is desirable, it often has to respect the traditional boundaries. As far as literature is concerned, the idea was wisely put by the Dutchman R. W. Zandvoort: "Though 'American Studies' cannot dispense with the study of American literature, the latter would be acting against its own interests by regarding itself merely or mainly as a department of the former. On the contrary, it will have to beware of any encroachment on its autonomy, and to maintain its primary connections with the study of literature as such, and with English literature in particular".[34] This opinion is doubtless shared by a majority even of American scholars, and, *mutatis mutandis*, not only in the departments of Literature.

The effort to establish more departments of American Studies in American universities and colleges, and to develop further those that already exist certainly will and should continue. But these establishments are not supposed to emulate those of the traditional type. Their internal unity, as far as it goes, will have to rest on their subject, "American Civilization". This material has its limitations in time and space, and is both sprawling and vague. But at the same time it has strong traits of coherence, and distinctive qualities. It is overwhelmingly rich, with a wide range of possibilities. And because of its modernity it is more easily accessible than are the subjects of many specialized departments, — "an immediate culture of recent development and a high degree of sophistication as well as complexity".

In their work with this culture the American Studies departments admittedly will be held together less by specific procedures and techniques than by a scholarly attitude and direction, a concern with synthesis, an emphasis on general forces and organic connections. In practice the departments will obviously have to establish their systems of courses, examinations and degrees. But their main task will be to serve as centers of mediation, informal meeting grounds, — in the words of a Briton: academic "common-rooms", — for scholars "working from within existing academic disciplines but attempting to widen the boundaries imposed by conventional methods of inquiry".

This cooperation will also be inspired by the hope that through "repeated criticism of practice" such parallel inquiries will ultimately converge. But whatever unity may thus emerge, the movement believes not only in the "dualism", but in the fundamental multiplicity of civilization itself, and of the scholarly way of studying it. All sound research has to be guided by the principle of "complementarity" that is also strong in modern Science, and which makes various approaches "mutually supply each other's lacks".[35] Far from presenting one method, or searching for one, American Studies will be characterized by "differences rather than similarities". The movement will aim, not at a diminution of the number of questions, but at an increase, using relevant knowledge and methods wherever they may be found, in a procedure of "principled opportunism".[36]

The undoubted danger of dilettantism involved in such transgression of boundaries can only be countered by a sharpened critical attitude within each individual field concerned. There is evidence of a development in this direction. The growth of such critical awareness has even been called one of the most significant features of the movement in recent years, "the realization that the study of an American painting or social institution or landscaped garden or poem as a cultural artifact first involves comprehension and evaluation *within its own universe*".[37]

To the present writer the strongest guarantee against cheap generalization is, however, that "piecemeal", "one-problem" approach that is now being recommended by some of the outstanding leaders of the movement, although most universities are slow in recognizing it. "Integration" should not start from theories, but from a study of the specific, concrete case. It should try to "take into account as many aspects of it as possible", based on material from as many fields as possible, selected because of its relevance to the individual problem more than to the particular disciplines. The work should proceed in the conviction that such really exhaustive knowledge of detail embodies "whatever uniformities may exist".[38] And such integration should no longer be felt as a permanent duty, but as *one* approach beside others, to be applied when the material asks for it — as is actually the case in the practical work of many American scholars today, without much concern about coherent theory.

The credo of these American Studies was stated succinctly in 1963 by the editor of the *American Quarterly*, H. Cohen: American Studies are "still fluid, experimental, and highly individualistic . . . while certain useful methods and devices have evolved, no synthesis has taken place. [The work] has not become a discipline. It remains an approach, a congeries of various skills and bodies of information [held together by] the interdisciplinary approach and the willingness to experiment". In the metaphor of R. E. Spiller: American Studies will be "the yeast rather than the dough" of research. It is for good reasons that they call themselves American Studies: their pluralistic looseness points to their real strength.[39]

Whether work organized along such lines should be called a "discipline" in the traditional sense seems to be an academic question in both meanings of the word, considering the obvious need for exactly that kind of work in present-day scholarship, and the evident usefulness of the movement in performing it. There is a feeling within many fields of research today that interdisciplinary cooperation in the widest sense is the catchword of the time. This idea is corroborated by the fact that in many subjects recent progress has sprung from such cooperation. But outside some areas of Science the fusion has in practice proved extremely difficult; and both in the Social Sciences and the Humanities strong currents are now running in the opposite direction. Everywhere there is more lip service to integration than organized effort to achieve it. The American Studies departments in the United States embody such an effort. Their development in recent years may have equipped them to serve as real points of contact, and their influence may not be limited to their own area.

In its ideas and its emotional atmosphere the American Studies movement is colored by its background in post-war United States. In a recent discussion one of its leaders tossed off the statement that there is an American culture today "largely as a result of the American Studies movement". This is a truly Western exaggeration. But doubtless the organized effort to see American life as a whole is a contributing factor in establishing national selfunderstanding and selfcriticism within the United States. In the present world that understanding is of concern not only to the Americans.

Even more important is the possibility opened up by the American Studies movement of having basic problems of cultural development discussed on an experimental basis with an American lack of formalism, and (at least until recently) with large scale financial support. There are other centers in the United States with similar aims and scope. But the movement combines concentration on specific material with an openness of mind and a willingness to penetrate unexplored territory which is hardly equalled anywhere else. The very ambiguity of its ideology may here prove an asset. Even its wildcat ideas harbor a nucleus of truth, and may prove creative if combined with criticism.

"We must insist upon asking the big questions", one of the theorists recently stated, "for the answers we receive can never be better than our questions". This pioneering spirit is in the best American tradition, and recently made a scholar call American Studies "one of the most exciting areas in the humanities today". It made a highly critical observer like Lionel Trilling rank the movement among the most remarkable events in the intellectual history of the last decades.[40]

In the long run the movement can only justify its existence by its results in scholarship. The time has not yet come for large scale syntheses. But in monographic research originating within the movement there is much of obvious value. While the frontier crossing may not always seem revolutionary to European eyes, the opening of vistas is often inspiring. One may mention as a striking example John W. Ward's analysis of the Lindbergh myth.[41] In H. N. Smith's *Mark Twain. The Development of a Writer* (1962) the method is applied to one literary figure in a way that points far beyond the American material. And on a larger scale H. Nash Smith's *Virgin Land* (1950), R. W. B. Lewis' *The American Adam* (1955) and Leo Marx' *The Machine in the Garden* (1965) have given to the history of ideas a breadth and depth that is rarely equalled anywhere.

But so far, the movement has probably made its most weighty contribution in teaching. Its importance in scholarly education should not be gauged exclusively by the number of formal American Studies programs at the universities. Even more momentous may be its impalpable influence in the much more extensive studies of American civilization that are carried on within the many traditional disciplines.

At the same time the recent decades in the history of the movement have brought out, not only the inherent limitations of its theory, but also its special character in a more practical sense. The "American Studies" are an American creation, and in their typical form are not immediately an article of export. In many features they show the mark of that national system of education and scholarship which they have reacted against, and which has no exact counterpart anywhere else.

This American experience was unexpectedly put to the test and in many ways borne out by the development of American studies in the post-war world outside of America.

The results of the great conflict 1939—45 made it inevitable that the study of the United States and its civilization experienced a further expansion, this time all over the globe. The omnipresence of the Americans and the impact they made challenged mankind to try to find out what their civilization really was about. Much of this swiftly accelerating activity in war-devastated countries needed American help. By a coincidence of circumstances part of this assistance came to be closely tied to the ideology of the American Studies movement. And both its strength and its weakness were revealed thereby.

Behind the Iron and Bamboo Curtains there was no possibility of such direct contact. On the contrary, the Cold War initially led to a further strengthening of the propagandistic trend that had been typical of American Studies in the communist world before the war. The thaw since 1953 is doubtless modifying the traditional rigor in the Soviet Union and the former satellite states. But so far, little is known about these changes; how long they are going to last is no less uncertain. In any case, nothing radically new seems to have been added to the study of the subject as yet, in those parts of the world.

In Western Europe the situation was different, above all in Germany. And as before, the German problem created a discussion that is relevant to the situation in other countries as well.

In the American zone of occupation in Germany the United States government from 1945 onward made a carefully planned attempt to reorganize the German educational system completely. The traditional rigidity, isolation and specialization in the work of the universities were regarded as one of the main obstacles to democratic reform; and because of the presence of some American Studies specialists in strategic positions that subject came to play a considerable part. An effort was made to introduce "integrated" and "cross-departmental" American Studies both in schools and universities as a lever for more general educational policies. Much effort and money was expended on the establishment of American Institutes with a program independent of the traditional system. The American Institute in Munich (founded in 1949) with its "horizontal" methods was planned originally to serve almost as a separate university, a model of scholarly procedures aggressively different from those of its German surroundings.[42]

These efforts failed almost completely, however. There was much willingness in Germany to build up serious work in the American field. Ever since economic recovery got under way the number of chairs, libraries, and teaching hours has increased steadily. But there was a stern determination that this development should take place within the old academic framework. This was the case even in the American occupational zone, let alone in the others. To some extent this determination was due to conservatism, but even more to a critical reserve which parallels that of many American scholars, but has its somber background in Germany's own experience.[43]

Some of the arguments were practical. It was pointed out that the American variety of American Studies sprang from national conditions that did not exist in Europe. As seen above, many such programs in the United States apply to younger students than those who are normally found in a European university. Equally important, these students have a different background: they are born into American language and civilization. Outside of the English-speaking nations even an elementary knowledge of this background has to be acquired with sweat and tears, and always imperfectly, within the framework of the established disciplines; there is no "integrated" approach to English intonation. And this effort is bound to take most of the time and working power both of teachers and students.

If, therefore, in European universities, an "integration" is to mean more than preoccupation with simple generalities, it makes demands that can be satisfied only by the select few, even more than is the case in the United States. Prosaic considerations are bound to limit possibilities even further. In the Humanities the bulk of European students are preparing for a teaching career, mostly in secondary schools. To such students American Studies as a separate discipline would offer even smaller prospects than they do in the USA.

There were also reservations of a theoretical kind; many of them have been recently summed up by one of the German leaders in American Studies, H. Galinsky.[44] Not only was the "area" approach generally suspect because of its previous connection with Nazism. Both in Germany and Europe generally academic studies have a universalistic trend, and there is little sympathy with a selective concentration on one national culture in its entirety like the one practiced in American Studies. German universities know no synthetic or comprehensive "area study" even of German civilization, except in vacation courses, and most scholars lack the conceptual equipment for it. In Germany as in the United States such negative tendencies are strengthened by structuralist and a-historical trends in modern research generally. Moreover, while many German scholars are genuinely attracted by the broad sweep of American Studies which differs so strikingly from accepted methods, they also often share the more specific scholarly hesitations of their American colleagues which are discussed above.

The result was a compromise. German professional meetings in 1951—53, heavily dominated by scholars of literature, language and history, produced warm protestations of goodwill in principle toward American Studies in the widest sense, and work along such lines was encouraged. But the details of arrangement it was decided to leave to the individual universities. In practice this has proved to mean, that even more than in the United States the study of American Civilization in Germany takes place within the existing disciplines and departments, above all in English and History.

Almost everywhere teaching of American material is now being provided in the old subjects, and American requirements are being tightened, particularly at lower examinations. But smaller universities normally go no farther than that. "Integration" in the American sense does not enter into the picture at all; the independent subject "Americanistics" exists in a few universities, but is of little importance. Some universities have separate chairs both of American Literature and American History (or Social and Intellectual History), sometimes even of other American fields; and more often than not all lectures on American subjects are listed under a separate heading. But this unity is in itself unusual, and as a rule it exists on paper only. The juxtaposition of courses on the Civil War, Ezra Pound, and American Patent Law (given in various departments) has little "synthetic" value. In H. Galinsky's ironical expression: integration between the subjects is hopefully supposed to take place within the mind of the ideal student who attends all these heterogeneous courses.

Teaching of a directly inter-disciplinary character is almost non-existent. There is of course no counterpart to the General Education courses in American Civilization that are natural in the States itself; and the graduate schools show little interest. In the Winter Term 1962 —63 111 courses were given on American subjects in all German universities taken together, but only two of them could be called "integrated".[45]

This does not mean that integration is being neglected. But even more than in the States it is left to specialized work on the highest level, particularly in the large universities. Committees of cooperation on the American pattern, with members representing the various established departments, organize doctoral work as they do in the States. They normally emphasize cross-departmental studies; in some of the universities such work is facilitated by the existence of general American Institutes with important research libraries. Most ambitious is the recently established John F. Kennedy-Institut für Amerikastudien at the Free University in West Berlin, where a Ford Foundation grant has made it possible to expand "integrated" studies of the American area on a scale that has no parallel outside of the United States itself.

But the work remains purposely experimental. No definite or elaborate "method" is aimed at. And the activity remains supplementary, and somewhat extraordinary. From the University of Mainz, where American Civilization is being studied with care, Professor H. Galinsky reports on a total of three seminars of a wholly "integrated" character during the recent decade. All of them were tentative, and the results somewhat uncertain.[46] Even at the John F. Kennedy Institute the bulk of the teaching moves within the border lines of the established disciplines.

As a source of general inspiration the American Studies movement is nevertheless important. In Germany as in the USA the American Institutes and the departments of cooperation offer constant reminders of a more synthetic approach; and with the growing recognition of American subjects within the educational system these departments increase their chance to exert a direct influence. It is even possible that their basic ideas may prove fruitful in a more general way. Several new universities are now being established in Germany. And at those in Bochum and Konstanz, at least, the planners visualize a radical reorganization of the old faculty and department system in favor of a more integrated approach. But within the old ordinary universities, tied as they are to the traditional school systems and requirements of each individual "Land", the importance of such work is still quite limited as compared to the normal teaching of American subjects in the established manner.

In 1959 Robert E. Spiller expressed the hope that the reorganized American work in Germany might "offer . . . much of the theory and system for the movement" as it had done in the past. This hope has not materialized. As late as 1964 an observer as sympathetic as Professor H. Galinsky was still hesitant to say whether American Studies in Germany should be called "a problem child", or — more hopefully — "the experimental thorn in the academic flesh".[47]

If this German situation has been gone into in some detail, it is partly because of the central position which the country has held within the European discussion of the subject. But it is also because in important features the problems in Germany are analogous to those in other countries of Western Europe, and the solutions as well.

In Germany, the size and resources of the respective universities have been a decisive factor in the development of American Studies. This factor is no less important in the small European nations. Several of them are actively developing American Studies, but almost completely within the old disciplines, particularly in the English and History departments.

Austria, Holland and Switzerland can be mentioned as examples. There is a general effort to increase teaching of American civilization, not only as "background" material and on the elementary level. But no special arrangements are made for "integrated" work, even if subjects for doctoral theses may be chosen quite freely. The five small Scandinavian nations may be mentioned as other examples. In two of them (Denmark and Iceland) American Studies are still in their infancy. In Finland, Norway and Sweden the subject is now firmly entrenched in the traditional departments, with specialized chairs, obligatory requirements, and important research libraries covering many fields of American civilization. But so far, there has been hardly any time to spare for organized integrated work. And it may safely be said, that if a different road had been chosen during the last two decades, American Studies in these countries would now have been isolated and powerless, and with few regular students.

A unique situation exists at the University of Amsterdam, where American Studies are *not* developing within any long established discipline. An impressive American Institute is attached to the Faculty of Social Sciences, for the students of which it serves as a "workshop of area study"; it is also used on an advanced level by students of many other subjects.

In the great nations within the Romance language orbit the attitude of caution is pronounced. France since the War has vigorously developed its national combination of American Literature and Civilization taught through *explication de texte*, and holds its strong position both in study and research. But little attention is paid to the more sweeping claims of the American advocates of these studies. Italy is following the same road. A great number of chairs have recently been established in American Studies, and some universities also have interfaculty institutes with courses offered in American History, Literature, Geography, Education, etc. But it seems doubtful whether this effort involves more than the collected listing of separate lectures that is known from other countries.

Promising in many ways is the post-war development in Great Britain. As before, the old British universities are generally unwilling to adopt an "integrated" method in the American sense. But even there, much work is now going on in the traditional disciplines; and several of the more recent establishments are also eager to discuss and study the American ideas, and to experiment with them. Noticeably Manchester, North Staffordshire and Nottingham long ago organized American work along lines comparable to the American system. Hull recently set up a Department of American Studies, and the University of London has just created an Institute of United States Studies. In some of the new universities that are being founded in the 1960's, particularly those of East Anglia and Sussex, all studies of the Humanities are being integrated and brought into contact with each other in a way that resembles both the American system and the plans for the new German universities. American Studies form a part of these experiments, and some of them are guided by specialists in American Studies. If successful, they may influence both the study of American Civilization and British university life generally.

European research in American Civilization is slow in applying the new methods, for reasons that have already been touched upon.

Materials are scarce in most countries, and work along traditional lines is often sufficiently demanding. Nevertheless, even here an impact of the "integrated" efforts is noticeable.

The European Association for American Studies and the various regional Associations of the same type have been constantly aware of the problems of integration, and the programs of their conferences show it. The German *Jahrbuch für Amerikastudien* is by definition an outlet for cross-departmental research. A good deal of such work is being done in fields where an integrated approach is natural, not least in comparative studies of American and European developments, of the American impact and image, of European emigration and its consequences, and of transatlantic relations of other kinds, often with a broad sweep.

At the same time, even in the German *Jahrbuch* most of the articles are of a quite traditional type. One receives the same impression by looking into the annual bibliography of European research that is published in the *Newsletter* of the European Association. In certain countries the special American methods are almost ignored. In the impressive Italian annual *Studi Americani* the editor of the series would like to cover a wide field of American Civilization. But his contributors are almost exclusively concerned with literary analyses in the vein of the New Criticism.

In the 1950's and 1960's even the Far East has unexpectedly entered this world picture of American Studies.[48]

In India such work got under way only in the late 1950's. Programs were established or planned, and permanent teaching by nationals began on a tentative scale. But the activity is still in its beginnings both with regard to resources and personnel. A report issued in 1963 by the United States Educational Foundation in India stated, as the result of a specialists' conference, that according to general opinion, "since interdepartmental cooperation in India is so limited, 'American Studies' involving several disciplines is not feasible at present".[49]

In Japan progress is much more advanced. Some American studies were organized soon after the conclusion of hostilities in 1945. An American Studies Association was active from 1946 to 1958, and a good deal of teaching developed under the American occupation. Growth has continued ever since, in several universities and in many fields, but with a predominance of literature and history. Both in India and Japan a surprising number of articles are already appearing on American civilization, in particular on American literature.

American encouragement and aid have been essential to this development, and so has the activity of American Fulbrighters. Many of them were educated in the American Studies movement in the USA. So were several Japanese scholars, and they have tried to introduce similar arrangements in their own country. A report from 1962, written jointly by a Japanese and an American, points out as "the ultimate goal" of this work the establishment of area studies on the American pattern. The same words were echoed in the following year by the recently founded Japanese American Studies Foundation. Of the 45 Japanese institutions of higher learning about half a dozen have now departments of American Studies in the "integrated" sense of the word. It is interesting that in some universities the younger generation of scholars is simultaneously pressing for these studies and for increased study of contemporary Japanese subjects, which are still frowned upon within the traditional departments.

This policy has also met with some skepticism, however. In Asia as everywhere a certain generalization in the teaching of American Civilization is obviously pedagogically desirable at the elementary stage. But the critics warn that before "integrated" experiments be pushed too strongly on a higher level there should be a solid basis of training and knowledge in the traditional disciplines. Such aims have hardly been realized in Japan as yet, let alone in India. It has taken much time and effort to lay the necessary foundations in Europe, which after all is so much more close to American language and civilization than is the Far East; and serious obstacles are still hampering integrated work in the great Western nations. Under these circumstances one can understand the hesitations in Japan and India. And they are borne out by recent American reports about the "lack of scholarly sophistication" in the printed output from these countries.[50]

Similar doubts were also voiced by some of the Japanese scholars at the American Studies Conference in Tokyo in 1964. While there was much interest in an "integrated" approach, these speakers reminded the conference that "interdisciplinary study assumed individual disciplines", that there is danger involved in "producing an expert in American civilization without any particular discipline as his tool of research", that there are "special problems and difficulties" in the contrast between area studies and other conventional fields with established methodologies, that Japan at the moment needs "encouragement of American Studies both in the strict and broad sense", and finally, that Japanese scholars "should have their own approach and point of view".[51]

In conclusion, it is worth while pointing to that caution which, in this respect, the recently organized Canadian Association for American Studies found it useful to express in its Constitution and at its first Conference in 1964. There was general agreement that "American civilization is a valid field of study in itself". At the same time the organization emphasized that it wished to "include among its members both those who favor the newer interdisciplinary approach and those who see American Studies as a number of separate but related studies within the framework of the traditional disciplines". The Association as such "takes no specific position" in the question.[52]

That problem of scholarship which American Civilization presented to the world has proved to be knotty. From the very beginning the subject was marked by the range of contrasts that are typical of American life. And complication increased when after the two great wars the United States became a decisive factor in the world both intellectually and physically, and everywhere championed its own ideas about the study of its civilization.

The result was that long and inconclusive bickering that is outlined above. And the outcome remains ambiguous and is bound to continue to be so. There is widespread recognition in the scholarly world of the general goals of the American movement. But there are equally strong reservations and qualifications. Universities in Europe and Asia are often unable to adopt arrangements and ideas that have grown as a pragmatic solution to immediate needs on the different soil of the United States. And even in America itself the American Studies movement runs counter to deeply rooted ideas and traditions.

No simple or uniform solution is in view. There is some truth in most of the conflicting opinions both theoretical and practical. From university to university the arrangements adopted are a result of conflicting forces, more daring and experimental in the States, where American Civilization is studied from the inside, more cautious and hesitant in other parts of the world, where the subject is viewed from a distance. And this situation is there to stay. Many transitional forms doubtless are destined to live beside each other for quite a while to come.

Those who are concerned with American Studies and personally committed to the promotion of them will have to serve this development each in his own place in accordance with these varying possibilities. But through the unavoidable compromises it should be kept in mind, that the main contribution of the American Studies movement is no chauvinistic program for the study of *one* culture, but a general ideal of scholarship. "Integration" has always been important to the study of American civilization, more vaguely in the beginning, more consciously in recent decades. Today the idea of integration points to a basic weakness in modern academic teaching and research; and no similar movement in our time raises the protest against this weakness with comparable force and consistency. We are fast approaching the society of mass education, with an explosive growth of the student population even in the universities, with ever more insistent practical demands, and with a corresponding tendency to reduce teaching and requirements to the quality of intellectual emergency rations. If, in this society, the American Studies movement proves able to maintain its standards of solid research, it is bound to become ever more important, even outside of its own field.

In many ways the movement represents an American ideal; and once again in history the ideal is important to the world *because* of its distinctive American character. One of the tasks of American Studies in the future, wherever they exist and whatever forms they may take, will be to see to it that this salt does not lose its savor.

## NOTES

This article was originally read as a paper at the Second Conference of the Nordic Association for American Studies, held at the University of Oslo in June, 1964. The discussion at the Conference session made the author rewrite the paper and pay attention to even more recent material. The article appears simultaneously in the Proceedings of the Oslo Conference, *USA in Focus. Recent Re-Interpretations*, ed. Sigmund Skard (Oslo, 1966), pp. 140—173.

A number of American and European scholars of highly divergent opinions have been kind enough to read the manuscript and give the author the benefit of their criticism.

[1] American theoretical discussion of the subject, as well as information about recent research, are conveniently brought together in the bibliographies in *American Quarterly*. For the historical section about Europe in the article the reader will find more extensive documentation in my books *American Studies in Europe*, I—II (Philadelphia, Pa., 1958) and *The American Myth and the European Mind* (Philadelphia, Pa., 1961), and references to these books are only given sparingly below.

² E. E. Doll, "American History as Interpreted by German Historians from 1770 to 1815", *Transactions of the American Philosophical Society*, N.S. 38/5 (1948), 457 and 500.

³ S. Skard, *American Studies in Europe*, I, 54.

⁴ *Revue internationale de l'enseignement*, LXXIII (1919), 247—265.

⁵ S. Skard, *American Studies in Europe*, I, 261.

⁶ Tremaine McDowell, *American Studies* (Minneapolis, Minn., 1948), pp. 10, 28 f., 31—33.

⁷ R. E. Spiller, *The Third Dimension. Studies in Literary History* (New York, 1965), pp. 203 f.

⁸ R. H. Walker, *American Studies in the United States. A Survey of College Programs* (Baton Rouge, La., 1958), p. 158; R. E. Spiller and Henry Wasser in *American Studies in Transition*, ed. M.W. Fishwick (Philadelphia, 1964), pp. 235 and 166. Compare protestations that American Studies *are* a "discipline" by J. F. Stone, *American Studies*, I, No. 4 (Febr. 1956), p. 3 and W. Randel, *College English*, XIX (1958), 361.

⁹ The promotional leaflet of the American Studies Association (1965).

¹⁰ R. H. Walker, *American Studies in the United States*, p. 158.

¹¹ *American Studies in Transition*, p. 129.

¹² Merle Curti in *American Scholarship in the Twentieth Century*, ed. M. Curti (Cambridge, Mass., 1953), p. 5.

¹³ *Studies in American Culture. Dominant Ideas and Images*, ed. J. J. Kwiat and M. C. Turpie (Minneapolis, Minn., 1960), p. 5. H. Cohen in *Saturday Review*, Jan. 16, 1965, p. 32.

¹⁴ H. Cohen, "American Studies and American Literature", *College English*, XXIV (1963), 550.

¹⁵ I. Howe in *American Literature*, XXXVII (1965), 81. For a much more violent criticism, see K. B. Murdock in *Amerika och Norden*, ed. L. Åhnebrink (Stockholm, 1964), p. 191.

¹⁶ *American Studies*, I, No. 4 (1956), pp. 1f.

¹⁷ A description of courses of this type at Michigan State University is found in *American Studies in Transition*, pp. 181—195.

¹⁸ Richard E. Sykes in *American Studies in Transition*, p. 143.

¹⁹ J. A. Kouwenhoven ibid., pp. 16 and 27; promotional brochure from the American Studies Institute, University of Delaware (1965).

²⁰ Patrick D. Hazard in *American Studies in Transition*, pp. 59, 63—65.

²¹ J. Higham in *American Quarterly*, XIII (1961), 220.

²² R. B. Posey in *American Studies*, VI, No. 1 (1963), 6.

²³ R. H. Pearce, "American Studies as a Discipline", *College English*, XVIII (1956—57), 185.

²⁴ A. E. Bestor, Jr., "The Study of American Civilization: Jingoism or Scholarship?", *The William and Mary Quarterly*, Third Series, IX (1952), 7.

²⁵ R. Gabriel in *American Studies*, VI, No. 1 (1963), 1.

²⁶ H. N. Smith, "Can 'American Studies' Develop a Method?" in *Studies in American Culture*, p. 14.

²⁷ *American Perspectives. The National Self-Image in the Twentieth Century*, ed. R. E. Spiller and E. Larrabee (Cambridge, Mass., 1961), p. VI; *American Studies in Transition*, pp. 8 and 10.

²⁸ R. E. Spiller, *The Third Dimension*, pp. 205, 212, 216.

²⁹ R. E. Spiller, "American Studies, Past, Present, and Future", *Studies in American Culture*, pp. 207—220, and "Value and Method in American Studies", *The Third Dimension*, pp. 199—216. The omitted passages are on pp. 212 and 215 in the first version; other characteristic changes on pp. 211 (compare the second version pp. 203, 204), 212 (205) and 216 (211).

³⁰ H. N. Smith, "Can 'American Studies' Develop a Method?", p. 14 f.

[31] *American Perspectives*, p. VI.

[32] R. H. Pearce, "American Studies as a Discipline", pp. 180 ff. and 185.

[33] M. W. Fishwick in *Social Education*, XXVII (1963), 421.

[34] Quoted from *American Studies in Transition*, p. 242.

[35] R. E. Spiller, *The Third Dimension*, p. 204; H. N. Smith, "Can 'American Studies' Develop a Method?", pp. 14 f.; D. C. Watt and Henry Wasser in *American Studies in Transition*, pp. 245 and 166—180.

[36] M. W. Fishwick in *American Studies in Transition*, p. 9; R. E. Spiller, *The Third Dimension*, p. 211; H. N. Smith, "Can 'American Studies' Develop a Method?", p. 15.

[37] H. Cohen, "American Studies and American Literature", pp. 552 f. (my italics).

[38] H. N. Smith, "Can 'American Studies' Develop a Method?", pp. 3 and 15; S. Diamond, "Do Good Fences Make Good Scholars?", *American Studies in Transition*, p. 98.

[39] H. Cohen, "American Studies and American Literature", p. 551 f.; R. E. Spiller, *The Third Dimension*, p. 205.

[40] B. Hindle, "A Bridge for Science and Technology", *American Studies in Transition*, p. 126; Ch. Boewe, *American Studies*, VI, No. 1 (1963), 6; L. Trilling quoted from *American Studies in Transition*, p. 12.

[41] "The Meaning of Lindbergh's Flight", *American Quarterly*, X (1958), 3—16.

[42] See, in particular, the inaugural lecture by the founder and first director of the Institute, H. F. Peters, *Ziele und Methoden der Amerikanistik* (München, 1950).

[43] The entire discussion is summarized in S. Skard, *American Studies in Europe*, I, 291 ff.

[44] H. Galinsky, "American Studies in Germany", *American Studies in Transition*, pp. 232—252.

[45] *American Studies in Transition*, pp. 238 and 251.

[46] ibid., pp. 236 f.

[47] ibid., pp. 234 and 249.

[48] See for the following R. B. Davis in *American Studies in Transition*, pp. 285—288; R. Denney and S. Lutzky, *American Studies in Asia. A Brief Survey* (Wilmington, Del., 1964), pp. 7 f. and 20—29; *American Studies Conference, Report* (Tokyo, 1964), pp. 21 ff.; W. Johnson, *American Studies Abroad. A Special Report* (Washington, D.C., 1963), pp. 38—46.

[49] R. Denney and S. Lutzky, *American Studies in Asia*, p. 15.

[50] W. Johnson, *American Studies Abroad*, p. 45 f.; *Report to the MLA American Literature Group 1965* (mimeographed), p. 5.

[51] *American Studies Conference, Report*, pp. 22 and 31—33.

[52] *CAAS Bulletin*, I, No. 1 (Montreal, Quebec, 1965), pp. 2, 14, 20.

# LUDVIG KRISTENSEN DAA
## AND THE USA

### By Petter Christian Steenstrup

The American impact on Norwegian political history is in its main
features similar to that observed in other small democracies in Europe.
But the details in Norway, while mostly unexplored as yet, show many
nuances, that are sometimes of more than local interest. The following
article will sample this material by analyzing thoroughly the influence
of America (the United States) in the thought and public activity of the
Norwegian scholar, publicist and politician Ludvig Kristensen Daa
(1807–77).

L. Kr. Daa is a marginal figure in Norwegian history. His burning
ambition was never really satisfied. But partly for that very reason he
offers instructive material for a pilot study of this type. He had a keen
and versatile mind; and more than most of his Norwegian contemporaries he was open to the ideas of the world. Since large-scale action
was denied to him, he became doubly eager to put his views before
the public, and frequently gave them added prestige by presenting
them in their international context. Thus, indirectly, Daa's writing
on the United States may also contribute to a better understanding
of his own controversial political career.

The aim of this article is to present Norwegian material. The earlier
phases of the American political impact in Norway are outlined in
some detail, since that has never been done before. The extensive
literature about the impact elsewhere in Europe is referred to only
when necessary as a background.[1]

## 1.

The Norse expeditions from Greenland and Iceland to the American
continent in the Middle Ages left few traces in Norway itself, except
as proud memories. During its subsequent four hundred years of uni-

on with Denmark the country was only influenced indirectly by the second discovery of America, and played little part in the following settlements. But beginning with the revolutionary period, America became an influence in political thinking and action in Norway as elsewhere in Europe.

From the 16th century literate Europeans had worshipped the "noble savage" of the Western world, remnant of a past Golden Age. This idealization was later transferred to the British colonists in what was sometime to become the United States, in particular to the Quakers, and the image was further elaborated by the enlightened philosophers in the spirit of Rousseau. Their concept of simple purity flowering in the wilderness deeply influenced even the colonists themselves. Such generalizations were built on scant knowledge of America and its diversity. But in their struggle for liberty and the formulation of their political tenets the new American states came to represent some of the deepest longings of the time, and also the double trend which they involved.

In earlier periods of history the developing bourgeoisie in Europe had needed the power of king and government as a protection against semi-feudal restrictions. In the eighteenth century the middle classes had reached a position of strength which made them turn against their former ally, and demand liberty even from the state and its mercantilistic system. The idea gained ground that "that government is best that governs least". Apart from their stabilizing function in society king and government should have as little power as possible, leaving a free field to the utilization and increase of property by its owners. Freedom of press and opinion, religious liberty, and also a certain political freedom limited by census, should all serve the same purpose, opening the widest possible leeway to the individual. The rebellion of the idealized British colonies in America against the political and economic tyranny of the British King therefore gained keen sympathy among European liberals, even among those who socially were quite conservative. America is the hope and the model of mankind, wrote Turgot: "l'exemple de la liberté politique, de la liberté réligieuse, de la liberté de la commerce et de l'industrie".[2]

But the American revolutionaries did not only demand political liberty. In the Declaration of Independence Jefferson also proclaimed that all men were created equal, with the right of selfgovernment; and to Jefferson that meant government by the law of majority.[3] He thus came to voice the claims even of the developing lower classes, which everywhere in the eighteenth century began to make their demands heard. Such democratic ideas were no more generally popular in Europe than they were in America itself. Many liberals saw in equality a danger to their own position, to property, and even to liberty itself. And they soon found their worst misgivings justified by the excesses of the French Revolution.

But in the long run this development strengthened the idealization of the USA in liberal circles in Europe rather than destroyed it. The radical American democrats soon proved to be models of balance and caution. There was a social element even in *their* change of government. But in the new state the "men of principle and property" soon were back in power, making the American lack of a nobility appear as an innocent and almost romantic peculiarity. The English statesman C. J.Fox, a member of the opposition to the British government, but no friend of a democratic franchise, could declare the cause of the American colonists to be "the cause of freedom, the cause of the constitution, the cause of whiggism".[4] Edmund Burke, who hated the French Revolution because of its "inorganic" character, saw no such violation of natural development in the American Revolution.[5] To many European liberals the free Americans and their leaders called to mind the venerable Romans of classical antiquity with their virtuous moderation.

The merchants and officials who in 18th century Norway made up the intellectual élite of the nation, were deeply imbued with these ideas of contemporary Enlightenment, including the conflicting attitudes toward America. But beneath the autocratic Danish domination Norwegian society had developed a democratic structure which made even the more radical aspects of the new ideas more acceptable to the upper classes than was sometimes the case on the Continent. And the Norwegians had a special reason to feel akin to the new states that were springing up on the Atlantic seaboard: like their American counterparts they had a grievance against an arbitrary and semi-foreign government across the ocean. The first signs of sympathy toward America in Norway occurred in 1779 during the War of Independence. When one of John Paul Jones' squadrons brought some English prize ships into the port of Bergen, the citizens protested the surrender of the vessels to the British by the Danish authorities.[6]

The expression of interest soon became more articulate. In 1777 the leading Norwegian man of letters of the time, Claus Fasting, wrote that "most Europeans are fighting for America's cause in their hearts, as for their own".[7] And probably he was right about his fellow countrymen too, at least with regard to the more conscious patriots. America was felt to be the standard-bearer of freedom in a world of tyranny, and the Norwegian eulogies sometimes had a ring of revolutionary fervor. In 1781 the radical clergyman Hans Hammond wrote in his letters: "Three of my children have now died; they enjoy the land of eternal liberty, and know nothing of the slavery and the prevailing suppression in Europe. God help at least America to fight its way to freedom, lest all mankind shall perish in serfdom... That the Emperor of Russia will assist in the subjugation of America is inhuman. Whence shall the suppressed escape now, and where in the world is the land of liberty to be found any more then?"[8]

With other Norwegians, however, such enthusiasm was seasoned by conservative qualifications, as was often the case on the Continent. The poet and playwright Johan Nordahl Brun (1745–1816), in his later years a bishop in the Dano-Norwegian Church, was also a great Norwegian patriot, and the author of a song which in disguised metaphors prophesied a Norwegian rebellion against Denmark. He praised the freedom-loving Americans in no uncertain terms. But by temperament and background he was a conservative, and the next moment praised the cautious character of the American Revolution: George Washington was no radical Hotspur, but emulated the thoughtful Roman general Fabius Maximus Cunctator. "He never said tactless things to the princes of Europe. He did not regard himself as an apostle of liberty, bent on converting the people of all monarchies to the true faith and seeking for proselytes all over the world" — as did the infiltrating demagogues of contemporary France![9]

This typical fusion of conservative and radical elements in the attitude toward America is found in a more elaborate form in the writer and Justice of the Norwegian Supreme Court Envold Falsen (1755–1808), a man who in his youth had been a fervent liberal, but later turned conservative under the impact of the French Revolution. In 1802 Falsen wrote an article: "What is liberty, and where should we look for it?"[10] His main contention was, that the question of the best form of government remains eternally unsolved because it is futile: the form is not decisive, but the spirit. Liberty can well exist even under a government with absolute power, "when the monarch, having made the law, remains its first servant, and secures peace for all citizens by keeping it with a strong hand". On the other side, a parliamentary and constitutional system is no guarantee of freedom, as demonstrated in England, where "the *habeas corpus* Act through considerable periods was suspended". Is was for that reason that dissatisfied Englishmen "moved to the Antipodes, in order to seek out in the deserts and woods of North America that liberty which did not, or in their estimation did not, shelter them by their original hearths".

But if the Americans found liberty on their own soil, it was not because of their form of government. In Falsen's reasoning on this point there is a touch of Rousseau, whom he himself quoted in the article. "There they stood," he wrote about the Americans, "almost reduced to the original situation in which man left the hand of the Creator, released from all the bonds which by use and misuse have weighed down the ageing states". But the human factor was decisive (and now comes the conservative praise): "If the tree of liberty flowers on the soil of North America, this good fortune is due to the experienced hands which planted it, protected the young stem by fencing it in, and wisely knew how to keep it free of straggling growth".

Men of self-denying virtue, faithful to the voice of conscience, created America, as "virtue alone can preserve it" (here comes Washington again, the North American Fabius, Cocles and Cincinnatus combined). And the idealization is clinched by the contrast to France. The forms of liberty created during the French Revolution apparently were built on principles. But "to organize a republic in the middle of frivolous Paris was to conjure virtue from the cave of vice, and ask liberty to spring from depravity". The article curiously demonstrates how a loyal official of the Dano-Norwegian autocratic monarchy could combine a liberal praise of free America with a complete disregard of its constitutional forms, one of the lasting gains of the revolutionary period. And Envold Falsen's opinion was certainly shared by many of his colleagues at the time.

This situation was changed radically when, by the vicissitudes of world politics, Norway itself in 1814 was suddenly turned into a revolutionary state. The Dano-Norwegian king had been clinging tenaciously to his alliance with Napoleon. In the consequent war with England a British blockade cut Norway off from Denmark, made it largely dependent on its own resources, and strengthened the trend toward independence. When in 1813 the powers of the anti-Napoleonic coalition brought the Danish king to submission, and in January 1814 forced him to cede Norway to one of them, Sweden, the Norwegians rebelled, declared their independence, and in the following spring gave themselves a free constitution.

4

In itself this rebellion was bound to strengthen the Norwegian feeling of fellowship with the Americans. Like Norway, the USA in 1814 was at war with Great Britain, which was starving the Norwegians by its naval blockade and tried to force the country to accept Swedish domination. In the summer of 1814 the free Norwegian Government formally approached President Monroe and asked for American support of their newly-won liberty.[11]

This sympathy paved the way for a much more direct American impact. In the Norwegian Constitutional Assembly there was still a group of conservative delegates who looked nostalgically back to the period of Danish autocracy. But to most members the idea of national independence was now combined with a strongly democratic attitude. The feudal system had never become entrenched in Norway. The country had little nobility; the yeomen, who still constituted the great majority of the population, had never lost their personal freedom. In spite of the fact that the Assembly largely consisted of merchants and officials, the majority, in a mixture of radical and national enthusiasm, formulated a Constitution which, considered as a whole, safeguarded liberty, equality and majority rule more consistently than did any other European constitution of the time.

This document drew its inspiration from many sources. Even more was this the case with the many Draft Constitutions which were evolved by individuals or groups of members of the Assembly. It is often impossible to trace the details back to their origin. But obviously the American constitutional documents played an important part, both the constitutions of the individual states, the federal Constitution, and the federal Declaration of Rights; they were all well known to the Assembly. The forms of Norway's future political life now became all-important, and the influence of the American models is manifest in several of the Draft Constitutions. The most important among them, which was worked out by J. G. Adler and Christian Magnus Falsen (the son of Envold Falsen), opened with a Declaration of Rights that has its direct counterpart in the Massachusetts Constitution of 1780. The sentence which has been called the basic principle of the Norwegian Constitution ("Laws, not men should govern") is a translation from the American source.[12]

The young judge Chr. M. Falsen, often called "the Father of the Constitution", was himself a great admirer of Washington and Franklin. When a boy was born to him during the Assembly's session, he had him baptized Georg Benjamin, and later wrote a highly laudatory "biographical sketch" of Washington.[13] But Falsen's enthusiasm for America also included those constitutional forms which to his father had appeared unimportant. When the Assembly discussed the question of having one or two houses in parliament, both Falsen and the equally respected leader Georg Sverdrup reminded the members that their proposal was borrowed from the best constitutions in existence, the English and the American.[14] In retrospect, Falsen in 1817 could write with some exaggeration that the Norwegian Constitution, "in particular when it comes to the representation of the people, almost exclusively kept the American Constitution in view".[15]

The events in 1814 were decisive to the future Norwegian attitude toward the United States. The admiration of America became closely tied to the concept of its ideal political and social system; and Norway itself now joined America as one of the first constitutional states in the world. This feeling of fellowship and common cause was symbolically expressed in the proposal made to the Constitutional Assembly that Norway adapt the Star-Spangled Banner as its new national flag, with five stars, one for each of the dioceses. The analogy was found to be lame, and the proposal was not passed. But the final outcome was a national flag in the form of a cross, with the colors red, white and blue, "which now signify freedom, as we have seen it in the flag of French liberty, and still see it in the flag of the Dutch and the Americans and in the Union Jack of the English".[16]

But the spring independence of little Norway in 1814 was a tiny eddy, actually almost a mistake, within the swirling currents of contemporary history. Those general contrasting forces that had come to the fore with the French Revolution were lining up for battle in the new century, and they were going to shape the political life of the globe for a long future. The coalition against Napoleon, Son of the Revolution, was the beginning of a counter-revolution that found its organization in the Holy Alliance, and soon effectively checked the libertarian movements, political, social, and cultural, in one country after another on the European continent. On the opposite side liberalism gradually gathered its forces into an international movement, which became more and more radical, and was to show both its weakness and its strength in the revolutions of 1830 and 1848.

In this development America came to play an increasingly important part. Everywhere in Europe the country became better known than before through a surprisingly voluminous literature of information, but above all by emigration, which in the new century soon became an international movement and everywhere strengthened the positive image of America, not only as the paradise of political liberty, but as the "Common Man's Utopia". As time went on, the American Government itself sometimes helped in building up the same picture, by showing an active interest in the revolutionary movements in Europe. To liberals and radicals of all shades America became the great symbol of hope. Mme de Staël in 1817 called the United States "the vanguard of mankind", and her words were echoed during the following decades by freedom fighters everywhere.

But even the conservatives now had more to build on. The political thinkers of the Holy Alliance still largely moved on the level of theory, when they pointed to the abstract and articifial character of American political life. But America's own development from the 1820's soon furnished its denigrators with more striking material. The great democratic breakthrough under Andrew Jackson and his successors seemed to confirm the somber prophesies of European conservatives. So did mass immigration with its corollary of lawlessness, corruption and materialism, let alone the continued slavery of the Negroes, which had long been manifest as a blemish on American freedom. The "letters home" of the emigrants did not conceal these less attractive sides either. And in many countries propaganda against emigration made this negative image of America systematically known: the USA was described as a nation where equality had promoted mediocrity and liberty led to anarchy.

In the 1830's Alexis de Tocqueville added fresh fuel to this fire, and in the original and in translation his famous book reached a great part of the European intelligentsia. Tocqueville was much aware of the virtues of the democratic system, and firmly believed that society "was tending every day more and more towards equality". But his objectivity also made him stress many of the shortcomings and dangers of American life. In a way unknown before, he thus made America the fighting ground of the burning issues of his time; and he did so with an authority that gave the political and social debate a new substantiality. Typically, his book became an arsenal for radicals and conservatives alike.

These gradual changes can be followed in Norway too, during the period from 1814 to 1850. But the development here shows its own characteristic features both in direction and speed.

The first decade following the revolution of 1814 saw no radical shift in the political and social set-up of the country. The old class of patricians had been seriously weakened during the financial crisis caused by the Napoleonic wars. The farmers were not yet sufficiently aware of the political possibilities opened up to them in the Constitution; the small beginnings of an artisan and labor class were even less so. The officials still dominated the scene and filled the Ministry. They alone had the administrative and political training and the economic and cultural prestige which was necessary in order to make the new state a going concern.

Moreover, their ability was sorely needed. Down to the 1830's the energy of the group was almost completely absorbed in the defense of the national and political gains embedded in the Constitution. In the fall of 1814 the Norwegians after a brief war with Sweden finally had been forced to accept a union with that country under a common king. But they maintained the essence of national and political liberty. As king of Norway the Swedish monarch had to reign in accordance with the Norwegian Constitution, which left him little power. As reaction strengthened its hold on the Continent, the Swedish king tried time and again to change the Constitution in his favor. The Norwegian Government and officials here followed the line of the European liberals, and they were supported loyally by all other national groups. There was hardly a sign of sympathy with the Holy Alliance and its policy, and practically all of the royal attempts at revision were successfully warded off.

This did not mean that there were no efforts towards an organized opposition in internal politics. The lower classes soon found that their interests were not paid sufficient attention by those in power. In the parliament this dissatisfaction found a point of condensation almost immediately in a group which was named the "Flor-Hoel group" after its leaders (political parties in the modern sense did not yet exist). This group consisted of a circle of farmers and town-dwellers with an economic and national program directed against the Ministry and its bureaucracy. In particular the influence of the group made itself felt in the parliamentary sessions of 1818 and 1821, and its ideas were propagated by a journalistic activity that, for the period, was quite extensive. In this propaganda somewhat "radical" principles came to the fore, and the idea of liberty was stressed emphatically. In fact, however, these "patriots", as they called themselves, were not as yet much more radical than their adversaries were reactionary. In the main, all parties paid homage to the system established by the Constitution. At most there was a difference of intensity in the libertarian enthusiasm.

This lack of violent contrasts within a strongly democratic framework was also demonstrated in the Norwegian attitude toward America during this first decade of independence: the devotion that had been typical of the year 1814 continued almost unabated. So did the somewhat theoretical note of discussion. Factual information about America remained extremely scant, emigration had not started yet. The warmth of the praise showed some shades of difference. But these differences did not clearly indicate a conflict of principle, as was the case in other parts of contemporary Europe.

In one important point the Norwegian Constitutional Assembly had deviated from its general ideals: it had not accepted full liberty of religion. The issue soon was raised in parliament, in the first instance with reference to the Quakers. The opposition leader Jacob Hoel spoke in their favor. He admitted that he did not know the American Quakers very well; "but I have always assumed that the foremost of the constitutions of all nations would not have granted these great liberties to them if they were regarded as citizens detrimental to society".[17] Thus, Hoel regarded the American Constitution as a document above all criticism. Hoel's colleague Isaach Isaachsen, formerly a member of the Club of the Jacobins in revolutionary Paris, also referred to America motivating his proposal for full religious liberty.[18]

The motion was not carried; but it is typical that the other references to America in the debate struck the same polite and friendly note. In its report the parliamentary committee warned against direct comparison of the two countries, but was careful to explain the American position: Norway never recognized more than one official religion, but in America "most of the sects have, so to speak, grown up together with the new state".[19] The philosopher Niels Treschow had many doubts about religious liberty, but admitted that tolerance and forbearance had proved to be without dangerous consequence either to state or religion in many states, such as "Old Rome, North America and Holland".[20]

It is worth noting that a hint of objection to the "seductive" example of America on this point is found in the oppositional paper *Patrioten*. In a series of articles (certainly approved by the editor) one writer came out against giving the religious sects a free hand; in this connection he stated that after all the Quakers had caused no little trouble during the American War of Independence.[21] *Til-skueren* (the Spectator), a journal which strongly supported the Ministry, was to be found on the other side; one of its main contributors was Chr. M. Falsen, who since the 1820's had become increasingly conservative. The journal reminded its readers that complete religious liberty in America was one of the strongest allurements to European immigrants.[22] America was not yet monopolized by any special political group.

When it came to liberty in industry, the conservative *Tilskueren* was not so enthusiastic. The journal *Patrouillen* had maintained that it was the unrestricted liberty in the economic field which had brought to the US so many able hands and "helped bring the country to its present position by leaps and bounds". *Tilskueren* made mild fun of this liberty in industry in a nation where some persons "are artisans one year, farmers the second, solicitors the third, preachers the fourth and newspaper-writers the fifth". The journal itself saw the corporative spirit as a social advantage, in contrast to that chaos which in its opinion was bound to be the result of economic liberty. But typically, the attack was not directed against the American example. Again, the difference of background was pointed out: "That countries where artisans are in demand, do not oblige arriving artisans to enter a guild immediately upon their landing, is sensible and rational".[23]

Another problem touching upon the principle of equality had been temporarily postponed by the Founding Fathers: the abolition of nobility in Norway. The institution was finally done away with by the Parliament in 1821, perhaps the greatest victory of the Flor-Hoel opposition group. Most members of the ministerial party voted for retaining nobility, allegedly because of the dangerous international consequences of a more radical measure. The opposition did not believe this to be the sole motive, and in the debate played on the principle of equality, with America as an example. One of the few officials to vote for abolition, S. G. Bøckmann, emphasized the futile, unfair and socially harmful character of nobility, and referred his opponents to the states of North America and the Swiss Confederation, where the constitutions had made nobility illegal: "Who can point to states where true civil liberty is more successfully established by law?"[24] *Det norske Nationalblad* stressed that "Franklin and Washington were not noblemen. Nobility is no stamp of value".[25]

The opposition was, however, right in believing that nobility still had its advocates in Norway. In 1824 the Swedish king proposed to

Parliament the establishment of a new Norwegian nobility. When in its protest the oppositional *Patrioten* again referred to America, the ministerial journal *Tilskueren* retorted that "with regard to the North American free states we will only say, that the representatives of that nation are elected almost exclusively from amongst the wealthy and enlightened proprietors of great estates, who lack nothing of nobility but the name".[26] Such qualifications did, not, however, prevent the editor of *Tilskueren* from being quite eloquent in his enthusiasm for America on other occasions. A few years later he wrote in a historical survey that with the American Revolution "doubtless a new and better era was beginning".[27] Obviously Norway was not yet ripe for a clear clash of opposing political theories. An equally strong reason was doubtless the one referred to by *Tilskueren* in its discussion of nobility: American political life itself was still largely dominated by the upper classes, and therefore less alarming to conservative opinion.

Even in Norway a few observers of America early sensed that a change was in the offing in that respect. In 1822 the conservative writer Nicolaj Tidemand discussed the organization of federal states. Pointing to the democrats as "the most wild, vulgar, popular, rash, and dangerous among all political sects", he prophesied "a great catastrophe in this Union", because of its "dangerous electoral system".[28] Such ideas were still unusual in Norway. But they were soon to have a greater following.

The change became obvious around 1830: the period of idyllic unanimity was over.

After a final crisis in 1835 the pressure on the part of the Swedish king abated, and internal strife came to the fore. The dominant feature of the new political situation was the advance of the majority of the people, the farmers, toward that position of power which the Constitution had granted them. While the July and February Revolutions had few violent repercussions in Norway, they sharpened existing contrasts and increased the popular demands. Behind the farmers loomed the new industrial class, which to the panic of the Ministry made its first attempts at organization in the late 1840's. The "patriots" were assessing their cause more and more under the impact of the great international conflicts. Above all this was the case with their spiritual leader, the poet and popular hero Henrik Wergeland, who drew his inspiration from the Western democracies, condemned the influences from autocratic Germany, and saw his work in his own nation as part of the liberal world struggle against the oppressive spirit of the Holy Alliance.

This rallying of radical forces was bound to create a similar consolidation on the conservative side, and a similar clarification of principles. Against the "patriots" a new group which called itself the "intelligentsia", began voicing general doubts about the ideas of democratic progress. In its new journal *Vidar* (named after the Norse God who battled the wolfishness of brute force) Carl Fougstad complained that "the period of political innocence has come to an end, the peasantry begins to know the Constitution and its advantages, the demagogical element, the development of which is so well favored by our Constitution, has begun to show its effect".[29] "Demagogical" was the very catchword of European reaction. Here were the beginnings of a really conservative party, which gradually was to use the power of the Government systematically as a means of holding back the popular forces, in the political as well as in the social and economic fields. The ruthless repression in 1851 of the not too radical labor organizations showed how fast the political climate had toughened.

In this new situation the USA now came to play about the same part in Norwegian political discussion as it did in the rest of Western Europe. Some of this material, in particular on the liberal side, showed a repetition of old slogans. Quite a few of the poems of the 1830's written in honor of free America might as well have been produced in the 1780's. But the political situation put a new edge on old ideas. When international reaction swallowed up one after another of the free constitutions which had served as models to that of Norway, the feeling of real fellowship was bound to strengthen toward those free countries that still survived: England, "freedom's bastion amid the ocean", and America, "where the kernel of my own liberty grew in the shadow of the sycamore" (H. Wergeland).[30] The new contrasts at home were reflected in the American material: in both countries the issues were increasingly the same. New knowledge offered fresh possibilities of comparison. American literature became known (Cooper). The Government had Tocqueville's survey of American prisons translated (1839). His great book on America played a considerable part in Swedish political debate in the 1840's,[31] and also gradually became known to Norwegian readers, in particular from 1848 on.[32] But above all, emigration made the American problem more immediate and serious than was the case in most other nations.

Very few Norwegians had travelled to the States before the 1820's.

To the common man the country was largely unknown. An early immigrant farmer admitted that home in Norway he had never heard of America before he made a trip to town in 1836.[33] But beginning with the first organized crossing in 1825 the exodus soon swelled with irresistible force, in itself a sign of the growing economic and social pressure. In the second half of the nineteenth century Norway was to have the heaviest emigration to the United States in proportion to its population of all European nations with the sole exception of Ireland. Soon, there was hardly a family in the Norwegian countryside which hadn't relations and friends "over there". The letters home, often extensive surveys of conditions, the printed pamphlets about the country, and the oral reports of returning emigrants soon created among ordinary Norwegians a knowledge of America more personal, intimate and concrete than was the case with any other foreign nation.

This information took on a political character almost right away. The experience of the individual emigrant was by necessity limited. But the general image was largely the same, and it made an overwhelming impression. Practically all emigrants were farmers, with a sprinkling of artisans from the cities. They went to America because — in the words of one member of the pioneer group from 1825 — they "expected to find a Land of Canaan", and they really did. In the words of an opposition farmer who had suffered a good deal at home because of his views: "Now at last I can breathe freely".[34] The reports about America's political freedom, its general franchise for white men, its unheard of social equality, its complete religious liberty, and its unlimited economic opportunities, presented to the average Norwegian the most striking contrast to his own poor little country, dominated by officialdom politically and socially, and with many kinds of restrictions. In the continued democratization of modern Norway all through the 19th century this image of America was to be one of the strong motive forces.

But the image was also bound to create its counterimage. There were immediate practical considerations. The extent of emigration soon created misgivings even among the friends of America such as Henrik Wergeland. In Norway too it was attempted to give the "bloodletting" more moderate proportions; and the obvious method was to distribute more sober reports than those of the emigrants and the emigration agents. A clergyman put together a scheme in which American and Norwegian conditions were compared, one after the other; and everywhere Norway came out better.[35] Charles Dickens' very negative notes on America were published in Norwegian in 1843, soon after their appearance, at a time when foreign translations of that type were almost non-existent in Norway.

Almost of itself this activity took on political undertones; and they became increasingly explicit as the advocates of emigration pressed their point. A blackening of the glossy picture of America was bound to reflect favorably on existing conditions at home, which perhaps were not so bad after all. And the shortcomings of the United States could easily be traced back to that exaggerated liberty and equality, those "demagogical" traits, which the Fathers of the Norwegian Constitution and their successors had wisely avoided, and which some shortsighted radicals now longed to introduce. "If you declare that nothing is bad in a country, you reveal at once how unreliable you are", was a newspaper comment in 1837 on a letter from America. But that is the method of these propagandists, the paper continued: they "praise America for things which are exactly the same here with us, keep silent on America's deficiencies, and in their ignorance have found some conditions glorious which are the supreme disgrace of the country".[36]

This reevaluation of the America myth — on both political wings, but most strongly among the conservatives — was unavoidable because of the explosive internal development of America itself, which brought many conflicting elements to the surface. But the heat of the discussion, and the intensity in the confrontation of opposite views, came from the direct relevance of American political and social problems to similar problems at home in Norway. For the same reason the lack of synthesis is striking. To some extent it may be explained by the scarce and arbitrarily selected material that was available, and by the lack of competent commentators. But it was due even more to the purposes for which the material was largely used. Instead of a picture with added depth and shades, there were more often two contrasting pictures, in black and white respectively. Such was the situation at the time when L. Kr. Daa entered Norwegian political life.

## 2.

L. Kr. Daa came from a family with traditions in public service; his father, grandfather and great grandfather were clergymen.[37] He prepared himself for a scholarly career, and his interests ranged widely, from History, Ethnography, Geography and Languages to Economics and Law. Actually this range proved to be a handicap: he did not manage to sound beneath the surface anywhere. According to a political adversary Daa "knows a little of everything, but where did he get to the heart of the matter? His superficiality and carelessness are notorious".[38] His own nephew, the historian L. L. Daae, famous for his vitriolic characterizations, wrote that it was "almost unbeliev- able to what extent Daa despised, and consequently also lacked, the usual foundation and method of the historian. He was rather indif- ferent about bibliography, and oftener than not it was a matter of chance what sources he happened to use or overlook. He pursued his studies primarily in order to find support for results which had been decided in advance".[39]

Such words should not be taken literally. Notwithstanding, Daa was hardly wronged when he was twice passed over for professorships at the University of Christiania (Oslo), one in History, one in Statistics, although he was originally nominated for both. Daa himself and many of his contemporaries believed that this slight had something to do with Daa's "patriotic" views; his two rivals belonged to the minis- terial "intelligentsia". We have to admit that they were men of genius as well, while Daa himself was just a man of talents. When, in the 1860's, in his middle age, Daa finally had a lectureship and later a professorship at the University, both in History, it was too late. He is now primarily remembered as a politician and publicist. But in that field his special type of gift showed to its advantage. "He had at his disposal a rich treasury of polyhistorical knowledge, and better than most he knew how to master and utilize it".[40] Perhaps it was just with large-scale political activity in view that he branched out so widely in his studies.

Daa early joined the oppositional camp of the "patriots". As a schoolboy in Bergen, during the tumultuous celebration of Constitu- tion Day 1826, he suggested to his classmates that they should break the windows in the Governor's house, this official being at the time Chr. M. Falsen, now a bitter adversary of the "patriots". Out of school, Daa was for a time family tutor in the home of the liberal cabinet minister Chr. Krohg, who according to Daa himself strongly influenced his political views. Daa early became a fervent admirer of Great Britain and the British; English history was his favorite lecture subject at the university. He saw his own ideal in the British political system generally, and the moderately liberal reformism of the whigs in particular.[41]

At the University he became a leader among the students. During this period he was a close friend of Henrik Wergeland, and the friendship lasted for many years, while Daa swiftly ascended in politics, and for a while was the undisputed leader of the opposition. Both men were national and liberal, and both abhorred all attempts to restrict civil liberty. Like Wergeland, Daa regarded the celebration of Constitution Day (which was frowned upon by the Swedish king) as "a starting point in the battle against excessive official power". Like Wergeland, Daa reacted against the cultural influences from Central Europe which reached Norway by way of Denmark. Instead, both put their faith in the liberal tradition of the countries of Western Europe and America, and fought those ideas which "made liberty shrink to a sun-mote under the eye-glasses of Haller or Hegel".[42]

But the two friends also diverged in some of their views. Daa never could follow Wergeland in his republican sympathies, which were out of keeping with his enthusiasm for the British constitutional monarchy.[43] Likewise there was a difference in their ideas about the lower orders in society, "the people". To be sure, even Wergeland maintained that the right of voting should be limited to those "in possession of land, house, or office". Only thus would it be possible to preserve order at public proceedings and stimulate the urge toward economic betterment.[44] But the aim of the immense educational activity of Wergeland was to raise the lower orders to political maturity; and he firmly believed that this could be done.

Daa harbored no such dreams. When *he* demanded "a civil and private liberty as complete and a freedom of speech as extensive as is consistent with an ordered state", it was because such reforms would allow "those not granted the right to vote" to feel the benefit of liberty as far as was just and possible, and thus prevent dissatisfaction among them: "What they never could use, even if it were granted them, namely direct participation in government, they do not appreciate anyway". There was in Daa an element of social conservatism. Wergeland was a democrat, and believed in the lower classes. Daa's primary concern was to make certain that these classes be not dammed up so as to evoke a democratic overflow.

Liberty, not equality was to Daa the decisive demand. A further liberalization of franchise would in his opinion spell disaster. Still, liberty of speech, religion and industry would prevent the growth of a possible aristocracy, a class which was not to his mind either. The lower orders were not fit to participate actively in government. But neither should they be kept under guardianship: they should influence government through free public opinion, where the contrasts are balanced and are inclined to strike a middle road.[45]

This good whiggism made Daa praise the parliamentarism and political party system of the British, at a time when the idea of political parties was regarded as almost immoral in Norway. And in the early 1840's it became his own political dream to create a Norwegian opposition party which did not represent social classes, but political principles, a union of liberal merchants, university men and officials in alliance with the farmers. The failure of this undertaking led to Daa's political downfall. In the parliament of 1842 he had been one of the leaders of the opposition, and even in 1845 he was several times elected chairman of the "Odelsting" (second chamber). But when his master plan did not succeed, largely because he could not collaborate with the farmers, Daa suddenly broke with the opposition. This unexpected change of allegiance left him politically isolated. He was returned to parliament only once (in 1854), and never more regained a leading position.

His former political friends found it to be an inexplicable breach of principles that a man who had once published *Granskeren*, "one of the most radically democratic organs this country ever had", could now "throw himself into the arms of persons and conditions he had formerly fought against".[46] Daa did not deny having changed his views with regard to persons, but he could not admit having changed his political opinions. If in the parliament of 1845 he was forced to leave the opposition, he asserted, it was because of a change of attitude on the part of the government, which now, in the most important questions, showed a spirit that attached to it the friends of liberty.[47] At the same time Daa's own former friends had deserted exactly these ideals on one point after another, above all in the question of religious liberty, always one of the causes most close to Daa's heart. His former allies doubted that these were his real motives, however. To them his "berserk fury" seemed to have no connection with vital political matters, only with "pure trifles". Neither the opposition nor the adherents of the Ministry had changed their politics: "everything remained as before, except that L. K. Daa was now an apostate".[48] His opponents explained his defection by a want of character, an inability to cooperate, and an urge to domineer.

The matter has remained controversial even among the historians. Ernst Sars agreed with Daa that his real concern was the liberal cause.

In 1845 the Government itself, after previous resistance, seized the initiative and reached a solution on a number of the most important issues, while the farmers remained untouched by anything but their own class interests and sacrificed liberalism wherever it was to their advantage to do so. Sars thus accepted Daa's own interpretation: it was natural that he had joined up with the farmers' group, but at the same time had tried to change it from a coterie to a real party with a consistent liberal program. There was nothing wrong with this policy, except that it came too early.[49] — Against this opinion Arne Bergsgård maintained that the decisive factor in the shift was Daa's personal friction with the other opposition leader, a rivalry in which Daa was the loser. When he blamed the farmers for lack of liberalism, it was just a rationalization. The basic facts remained the same, and so did the Government.[50]

The present writer agrees with Sars, and with Daa himself. If looked into carefully, his policy appears as the logical expression of consistent ideas. This nucleus of conviction will become apparent if attention is paid not only to Daa's work in parliament and his activity as political orator and pamphleteer, but to the field where he really was original and creative, journalism. For this purpose his discussions of international questions are particularly significant, and not least his comments regarding America.

Daa's first great achievement as a journalist was the publication of the review *Granskeren* (The Inquirer) 1840–43. For the first time in Norway he created a journal with a thoroughly personal flavor. All articles were anonymous, as was customary at that time; he even declared that "as far as possible" he had tried to remove from the journal what was individual. Actually he wrote most of the review himself, and he is easily recognizable. This makes the journal an invaluable source for the period when Daa was in a leading political position. In its first issue *Granskeren* declared itself to be "a liberal party-paper", working for a progressive policy along the lines pointed out in the Constitution.[51] But both before 1839 and after, Daa had written in *Morgenbladet,* which at that time was also in opposition; from 1839–47 he was a permanent contributor, and editor of its foreign news section.[52] From 1848–51 he held the same position in *Christianiaposten,* and was the editor of this paper from 1853 to 1856. In addition, from 1851 to 1853 he published *Den norske Tilskuer* (The Norwegian Observer), and in the 1870's again was the editor of his own journal, *Tids-Tavler* (Tables of the Times).

These publications covered an amazing range of subjects. But in most of them the foreign news section played an important part, in a way that had no parallel in contemporary Norway. In the Norwegian press of the time foreign news consisted largely of extracts from foreign newspapers, and they were just called Summaries ("Referater"). The material reveals the poverty of the resources, both financially and otherwise. The editors frankly admitted that their news coverage depended on the number of foreign publications — if any — which they could afford to subscribe to. The news items were normally presented without comment, because there was nobody qualified to discuss them. The poet and journalist A. O. Vinje in 1852 bluntly demanded that the papers should rather stick to mere translation, since "the original stuff which can be provided in this country, is mostly one-sided and poor".[53]

In particular the American news was bound to suffer from this state of affairs. We learn in 1837 that "papers from the New World rarely come to us and are used only to a limited extent by those who report on foreign news".[54] American events therefore largely reached Norwegian readers as reported in British newspapers. In *Morgenbladet* even the Civil War was still essentially covered by clips from the London *Times*, reflecting the point of view and bias of certain circles in England. American conditions outside the sphere of politics were mostly discussed in letters from emigrants and comments on them.

Here, L. Kr. Daa moved on a different level. In the first issue of *Den norske Tilskuer* he criticized his political colleagues for concentrating short-sightedly on so-called "useful" and "practical" home events, while contemptuously neglecting almost all foreign affairs, "even as examples or models". His own program was "to survey events in Norway and abroad, and to compare Norwegian and foreign conditions".[55] And he was better equipped for this ambitious task than most of his Norwegian contemporaries. He was much more widely read than the ordinary journalist. He had the necessary knowledge to discuss the material, both national and foreign, in a larger context. And he did so not only in newspapers, but also in his periodicals, pamphlets, and books.

While we thus have quite extensive material in the way of foreign comments from Daa's hand, to interpret it is not always easy. He was once accused of using his foreign news reports in *Morgenbladet* as propaganda for his own opinions. He answered that his single duty was to "mirror European opinion faithfully", and that he was supported in this attitude by the editor.[56] While these assertions certainly should not be taken at face value, they demonstrate the generally accepted idea about the impersonal task of the foreign editor in the ordinary papers. Opinions expressed in "Summaries" cannot without caution be attributed to Daa himself. And the journalists of the time did not yet know the modern technique of giving neutral news a personal slant by means of the headlines.

Nothwithstanding, even in the newspapers a good many comments and connecting remarks doubtless originate from Daa, not from his sources; and much other material is signed, or can otherwise be attributed to him. Judging it as evidence of his own "opinion" is a different matter, however. His remarks on any specific subject are often written at long intervals, and have to be pieced together from different kinds of publications. It would be demanding too much to expect consistency in details. Moreover, there was certainly some truth in the criticism referred to above: some of the foreign news items clearly were geared to Daa's journalistic needs at the moment. Once in a while he may also be found to be contradicting his own earlier statements on a subject, whether he realizes it himself or not.

As a whole, however, if Daa's anonymous newspaper work is studied carefully, and compared with material doubtlessly written by him, the main impression is one of consistency and coherent development, even in his handling of foreign affairs. This also holds good of his attitude toward the United States. Throughout his entire career as a publicist America was, for good or bad, one of his most frequent points of comparison. By necessity he sometimes theorizes and generalizes, — he never visited the States himself. But his writing reveals an unfailing interest in American history and a good deal of real knowledge; in his scholarly work he was also actively interested in American ethnology. There are some problems to which he often returns, and not always consistently. But generally speaking there is a clear line of development, with its turning point in the late 1840's when his own political career passed its zenith.

### 3.

Among the questions which, from the 1830's onward, increasingly brought the American example into Norwegian public discussion, that of *religious liberty* remained one of the most important. The problem was raised particularly by the preaching of the dissenters,

5

which at that time was still forbidden by law. America in the same period went through a series of broad religious revivals, with a luxuriant growth of sects. Their manifestations were often surprising; through the emigrant letters they became widely known in Norway, and were naturally brought into the debate. But the noticeable change of attitude toward America generally which is revealed in the material studied, was as much connected with the sharpening of ideological contrasts in Norway itself.

To liberal circles America in the 1830's remained the ideal that it had been before, — the nation which "did not only erect the altar of political, but also that of religious liberty".[57] But beside such obligatory praise there were now dissenting voices, which maintained that liberty might be detrimental both to religion and state. And now the critics no longer contented themselves with rejecting the American example because of differences in historical background.

The liberal clergyman Iver Hesselberg was one of those who still referred to America as an example of "the creative power of the free forms".[58] But a number of other theologians thought differently about the creative power. W. A. Wexels would recognize no liberty which had its roots "outside of the life which is in God".[59] Christian Delphin pointed to the passions which are released when liberty lacks that foundation: examples abound in "the free North America, which is praised so highly, and is generally proclaimed as the home of civil happiness".[60]

In a book by William Sverdrup it becomes particularly clear how America could now also be used as an argument *against* religious liberty. One shouldn't ask "what man is as man, and as citizen of a civic community", Sverdrup wrote, "but what man is as an organic member of an organic state". Liberty is realizable through the state only, as demonstrated by Hegel. Those who refer to North America as a model of liberty, reveal that they "have not risen to the organic concept of state and state liberty, but only to the concept of a civic community and a civic liberty. — Free in a true and noble sense the North-Americans are not".[61]

This challenge Daa could not leave unanswered. As early as in 1831 he had himself protested against the philosophers of reaction, Haller and Hegel (above, p. 61). He used as his starting point the proposal of a law about religious liberty that had been worked out by Claus Winther Hjelm and commissioned by the Ministry of Church and Education; Daa opened his attack on a broad front in the first issue of *Granskeren*. The author of the proposal had maintained that the section about religious liberty in the American Constitution was "one of its weakest sides". He regarded the state as the common denominator, and the church as "the main wheel in our machinery of state": if it should be destroyed, conflicts which Norway now happily did not know would be unavoidable. If state and church were separated, they would be opposed to each other, and "in our times" many would then rather serve the state than the church. "Whoever knows something about the history of the American sects, must pray God keep us from introducing a similar liberty!"[62]

To the liberal Daa, the relation between state, religion and individual must appear as totally different. To him the state was nothing but a means of realizing the freedom of the citizen, it was no goal in itself; and liberty was a condition of civic happiness, just because it was the most effective means of creating it. Daa did not for that reason regard religion as being of no consequence to society, and he was careful not to provoke the suspicion that he wished to separate church and state in Norway. A very few among his contemporaries did harbor such ideas, however, and they referred to America as a model.[63] Daa felt differently. He even thought that the USA rather "ought to have established a regular and well founded state church, and granted religious liberty beside it". That was the arrangement he hoped for in the future in his own country, and which also, eventually, came to be realized. If, nevertheless, he referred to America, it was because the country was an example of the importance of liberty, not only as a goal in itself, but as a means to an end. America showed that "too much liberty in matters of conscience is more beneficial than too much restriction", and this principle was equally applicable to religion, church and society.[64]

"When many of our intolerants assert that greater liberty in religious matters would produce disbelief, .... the example of the US refutes their contention most clearly".[65] Many facts made it obvious to Daa that on the contrary, religious liberty in America had strengthened the intensity of religious feeling: no Protestant country in Europe had nearly so many temples and clergymen as had the USA, where everything was based on voluntary contributions. And this strength of organized religion was not just sham and pretence: the fear of God was really greater among the Americans than in our own hemisphere.

Daa here referred to the work of a Frenchman another of whose books had ealier been translated into Norwegian at Government expense. He was thinking of A. de Tocqueville's *De la démocratie en Amérique.* "By comparing the formerly so intolerant and now so free-thinking France with the always tolerant and god-fearing America, he [Tocqueville] comes to exactly the reverse result of that which our home-bred legislator-philosopher [Winther Hjelm] formed in his arm-chair. Tocqueville assumes that the fear of God being so remarkably general in the United States, is due to the government's complete unconcern about religion and the clergy, and to the fact that the clergy likewise abstain as much as possible from interfering with the business of government".[66]

Winther Hjelm saw America as the example demonstrating how religious sectarianism let loose "slackens all the bonds of humanity and dulls all sympathies".[67] The liberal Daa saw the same country demonstrate how a natural harmony was created when the activity of the state was limited as much as possible even in the religious field. He did not only believe that religious liberty was favorable to religious faith in a more restricted sense: he maintained that it strengthened moral feeling and social understanding generally. In America there was "a sense of public decency, a respect for good moral and humanity" which Europe could only admire.

To Daa one of the proofs of this high moral standard was the American work for temperance, one of the much needed movements in his time. It was of American origin, and it made progress in Europe "exactly to the same degree that religious life is similar to that in America" — that is, "in countries where a living faith is called forth by the free conflict and activity of several sects".[68] Free competition created initiative even in religion. Just those itinerant preachers, who were so feared by the adversaries of religious liberty, were leaders in the temperance movement, which even Norwegian clergymen regarded as one of the most delightful fruits of godliness.

Daa's liberalism was consistent even to the point of believing that temperance would be most effectively furthered in Norway if the Government refrained from prohibiting distillation. The authorities ought rather to behave "like an American or Englishman, who ad-dresses himself to the people by persuasion and conviction alone".[69] Work in the cause of sobriety by moral warnings and by state regula-tion simultaneously would be of no avail. Daa felt that success could not be achieved through legislation, but through the activities of travelling agitators such as, e. g., Robert Baird, who around 1840 appeared as a temperance speaker in many parts of Scandinavia.[70]

One more example proved to Daa that "the republicans of the West do not live for self-interest alone": America was the pioneering country in the field of prison reform. After all, religious liberty perhaps did not slacken all human bonds of sympathy! The Norwegians of the time disagreed about whether they should choose the Philadelphia or the Auburn prison system, and Daa had a very definite opinion on that point. He alone called attention to the fact that both systems were American: "Europe has been unable to do more than to ponder which of the two institutions — it will imitate".[71]

Behind such individual issues Daa saw a general principle which made the United States a model even to his own nation. "The Americans consider it the safest method of obtaining a good government — and at a reasonable cost — that the authorities leave as much as possible of the affairs of civic life to the decision and management of those men to whom they are of most immediate concern. Thus, the authorities in America never take charge of any matter before they have convinced themselves that it can by no means be left to take its own course: they always recognize their own administration as a necessary evil, which flows from the imperfection of things human".[72]

This general demand that the state keep passive as far as possible, of course was particularly relevant in the field of *economic* legislation. "Monopolies reduce enterprise . . . . The sentence which Economics long ago substantiated, that particular or exclusive privileges create indolence, but competition activity, is as completely corroborated by experience in Norway as in any other country". Again the USA offers striking material for comparison: while in Norway one still finds many "absurd restrictions", America maintains "a wise liberty of business and trade", contenting itself with taxes for fiscal purposes, and regulations necessary for the maintenance of order.[73]

To Daa, as we have seen, liberty was essential because it was an effective means of creating civic happiness. What he actually had in mind, however, was that the means should rest in the hands of the bourgeoisie. This important qualification transpired when, for once, he took exception to the liberty of industry. He wrote, that freeing commerce from traditional regulation would make it necessary to provide protection for the old merchant class, and create guarantees hindering that "all towns and rural districts be flooded by good-for-nothings and pedlars". And it was necessary to make certain that this crowd of new tradesmen were not enabled by sheer numbers to use the assessment of taxes for pushing the heaviest economic burdens onto the shoulders of the old merchant class. To Daa the existing system of assessment had established a "mob rule".[74] If liberty conflicted with his social ideals and created equality in any form, he was willing to make a compromise with it. Even his enthusiasm for America applied to its free legislation, not to its social and political equality.

To Daa as to most of his contemporaries an important factor in their attitude toward the United States was *emigration*.

The motives of the emigrants themselves for leaving can be outlined quite simply. Apart from a spirit of adventure, the majority was largely attracted by information about the leeway left to individual initiative in the States, the rich natural resources opened up to the newcomers, and the equality in rank and opportunities. But the reactions to emigration among those who remained in Norway cannot be schematized that neatly.

Members of the opposition did not automatically advise people to leave. Conservatives did not simply denigrate America in order to defend existing conditions at home. A. O. Vinje can serve as an example. In his radical period in the 1840's he indignantly criticized the policy of Norwegian officials in putting obstacles in the way of the emigrants. But when later he approached the Ministerial party and became quite conservative himself, he nevertheless insisted that people be freely allowed to emigrate. In part the reason may be that Vinje knew the poverty of many Norwegians from experience. But he also quite simply regarded it as an advantage that the discontented left: "That is the most emphatic opposition".[75]

On the other side the international revolutionary firebrand Harro Harring, who made a brief appearance in Norwegian political life around 1850, regarded emigration to America as an unworthy escape from difficulties. The Americans themselves, Harring wrote, would have despised their ancestors if, instead of fighting and gaining liberty at home, they had taken refuge in Australia. Emigration was just a temporary relief to the individual, not to the nation.[76]

Political considerations alone did not decide this attitude toward emigration, however. Often a national motive was equally important: the exodus of so many able-bodied men and women was regarded as a deplorable bloodletting of the people. This consideration played a great part in the reflections of the leading "patriots" in the 1830's, H. Wergeland and L. Kr. Daa. But even here there were shades of difference.

We have seen how often Daa in his polemics of this period referred to the ideal of American liberty. On this point he agreed with the emigrants — but only in their premises, not in their conclusion. In spite of his opposition views he was far from happy about that reaction against Norwegian shortcomings which emigration implied. Daa came closer to Harro Harring when he maintained that the American model should not seduce to emigration, but stimulate reforms at home. To those who complained about restrictions on business he answered: "The Norwegian nation makes its own laws. Let it elect an energetic parliament, which either pulls the reluctant government with it along the road of the rest of the civilized world" — or provide itself with a better government![77] America should be an example, not an asylum.

Daa realized, however, that appeals to patriotism or reformatory zeal were not enough. While in his liberal polemics he wrote eulogies in honor of America, he at the same time found it to be "a useful deed to counteract that praise of America which in many regions is prevalent among the farmers".[78] His main argument was that of natural resources. He admitted that "most of the other nations which go to America [as emigrants], do so of necessity", because their soil cannot any longer support an increasing population. But that was not the case in Norway; here Daa struck a strongly national note. What Norway lacked, was not economic chances, but "common sense, unity and conscientiousness": actually, "our entire land is in some ways an America". Northern Norway in particular had large uncultivated areas which were waiting for pioneers, where the newcomers could live among their own people, in a climate which they knew and which was not detrimental to health, as was the case in America.

Daa asked for information from his readers about possibilities for new settlement in the country itself: such assistance would "do more good than all the other warnings against listening thoughtlessly to the heralds of emigration to America".[79] He was delighted to read in the above mentioned Robert Baird's book *Visit to Northern Europe* (New York, 1841) that in his view the Norwegians are well off, have what they need, and inhabit a country that by better cultivation could yield even more, " a statement from the mouth of an American which could not easily have been dreamt of by any of our emigrants, or declaimers about emigration".[80]

Daa knew that many people were skeptical toward critics of America and suspected them of egoistic motives. It was often assumed that such criticism originated from the rich, who were afraid of raised wages as the labor supply decreased. These suspicions indicate how clearly emigration was felt as a social movement, and Daa was careful not to leave any doubts with regard to his own attitude. He maintained however, that such assumptions were false: the ocean crossing was so expensive that in fact few workmen could afford it. Most emigrants to America owned some property; and in that case emigration actually benefited those who remained, and who bought cheap what the emigrants had to dispose of. Daa warned that more often than not exaggerated descriptions of America were apt to originate from Americans who wished for cheap labor, or captains of ships who needed cargo. Such profiteers would also reckon with the fact that distance often made it impossible for the emigré to return from America, even if the country proved to be less attractive than expected, a suspicion which Daa found confirmed in Charles Dickens' *American Notes*.[81]

In his eagerness to have misinformation corrected from reliable sources Daa went to the length of printing in *Granskeren* an advertisement asking for information about a Norwegian emigrant who reportedly had returned disappointed from America. Daa was "not averse" to having it confirmed by a man who knew the facts from his own experience that it was "quite inadvisable" for Norwegians to emigrate to the States.[82]

This propaganda against emigration in Daa's articles moved on the material and practical level, however: he discussed the climate, the possibilities of livelihood, and other disadvantages of leaving. Henrik Wergeland's reactions are interesting in comparison. He was the poet of liberty beyond all others in Norway. As such, in the 1820's and early 1830's he praised America as a nation where "the state has few shortcomings". When emigration began, he found that "our own legislation, so unfree in many respects, is the real motive". If Norway established liberty of religion and industry, the inclination to emigrate would disappear, and the longing toward liberty would no longer look for satisfaction beyond the Atlantic. But even if Wergeland understood the motives, he regarded emigration as "a great national disaster". And its explosive growth in the following years made it appear to him as "the most dangerous disease of our time, bleeding the country to death".[83]

In his patriotic efforts to find a remedy Wergeland also directed his attack against America itself, as did L. Kr. Daa. But he went much farther: when necessary, he abandoned the myth of the land of liberty. In his struggle to have removed the paragraph in the Norwegian constitution which banned Jews from the country Wergeland still pointed to "America where the liberty of hand and mind exists". When he wrote for people who might themselves consider emigration, however, as he did in the paper which he published for the laboring classes, he did not only, like Daa, question the material possibilities across the ocean, and appeal to the "renowned patriotism" of Norwegians in order to hold people back: he directly raised doubts about American liberty and equality. He wrote that Norway deserved to be "loved by the Norwegian laborer beyond any other country, beyond America, which only offers liberty to those who can avoid selling themselves as bond servants for many years". He wrote that "the extreme of inequality really exists *there*, where even children are born a merchandise, namely to be sold for slaves. But the soil of Norway tolerates slavery so little, that the negro slave is a free man the very moment he puts his foot on it".[84]

Daa used different arguments. For him, too, emigration ran counter to his national feelings. But at this stage he did not, like Wergeland, try to lessen the idea of America as the land of liberty. Doing so would have been at variance with his other statements at the time, both in his parliamentary speeches and in his writing, and certainly also with his own sincere conviction. Slavery was a deviation from the libertarian ideal; while of course Daa was aware of it,[85] in his propaganda he preferred to keep silent about it. He might, like Wergeland, have pointed to other American shortcomings in the field of equality; he must have read about them in plenty in Tocqueville. But Wergeland did so because he regarded equality as a blessing. Daa did not, and therefore could not well use the argument. He rather saw an exaggerated equality in America; but that could not easily deter Norwegian emigrants from leaving. It was in a different context that Daa was to return to that group of problems.

### 4.

His generally positive attitude was not going to last, however. Toward the middle of the 1840's signs of a change became increasingly noticeable in Daa's writing. And there were indications of it even before that.

Daa's oppositional program was to limit the power of the bureaucracy. To him, government should have its center of gravity in the parliament. But this did not imply that he would give parliamentary representation a broader foundation in the people. Similarly, he saw decentralization as another useful limitation of governmental power: people should be encouraged to manage their own business as much as possible. Therefore he referred to America as "the favorite soil of individual liberty and municipal institutions", and fought excessive domination by the officials because they represented governmental power.[86] But when for these reasons he was accused of being "ultra-radical and bent on levelling everything", he protested peremptorily: "The era when one couldn't mention liberty without mentioning equality, passed quite some time ago".[87]

His fight against the power of the officials was not a struggle for equality. On the contrary he asserted that equality represented a danger to liberty, and that it was the enemies of liberty who wished for it. And these enemies he found not least among the representatives of officialdom. If Claus Winther Hjelm and his colleagues should succeed in bringing all sheep into the same Christian herd, then it would also be easy for him "to rule and shear his pious flock under the sacred law of equality".

To Daa, liberty and equality did not of necessity go together. On the contrary: he rather posed them as thesis and antithesis. In 1840 the outstanding Norwegian conservative economist and statesman A. M. Schweigaard suggested that from the point of view of Economics the Norwegian land would yield larger crops and be cultivated more efficiently if it belonged to many small freeholders, than if it had to be leased from the great land-owners. Daa protested against this "parcelling out" and this "hatred of privilege". The political consequence of such measures would be, that when all were alike, the king would govern easily through his aristocracy of officials. In order to avoid such absolute domination one should make certain that the officials were counterpoised by a well-to-do upper class of farmers and bourgeoisie. Equality would mean a leveling-down of everybody except the officials themselves. In that way "the most humble Norwegian-French egalitarians" would crush liberty and extend governmental power by making certain that nobody else would be qualified to govern.[88]

No doubt Daa was here again influenced by Tocqueville, who maintained as his thesis that tyranny could most easily originate in a state where the differences of station are leveled down. When Daa talked of the "Norwegian-French" egalitarians, he was in agreement with Tocqueville, who pointed out (in the introduction to Part I of his book) that it was precisely such policies that the kings of France had pursued most consistently. The public servants in Norway, Daa maintained, planned to dominate society in a similar way. But Tocqueville had primarily investigated the effect of equality in a society like free America, and showed how "the tyranny of the majority" in many ways also represented a danger to liberty. Following him, Daa placed beside the "Norwegian-French" kind of egalitarianism a different type, namely "the rebellious-American" kind, which intended to "turn away privileges and differences of property as far as is feasible, and then chase king and officials after them, and eventually play Yankee-doodle in the tidy house".[89]

This critical awareness of dangerous democratic tendencies in American society appears early in Daa's writing, and may also reflect the English influence which is so important in his thought. The circles which in Great Britain had championed the "Reform Bill" to victory, but then intended it to be "final", earlier in the battle had referred to the American example, but after 1832 became more critical toward American democracy.[90] Daa visited England in 1838, and may well have run into such criticism there. In a letter from London to *Morgenbladet* he maintained that the demands of the Chartists of a widened franchise were too radical: "most visitors *other than Americans* presumably find that a liberal Englishman couldn't wish for much more in the way of political rights".[91] But he did not yet mention excessive democracy as an essential objection to America. He only touched upon the problem at long intervals, showing incidentally that he was aware of it.

C. Winther Hjelm in 1840–41 asserted that "extravagant ideas of liberty are always close to tyranny", and he repeatedly supported the axiom with American examples.[92] Daa was willing to admit that America also had its mob, which sometimes encroached upon the rights of "a party it does not like". He even called this "a sad and dark side of the picture of the Republic". But he denied any connection between such shortcomings and the liberal legislation, which was the point made by Winther Hjelm: they only confirmed a fact which we knew already from Europe, namely "the savagery of the needy classes". It was not the educated citizens in America that were obsessed by "the Satan of intolerance": violence was typical of the mob.[93]

Daa's line of reasoning is consistent enough, remembering his own position at the time. What he was now fighting, was the "Norwegian-French" egalitarians among adherents of the ministerial party, not the "rebellious-American", who were "extremely few" even in Europe,[94] let alone in Norway. Also toward the latter group his front was clear enough; only he did not at the moment need to guard it continuously. America was still important to him primarily as a model and a piece of propaganda against the enemy toward whom he was just now aiming his guns. He couldn't weaken their effect by simultaneously specifying the aspects that he feared in American life.

But this strategic situation changed basically when in the early 1840's the Government itself took up and planned to solve several of the problems for which the liberal Daa had battled most vigorously, and at the same time the farmers appeared to him to desert the cause of liberty. Simultaneously, the democratic forces made themselves felt more and more as a general and real danger, in the world at large and even at home in Norway. The February Revolution was approaching, and so was the first socialistic Norwegian labor movement of 1850. This situation called for a revaluation even of Daa's foreign alliances. In the years to come his writing about America changed deeply both in ideas and mood.

In 1850 A. O. Vinje, still in his radical phase, accused Daa of having broken with his own past. "Will he, as it were, wash off the sin of having once been a republican, by blindly hating revolutions and republics?"[95]

The change of political ideas which many believed Daa guilty of following his break with the farmers' opposition in the parliament of 1845, seemed to be further confirmed in his foreign news section in *Christiania-Posten*, where he had been a contributor since 1848. But it is hard to desert views one has never held, and Daa certainly never was a republican. Nor had he ever been a revolutionary. Therefore it was equally misleading when, a few years later, Vinje asserted that Daa had been "crimson" in his *Granskeren*.[96] Daa's opposition at the time was constitutional on the English pattern, and had no social content as had the revolutions of 1848. In his defense of Daa, Ole Richter stressed this point quite appropriately: what had been said about Daa's republicanism and admiration for the North-American constitution doubtless was "*in part* due to a misunderstanding. He is a democrat to the extent that he wishes the educated, economically and intellectually independent part of the nation to have the weightiest vote in the affairs of the state".[97]

While it could justly be said that Daa was not exactly enthusiastic about the revolutions of 1848, this did not hold good about all of them: he could sympathize with national insurrections which had no social background. Thus, in the beginning he accepted the war of independence of the Italians against the Austrians, and he enjoyed the fact that the Italian nobility and the old, historically famous families of the country came forward as "the natural leaders of the popular movement": in Italy, "communist riots did not occur, — not even among the tramps of Naples".[98] History thus could teach us, he felt, that "an enlightened and rich nation has the natural authority to govern itself. During an insurrection it knows how to use the right means to vanquish those it chooses to regard as its enemies, while political barbarians only use their liberty for pieces of folly and errors which make them forfeit their freedom".[99]

The mistake of the Italians was that in the end they did not show maturity after all: their revolution assumed a social character, and therefore was bound to fail. Since the rising in Belgium in 1830 and in Schleswig-Holstein in Daa's own age, "like that of the North Americans in the days of our ancestors, were *purely political without an admixture of one mustard-seed of social or democratic ideas*" (Daa's italics), this explains the fact that these nations had more success than the Italians had in their "suicidal battles in the face of the Austrian guns, their scoffing at the sacrifice of Charles Albert, their hatred of the idea of monarchy, their threats against religion, property, and family". The "suicidal revolutionaries" alienated the best in society, and their game was lost. In order to show how little social tinder there was in the American revolution as distinct from the Italian rising Daa even pointed to slavery as an explanation of why America managed to carry its War of Independence through to victory (of course without for his part accepting slavery as an institution): the maintenance of slavery demonstrated that "the moneyed aristocracy and vested rights of Europe had nothing to fear from supporting this insurrection".[100]

Daa certainly was no reactionary, his sympathy was with liberty. But he believed that liberty can never be enforced by the slave, who "in a desperate rage thrusts the dagger into the hard heart of his master or smashes his head with all its evil plans". The slave surely can overthrow the tyrant, but he is not himself able to build the kind of liberty which "requires time and orderly, considerate effort".[101] Democracy cannot solve a task of this kind. Therefore, in France, "the result of the general suffrage was the saddest thing one can imagine".[102]

But why did not Daa in his comments on foreign affairs turn with more violence against America now, when the egalitarians of the "rebellious-American" type had gained such influence even in Europe? He actually made a note of the fact that "the press in the US has greeted the most recent French revolution as a new social gospel".[103] And in purely general meditations he could say with direct reference to America that in democracies so far it hadn't so much been "a question of the benefit of the people as of its leaders".[104] But decisive to him was the fact that at the moment America certainly was not "rebellious". "The United States rejoices in peace, happiness and rapid development", and in spite of "all the red and socialistic bragging" to be heard over there, "the general suffrage has placed at the head of the republic that man whom the moderates and the enlightened regarded as the most honest", namely Zachary Taylor, "the first candidate for many years who has come from the ranks of the moderates, the intelligent".[105]

It is reasonable that Daa could not attack America for its democracy when it brought forth such a fortunate result. However, he did not think that this had happened because of democracy, but rather in spite of it. If the United States in 1848 had avoided revolution and mob rule, the reason was not that the country already had a political system which made revolution unnecessary. Daa found the explanation in the material circumstances, the rich economic opportunities of the country. "The United States has a mob which, when once its passions have been roused, is able to perpetrate just as gross acts of violence as any mob in Europe. The difference is only that the American mob more rarely is forced by want to proceed to disorder".[106]

"The great demand among all individuals is now what the Americans so appropriately call 'more leeway'. Russia, England and the USA have already acquired this inestimable goldmine of civic well-being. Whoever in these countries is hungry and has a mind to work, can be assigned a place where he is needed. He is received with open arms, and can gain those necessities and that prosperity to which he aspires". If these three countries avoided "the concussions of the years 1848 and 1849", it was "not due to their policies alone, but also to the simple material thing with the simple name 'leeway'".[107]

Even Daa's old enemy from the "intelligentsia", the historian P. A. Munch, seized upon this argument, and asked whether it was not more reasonable to explain the phenomenon by means of "the popular liberty which already exists [in America], and which leaves the people nothing to be desired of the more important political blessings". That everything was quiet and peaceful in Russia, was to Munch a totally different matter, more connected with the predominant despotism than with leeway.[108]

Daa's remarks in 1848–49 about the great material opportunities in America do not tally too well with his attempt in the early 1840's to find arguments against emigration. At that time his strongest point was that a Norwegian could not more easily earn a livelihood over there than he could in his own home-land. To be sure, he then admitted that America was better off than most of the other European countries, making Norway an exception. But according to his more recent articles it was obvious that he now saw an essential difference in America's favor, even when compared to Norway. Consequently, he now abandoned his strong resistance to emigration. Unfortunately the sources are silent on this point in the actual years of revolution. But from 1853 there are some statements which unambiguously reveal a change of views.

The novelty is not the fact that Daa speaks with a certain pathos about emigration as "the only popular movement which no tyrant or despot presumes to curb"; such words he might well have used even in 1841. The novelty is his admission that even Norwegians might be better off in America, "even if we think that industrious people still can make both ends meet in Norway".[109] Actually, Daa's arguments about emigration had now been turned upside down as compared to the early 1840's. At that time he used the material disadvantages as a warning, but admitted that the American Constitution was a model, even if this was not a reason good enough to justify emigration. Now he found the material opportunities to be better over there, but turned against "those who wish to emigrate to America with the idea of gaining more political influence in that country, or who advise people to emigrate from our country because it is dominated by bureaucracy".[110]

It may be reasonable to assume, that if Daa now accepted Norwegian emigration, part of the explanation, at least, may be that like Vinje he regarded emigration as a safety-valve to social unrest. In spite of the prevailing economic boom in Norway emigration reached a new peak in the year 1853, a secondary effect of the crisis in 1848 and the violent repression of the labor organizations. But if, nevertheless, Daa now protested against the ideas of those emigrants who gave political grounds for leaving, it was, among other reasons, because he had begun to think that "neither the political

wisdom of the Yankees nor the quality of their institutions come true
when difficulties arise".[111] Behind such words lies the fact that from
now on Daa appraised in a different way what was essential in the
American Constitution.

Early in the 1840's Daa pointed out that the Norwegian Constitution was based on the assumption that "the farmer should have more
sense and more independence than a hired man". And he warned
that if his country in the future did not have "more enlightened electors, with more ability for independent thinking than is now the case,
then a Constitution like ours must beyond any doubt go to ruin".[112]
He feared that "the common worshippers of the absolute rule of the
majority" represented a serious danger to liberty, and he found this
thesis confirmed in 1845 when he pointed to the fact that the Norwegian
farmers who voted against the liberals were those from the Western
districts where there was no social difference between farmers and
hired men, not those from the East, where such differences were more
pronounced.[113]

Of special interest in this connection is Daa's attitude toward the
new demands of labor, as propounded around 1850. There are few
sources about his views of interior politics at that time. But when
from 1851 onward he again had a forum for his opinions in the
journal *Tilskueren,* his enemies tried to prove his political fickleness
by maintaining that he there supported some very radical proposals.
And sure enough, he did advocate an extension of franchise to include
cotters with a minimum of five years' lease. He ridiculed the Labor
Committee of the parliament for its verdict that political equality
is impossible. He even maintained that the new trade unions were
"the only political organization in Norway with a program or credo
containing something intelligible or intelligent, even if not all of their
contentions can be called correct".[114]

Upon close inspection this inconsistency is only apparent. To
Daa it had always been a horrifying idea that the people should be
divided into two hostile camps locked in uncompromising conflict.
Even in the early 1830's he stressed that the lower orders must be
granted indirect participation in political life lest they should feel
ostracized and store up discontent. When he broke with the farmers
in 1845, it was also because they frankly followed a class policy.
And Daa was scared of any class conflict, "which is so different from
a clash of principles": the nation must not be divided into the parties

of "intelligence or coarseness".[115] Now, in 1852, he again maintained that "the great task in order to avoid a serious civic strife, is to manage affairs so as to make the distinction between the classes imperceptible, to the extent that nobody can tell where the one begins and the other ends".[116]

The February Revolution and the labor movement did not turn Daa into a democrat. But they made it clear to him, that in order to "preserve the essentials" one must not "fob the masses off with a mere pretense and give them stones for bread and serpents for fish".[117] Parades on Constitution Day would no longer offer sufficient release. The franchise granted to the cotters would smother some of their dissatisfaction. At the same time, by limiting the franchise to those with five-year contracts, democracy would not be carried too far, and the extremists would be left out, those who "look at everyone outside their own class as enemies": the landowners were free to deny long contracts to such people.[118] As to labor, Daa showed a human sympathy for their imprisoned leaders and felt that they should not be treated too severely. But if he was willing to make more concessions than many others, it was only because he felt it to be necessary. His apparent radicalism actually sprang from his social conservatism.[119]

As before, these views are also reflected in his American parallels. Daa's comments upon American internal politics at the time clearly demonstrate, that no more than before did he sympathize with the ideas of greater political equality, beyond what he felt to be a virtue of necessity.

The victor in the presidential election of 1852 was Franklin Pierce. Daa in 1848 had greeted the whig Zachary Taylor as a representative of the moderate and intelligent electors. The slavedemocrat Pierce he saw as "a man of mediocre ability, mediocre culture, and the slackest morality", marked by materialism and egoism "which the vulgar mass values the more because it knows them thoroughly".[120] The question of slavery had increasingly come to the fore in America in these years since the compromise of 1850. In particular the enforcement of the refugee slave law aroused violent exasperation among the abolitionists. When Pierce insisted that the compromise be acted upon, Daa reproached him, and found him to be more a party-man than a president.

This reproach called forth a public debate with the lawyer Ole Munch Ræder, who in 1846–49 had himself visited England and the USA by government commission in order to report on the jury system, Daa himself being one of the proposers.[121] No more than

Daa did Munch Ræder defend the institution of slavery. But he maintained that at all events it was Franklin Pierce's duty to make sure that the compromise bill was enforced. Pierce did not do so as a party-man, but in the capacity of president. The question of slavery itself was not on any consideration the concern of Congress or President. It was beyond their competence, and a matter for decision by the individual states who had voluntarily joined in a union. "Any invitation to reform in this question has thus to be directed to the states, not to Congress". The compromise was necessary for the preservation of the voluntary union.[122]

In his reply Daa called Munch Ræder's statement a strictly juridical line of argument, of the kind which always comes in handy when it suits the purpose. Such rationalization of foul motives was exactly what America was guilty of. The compromise on slavery weakened any confidence in the morality of American statesmen. The policy of president Pierce did not spring from a respect for the Constitution, the voluntary agreement, but was connected with the entire political system, the majority rule. As early as 1849 Daa had suggested (above p. 78) that in America as in other democracies the benefit of the popular leaders was the real motive. This was now to him the key to an understanding both of the slavo-cratic politicians in the South and the compromise-makers in the North. "The same men would have said and done exactly the opposite, if the stronger power, the majority, had been of the opposite opinion".[123] The politicians did not lead the people, but let themselves be led by it. Because power was with the masses, politicians had to play up to them in order to gain their favor for their own benefit.

In a discussion in the Norwegian parliament of 1845 about the dissenters Daa described the two ways in which, in his opinion, a representative of the people could behave. He could lead the masses and show the way toward the future, or he could follow them, "make out what marauders and old crones yell to the rear guard, and shout it with an air of pronouncing a public opinion", dragging the people backward to coarseness and barbarism.[124] He now saw the same contrast in the contemporary United States. The top men among the Americans chose the latter of the two modes of behavior, because the system itself did not generate independent personalities able to lead the way. The people preferred "quite unknown party fools to men with such ability that they must also presumably have a certain degree of intellectual independence".

The political issue in America was not ideas or principles, but power and public office. Opinions were used as passwords rather than in their true sense. In reality one may safely say, Daa wrote, that "the chance of the hereditary system has given Europe no less talented rulers, on the average, than the Americans have given themselves by these elections, where envy is one of the most important factors in deciding the result". Thus, the United States had succeeded in "debasing the executive power to a puppet or a tool without conscience". But if the nation had to suffer, this served it right: "the people that chooses to be governed by unscrupulous slaves, deserves to learn that it has acquired unscrupulous tyrants".[125]

The dependence of statesmen on the favor of the masses was also to Daa one of the most reasonable explanations of the often repeated statement that "so far the democracies have most frequently been warlike". To provoke a war is "the easiest way of making oneself conspicuous, important, or even perhaps indispensable". For that reason James Polk, "the least remarkable man whom party spirit ever elevated to the presidential chair of the United States", started the war against Mexico.[126] War was a means by which the slave-party could keep its majority, in the long run "the only trustworthy means of securing the survival of the institution [slavery]". The statesmen met the demand because it was the wish of the majority, and democratic America was so martial that "there is no neighboring state with whom the Americans have not a cause of war in store, and toward which they have not turned their greedy eyes".[127]

Daa also tried to show how popular rule actually limited liberty in America: freedom was for the majority alone. Benjamin Franklin is once reported to have said that the freedom of the press must be joined by the freedom of the stick; this method of decision Daa found to have become "national" in America. People were tarred and feathered, flogged and shot to death if they used their freedom of speech too liberally. "King Mob has taken over the task of keeping the liberty of the press within the right limits". And such indecency certainly was not found in the slavery states alone, as Harriet Beecher Stowe had learned by personal experience. The American newspapers had become nothing but "willing tools to the wickedness of the people. . . . slavish servants of its aberrations, or self-seeking provision-dealers in its vices. The newspapers proffered only that drink which was to the taste of the public".[128]

In spite of all this, Daa did not regard the development in America only with pessimism. In the long run he believed that the politicians of the North would eventually reverse the compromise to which they had agreed in order to please the majority. But they would do so not for idealistic reasons, but because the majority itself was going to demand it. "The American people, and even more its statesmen, trained as they are to obey the national will, are remote from any kind of stubborn aristocratic consistency. As soon as it is fully ascertained where the power is, laws and Congress bills will go the same way as the opinions and conviction of their authors". The time was bound to come when the flood of the immigrants had saturated the country in the North and the West, and wages would be put under pressure. Then those states would no longer put up with the closed labor market in the slave territories, and the compromise would be doomed. A revolution would follow, and liberate the Negro slaves, "not for their sake, but for that of the Whites themselves".[129]

This change in Daa's opinions also affected that former idol of his, the American Constitution.

As shown above, developments in contemporary America itself of course played their part in this revaluation, as the internal contrasts in the United States were coming to a head and American society moved toward the Civil War. Many features of the conflict were far from flattering, and worried even confessed friends of American democracy.[130] But Daa's new accusations have about them a bitterness and violence which also doubtless came from sources closer at hand. In the 1840's the problems of liberty were uppermost in his mind, and the American Constitution represented his libertarian ideals. Of course he knew that the Constitution was also extremely democratic, much more than he liked. But as yet, that aspect did not mean so much to him personally. Around 1850 the issues had changed. Now the problems of democracy faced him everywhere in scaring manifestations, on the European continent and in Norway itself. And it appeared to him that in America the excesses of popular rule were particularly glaring. This put even the Constitution in a different light: the form of government was the root, not only of America's political glory, but of its political decay as well.

There was to Daa a deep disappointment about this realization; and sometimes he can hardly find words harsh enough. "It's a dangerous shortcoming", he wrote, "that the American Constitution has to be ashamed of itself".[131] Three years later he found it to be undeniable that "the great American republic, which Europe had long desired to regard as the ideal of perfection among states established by man, and its citizens as superior to the weaknesses of the old societies, now is on the point of becoming, in the opinion of the great public, a scandal among the nations".[132]

The thoroughness of this new attitude is revealed in the fact, that contrary to his previous opinion Daa now did not only see present day America as scandalous: he revaluated the very history of the United States.

In 1842 he had, as an argument in the discussion of temperance, pointed out some of the most prominent advocates of that cause in America, namely three presidents: Jackson, Madison, and Quincy Adams, "three men who for twenty years have been at the head of the greatest republic in the world and guided its fate with such renown that kings ought to envy them, men who had by talents and by merits as citizens reached the highest post of honor which general esteem and gratitude can give".[133] Ten years later, according to Daa, "the man who is elevated to the throne of the great republic need not always be a great man. On the contrary, no more than three of all the presidents of the Union have shown that they had the slightest claim to that title. With the exception of Washington, Jefferson, and Jackson (of whom the two latter must in several respects almost be ranked among bad men), not one single American president has had a higher reputation among his fellow-countrymen than that of being an able official".[134]

Madison, Quincy Adams, and Jackson had left the political scene long ago, and all were now dead. Nothing had happened in the meantime to explain the fact that Daa was no longer willing to recognize the talents of the two first, or that to him the memory of Jackson's merits as a citizen was darkened by the impression of his bad character. The simple explanation was, that in Daa's mind the American presidents no longer in the first instance represented the liberal constitution, which he revered, but government by the people, which he had come to fear and hate.

Daa warned America that it had rather learn from the experience made by the February Revolution: if democracy is not kept within bounds, it ends in tyranny. "The latest republican constitution of France, of November 4, 1848, was an imitation, albeit imperfect, of the American. The way in which it was overthrown, could serve as an instructive warning, if it were possible for one nation to learn from the mistakes of the other".[135]

## 5.

One special problem of American political life occupied Daa a good deal, particularly in his later years, namely the federal aspects of the Constitution seen in the light of *Scandinavism*, the organized effort to establish closer ties between the states of Northern Europe.

We have already (above, p. 56) referred to a book on federal government, published in 1822 by Colonel Nicolaj Tidemand. For strategic reasons, and especially in fear of a Russian attack, the author of this book advocated a close union of Norway and Sweden. But he was not in favor of the kind of union that had been established in 1814. Every regent of a union, Tidemand believed, is bound to strive towards "changing an incomplete union into a more complete political association", or, instead, turning it into one single monarchy. With the former solution, which Tidemand preferred for Norway and Sweden, he had in mind a federation like the North American union, with the one qualification that to him the American central government was too weak since the president had to be elected. A monarch would serve the purpose better. Scandinavian federation would guarantee the liberty of the two countries, but add much to their combined striking power, as compared to the present union, which had no central government.

In 1825 Professor H. N. L. Steenbuch added the argument that a more complete union would also better neutralize rivalry between the two parties: "Who ever heard of a war between the states of the North American union? Who ever experienced there an uneasy dread of amalgamation, a dangerous national envy, an offended patriotism, or a restless urge for independence?" Even to Nicolaj Tidemand it was one of the central ideas that in a federation of the American type one would avoid the danger of creating a "predominant, leading state".[136]

L. Kr. Daa has related that he knew Henrik Wergeland to harbor a similar Scandinavian conviction in the years immediately following 1830. Daa knew, he says, because he had himself "formed one even earlier, or rather from the very time I began to consider the development of historical conditions. The July Revolution, the Belgian and Polish insurrections, and the publication of Tidemand's book on federal states made the idea of nationality, from being a scholarly problem of ethnology become for me one of the foremost among practical questions; and the idea of a federal state followed next to it. I remember that at the time I often expressed my opinion to Henrik Wergeland, or in his presence. Not only did he not disagree, but even loudly applauded".[137]

In the early 1830's Wergeland himself wrote a poem called "Unio robur Gothorum. Tria juncta in uno. Trinitas Gothorum", where he expressed his dream of a Nordic trinity to add strength to the tribes of the Nordic "Goths". In an article he discussed the idea in more realistic terms. He declared that the "flourishing condition" of the American republics was due in particular to "the characteristic advantage that they are federal states, each of them retaining their independence". However, he did not believe such a federation to be possible between two parties only, because one of them would then always assert itself as the leading state to the discontent of the other and "eventually make it tired of playing the part of the step-brother". Therefore Wergeland extended the idea put forward by Tidemand, and suggested a political union of the three Nordic countries (Denmark, Norway, and Sweden), "each of them with its own and independent, free constitution, but under a joint representative government and with joint diplomatic representation abroad, imitating excatly the North-American arrangement".[138]

The priority of Daa or Wergeland in this matter is of small importance; so are the details in the further discussion. The interest in our connection is concentrated on their agreement, and their joint reference to America. Daa had early realized that "the tendency of the world is toward an association and levelling of nationalities".[139] The events in 1848 convinced him that the existence of the small nations was threatened. From then onward he was a consistent advocate of a political Scandinavism, preferably based on a union of all three states. "The number of members and the multiplicity of interests would [then] remove the fear of mastery and prejudice, as palpably as is the case in the homelands of Washington and Tell".[140]

The historian P. A. Munch was friendly to Scandinavian cooperation in many fields, but did not approve of a political union. "The great accumulations of nationalities are not favorable to liberty", Munch wrote. "An empire needs a powerful central government. And even if it is quite republican in its constitution, in the more distant parts of the realm this government is bound to act in a way that harmonizes badly with the true idea of liberty. Properly speaking, a great republic is inconceivable, if it is really to correspond to its name". Neither did Munch believe that in the future the small states would need to join in a union for defense. In his opinion the urge toward expansion in the great powers of Europe would abate as the present movements toward liberty, equality and nationality developed in strength and found their proper balance.[141]

On both points Daa had different ideas. As mentioned previously, America to him had strikingly demonstrated that democracy is no guarantee against aggressive tendencies. On the contrary: some Americans had dreamt of "attaching all adjacent countries to the great democratic whole... Hardly any state in our days has begun war for reasons as insignificant as have the Americans".[142] Thus, the small states still certainly would need to join forces even in Europe. But on the other hand, America was not to Daa an equally disquieting example when it came to the liberty of states within a union. On the contrary, it was admirable how the American federal constitution guaranteed full independence to each of the states, and at the same time had been able to "fuse their forces into a unity which has made the North-American Union make giant strides in power, influence and well-being".[143]

A Scandinavian union would need a more solid foundation than political necessity, however. To Daa, the countries of the North ought to unite not only because they were close neighbors, but also because to all practical purposes they formed a cultural unity. In particular their languages were closely related; during its long union with Denmark Norway even had adopted the Danish written idiom and by 1850 still used it with little admixture of Norwegian forms. A movement to create a separate Norwegian language was under way, however; Daa strongly opposed it, and on the contrary worked toward bringing the Scandinavian languages more closely together. Again he used the United States for reference. In spite of much "patriotic conceit", he wrote, the Americans had not thought it necessary to develop a language of their own. Federations in our time do not seem to need that kind of putty in order to stick together; in America the free institutions had proved sufficient for the purpose. Instead, the Americans had been able to turn their free forces to "investigating external nature with such energy" (Daa mentioned the inventors Samuel Morse, Samuel Colt, Isaac M. Singer, and John Ericsson as examples). The community of language with the British also had opened a wider field to authors such as Longfellow, R. H. Dana, Washington Irving, Cooper, and Prescott.[144]

Here as elsewhere one should not demand pedantic consistency in

Daa's views. In the 1850's and 1860's America was referred to in his writings less frequently than before. The material itself became more self-contradictory, and his use of it more arbitrary. His American parallels in support of his theories on Scandinavism sometimes differ a good deal from simultaneous statements in another context. His discussion of the Norwegian language problem against an American background is curious, to say the least, and does not bear close scrutiny. There are other examples of a similar kind. During the Civil War Daa lavishly praised the Canadian and US governments for a political wisdom beyond anything found in Norway. The main reason for this homage was that the two nations had signed a treaty of free trade, which was Daa's ideal for Norway and Sweden.[145] In his eulogies of the freedom of the states belonging to the American federation he completely disregarded how severely he had earlier condemned the insistence on states' rights as the very foundation of slavery.

But more often than not Daa's own basic opinions are clear enough, and sometimes are brought out particularly well in such contradictory material. In his book on the problem of nationalities (1869) he condescendingly patted on the back the "bold and inventive Yankee" who had "with the most extreme daring built his political life on new and untried foundations" — after having described at length the terrifying structure of slavery based on exactly those foundations. But Daa's reasoning is typical, and well sums up his final judgment of America and the axioms on which it was built.

The contempt of the Negro is not only deeply imbedded in human nature, Daa wrote, but no less strongly conditioned by the American political system. At elections over there, an unparalleled equality has abrogated the difference between rich and poor, cultivated and vulgar, and in a way made the lowest social order, the majority, the privileged and almighty ruling class. "As a counterpoise against this absurdity contempt of the Negro was developed with insane inconsistency to the point of abolishing his legal rights. This socalled 'sweet prejudice' became the favorite doctrine of the Democrats. The white man, who was voted down by the rabble of his own color, felt compelled to have around him people of a different color who were obliged to recognize his own superiority without a word of objection". Daa characterized the situation in the South during the reign of the carpet-baggers in a similar way: the same unqualified majority rule without distinction of culture and wealth "in certain regions placed government in the hands of quite savage Negroes".[146]

At the same time, however, these words make it clear, that if Daa reacted to having Negroes in leading political positions, it was not because of their race, but for social reasons. Race to him was an external difference. The doctrine of the biological dissimilarity of man, and the belief in segregation, which had appeared "in its most extravagant extreme" in America, had also "brought about the most overwhelming calamities which may befall a nation through evil passions": "the sanguinary civil conflicts, by which its colossal wickedness has to be chastized".

But Daa's somewhat surprising conclusion was a warning, presented in the American example, against hatred and contempt among the Scandinavian nations. The differences between the countries of the North were due to their surroundings, and would be leveled by "connection and communication" to the benefit of civilization. In a similar way the excellent qualities which the Americans like to ascribe to themselves and which they feel give them precedence over the Europeans, may actually be due, in part at least, to the fact that they are a new nation, originated from a fusion of many tribes and forms of civilization in Old Europe.[147]

6.

America was not to L. Kr. Daa a subject of scholarly investigation, but a tool in his political career. That career was not a success.

In part his failure was the result of personal qualities. Daa never was popular, and for good reasons. His manners were brusque and his form offensive, "he was delighted to give even his best friends a punch on the nose".[148] Adversity early made him bitter — Henrik Wergeland called him Mr. Vinegar; his political colleagues complained about his suspiciousness and general oddity. Above all he was obstinate. Faithful to his basic convictions, he lacked the gift of adjustment which is the secret of practical politics.

But these handicaps were emphasized by the political ideology to which he adhered so rigidly. It was his dream to become a statesman of the English type. Liberalism and social conservatism were insolubly fused in his mind; his ideal was a society where an extensive economic and political freedom was largely limited to a dominating middle class. In his own country these were imported ideas which needed modification. The Norwegian bourgeoisie could not form a liberal opposition party without the support of the majority of the people, the increasingly class-conscious farmers; and the two groups could only be united by a compromise on broadly democratic foundations. When this compromise materialized a few decades later, it changed Norwegian politics for generations; L. Kr. Daa was too stubborn and at heart too antidemocratic to effect it. Instead he was left in an intermediate position which was politically hopeless. He fought his enemies above and below in the name of an abstract libertarianism which was not understood or appreciated by anybody. When finally he believed he would find support for his ideas with his former conservative adversaries, he gained nothing but the destruction of his own political future.

From a personal point of view this story is somewhat sad. But it is the background for his views which above all lends interest to Daa's attitude toward the United States. The details are far from unique. There are not many of his comments that are not paralleled in the political history of other countries with an American impact. Neither do we know to what extent America and its political institutions originally moulded Daa's ideas; Great Britain doubtless played the major part in that respect. But all through his life the United States offered him a continuous sounding board and frame of reference, which made his reactions reflect both the curve of his own career and the basic tensions of his time. The dichotomy of liberty and equality which had vexed the Europeans in their judgment of America from the Revolution onward, in the 19th century became a clash of irreconcilable contrasts. Daa was himself torn to pieces in the conflict, and he made America the image of his struggle. In their apparent incoherence his scattered remarks reflect both sides in the battle, with that sullen and unyielding honesty which was at the same time his undoing and his honor.

## NOTES

[1] Little is written about the American impact in Norway. Useful for the general background are H. Koht, *The American Spirit in Europe. A Survey of Transatlantic Influences* (Philadelphia, 1949); S. Skard, *American Studies in Europe, Their History and Present Organization*, I–II (Philadelphia, 1958); and H. Elovson, *Amerika i svensk litteratur 1750–1820* (Lund, 1930) — with bibliographies. Much material focussed on emigration is found in Th. Blegen, *Norwegian Migration to America 1825–60* (Northfield, Minn., 1931) and I. Semmingsen, *Veien mot vest. Utvandringen fra Norge til Amerika 1825–1865* (Oslo, 1945). Brief sketches are Fr. D. Scott, "American Influences in Norway and Sweden", *The Journal of Modern History*, XVIII (1946), 37–47, and S. Skard, "Studiet av amerikansk litteratur", *Samtiden*, LVII (1948), 225–242, and in English translation, *The Study of American Literature* (Philadelphia, 1949).

[2] Quoted from H. Elovson, *Amerika i svensk litteratur*, p. 24.

[3] Th. Jefferson, *The Papers*, XVII (Princeton, 1965), 195 (July 15, 1790).

[4] Quoted from G. H. Guttridge, *English Whiggism and the American Revolution* (Berkeley, 1942; Univ. of Calif. Publ. in History, 28), p. 142.

[5] Compare F. J. C. Hearnshaw's article on Edm. Burke, *Encyclopaedia of the Social Sciences*, III (New York, 1930).

[6] See H. Koht, *The American Spirit in Europe*, p. 21, and his article in (*Norsk*) *Historisk Tidsskrift*, XXXIV (1946–48), 87 f.

[7] Claus Fasting, *Provinzialblade*, III, No. 40 (1780), 314.

[8] F. Rønning, *Rationalismens Tidsalder*, II (København, 1890), 389. For other expressions of similar opinions, see Sverre Steen in *Det norske folks liv og historie*, VII (Oslo, 1933), 77.

[9] J. Nordahl Brun, *Republikken paa Øen. Et Skuespil* (Bergen, 1793), pp. 47 f.

[10] E. Falsen, *Skrifter*, I (Christiania, 1821), 131–166; F. Rønning, *Rationalismens Tidsalder*, III, 2 (København, 1899), 37.

[11] H. Koht in (*Norsk*) *Historisk Tidsskrift*, XXIV (1946–48), 85–96.

[12] Johs. Andenæs, "Menneskerettighetserklæringene i det 18. århundre og den norske grunnlov," *Tidsskrift for rettsvitenskap*, LV (1942), 474–96; Paal Berg, Fr. Castberg, Sverre Steen, *Arven fra Eidsvoll. Norges grunnlov* (Oslo, 1945), p. 185.

[13] H. Koht in his article on Falsen, *Norsk biogr. leksikon*, IV, 29 (Oslo, 1929). Falsen's biography of Washington in *Snotra. Nytaarsgave for Aaret 1821* (Bergen), pp. 25–86.

[14] V. C. W. Sibbern's diary during the Constitutional Assembly, (*Norsk*) *Historisk Tidsskrift*, I (1871), 255.

[15] *Den norske Tilskuer*, 1817, p. 60.

[16] *Storthings-Forhandlinger*, May 1821, p. 532 f.

[17] *Storthings-Forhandlinger*, May 1818, p. 329.

[18] *Storthings-Forhandlinger*, June 1818, pp. 648 f. About Isaachsen's Jacobinism, see Sverre Steen, *Kristiansands historie*, I (Oslo, 1941), 386. I. Isaachsen's brother Peter was appointed American consul for Norway in 1814; see H. Koht in (*Norsk*) *Historisk Tidsskrift*, XXXIV (1946–48), 86.

[19] *Storthings-Forhandlinger*, June 1818, p. 642.

[20] N. Treschow, *Lovgivnings-Principier*,

[I] (Christiania, 1820), 152 f. Compare Bj. Svare, *Frederik Stang*, I (Oslo, 1939), 80.

21 *Patrioten*, 1824, Sept. 10, p. 85 and Sept. 17, p. 92.

22 *Tilskueren*, 1824, June 20.

23 *Patrouillen*, 1824, May 31, p. 99; *Tilskueren*, 1824, June 17 and 20.

24 *Storthings-Forhandlinger*, April 1821, p. 243.

25 *Det norske Nationalblad*, 1821, April 28.

26 *Tilskueren*, 1824, February 8.

27 P. Treschow Hanson, *De mærkeligste Tildragelser i Verden siden Katharina den anden*, I, 2. ed. (Christiania, 1832), 94.

28 [N. Tidemand], *Om de sammensatte Staters Foreningsmaade* (Christiania, 1829), pp. 43, 87. Written in 1822.

29 *Vidar*, 1834, January 11, p. 171.

30 H. Wergeland, *Saml. skrifter*, I, 3 (Kristiania, 1919), 126, 197.

31 Berit Borell, *De svenska liberalerna och representationsfrågan på 1840-talet* (Uppsala and Stockholm, 1948), pp. 61 and 66.

32 Lending record of the University Library, Oslo.

33 I. Semmingsen, *Veien mot vest*, I, 44.

34 "Land of Canaan": *Den norske Rigstidende*, 1825, No. 59. The oppositional farmer: Hans Barlien; see I. Semmingsen, *Veien mot vest*, I, 58.

35 *Morgenbladet*, 1839, Oct. 10.

36 *Morgenbladet*, 1837, June 18.

37 There is no biography of Daa. The best modern survey is that by H. Koht, *Norsk biografisk leksikon*, III (Oslo, 1926).

38 J. H. Thoresen in *Morgenbladet*, 1859, No. 123, May 6.

39 Obituary in *Morgenbladet*, 1877, No. 163 A.

40 Ludvig Daae in *Morgenbladet*, 1877, No. 163 A.

41 (*Norsk*) *Historisk Tidsskrift*, 2. R. V (1886), 269–70; L. Kr. Daa in *Tids-Tavler*, I (1872), 313 and *Varsko*

*formedelst den offentlige Stemning.....* (Christiania, 1846), p. 79.

42 L. Kr. Daa, *Syttende Mai og Politiet* (Christiania, 1831), pp. 17 and 22.

43 *Tids-Tavler*, I (1872), 313.

44 H. Wergeland, *Saml. skrifter*, IV, 6 (Oslo, 1928), 252.

45 L. Kr. Daa, *Syttende Mai og Politiet*, pp. 38 f., 42, 54.

46 Rolf Olsen in *Morgenbladet*, 1849, No. 125, May 5.

47 L. Kr. Daa, *Varsko* ....., p. 84.

48 *Morgenbladet*, 1846, No. 165, June 14; Rolf Olsen in *Morgenbladet*, 1849, No. 125, May 5.

49 J. E. Sars, *Norges politiske historie 1815–85* (Kristiania, 1904), p. 328.

50 A. Bergsgård, *O. G. Ueland og bondepolitikken*, I (Oslo, 1932), 472 ff.

51 *Granskeren*, 1840, Sept. 16, compare Oct. 24.

52 He did *not* also write the monthly "Politisk Omrids", as stated by H. Koht in *Norsk biografisk leksikon*: see *Morgenbladet*, 1843, April 1.

53 *Drammens Tidende*, 1852, January 9.

54 *Morgenbladet*, 1837, June 5.

55 *Den norske Tilskuer*, 1851, Oct. 4, p. 1, Nov. 8, p. 41.

56 *Morgenbladet*, 1843, April 6; *Granskeren*, 1843, April 13, p. 375.

57 *Statsborgeren*, 1833, Febr. 10.

58 Iver Hesselberg, *Christelig Liberalisme* (Christiania, 1837), p. 18.

59 W. A. Wexels, *Religiøs-politiske Betragtninger fra christelig-moralsk Standpunkt* (Christiania, 1837), p. 45.

60 Chr. Delphin, *Et Sendebrev til Hr. Sognepræst Hesselberg* (Christiania, 1837), p. 27.

61 *Tidens Tarv og Tidens Brøst af N.F.S. Grundtvig*. Betragtet af W. B. F. P. Sverdrup (Christiania, 1840), pp. 1 and 48—49.

62 Cl. Winther Hjelm, *Betænkning og Forslag til Lov om Grændserne for Religionsfriheden* (Christiania, 1840), p. 70; *Morgenbladet*, 1841, January 8.

[63] *Statsborgeren*, 1833, Febr. 10.

[64] *Granskeren*, 1840, Oct. 31, p. 61; 1841, Febr. 6, p. 176.

[65] *Granskeren*, 1840, Oct. 10, p. 35.

[66] *Granskeren*, 1840, Oct. 10, p. 39.

[67] Cl. Winther Hjelm, *Betænkning*, pp. 7 f.

[68] *Granskeren*, 1840, Oct. 10, p. 36.

[69] *Granskeren*, 1843, June 29, p. 462.

[70] *Storthings-Efterretninger*, 1836–54, II, 366. Compare Fr. D. Scott, "American Influences in Norway and Sweden," *The Journal of Modern History*, XVIII (1946), 39.

[71] *Granskeren*, 1840, Oct. 10, p. 36.

[72] *Granskeren*, 1840, Oct. 17, p. 41.

[73] *Granskeren*, 1840, Dec. 19, p. 118; 1841, March 17, p. 223; *Morgenbladet*, 1839, Jan. 2.

[74] *Granskeren*, 1841, Oct. 8, p. 488; *Storthings-Efterretninger*, 1836–54, II (1842), p. 296.

[75] Letters to S. Jaabæk 1845, June 5 and July 5, *Syn og Segn*, XVIII (1912), 315, 317; *Drammens Tidende*, 1853, Febr. 27. See also A. Bergsgård, *Aa. Vinje. Norsk nasjonal konservatisme* (Oslo, 1940), passim.

[76] *Folkets Røst*, 1850, No. 5, May 15 and No. 7, May 22.

[77] *Granskeren*, 1841, March 17, p. 223, compare p. 221.

[78] *Granskeren*, 1841, Sept. 20, p. 468.

[79] *Granskeren*, 1841, March 17, pp. 221 and 223.

[80] *Granskeren*, 1843, jan. 26, pp. 313 f.

[81] *Granskeren*, 1841, March 13, pp. 218 f.; compare 1841, Sept. 20, p. 468 and 1843, Febr. 2, pp. 317 f.

[82] *Granskeren*, 1841, Sept. 20, p. 468.

[83] H. Wergeland, *Saml. skrifter*, III, 1 (Oslo, 1932), 170; III, 3 (Oslo, 1943), 154 f., 138 f.; IV, 6 (Oslo, 1928), 379–85.

[84] H. Wergeland, *Saml. skrifter*, I, 3 (Kristiania, 1919), 29; IV, 6 (Oslo, 1928), 329, 251 f.

[85] See *Historisk Repetitions-Haandbog* af

Chr. Christensen, 2. Opl., gjennemseet og fortsat fra 1814 til 1839 af L. Kr. Daa (Kristiania, 1839), p. 161.

[86] *Granskeren*, 1840, Oct. 17, p. 41.

[87] *Granskeren*, 1841, Nov. 2, p. 519. Compare *Den Constitutionelle*, 1841, No. 302.

[88] *Granskeren*, 1841, Nov. 2, p. 519; A. M. Schweigaard, *Norges Statistik* (Christiania, 1840), pp. 45 f.

[89] *Granskeren*, 1841, Nov. 2, p. 519.

[90] E. D. Adams, *Great Britain and the American Civil War*, I (London, 1925), 26 ff.

[91] *Morgenbladet*, 1838, Oct. 18; my italics.

[92] *Morgenbladet*, 1841, Jan. 14. Compare Cl. Winther Hjelm, *Betænkning*, p. 69.

[93] *Granskeren*, 1840, Oct. 10, p. 39.

[94] *Granskeren*, 1841, Nov. 2, p. 519.

[95] *Tiden*, 1850, Sept. 1.

[96] *Drammens Tidende*, 1856, Nov. 7.

[97] [Ole Richter], "Ludvig Kristensen Daa", *Krydseren*, 1850, No.s. 41, 43, 46, 47. Richter refers to Th. Mügge: *Skizzen aus dem Norden*, I (Hannover, 1844), p. 150, where Daa is called "Republikaner und eifriger Bewunderer der amerikanischen Verfassung".

[98] *Christianiaposten*, 1848, May 29.

[99] L. Kr. Daa: *Danmark og Tyskland*, Aftryk efter Christianiaposten (Christiania, 1850), pp. 9 ff.

[100] L. Kr. Daa, *Danmark og Tyskland*, pp. 7–9, 36.

[101] L. Kr. Daa, *Danmark og Tyskland*, p. 10.

[102] *Christianiaposten*, 1849, June 1.

[103] *Christianiaposten*, 1848, May 25.

[104] L. Kr. Daa, *Om Professor Munchs antiskandinaviske Historik*, Aftryk efter Christianiaposten (Christiania, 1849) p. 75.

[105] *Christianiaposten*, 1848, Dec. 9; 1849, Jan. 15 and 23.

[106] *Christianiaposten*, 1849, June 11.

[107] L. Kr. Daa: *Danmark russisk eller*

*skandinavisk*, Aftryk efter Christiania-posten (Christiania, 1849), pp. 30 f.

108 *Morgenbladet*, 1849, May 25.

109 Compare his speech in Studenter-samfundet May 17, 1853 as reported by A. O. Vinje in *Drammens Tidende*, 1853, May 20. *Den norske Tilskuer*, 1853, March 12, pp. 601 f.

110 *Den norske Tilskuer*, 1853, Jan. 15, pp. 538 f. It may be worth while noticing that Daa's only son later emigrated to the USA.

111 *Christianiaposten*, 1850, July 31. Daa knew the usual meaning of the word "Yankee", but often used it about the Americans in general; see his *Lærebog i Geografien* (Christiania, 1859), pp. 321 f.

112 *Granskeren*, 1842, Oct. 27, p. 227 and Nov. 3, p. 232.

113 L. Kr. Daa, *Varsko*, pp. 12 and 62 f.

114 *Morgenbladet*, 1859, No. 123, May 6 (J. H. Thoresen); *Den norske Tilskuer*, 1851, Nov. 15, p. 49 and Oct. 25, pp. 25 f.

115 L. Kr. Daa, *Varsko*, pp. 63 and 14.

116 *Den norske Tilskuer*, 1852, Febr. 14, p. 157.

117 L. Kr. Daa, *Danmark og Tyskland*, pp. 9 f., 38.

118 *Den norske Tilskuer*, 1852, Febr. 14, p. 156.

119 If Daa is really the author of an article in *Christianiaposten*, 1849, April 12 about the labor movement, this view of his opinion is corroborated.

120 *Christianiaposten*, 1853, April 25.

121 *Storthings-Forhandlinger*, 9, 1845, p. 260.

122 *Christianiaposten*, 1853, May 8.

123 *Christianiaposten*, 1853, July 1.

124 *Storthings-Efterretninger*, 1836–54, II, p. 653.

125 *Den norske Tilskuer*, 1852, Dec. 4, p. 489; Dec. 18, p. 505.

126 L. Kr. Daa, *Om Professor Munchs antiskandinaviske Historik*, p. 75.

127 *Den norske Tilskuer*, 1852, Dec. 18, p. 506.

128 L. Kr. Daa, *Om Professor Munchs antiskandinaviske Historik*, p. 63; *Den norske Tilskuer*, 1852, Dec. 4, p. 491; L. Kr. Daa, "Om de geografiske Forholdes Indflydelse paa Kulturens Udvikling", *En Tylvt Forelæsninger*, udg. af Selskabet for Folkeoplys-ningens Fremme (Christiania, 1862), p. 76.

129 *Christianiaposten*, 1853, June 2 and July 11.

130 A benevolent observer such as O. Munch Ræder speaks of "the trans-atlantic party battles and their in-justices" (*Christianiaposten*, 1856, March 10).

131 *Christianiaposten*, 1853, June 2.

132 *Christianiaposten*, 1856, March 14.

133 *Granskeren*, 1842, Jan. 27, p. 605. In *Christianiaposten*, 1849, Jan. 23, Daa called Jackson "a kind of per-sonification of the activity, courage, and perseverance of the Yankee".

134 *Den norske Tilskuer*, 1852, Dec. 4, p. 492.

135 *Den norske Tilskuer*, 1852, Dec. 18, p. 505.

136 [N. Tidemand,] *Om de sammensatte Staters Foreningsmaade*, pp. 17, 37, 41, 43. Steenbuch's articles (*Morgenbladet*, 1825, July 26 to 28) were based on Tidemand's manuscript, see J. B. Halvorsen, *Norsk Forfatterleksikon*, s.v. Tidemand.

137 *Tids-Tavler*, I (1872), p. 332.

138 H. Wergeland, *Saml. skrifter*, I, 1 (Kristiania, 1918), pp. 229–240; III, 1 (Oslo, 1932), 261. Compare *Tids-Tavler*, I (1872), pp. 305 ff. (The poem pp. 339–45).

139 L. Kr. Daa, *Svensk-norsk Haandordbog* (Kristiania, 1841), Forord, p. XII.

140 F. B. Wallem, *Det Norske Studenter-samfund gjennem hundrede aar, 1813–1913* (Kristiania, 1916), p. 419. Compare *Christianiaposten*, 1848, Dec. 1 and L. Kr. Daa, *Danmark russisk eller skandi-navisk*, pp. 36 f.

[141] *Morgenbladet*, 1849, April 30 and May 25.

[142] L. Kr. Daa, *Om Professor Munchs antiskandinaviske Historik*, pp. 73 f.

[143] *Christianiaposten*, 1855, May 6.

[144] L. Kr. Daa, *Om Nationaliteternes Udvikling* (Kristiania, 1869), pp. 221–23.

[145] L. Kr. Daa, "Om større Statsenheder", *Forhandlinger i det Skandinaviske Selskab i Christiania* 1864–66 (Kristiania, 1869), p. 18.

[146] L. Kr. Daa, *Om Nationaliteternes Udvikling*, pp. 45 f., 221.

[147] L. Kr. Daa, "Om de geografiske Forholdes Indflydelse", pp. 79 and 99; *Om Nationaliteternes Udvikling*, pp. 2 and 81.

[148] [Paul Hjelm Hansen], *Norges Storthing 1845* (Christiania, 1846), p. 91.

The author owes a debt of gratitude to Professor Sigmund Skard. Without his encouragement, counsel and assistance this paper would not have reached publication.

# ORESTES A. BROWNSON'S *NEW VIEWS*

## BY PER SVEINO

From early childhood Orestes A. Brownson took great interest in religious subjects. Thus once, as a nine-year-old boy, during a muster of the local militia, he got into a hot argument with two old men on the doctrine of predestination.

At the age of nineteen he experienced a kind of religious conversion and became a member of the Presbyterian Church. He was, however, dissatisfied with the Calvinistic dogma of unconditional election and reprobation. After two years he left orthodoxy and turned to liberal Christianity. He joined the Universalists, a sect believing in the final salvation of all men. Both as an ordained minister and the editor of a small bi-weekly paper he advocated Universalism and the free exercise of human reason.

Yet even Universalism was not liberal enough for Brownson. He passed on to downright unbelief, and joined hands with the "free-thinkers" and social reformers Frances Wright and Robert Dale Owen. Together with them he took up the cause of labor and helped organize the Working-Men's Party in New York. But the former Presbyterian and Universalist soon felt the need of religion of some sort, and after only one year he resumed his work as a preacher, although at first independent of any particular denomination. His religion was a vague, undogmatic Christianity or, in his own words, a "religion of humanity,"[1] aiming at the creation of an earthly paradise.

However, he felt a growing sympathy with the Unitarians, and in 1832 he formally became a Unitarian minister. From that time on he took up methodical studies of philosophy and theology, and even learned French and a little German in order to understand literature in those languages. The foreign writers that he read with the greatest interest were Benjamin Constant, Victor Cousin and Saint-Simon. Leading Unitarians like William Ellery Channing and George Ripley came to know this self-taught Vermonter and wanted him to move to Boston to preach his social Christianity to the working-class people. As a free-lance Unitarian and former organizer of the Working-Men's Party he was supposed to be the right man to present Unitarianism to the laboring classes, which to a large extent had drifted away from religion.

So Brownson moved to Boston where, in 1836, he founded "The Society for Christian Union and Progress;" and he remained its minister or leader for about seven years. As its name implied, Brownson did not only stress the need for "progress" or social reforms. He also wanted to promote Christian unity.

His undogmatic conception of Christianity and especially his emphasis on "the inner light" or "the religious sentiment" made him open to the ideas of Transcendentalism. In politics his social-radical views led him in the direction of the Democratic Party. In his *Boston Quarterly Review* (1838—42), which he wrote almost singlehandedly, he expressed his opinions on a wide range of subjects. On the eve of the presidential election in 1840 his religious and social radicalism reached its climax in his two incendiary articles on "The Laboring Classes," in which Brownson made short work of all existing churches and proposed the abolition of all inheritance laws.

But to Brownson the election campaign of 1840 was disgusting with its "log cabins, and hard cider." Even more important, the defeat of the Democratic Party so upset him that he lost almost all confidence in the intelligence and instincts of the masses. From that time on he began to verge toward conservatism, both in politics and religion. Brownson, who had distrusted political and religious authority, now began to feel the need of strong institutions in state and church, in order to secure both progress and stability.

In politics, he became a keen supporter of what he called "constitutional republicanism," that is, a form of government securing the system of checks and balances established by the American Constitution, in Brownson's thought the only safe guarantee against the doctrine of the sovereignty of the people. Under the impact of the Civil War he wrote his best book, *The American Republic* (1864), in which he stated both his general long-cherished political views and his more recent theories of the Union.

In religion, his need for an authoritative institution led him slowly, but steadily toward the Roman Catholic Church, the oldest and most traditional of all Christian churches. In his autobiography, *The*

*Convert* (1857), Brownson is anxious to point out that his conversion, which took place in 1844, did not involve a rejection of human reason. On the contrary, it was allegedly the non-Catholic French philosopher Pierre Leroux who indirectly led him toward the Catholic Church through his doctrine of life and communion.

However, when reason had convinced him of the necessity and the existence of the one true Church, he had no great difficulty in accepting its authority. Yet the "Yankee" Brownson did not easily adapt himself to the Catholic *milieu*, which in the nineteenth century was not, for better or for worse, so "Americanized" as it is today. For some time around 1860 he inclined toward a liberal Catholicism, and even gently reproached his old friend the Protestant historian George Bancroft for being too lenient in regard to the Jesuits, "in our day the real *obscurantists*."[2] But on the whole, Brownson was a strong, thorough-going Catholic, and firmly believed in the authority of his Church as represented by its supreme pontiff. From his conversion until 1875, the year before he died, he edited *Brownson's Quarterly Review*, with only one intermission (1865—73). In 1855 he moved from Boston to New York.

During his life-time, especially before he became a Catholic, Brownson was accused of changing his opinions much too easily. This charge was not unfounded. True, Brownson was a keen logician, but also a man of swift temper and of great intellectual curiosity. The latter qualities often led him to change his premises. But the starting-point being given, his reasoning had an unmistakable stamp of logic. His importance in American intellectual history lies in his responsiveness to new ideas, an ability to expose the most diverse religious and philosophical trends of his time, combined with an ingrained sense of tradition, and great emotional and intellectual force in the presentation of his views.

Just after organizing "The Society for Christian Union and Progress," Brownson wrote a small book, *New Views of Christianity, Society, and the Church* (1836).[3]

The author intended to state the principles on which his own association was based and on which a new church — the "Church of the Future"[4] — might be organized. However, he was concerned with the general ideas, not with the precise form of organization.

The views set forth in his book were, as the author himself admitted, to a large extent derived from the writings of Benjamin Constant,

Victor Cousin, Heinrich Heine and the Saint-Simonians.[5] Properly speaking, then, his ideas were not original. But in New England of the 1830's they doubtless had about them an air of newness and originality.

Brownson opened his book with the thesis of Benjamin Constant that religion is natural to man, and stated that "Christianity, as it existed in the mind of Jesus, was the type of the most perfect religious institution to which the human race will, probably, ever attain."[6] To Brownson, however, neither the Catholic nor the Protestant churches had succeeded in realizing the perfect religious institution.

As for Catholicism, it fulfilled in its time an important historical mission. The Catholic Church met the wants and needs of the people and even aided the growth of the human mind. But Catholicism was founded on an exclusive principle: spiritualism. This principle was no doubt well fitted to prepare men for heaven, but hardly fitted to prepare them for life on earth. For this very reason Catholicism had not been able to keep pace with the progress of mankind.

The historical task of Protestantism was to demolish this system of pure spiritualism. However, Protestantism went more and more to the other extreme of exclusive materialism, while denying or depressing the spiritual. Protestantism recommended the acquisition of material wealth, rehabilitated the flesh, elevated humanity at the expense of divinity, and in principle represented a revival of the ancient civilizations of Greece and Rome. This revival of ancient paganism reached its climax in the great French Revolution of 1789, when churches were changed into pantheons and prostitutes were adored as goddesses of reason. To Brownson, Protestantism thus ended its work of destruction.

True, Protestantism stood for civil and political liberty, and also had a distinct democratic tendency from a social point of view. Yet these qualities, however valuable they may be in themselves, are not essentially religious. Within Protestantism even the traditional, central dogmas were being sloughed off: "The vicarious Atonement has hardly a friend left. The Deity of Jesus is questioned, his simple humanity is asserted and is gaining credence."[7]

To Brownson, German rationalism and English-American Unitarianism represented the last stage of Protestantism before complete infidelity. However logical this development might be, logic and consistency were not enough to outweigh the loss of true religion. For this very reason Protestantism was retrograding, whereas Catholicism, or spiritualism, was recovering lost ground: "Catholicism has revived, offered some able apologies for itself, made some eminent proselytes, and alarmed many Protestants, even among ourselves."[8] Loathing the "dead body" of Protestantism, men were beginning to look out for something else which might satisfy their longings for a really religious life.

Yet a complete return to spiritualism was to Brownson not only undesirable, but altogether impossible. During its progress mankind had definitely passed by and discarded the exclusive principle of spiritualism. What was now needed was a combination and reconciliation of these two principles of spiritualism and materialism. Such a reconciliation, or atonement, was possible, since both principles were inherent in man's own nature. All through history the great mistake of all the religious sects was their attempt to form human nature according to their particular creeds instead of doing just the opposite. For "human nature is well made, its laws are just and holy, its elements are true and divine."[9]

On the basis of human nature, then, all opposites would be reconciled: the spiritual and the material, the eternal and the temporal, the heavenly and the earthly. The Christian dogma of the God-Man symbolizes the truth of this doctrine of atonement. Brownson was convinced that the second coming of Christ, as foretold in the Bible, meant the complete realization of this doctrine among men on earth.

True, the author did not believe in a speedy realization. However, the idea of human perfectibility and the idea of the essential holiness of all things warranted the establishment of this new civilization, when church and state would be a holy unity. What really mattered for the present was to believe in these great ideas themselves, for "ideas, if they are true, are omnipotent."[10]

Obviously, Brownson rejected extreme spiritualism as well as extreme materialism. What he wanted to reconcile, was "the affirmative or positive" principles of both systems.[11] This presupposed an eclectic method of reasoning, and the very term "eclectic" at once leads us to Victor Cousin, whose philosophy was called Eclecticism.

Brownson became acquainted with Cousin's philosophy in 1833. One year before, H. G. Linberg's English translation of Cousin's lectures on the history of philosophy had appeared in Boston. Brownson, then, was not the first one to introduce Cousin and his philosophy in the United States. But as long as his enthusiasm lasted he was one of his most ardent admirers and strongest supporters in the country.

Cousin's main thesis is that all philosophical systems are true in what they affirm. They err only to the extent that they are exclusive, that is, strictly narrow or onesided. He maintains that the history of philosophy shows the interplay of four great systems: sensualism, idealism, skepticism, and mysticism, which, taken together, are supposed to cover all the phenomena of human consciousness. There will never be more philosophical systems than those four. When regarded separately, each of them is only a fragment of the truth. But in its constant progress the human mind will increasingly be able to combine them into one harmonious whole. Cousin's object, therefore, was to mould these philosophical systems into a higher unity, called Eclecticism.

But in Cousin's writing this term also meant the method by which to arrive at this comprehensive philosophy. And it was, above all, this method that caught Brownson's attention. He concluded that if Cousin's method could be applied to philosophy, it could be used in religion as well. By means of the eclectic principle he set about analyzing spiritualism and materialism with the view of breaking their isolation and combining them in a higher unity.

In Brownson's little book Cousin's eclectic method thus offered the framework of ideas. But much of their substance he borrowed from the German author Heinrich Heine. The latter's work *Zur Geschichte der Religion und Philosophie in Deutschland* was published in 1834, and a French translation with the brief title *De l'Allemagne* appeared in the following year.

Heine's immediate purpose was to inform the French of German religious and intellectual history, particularly after the Reformation. Despite his pessimistic mood and ironic temper Heine shared the general belief of the age in constant human progress, which he considered in the light of a conflict between "sensualism" and "spiritualism." Brownson replaced Heine's term "sensualism" by "materialism." Thus he did not fully adopt the German's terminology; but the two words as used by the two writers cover the same idea.

Heine maintained that the real idea of Christianity was the mortification of the flesh. More particularly, this idea was to him the core of Catholic Christianity. However, since this idea conflicted too sharply with human nature, it never was fully realized. Instead, the Catholic Church was forced to make concessions to human nature.

Unlike Brownson, Heine contended that the Reformation initially was a revolt of spiritualism against the glaringly materialistic tendencies of sixteenth-century Catholicism. Not long afterwards, however, sensualism again raised its head. Monasteries were closed, and monks and nuns, together with the clergy, were allowed to marry. Luther's historic statement that the Bible and conscience should be the sole judges in matters of faith inaugurated a new era. This statement, stressing the importance of reason and individualism, reduced the power of the hierarchy and made way for "religiöse Demokratien."[12] A skeptical attitude made itself felt more and more in philosophy, literature, and science, and even fundamental Christian dogma was questioned.

Obviously, neither Heine nor Brownson intended to give any detailed historical treatment of their subject. They simply intended to present certain main ideas. To both of them the Reformation had a marked democratic tendency, furthering civil and political liberty; Brownson even regarded the French Revolution as a direct consequence of the Reformation. Yet he did not give any answer to the question why the Protestant Reformation should have had so strong an impact on a basically Catholic country. Probably Protestantism to him was a general principle, an idea, more than a particular historical phenomenon.

They also agreed that both in religion and philosophy the work begun by the Reformation had ended in rationalism. Certainly, they knew that rationalism met with opposition from Protestant orthodoxy. But neither of them thought this opposition to be of any great importance. Both men emphazised the rationalistic and materialistic tendencies latent in the Protestant Reformation. In so doing they doubtless went too far in identifying Protestantism with Renaissance and Humanism, and seemed to overlook the specifically religious import of Protestantism.

But although Brownson thus borrowed much from Heine, the two men differed widely in their basic attitudes, and they did not arrive at the same conclusions. Heine, for his part, was far from regretting the socio-religious development of mankind from spiritualism to sensualism. On the contrary, he apparently did not want to retain any element of spiritualism as a religion, much less revive it. What made the religion of spiritualism particularly suspect in Heine's eyes, was that its representatives so often in history had made common cause with authoritarian regimes and moneyed interests. To Heine this alliance was formed in order to suppress the popular demand of freedom, a demand which, in principle, originated in Protestantism, as "die wahre Religion des judäisch-deistischen Evangeliums."[13] Through this form of religion, matter had been greatly rehabilitated.

Brownson, on the other hand, reacted just as strongly against exclusive materialism as against exclusive spiritualism. In distinct contrast to Heine he stressed the strong anti-rationalistic tendencies of the age, indicating that pure materialism had reached its end. Heine, in his work, had a social-political aim; Brownson, in his work, was particularly concerned with the religious aspect.

While Brownson derived his two terms "spiritualism" and "materialism" from Heine, it was the Saint-Simonian school that provided him with the doctrine with which to justify their synthesis.

To Saint-Simon and his followers there is no essential antagonism between the spiritual and the temporal, the holy and the profane. In fact, there is no basic dualism: all things are holy. By virtue of this idea the Saint-Simonians wanted to erect the Universal Church, which was to comprise and hallow all human activities.[14] Brownson reasoned along the same lines when he argued for the reconciliation of the spiritual and the material: "But the new doctrine of the atonement reconciles these two warring systems. This doctrine teaches us that spirit is real and holy, that matter is real and holy, that God is holy and that man is holy...."[15]

In his book *Nouveau Christianisme* (1825) Saint-Simon maintained that at any rate contemporary Catholicism tyrannizes the people and keeps them in ignorance, since it is building its organization on external power. Protestantism, on the other hand, is wrong in giving the church an inferior position as compared to the State. Saint-Simon called for *one* religion and *one* organization, comprising state as well as church. Brownson, too, wanted to put an end to the separation between church and state. He visualized a future when "both [that is, church and state] will aim at the same thing, and the existence of one as separate from the other will not be needed. The church will not be then an outward visible power, coexisting with the state, sometimes controlling it and at other times controlled by it; but it will be within, a true spiritual — not spiritualistic — church, regulating the heart, conscience, and the life."[16]

The great purpose of the new church based on Saint-Simonian principles was the speedy and continuous amelioration, moral, intellectual, and physical, of the poor and more numerous classes. Thus the new church had, above all, a social aim. Brownson's "Church of the Future" was to be devoted to the same end. Inspired by the utopian vision of Saint-Simonism he pictured a future when the idea of the holiness of all things had been carried into practice. In this social millennium men were to be "personally holy," governments "sacred," industry and agriculture "the worship of God." Slavery and wars would cease, briefly: "The universe will be God's temple, and its service will be the doing of good to mankind, relieving suffering and promoting joy, virtue, and well-being."[17]

In contrast to Saint-Simon Brownson emphasized that he did not want to introduce a new Christianity, only a new church.[18] Thus he made the nice though somewhat debatable distinction between "the Christianity of Christ" and "the Christianity of the church."[19] The former is permanent; the latter is temporary.

What, then, is "the Christianity of Christ"? Brownson willingly conceded that the church has always considered Jesus as making an atonement. But the church misunderstood the real character of this atonement. Instead of asserting the holiness of both spirit and matter, the church, by a false interpretation of the sayings of Jesus, stated that only spirit is holy. To the church, therefore, the mission of Jesus was not to effect the union of spirit and matter, but to redeem spirit from matter. Hence the symbol of the cross, hence spiritualism. On the other hand, "the Christianity of Christ" — or the Christianity of Brownson's *New Views* — "declares as its great doctrine that there is no essential, . . . original antithesis between God and man . . . . Neither spirit nor matter is unholy in its nature . . . . All things, spirit, matter, God, man, soul, body, heaven, earth, time, eternity, with all their duties and interests, are in themselves holy."[20]

Brownson, then, put forth a rather unorthodox view of the central Christian dogma of the atonement. His theory is so unorthodox that his criticism of the Saint-Simonians for advocating a new Christianity, and not only a new church, might be directed against himself. After all, since both the Saint-Simonians and Brownson reject Christian dualism, it matters little what the new thing is called: "nouveau Christianisme" or, simply, "new views of Christianity."

However, in one important respect Brownson differed from the Saint-Simonians. He could not accept their bold declaration about their prophet, that he was giving reality to the brotherhood that was preached by Moses and prepared by Jesus. To Brownson Jesus, though only a man, occupies a unique position in history.

At the time when *New Views* was written, Transcendentalism or "the New School" had begun to make itself manifest among New England Unitarians. In the same year — 1836 — the Transcendentalist Club held its first meetings, which were attended by Emerson, George Ripley, Frederic Henry Hedge, James Freeman Clarke, Convers Francis, William H. Channing, Brownson, and others. Their views were far from unanimous. Emerson, though admitting a common "sympathy of studies and of aspiration," said that "there was no concert" between the members,[21] and James Freeman Clarke, with a touch of humor, put it in this way: "We called ourselves the club of the like-minded, I suppose because no two of us thought alike."[22]

However, although Transcendentalism was a philosophical trend more than a fixed and clearly defined system of thought, the Transcendentalists shared some common beliefs or, at least, some common attitudes. They joined hands in their opposition against Calvinism. And more and more conspicuously they stood up against the "old school" Unitarianism, that is, the dogmatic creed represented by Andrews Norton, Professor of Divinity at Harvard.

Even if *New Views* is not exactly a Transcendentalist manifesto, the book contains some ideas that were typical of "the New School."

First, Brownson stressed that religion is "natural to man." The religious sentiment in us is "universal, permanent, and indestructible;" it makes us think and feel the Holy and prompts us to revere it.[23] By this insistence on the innate religious sentiment, Brownson reacted against the Lockean view held in esteem by the "old school" Unitarians, that the human mind is originally a blank sheet, a *tabula rasa*, regarding religion as well as everything else.

Second, in *New Views*, religion is above all presented as springing from the heart. Neither outdated orthodoxy nor barren rationalism can offer a suitable outlet for this deep emotion. Brownson, then, takes his stand both against Calvinism, and Unitarianism "on the plan of Priestley and Belsham."[24] But even if religion is primarily regarded as feeling, this feeling must concentrate on some central ideas, which constitute the religion or at least the religiosity in question.

The religion advocated by Brownson was essentially the Unitarianism preached by William Ellery Channing. The latter, though the founder of the American Unitarian Association, was no strictly dogmatic Unitarian like Andrews Norton, but cherished views and sentiments which heralded Transcendentalism. Therefore, Channing was hailed by the younger generation of Unitarian ministers as their great spokesman and inspirer. Later, however, when he realized where his "disciples" were tending, even the liberal Channing drew back in horror.

Brownson praised highly one particular sermon by Channing on the "Dignity of Human Nature." In this sermon, "the most remarkable since the Sermon on the Mount," Channing emphasized the essential similarity of the divine and human natures. To Brownson, Channing's idea of "the likeness of a kindred nature" implied another and even more momentous idea, namely, that the God-Man, or Jesus, is not "a being alone of its kind."[25] Thus in principle Incarnation loses its special character and instead becomes valid for every human being. The difference between Jesus and other men is not one in kind, but in degree. Channing himself, however, seemed to stop short of a similar conclusion. According to Brownson, Channing held Arian views on the person of Christ, or at least regarded him as a super-angelic being.[26]

The idea of the general Incarnation, which Brownson gave a fuller treatment in his article "Church of the Future," is no doubt representative of the Transcendentalist outlook.[27] Frederic Henry Hedge, for instance, believed "in the ever-proceeding incarnation of the Spirit of God in human life."[28] It is even possible that Brownson was the first among the Transcendentalists to state this doctrine. In any case, he was the one among them to emphasize it most strongly.

The doctrine of the general Incarnation, which in principle raises all human beings to the same level, expresses respect for and faith in every individual man and woman, and represents the religious-democratic aspect of Transcendentalism. To Brownson, if to anyone, this idea was indeed no abstract formula only:

The human mind, allied as it is to the divine, is too valuable to lie waste or to be left to breed only briars and thorns. Those children, ragged and incrusted with filth, which throng our streets, and for whom we must one day build prisons, forge bolts and bars, or erect gibbets, are not only our children, our brother's children, but they are children of God, they have in themselves the elements of the Divinity and powers which when put forth will raise them above what the tallest archangel now is. And when this is seen and felt, will those children be left to fester in ignorance or to grow up in vice and crime? The whole energy of man's being cries out against such folly, such gross injustice.[29]

In Brownson's view, it was just the common man who, 1800 years ago, went forth with glowing enthusiasm to conquer the world for Christianity. And the inspiration which in the first century dominated "the Christian movement of the people," is by no means extinct today. Manifesting itself in present-day associations of all kinds, the popular inspiration, helped by the Eclectic philosophy, will usher in the longed-for Christian renaissance, the synthesis of spirit and matter.

In two important respects, however, Brownson's views apparently differed from those held by most of the Transcendentalists.

First, he did not share their dislike of churches and institutions. He maintained that men "must and will embody their ideas of the true, the beautiful, and the good — the holy, in some institution."[30] However, this idea, which he later was to develop further and which led him in the direction of the Catholic Church, in 1836 was still in its embryonic stage.

Second, Brownson's skeptical attitude toward Protestantism as such was hardly typical of most Transcendentalists. Nor did they generally share his positive appraisal of medieval Catholicism; in his own words: the Middle Ages "are deemed ...to be 'dark ages' only because we have not light enough to read them."[31]

Such ideas were already pointing out the road of his own development. Though Brownson at that time did not dream of converting to Catholicism, which he thought to be hopelessly behind the times, Victor Cousin's Eclecticism and the writings of the Saint-Simonians had made him understand and appreciate the historical mission of the Catholic Church. And eight years later the former herald of a new church came to the conclusion that to him the Church of the Past was after all the "Church of the Future" as well.

## NOTES

[1] Brownson's autobiography, *The Convert* (*Works*, V, Detroit, 1884), p. 66.

[2] Henry F. Brownson, *Orestes A. Brownson's Latter Life* (Detroit, 1900), p. 459.

[3] *Works*, IV, 1—56. Hereafter referred to as *New Views*.

[4] *Works*, IV, 57—78.

[5] *The Convert*, p. 83.

[6] *New Views*, p. 5.

[7] Ibid., p. 22.

[8] Ibid., p. 27.

[9] Ibid., p. 34.

[10] Ibid., p. 50.

[11] *The Convert*, p. 86.

[12] Heinrich Heine, *Zur Geschichte der Religion und Philosophie in Deutschland* (*Gesammelte Werke*, hg. G. Karpeles, V, 3. Ausg., Berlin, 1909), p. 42.

13 Ibid., p. 53.
14 *The Unitarian,* June 1834, p. 286.
15 *New Views,* p. 47.
16 Ibid., p. 50.
17 Ibid., pp. 49, 50.
18 Ibid., p. 45.
19 Ibid., p. 1.
20 Ibid., p. 10.
21 Ralph Waldo Emerson, "Historic Notes of Life and Letters in New England," *The Complete Works, Concord Edition,* X (Boston and New York, 1904), 341–42.

22 Joseph L. Blau, *Men and Movements in American Philosophy* (New York, 1953), p. 110.
23 *New Views,* p. 3.
24 Ibid., p. 27.
25 Ibid., p. 46.
26 *The Convert,* p. 79.
27 *Works,* IV, 62–65.
28 Joseph L. Blau, *Men and Movements in American Philosophy,* p. 117.
29 *New Views,* pp. 48–49.
30 Ibid., pp. 28–29.
31 Ibid., p. 27.

# HAWTHORNE, AND THE SIGNIFICANCE OF HISTORY

## By Johannes Kjørven

Hawthorne's most characteristic trait as a writer is his awareness of an influential past which in the middle of the confusion of daily experience contains certain enduring elements or moral qualities. Contrary to the ideas of contemporaries like Emerson and Thoreau, to whom the past was without value, Hawthorne held that a people's attitude toward history deeply influences their opinion of themselves, their age, and their future. For the "lesson" of history was to him that the past is involved in the present through sin.

The purpose of this study is to investigate Hawthorne's treatment and understanding of history, and to point out that narrative technique and content in his work are based upon an imputation of guilt and eventual resolution through history. To Hawthorne the past dramatizes and makes vital one's connection with the eternal in the present and with the universal verities. Therefore his understanding of history becomes inseparable from his concept of the moral identity of his characters. They grow in moral stature as they come to see themselves not only against the background of their own life stories, but against the background of the march of ages. To nineteenth century America the image of man was under constant revision: man experienced and knew himself as different from time to time also in his own life. To Hawthorne this was fallacy, and as I hope to show, he used subtle and deliberate means to confront his readers with the lasting, moral implications of history.

I am concerned with Hawthorne's understanding of history, not with other possibly more influential themes within the total structure of his work. When I take up related problems, I discuss only their possible connection with the object of this study. Needless to say, many other aspects are important to the success or failure of his stories. Nevertheless, his understanding of history is a major factor. To a large extent it determines the treatment of his subject and forms part of his basic views.

More extensive studies have been made of Hawthorne's professional knowledge of history and his use of historical material.[1] Valuable insight is found in Marius Bewley, *The Complex Fate* (London, 1952), and particularly in R. W. B. Lewis, *The American Adam* (Chicago, 1955), Hyatt H. Waggoner, *Hawthorne: A Critical Study* (Cambridge, Mass., 1955), Chapter II, and Roy Harvey Pearce, "Hawthorne and the Sense of the Past or, The Immortality of Major Molineux."[2] I have also drawn much upon F. O. Matthiessen's *American Renaissance* (New York, 1941) and Roy A. Male's *Hawthorne's Tragic Vision* (Austin, Tex., 1957). But none of these tries consistently to interrelate Hawthorne's sense of the past with his deep artistic interest in the operation of moral laws.

## I. *Introduction.*

Hawthorne is concerned with history as a powerful influence in men's lives; he wants to find the "spiritual significance"[3] of the historical fact. This raises the basic problem of "fiction" versus "truth."

Historical records may reveal a certain order and direction in the historical process, but still be without any spiritual significance. Inversely, history as recreated by the romancer will not necessarily have to fit into an objective sequence of historical events, identified in time and place. As a writer, Hawthorne actually needs both aspects. In tales like "The Gray Champion," "The May-pole of Merry Mount," "Legends of the Province House," and "Endicott and the Red Cross" he recreates the New England past by letting significant associations invest the authentic history of New England. In "Roger Malvin's Burial" and "My Kinsman, Major Molineux" he tries to create the inseparable interrelation of authentic history and an imaginative and symbolical rendering of it. Still the result is not acceptable to the sober-minded historian. Therefore Hawthorne argues in the preface to *The House of the Seven Gables* that he is not writing an ordinary historical novel: " . . . to assign an actual locality to the imaginary events of this narrative . . . exposes the romance to an inflexible and exceedingly dangerous species of criticism, by bringing his [the author's] fancy-pictures almost into positive contact with the realities of the moment."[4]

As shown in "Edward Randolph's Portrait," Hawthorne regards any experience of a historical fact in terms of a reading imposed upon the fact. Yet he is still ambivalent when he compares his version to other readings; he often points out that "assuredly, it has a tinge of romance approaching to the marvellous."[5]

In one way, ambiguity is the very consequence of a setting in the past. R. H. Fogle, who stresses that Hawthorne's use of ambiguity is a means of pointing to the precariousness of objective, valid knowledge as well as to the complexity of human experience, says that "Hawthorne so employs the element of time as to warn us that he cannot guarantee the literal truth of his narrative and at the same time to suggest that the essential truth is the clearer."[6] It is this ambiguity which sets the general frame of reference for any inquiry into the historicity in Hawthorne's tales and romances. The historicity may manifest itself in "the authenticity of the outline"[7] and in a dramatic and poetic sense of general historical relations which have been integrated into the work of art. General Andros vs. the Gray Champion, Endicott tearing the cross from the royal banner, the Tory Major Molineux driven through the streets of Boston, and Hester Prynne on the scaffold facing the Puritan community are all *significant* images which recapture general historical relations and "truths."

The difficulty in proceeding from history objectively verifiable to a "true" and valid version of history as subjective experience implies a second dilemma which is connected with the significance of the past for the present. Hawthorne's problem is complex: how can he make history *significant* to human experience within an actual present when the past is considered dead and irrelevant? And when the difficulties are so complex and confusing if one tries to proceed from the sensible fact of history in experience to a sound theory of objective historical descriptions supported by logic, how can history then become meaningful? If the sense of time and history is not logically acceptable, the temporal sequence can very well become illusory and unreal. Reality can consequently be disassociated from time and history into something timeless and unchanging. Hawthorne is aware of the fact that the elements in the romance, his artistic medium, may sever reality from history, and he issues a warning in the preface to *The House of the Seven Gables*: "He [the writer] will be wise, no doubt, to make a very moderate use of the privileges here stated, and, especially, to mingle the Marvellous rather as a slight, delicate, and evanescent flavor, than as any portion of the actual substance of the dish offered to the public."

That is to say that the writer must not abuse his "right to present . . . truth under circumstances, to a great extent, of the writer's own choosing or creation."[8]

After this short discussion we can temporarily suggest that to Hawthorne any literary recreation of the past must fuse authentic history and the imaginative sense of it in order to be really significant for human experience,[9] of which the former is not merely of minor importance. Hawthorne is so much of a historian that he knows the value of primary historical sources, such as newspapers and almanacs.[10] They are the very media through which historical reality manifests itself. This reality is not *only* objectively rational as a treatise written by a man who sets himself apart from the age may be: nor is it exclusively a timeless, unchanging reality beyond the world of experience. The creative recall of historical time cannot contain the one without the other. Nevertheless, the recapture of history does not have to be objectively valid in order to be morally and aesthetically significant. The significance of history must be grasped by the poetical sensibility and not enforced by the logic of "an iron rod."[11]

## II. *Hawthorne and history as fact.*

Hawthorne thus needed his professional knowledge of history in order to recapture the past creatively.[12] His knowledge of recorded Puritan history was extensive; according to Norman Holmes Pearson, "What the life about him could not give, he got from books . . . from older histories like Cotton Mather's and newer ones like Peter's *General History of Connecticut*; in English *Annual Registers* and *State Trials*; in the newspapers and court-records of New England he steeped himself until his intimacy with the past was worthy of a professional historian."[13] Hawthorne even played the historian when he co-authored *Peter Parley's Universal History* and later wrote *Grandfather's Chair*. But the young Hawthorne's interest in history was not primarily professional.[14] The mere collection of valid historical descriptions was as useless to him as the lieutenant's explanation about the battle of Ticonderoga. "His description . . . would be as accurate as a geometrical theorem, and as barren of the poetry that has clustered round its decay."[15]

Hawthorne's dilemma is that a record of history which possesses some kind of objective validity does away with certain *qualities* of significant associations, which, on the other hand, are immediately present to the subjective experience of history. Therefore he is very much concerned with those qualities which are an integral part of human experience but not a part of any objective record of history. In a review of W. G. Simms' *Views and Reviews in American History* Hawthorne says: ". . . we cannot help feeling that the real treasures of his subject have escaped the author's notice. . . . To be the prophet of Art requires almost as high a gift as to be a fulfiller of the prophecy. Mr. Simms has not this gift; he possesses nothing of the magic touch that should cause new intellectual and moral shapes to spring up in the reader's mind, peopling with varied life what had hitherto been a barren waste."[16] For Hawthorne history interacts with and develops an ethical or spiritual theme. In the preface to *Grandfather's Chair* he himself "has sometimes assumed the license of filling up the outline of history with details for which he has none but imaginative authority, but which, he hopes, do not violate nor give a false coloring to the truth."[17]

Hawthorne's concern is intensely personal and it grows more out of "instinct" and a "home-feeling with the past"[18] than of a detailed knowledge of historical facts.

Hawthorne's hereditary affiliation teaches him as much about the significance of history as the Puritan chronicles. In his birthplace, Salem, he breathes the atmosphere of the past to the fullest extent. In "The Custom House" sketch he says that no one can conceive "of the oysterlike tenacity with which an old settler, over whom his third century is creeping, clings to the spot where his successive generations have been imbedded." Hawthorne is "conscious that it lay at . . . [his] option to recall whatever was valuable in the past."[19] His special "affection" for Salem, however, is due to its *significant* historical tradition and innate sense of a relevant past. The local tradition and way of life supports his version of the New England past by striking associations in him which stir "a thrill of awe."[20]

These significant associations are not only those springing from the evil and guilt of the past. In the historical tales, such as "The Gray Champion," "The May-pole of Merry Mount," "Legends of the Province House," and "Endicott and the Red Cross" Hawthorne intends primarily to recapture the past for its own sake, and history is more of an object of the past. In Salem Hawthorne can artistically and significantly live in the presentness of the past, and be "contemporary with" material which the past "hands down" to him under the guise of objectivity. The feeling of meeting the past personally is precisely the effect on Hawthorne after he has found the old documents after Mr. Surveyor Pue in the Custom-House. Out of the subsequent intercourse with the past, carried on in a presumed atmosphere of objectivity, arises the "intelligible truth for all times."[21]

Thus we can say that Hawthorne's thoughts about history are, as it were, impersonal in the sense that the significant aspects in the experience of the past are not only rooted in his personal innate "instinct." They find their "objective correlative" in the local tradition and in the objects and events of an enduring social system, and therefore the imputation of eternal verities seems more convincing. No doubt a long historical tradition is congenial to this kind of impersonal art. Henry James writing about Hawthorne thinks that "the flower of art blooms only where the soil is deep . . . it takes a great deal of history to produce a little literature."[22] As a young artist who writes his legend of New England, Hawthorne falls back on the history of his native state as a cultural and imaginative whole to which a general moral significance is imputed.[23] In "The Gray Champion" the objective, historical background and the poet's creative recollection of it are fused by the very existence of a vital tradition also presumably sensed by the reader. The vital tradition sifts and winnows the historical material and preserves the general image of history, such as we find it in the great scene of conflict in "The Gray Champion": "The whole scene was a picture of the condition of New England, and its moral."[24]

Obviously, the result is bound to be a compromise, and the success is not at all secured. The general image which "sometimes" suggests truth to Hawthorne [25] may lead to a generalized, limited, often ambiguous or fantastic treatment of the distilled historical material and the characters involved. What we finally get is the historical legend. When the authenticity is too thin as in "Old Ticonderoga: A Picture of the Past," the work of art becomes all fantasy, a *personal* sketch. On the other side, in "Howe's Masquerade," and frequently in *The Marble Faun* the authenticity is too heavy,[26] and Hawthorne is not able to infuse the story with sufficient significance.

There remains another dilemma which is stated in the preface. How can history be significant when man experiences the constant, successive changes even in his own life which demand an abandonment of the old for the sake of adjusting himself to new and invented things, and when man experiences himself as part of that constant, successive and discontinuous change even in his own life-time? Dominicus Pike, the tobacco pedlar in "Mr. Higginbotham's Catastrophe," is such a type: he lives in the temporal present, "always itching to hear the news and anxious to tell it again." By "blindly obeying the call of fate," he makes his fortune in a new society marked by a rising money economy.[27] The dilemma Hawthorne faces when he tries to make history significant to modern man, to a Dominicus Pike, can best be understood in relation to the climate of opinion in Hawthorne's own age, the nineteenth century.

The religious reformation, the revolution in science, economics, and technology, and the Renaissance interacted upon one another in the days when the Puritans settled in the promised land of New England, in such a way that to the Puritan chronicler and the Puritan community in general, the time after Luther was the period in history most loaded with meaning and significance.[28] Hawthorne's own works reflect how the upheaval is later extended to all areas of society and how it breaks down the traditional sense of enduring values. In "Earth's Holocaust" Hawthorne deals with the reformists' zealous demands for complete change and novelty; the modern age itself is seen in "The Celestial Railroad"; the characters of reform and their project are studied in *The Blithedale Romance* and through the portrayal of Holgrave in *The House of the Seven Gables*; the optimism of science is expressed in "The Birthmark" and "Rappaccini's Daughter." New vistas open themselves to Holgrave and ask to be realized in this world, a bid which is considered natural because of the evidence of constant change in natural and human history. Holgrave "had that sense . . . that, this very now, there are the harbingers abroad of a golden era." Time changes perpetually and is part of human life and history in this world. Consequently, as "The Celestial Railroad" shows, the concept of eternity within a constantly changing history is not paid attention to, or it is flatly rejected. "Tracts of land and golden mansions, situate in the Celestial City, were often exchanged . . . for a few years' lease of small, dismal, inconvenient tenements in Vanity Fair."[29] The stable framework of religious and moral values and eternal verities, and the apparently solid social and political framework all seem to break down, as Hawthorne suggests in "Earth's Holocaust."

Thus Hawthorne is conscious of living in an age which to a large extent is indifferent to one or all of these dimensions of eternity. Moral laws or verities are not absolute: truth becomes relative to the historical process and thus subject to change, or it is blurred by compromise. In *The House of the Seven Gables* Hawthorne indicates that the nervous and restless cerebration in Judge Pyncheon also suggests a loss of the sense of good and evil and a refusal to consider man's earthiness, the dark and animalistic in him, which paradoxically enough preserves the ideal, the eternal verity about man's destiny and moral conduct.[30] Hawthorne seems to say that once he has a conception of history (which the Judge has not), man will also discover how deeply he is rooted in earthiness and in wrong-doing.

How can history, then, in our age, be a *medium* for the discovery of eternal verities? How can one rely on the past for answers to the questions that one will put to the universe?

Hawthorne's concern with history is extraordinary only in *kind*. The historical interest of the age has been well characterized by Nicolai Berdyaev: ". . . historical research is apt to flourish not during periods when the human mind exercises itself in a deep, organic communion with actual, concrete history but precisely . . . when the mind has been jolted out of such communion, when it is sufficiently detached from the continuing flow of history to reflect self-watchfully upon it."[31]

Such research seems liable to the criticism which Hawthorne directs against the authors of theological treatises in "The Old Manse." The sense of an *enduring* quality and an organic interrelation between the past and the present is to him qualitatively different from ability in historical research. And it is the weakness of contemporary philosophy that it sees historical time as the only medium in which man can rise from birth and fulfil himself,[32] and "that it confuses penetration in space with moral insight."[33]

R. W. B. Lewis distinguishes between an antihistorical attitude which rejects past inheritance, makes a plea for new ideas, and on a deeper level wrestles with the facts of history in order not to make them a burden, and a non-historical attitude, represented by Emerson, Thoreau and Whitman, which admits and seeks no temporal distinctions at all, no past at one's back. To some it seemed that "as the present was cut away from the past, so the past appeared unexpectedly as an isolated, authentic object of inquiry." To others, like Thoreau, the past "should be cast off like dead skin."[34]

Hawthorne could hardly avoid being affected by these ideas of his age. His concern with constant, relentless change and transitoriness in human history echoes the shift toward some kind of historicism and the general interest in evolution and the process of growth. The "Rousseauistic faith in human perfectibility" is echoed in "The New

Adam and Eve."³⁵ But the concept of perpetual transitoriness and change is primarily *negative* to Hawthorne as it merely belongs to the context of human mortality. "There is a celestial something within us that requires, after a certain time, the atmosphere of heaven to preserve it from decay and ruin."³⁶ Nor does Hawthorne accept the view that man's place in history is defined and known by regarding him as subject to constant change and evolutionary processes such as they operate in nature.³⁷ Man may evolve biologically in history, but if he loses his soul he cannot evolve. "Evolution is not true, for we have a soul, and are very distinct from animals. The soul possesses an accumulation of wisdom, and an eternity to grow more in wisdom."³⁸ Finally Hawthorne does not attempt to make history "meaningful" in terms of a pattern or valid laws of continuity, or in terms of changing human aspirations and values which are temporarily relevant and valid within the historical process. "The world, nowadays, requires a more earnest purpose, a deeper moral, and a closer and homelier truth, than he [Walter Scott] was qualified to supply it with."³⁹ The very significance or "meaning" of history is that it can be an appropriate medium, as it was to the Puritans. And Hawthorne's historical sense manifests itself in the very act of discovery.

Thus, since history is a *means* to moral wisdom, Hawthorne is not over-serious about history in the scholarly sense of the word. The showman in "Main Street" does not present a historical drama or aim at an overwhelming impact of history in its totality and magnitude beyond the successive chronological episodes. In "Main Street" history as such consists of a series of episodes which exemplify or serve to evolve the eternal moral lesson through a creative imagination. Hawthorne is not interested in establishing empirically valid, historical laws which describe the general historical process. Such laws always answer the question about a conceptual *meaning* of history, and Hawthorne is not concerned with meaning in this sense.

Again the suppositions on which Puritan history was based are similar to Hawthorne's own ideas. The Puritan historian thought "history should be seen as a long revelation of divine intentions"; the historian "must not sort out his materials, suppress some facts and accentuate others, because they conform to patterns he has himself constructed."⁴⁰ The search for meaning in the nineteenth century sense implies exactly such a construction of a pattern.

Since Hawthorne is not concerned with the "meaning" of history, the term "significance" better indicates the extent to which historial facts, descriptions, and situations to him present themselves as with moral values, reflecting the transcendental eternal verities.

Because of the fundamental difference between knowledge of history and wisdom through history Hawthorne regards the science of history neither as "inferior" nor as "superior" to his own version.[41] The methods of research are proper for making objective and valid historical descriptions. But he suggests that this kind of history as contrasted with his own version, and we may say, even with Puritan history, lacks a certain direction and order. Holgrave in *The House of the Seven Gables* does see not the *quest* for the significance of history as a relevant one, even if he feels the weight of the past. " 'Shall we never, never get rid of this Past?' cried he." And the erudite but narrow-minded critic in "Main Street" pays attention only to the correctness of the historical paraphernalia. The train in *The House of the Seven Gables* and in "The Celestial Railroad" can be said to be a symbol not only for the modern age, but for an abstract idea about historical time.[42] Changes merely succeed one another so rapidly and unintelligibly that the individual is unable to understand his own past or the history of mankind. The train into which Hepzibah and Clifford plunge themselves seems to have no direction, no telos.

History viewed in this way can become a burden from which one tries to escape into dreams and timelessness. In "The Hall of Fantasy" Hawthorne says that the "burden of years rolls down from the old man's shoulders the moment that the door encloses" — and he enters the Hall of Fantasy. Another kind of escape from historical reality is the obsessive consciousness of antiquity as antiquity. In "Old Ester Dudley" the main character escapes into a past which "had once been a reality, but was now merely a vision of faded magnificence." She lives "in her own circle of ideas, . . . never regulating her mind by a proper reference to present things."[43]

Hawthorne is also suspicious of the nineteenth century's belief in progress. He disapproves both of the New England reformers and the Transcendentalists on this point. In his *Life of Franklin Pierce* the reformers are accused of moving faster than history itself and ignoring its lesson, which is intimately connected with any planning for the future.[44] History is a realm of conflict, not a realm of indeterminate growth and development. Hawthorne's reply to the belief that moral and social progress can be vindicated in terms of empirical knowledge of historical and social processes, is to seek out crimes committed in any historical time, by way of which he imputes evil and guilt to human nature and history. Commenting upon the Fall of Man, Austin Warren says that Hawthorne took the doctrine of the Fall "as empirically true."[45] In all of Hawthorne's romances sin has been or is being committed, and the reader must accept it as sin taking place in a historical reality. The "historical" setting can be the modern Arcadia of *The Blithedale Romance*, the Rome of all times in *The Marble Faun*, that is, both before, during, and after the Fall, or any historical period in which external national, religious, or social conflicts reveal the ambivalent interplay of good and evil.

We started this discussion by introducing the modern hero in "Mr. Higginbotham's Catastrophe," Dominicus Pike. Through sheer luck and vital curiosity he makes his fortune as a capitalistic manufacturer. He lives in the present "now," in the temporal present like Judge Pyncheon, "a devotee of the mechanical system in which time is measured spatially . . . [a man to whom] his unerringly accurate watch has measured the distance between his various engagements. One might say, indeed, that the Judge's watch has replaced his pulse."[46] It is Hawthorne's implicit argument against the believers in progress that evil and guilt ignored and unrecognized, *fragmentize* time and leave the self in the present "now." In an illuminating passage R. W. B. Lewis shows how Miriam's discovery of her own features in a sixteenth-century portrait helps her to see the similarity between her own relation to Donatello and that of Adam and Eve, "a saving shock . . . which restores the self to its relation with the world."[47]

Both Dominicus Pike and Judge Pyncheon represent a certain social and economic system, namely the system which the protagonists in "The New Adam and Eve" get acquainted with when they enter the bank.[48] The worst features of this system are the "big, heavy, solid unrealities" of material property which are all Judge Pyncheon cares about.[49] To him time is thus a commodity as it is the instrument for producing wealth; therefore the twelve hours of the day must be carefully planned.

Such a view affects also the view upon history. The modern producer of wealth looks upon historical time as useless and dead because it is past and therefore unable to reveal any purpose. In his greed Judge Pyncheon is certainly after the old claims to the family estate in Maine, but these claims turn out to be completely worthless to the present generation. *Real* time, and a vague sense of evil stemming from the past can, however, be said to be unconsciously in Judge Pyncheon's mind when he tries to enter the house by force. At least in the death scene the sense of *real* time which lurks all over the house encloses the dead figure of the Judge: ". . . the great world-clock of Time still keeps its beat."[50] But the effect upon the Judge's present is disastrous.

In "Alice Doane's Appeal" Hawthorne is more explicit on this point: "For my own part, I have often courted the historic influence of the spot [Gallows Hill]. But it is singular how few come on pilgrimage to this famous hill; how many spend their lives almost at its base, and never once obey the summons of the shadowy past, as it beckons them to the summit." A few paragraphs later Hawthorne gives a hint why this is so, namely because material prosperity and progress have blunted the sense of evil and guilt, hovering over Gallows Hill: "No blight had fallen on old Essex; all was prosperity and riches, healthfully distributed."[51] The ceaseless change and novelty of things make it hard to understand former ages and generations and particularly so on the level of moral significance.

In "Roger Malvin's Burial" Reuben Bourne is unwilling and unable to identify himself with the significant event of his personal history. Largely due to changes in the social and economic system and also on account of a pressure from without in general a disruption has taken place, both in one's experience of one's own past and in the theoretical connections in history: ". . . as we are not a people of legend or tradition, it was not every citizen of our ancient town that could tell . . . so much as the date of the witchcraft delusion." The date is important because to Hawthorne it signifies the representative example of the rising of moral confusion and guilt. If Hawthorne's contemporaries commemorate a past event by lighting bonfires it is "rather without an idea beyond the momentary blaze."[52]

The lack of a sense of a significant past, as "Alice Doane's Appeal" suggests, is largely the result of the instability of the social structure. On the whole, technology and industrialized society have limited man's perspective to the temporal "now." Man's control of space has extended, while his sense of history has contracted so that the past, the present and the future are not significantly correlated. In "The Custom House" Hawthorne hints that the extreme consequence of a patronizing democracy bodes ill since the paternal protection of Uncle Sam will prevent the citizen from living "throughout the whole range of his faculties and sensibilities,"[53] making him regard the "now" as the temporal stage in which all is included.

The social and economic developments have also led to the break-up of the family as when the ambitious Judge Pyncheon is able to crush the aristocracy represented by Hepzibah. In *The Blithedale Romance* a cause which is more psychological lies behind Zenobia's effort to get free from traditional family authority. In the same way Miriam resists her family's attempt to compel her into a planned marriage; she runs away and lives in the present "now" with Donatello.

What makes the disruption of the old family pattern important is that Hawthorne thinks this also has led to a contraction of historical time. The ardent democratic revolutionary, John Hancock, in "Old Esther Dudley," or the mob in "My Kinsman, Major Molineux" has no sense of what has gone before. Zenobia is so much part of the present "now" that her ordinary name linking her to common society, is not generally used. Nor is she willing to connect herself with her family so long as she stays on the farm. And Miriam remains so myste-rious throughout that Hawthorne has to add a special "conclusion" in order to unwind her knotty past.

Hawthorne's attitude to *his* family offers a valuable contrast to that of these disinherited characters: "The figure of that first ancestor . . . was present to my boyish imagination, as far back as I can remember. It still haunts me . . .." The feeling for family tradition is not nostalgic, but founded upon a sense of inherited guilt from persecuting ancestors. Hawthorne's almost desperate awareness of his Salem family does not lead to an effort of "liberation," even if he *hopes* that his children "shall strike their roots into unaccustomed earth." To him Salem is his family's "destiny" and "the inevitable centre of the universe."[54]

At this point Hawthorne's continuous effort to recapture the history of mankind, of his native region, or by way of analogy, of a family, would appear to be basically an attempt to discover the moral self in terms of belongingness and continuity with that which has gone before. It may even be that this sense of a significant continuity between past and future is more necessary because he feels that the unity of the family is about to be broken, or that he is about to be alienated from his family be becoming a professional author.

### III. *Hawthorne and the Romance.*

In the first two sections Hawthorne appears primarily as a writer who makes a certain significant response to history, and who, on the whole, is sensitive to the impressions from the world of the past. Now

I propose to show how he grapples with the historical material in order to make it artistically significant in his own sense of the word.

Historical time affects every aspect of Hawthorne's fiction, both theme, form, and diction. Therefore any discussion of the spiritual significance of historical time in Hawthorne's tales and romances will have to deal with these aspects, all of which involve artistic problems.

The artist cannot make an exact copy of reality as Hawthorne implicitly admits in "Edward Randolph's Portrait,"[55] for reality is ultimately non-verbal. Another problem is that, even if he describes a thing that has really happened in the past, he must yet create a sense of presence and presentness and recognition in the minds of his readers. In "Main Street" the showman who is after dramatic verisimilitude is indifferent to the criticism of the literal historian and the "acidously-looking gentleman" concerning the anachronisms and the lack of "things as they are." Instead he urges them to take the "proper point of view," to sense, as the Puritans tried to, the "overtones" which alter "the character of the bare fact."[56] Thus will they disregard the existence of a medium and its crude paraphernalia intervening between their eyes and the immediate perception of reality.

Further, the historical spectacles vary in appearance, so the truth of life that the author tries to reveal is not something fully itself, but is imposed on his vision by artistic as well as social conventions. Substantially, however, the spectacles are the same from one age to another. Life's stage, "Main Street," on the edge between the wilderness and the community remains together with the central rhythm of life and death. Perry Miller says that "Puritan history was posited upon the assumption of an eternal sameness in things."[57] So is Hawthorne's version of it in "Main Street."

In the great tales and in *The Scarlet Letter*, *The House of the Seven Gables*, and *The Marble Faun* Hawthorne is concerned with the world as it endures in history. But in this connection the formal conventions are more suitable to suggest the general artistic problem. Hawthorne is anxious to contrast his version of the romance with the novel, and thereby also the area of the possible with that of the probable. The preface to *The House of the Seven Gables* contains Hawthorne's theory of the romance, in well-known words: "When a writer calls his work a Romance . . . [he] has fairly a right to present that truth [of the human heart] under circumstances, to a great extent, of the writer's own choosing or creation. If he think fit, also, he may so manage his atmospherical medium as to bring out or mellow the light and deepen and enrich the shadows of the picture. He will be wise, no doubt, to make a very moderate use of the privileges here stated . . . . He can hardly be said, however, to commit a literary crime even if he disregard this caution."[58] Hawthorne's frequent preoccupation with the form of the romance suggests that he is not only anxious to characterize and describe it, but to discover and search out all its possibilities.

The romance is first and foremost a moral work which is true to human nature. The "truth" which to Hawthorne is of highest moral significance and value can best be indirectly hinted at through images and symbols; that is, the speech of the imagination, which crosses the border of the supernatural, "the Marvellous."[59]

The romance includes all experience in the largest, even in the most exaggerated, terms. The "latitude" which Hawthorne claims, makes it possible for him to choose and use the historical material freely. And this sense of the romance infuses all his New England tales and romances. Here the elements of experience which contain an allegorical and symbolical significance are integrated and interrelated with the characters who have those experiences, the community in which they live, and the moral sense of that community. And the sin and burden of the main character have both a particular meaning for the community and a typical one for all ages. In so far as the essentials of history used by Hawthorne do not violate human order and nature, and find their objective counterpart in the life of an organized community, they express the eternal verities.

In other words, though Hawthorne is concerned with the essentials of reality and must claim a certain "latitude" for the superficially real, the inherited tradition, history and the pattern of thought and morality, which I have traced in the two previous sections, prevent his best work from becoming mere poeticized sketches of historical facts. The subject-matter makes for an adequate and valid form. His works are not romances because of their sense of the past or their elements of "the Marvellous" and the mysterious, but because of the organic form given these materials: his art represents a way of perceiving truth from a happy point of view and a means to a significant end. When Hawthorne moves away from the moral reality which he knows, as he does in *The Marble Faun* and the unfinished romances, he mostly romanticizes the past. It is not recaptured so as to throw light upon his own or the reader's view of life. Emotion has substituted specific meaning.

Thus, however distant in time and place, however "Marvellous" — truth, character, situation, and setting must be based upon local fact which must be known immediately. The significance of history, the symbolical or allegorical impact of a character, has to grow out of a world where the symbol has a real existence, as the scarlet letter, the witchcraft superstition, or the belief in supernatural manifestations in seventeenth-century Salem. Only thus can we see how the past bears down upon the present.

Yet the medium, language itself, has to obey laws of order and sequence, not quite suited to the search after the eternal verities. Language which consists of separate discrete units cannot represent the unbounded and continuous which is the effect of historical time upon the mind. Hawthorne's difficulty is then that he will not merely reproduce a fair semblance to reality and present his thought about it, but also that he wants to evolve an intuitive understanding and unrational feeling for it. Therefore: "Articulate words are a harsh clamor and dissonance. When man arrives at his highest perfection, he will again be dumb!"[60] Truth can only be conveyed in words and becomes at best a collection of half-truths. But all forms of artistic thinking are verbal, and the author and the reader must strike a bargain pretending that the verbal account is as true as one is "likely to obtain from any other source."[61]

Hawthorne's images, symbols, and allegorical elements include within themselves the aspects of past, present, and future as dynamically associated and interrelated with each other. His historical sense manifests itself especially in his ability to find "historical" images, fuse them with the setting and action proper, and make them point both ways, both to the past and to the future. When John Endicott tears the red cross from the royal banner this means more than a rejection of the extrinsic power of the Church of England through the royal government. It "contains an entire era of American history in a single scene and action."[62] And the tearing away of the central Christian symbol, the cross, is the deepest level of significance which Hawthorne attaches to this historical event.[63] Equally, the growing predominance of Hester's scarlet letter which is given historical justification by being mirrored and thus externalized in the breast-plates and shining shields in Governor Bellingham's mansion, suggests various levels of meaning.[64]

In "Rappaccini's Daughter" Hawthorne confesses his "inveterate love of allegory."[65] When equating object and idea in an allegorical form, Hawthorne testifies to a Puritan influence. Puritan history "shows how common in New England was the tendency to interpret history as the limited and concrete dramatization of the play of supernatural forces."[66] This was also done by Hawthorne. In "The May-pole of Merry Mount" Hawthorne says that "the facts, recorded on the grave pages of our New England annalists, have wrought themselves, almost spontaneously, into a sort of allegory."[67] Allegory becomes a means to conceive of past history as revealing a definite and basic moral conflict which can be abstracted in terms of fixed moral values. And like the original Puritan one, it always tops itself in a decision of supreme moral importance — namely, whether to adjust one's self and further the divine plan in the world of brotherhood, or to decline the divine offer and search for natural liberty in a haunted wilderness or in an innocent Arcadia away from it.[68]

In other words, Hawthorne's characters must accept history or negate it by withdrawing from it. Allegory serves to give shape to a dualistic sense of historical conflict. And from my point of view the allegorical "focus" is upon the decision for or against historical and ethical reality.

As "The Custom House" shows, Hawthorne's world of reality is not the imaginary one nor the actual one *per se*, nor the absolute abstract reality of the allegory which merely depends upon the formal correspondence between object and idea, both of which are supposed to be given. Hawthorne is after "a neutral territory, somewhere between the real world and fairy-land, where the Actual and the Imaginary may meet, and each imbue itself with the nature of the other." The scarlet letter itself is a symbol which by being contemplated and observed recreates this world in a significant way. The world illuminated by the "A" "is at once physical and ideal. At its center are human beings who perceive the world by wearing the symbol in mind and body."[69]

I have already referred to Hawthorne's symbolical conception of history which reveals the complexity and significant ambiguity in life historically given. In many tales and romances we can watch the constant movement back and forth between the community and the wilderness which are symbols challenging the protagonists to choose between them, a decisive choice which will determine whether Arthur Dimmesdale, for instance, shall recognize his guilt in history, or escape from it.

Still the conflict is ambiguous. On the one hand Hawthorne recognizes the need for social fellowship and organized communal life. "Wakefield" and "The Man of Adamant" deal with the frozen individualist who has hardened into a stone-like character unable to draw strength from others. But Hawthorne is also aware of the deadening influence of too much civilization. Rome, which includes all that has been, is a heap of "broken rubbish" which covers the gigantic corpse of ancient civilization and makes it hard to breathe freely.[70] Hawthorne feels a considerable sympathy for the dwellers at Merry Mount as well as for Hester's and Arthur Dimmesdale's temporary relish of their freedom in the forest. Yet he grasps the reasons for the Puritans' distrust and fear of the wilderness, uncontrolled and unconcealed, the home of "devils and ruined souls." The preference for the community is due to its organization of human impulses and the restraint imposed upon their free expression. This is one reason why Arthur Dimmesdale does not give in to his impulses upon his return from the forest.[71]

Notwithstanding, the forest remains an ambiguous setting for moral decisions: it also affords hope, promises, and some kind of new insight. Arthur Dimmesdale and Hester gain vital power there to break the deadlock and return to the history of mankind. Edgar and Esther, the two lovers in "The May-pole of Merry Mount", find in the forest their mutual affection which will support them when they go back to the Puritan community. They abandon the mirth but not the mutual love in their new historical reality, "earth's doom of care and sorrow, and troubled joy." Similarly, Miriam's and Donatello's separate escape from Rome ends up with their recognition of their homelessness in Arcadia; as guilty human beings they are spurred back to Rome and historical reality, the "city of all time and of all the world."[72]

This is not a doctrine logically arrived at; the poetic truth grows out of Hawthorne's sense of a complete rhythm of experience. The ambiguity in history arises because Hawthorne sympathizes both with the withdrawal from the city as well as with the characters' integrity on their return to it. But ultimately he seems to possess a vision of a renewed light and strength because of his acceptance of historical reality.

This dialectic between the city and the wilderness, taking place in history, suggests three different types of character, disinguished in their historical sense of this dialectic. There is more to history than the shallow travellers in "The Celestial Railroad" are able to see. A deeper vision of the dark forces in life is seen in "the depths of every heart . . . a tomb and a dungeon, though the lights, the music, and revelry above may cause us to forget their existence." But there is also more in history than a predominance of guilt and darkness: a realization of the self and one's burden and responsibility. Having once gone through this rhythm of experience and acquired a new understanding of the march of history, one knows that the "'past, dismal as it seems, shall fling no gloom upon the future. To give it its due importance we must think of it but as an anecdote in our Eternity.'"[73]

In the last resort, however, Hawthorne is wary of mere symbolism which is not subject to any external discipline. Pearl is almost horrifying because she is not subject to any ruling principle, but enjoys "the freedom of a broken law."[74] It is characteristic of Hawthorne that he generally ends up on quite a different note, usually by bringing in the world of history and mortality in which he lives and writes. Therefore the allegorical view of history remains the stabilizing factor which he applies to his artistic vision. As allegory depends on a scheme of publicly accepted values, it does not blur the lines of demarcation in the moral conflict. Symbolism enriches and makes the significant historical episode more complex, while allegory defines it in the light of a long tradition.

There are some additional means to create a sense of the bearing of the past upon the present. One problem arises in connection with the different time-values of the reader, the writer, and the protagonists, which again involve a highly complicated structure. There is the illusion of historical completeness and continuity, of presence and presentness; the imaginative shift of the reader from his own present to the historical fictive past; and again, the translation of this past into a relevant fictive present which for Hawthorne's purpose is of primary importance. The author must solve such problems of technique as tempo, continuity, historical texture, and selection of material.

Instead of dealing selectively and historically with a whole generation and renouncing fictional density and rounded characters, Hawthorne usually deals with small units of time and concentrates on the psychology of the character within that unit. The history of the Pyncheons is compressed into a few summer months; in *The Scarlet Letter* the author concentrates on specific events within a span of seven years. All aspects of historical Rome in *The Marble Faun* "repeat" themselves in the story of Mirian and Donatello.[75] The historical tales centre on the *incident*, a vital climax, when it is too late for any slow resolution or compromise. (It is typical that in "Main Street" it is the

Great Snow of 1717, "a change, wrought in the twinkling of an eye, like an incident in a tale of magic," which marks the end of an era and is most loaded with significance).[76]

A device for bridging historical periods in the narrative is the inserted episode, such as Holgrave's story about Alice Pyncheon in *The House of the Seven Gables*, and Moodie's "exposition" in *The Blithedale Romance*, which brings Priscilla's past into focus.[77] Another solution in order to create an artistic illusion of historical reality and narrow the gap between truth and the *vraisemblance* is the attempt to generalize the particular human situation by giving cross-sections of society or a town.[78] In "My Kinsman, Major Molineux" Robin meets the simultaneous activity and obsession of a whole town; in "Young Goodman Brown" all the prominent leaders of the community are on their way to the devilish ceremony in the forest. In *The Marble Faun* the history-laden ancient city contains and generalizes all the stages Miriam and Donatello go through. Their history is analogous to Rome's: both are set down according to a pattern of life, death, and resurrection.

We have already (p. 117 above) referred to the idea of "the continuing flow of history." Hawthorne's own view is that existence neither originates in nor is determined by the chronological present. He says about time that there "is nothing new in him nor about him."[79] The enduring elements in time and history are interrelated with man's destiny in the world. The "lesson" in *The House of the Seven Gables* is "that, together with the seed of the merely temporary crop, which mortals term expediency, they inevitably sow the acorns of a more enduring growth, which may darkly overshadow their posterity."[80] The duration of evil in history can be perceived only by disregarding intellectual verbal formulations and by yielding to the direct impact of experience. Man carries his past on his back and continues an indefinite past in the living present.

A sense of enduring qualities is also projected into the transience of *things*. The ruins and "historic" dust of Rome and the Indian arrowheads at The Old Manse convey the same sense of time's flow which is so significant to Hawthorne's experience and secure for his sense of history a higher certainty and "authenticity," even if the concept of causality is not always comprehensible.[81] If the historical background provided by these empirical criteria is too thin to create a sense of history's flow, Hawthorne relies upon some person's memory as the objective basis for the past.

9

Memory, the store of tradition, is not only a substitute, however, to recapture a vague past. It is also continually at work within the action of the story and serves to recapture the historical time as experience from different points of view. Hence the use of traditional material, folklore, legends, and common superstition. As pointed out earlier, tradition is important to Hawthorne because it sifts the historical material through significant associations in the mind, and preserves what has a core of lasting, often ironical, truth in itself. Facts may turn into the fantasies of "the haunted mind," but through a sense of tradition they can also be reinterpreted and loaded with meaning in the light of the present situation, past guilt, and future hopes. The "historic influence" of Gallows Hill and Hawthorne's recollection of it are not simply due to the heritage of guilt stemming from his forefathers who persecuted the Quakers. He recollects also the *communal* conflict and guilt of the past which he proceeds to link with the communal attitude of the present. What he tries to do is to re-establish a lost tradition. The capacity to recall the unique events of the past helps to emancipate the individual and the community from the tyranny of the present; history proves to be a realm of freedom as well as of destiny.[82]

Tradition does not only sift the material. It also fuses it into significance in the sense that what seems void of significance can become full of meaning through the creative recall. Most of the New England tales recapture a historical incident which the community already thinks is value-charged. The author only has to give it artistic form.

Hawthorne writes about the past because that is the only way he can create something worth while. He has not "the insight and . . . the cunning" "to diffuse thought and imagination through the opaque substance of to-day"; "the rude contact of some actual circumstance" distracts him so that he cannot grasp "its deeper import."[83] Much of the contemporary scene is without symbolical significance: "Our labor symbolized nothing, and left us mentally sluggish in the dusk of the evening."[84] Hawthorne seems to have felt that even much of America's past is too fresh in the memory, and that any romantic treatment of it will be judged by the standards of realism. Therefore it is necessary to go back beyond the Revolution. It will be long "before romance-writers may find congenial and easily handled themes . . . in the annals of our stalwart republic."[85] Hawthorne is to some extent in the same position as the showman in "Main Street," for whom the scene will not move when he wants to leave the Puritan age. It is a long history Hawthorne misses when he complains in the preface to *The Blithedale Romance* that America has no "Faery Land . . . with an atmosphere of strange enchantment, beheld through which the inhabitants have a propriety of their own."[86] What Hawthorne needs is *distance* in time, "experience liberated, so to speak; experience disengaged, disembroiled, disencumbered, exempt from the conditions which usually attach to it."[87] By placing the subject in a remote past the author gives a broad representation of it and strikes a balance between the universal significance and the particular phenomenon.

Hawthorne's personal experience of the Puritan past is not only marked by distance, however, but also by intimacy. In the beginning, the Custom House is Hawthorne's enemy: it nearly destroys him as an artist and makes him feel old and decrepit. But when he discovers the scarlet letter he does not escape into the past: he is suddenly, for the first time there, being confronted with something of persistent significance. At the discovery of the letter Hawthorne's "inner" personal sense of the march of ages is related to chronological time. Unaffected by the thought and action of passing time, the scarlet letter brings about this realization. The letter has slipped into the unconscious, as it were, and is unaffected by any process of interpretation and falsification; it becomes in a way free of time and its effects. He says about the letter: "Certainly, there was some deep meaning in it, most worthy of interpretation, and which, as it were, streamed forth from the mystic symbol, subtly communicating itself to my sensibilities, but evading the analysis of my mind."[88]

Very pregnant is his sense that at the same time he is growing old through the pace of life. His mind can appreciate this more vividly because it can at last plunge itself into and then recapture the past with greater ease. The earlier sense of the *distance* of the past is superseded by a new feeling. Contemporary Salem "ceases to be a reality"; Hawthorne is "a citizen of somewhere else," of a past which is not static and objective, and whose shape shifts continuously and evades analysis. His entire life falls into a pattern in which the separate parts cohere. He is again a literary man, and as such he is about to remove the curse incurred by his ancestors; as such he can save his identity by pointing out how "strong straits of their nature have intertwined themselves with mine."[89] Thus Hawthorne can regain his sense of a significant historical past which is embodied in the letter "A."

"The Custom House" illustrates admirably how Hawthorne grapples with past material in order to make it meaningful experience. When he plunges into the past, it becomes all present reality; he seems to lose his separate identity in his own time and fuses into the series of ancestors in their several times. Actually "The Custom House" deals with Hawthorne's development on a double time-plane, first in terms of his growing old and maturing as an artist, and in terms of his inherited characteristics which were born 200 years ago. Also the future belongs to him. The town pump, and the water running through it, represent the endless flow of history, that is, the something which endures; thus it points to "the scribbler of bygone days."[90]

The real purpose of Hawthorne's works, as he puts it in "Alice Doane's Appeal," is "to assist the imagination in appealing to the heart." This taxes the author's skill to the utmost, especially because of the discrepancy between the reader's present moment of reading and the historical belongingness of the protagonists in the story. How can the reader sink into the historical past of the story?

"Alice Doane's Appeal" suggests three phases in the gradual immersion into a historical reality. Many never obey "the summons of the shadowy past," or are conscious of antiquity only for antiquity's sake, as an example of "antiquarian lore." The second phase is exemplified by the final reaction of the girls to the story of Walter Brome, Leonard Doane, and Alice Doane. Verbally all is past; psychologically, once the point of reference, the murder, has been set up, each event presented constitutes a point in a present experience, and the excitement and the horror are very deliberately raised by Hawthorne.

Yet to Hawthorne, a present experience of something which is past does not logically lead to a sense of the past's significance. Therefore he makes "a [final] trial whether truth were more powerful than fiction." He recalls an actual historical event, the witchcraft persecution at its peak of violence and fury; righteous Puritans are the guilty ones, and Hawthorne's contemporaries and he himself are their heirs. Thus Hawthorne transforms a present memory of something in the past into a present impression of sin and guilt which is made to be sensed as present but is yet familiar from the past: ". . . our kinship with the persecutors and the persecuted remains and will remain. We too know the evil passions of the wizard, the emotions of the murderer and the murdered, the fear of the victims . . .. The past has illuminated the present and thus has helped to educate the will, which is concerned with the future."[91]

One of the reasons why we are able to identify ourselves with history is that from our own life we are familiar with the things or events that we recognize in the past. What is finally sensed as present is that "the human heart has one infirmity that may result in crime." Thereby Hawthorne has achieved what he set out to do: "I had reached the seldom trodden places of their hearts, and found the well-spring of their tears. *And now the past had done all it could.*" "Alice Doane's Appeal" may not be quite successful in demonstrating this conclusion. Hawthorne's aim is nevertheless clear. His recapture of the past will not merely increase the knowledge of man's psychology. It is "intended to arouse the emotions of pity and terror, pity for the unfortunate dead and terror because they were so like ourselves."[92]

## IV. *Hawthorne's historical theme.*
## *The Tales.*

Hawthorne, then, in writing about history, or writing history, involves his protagonists, himself, and the readers in a central pattern or theme of guilt and reconciliation. History to him is ridden with disruptive and redemptive elements whose recognition is necessary in order to make it meaningful. This historical theme together with another which also takes the time dimension seriously, namely that of recognition and acceptance of guilt and redemption in the *present*, "make the whole that is Hawthorne."[93] In this section I intend to submit some of Hawthorne's works to a closer examination in order to see his historical theme in fullest perspective: four tales, "The Wives of the Dead," "The Gentle Boy," "Roger Malvin's Burial," and "My Kinsman, Major Molineux," and three novels, *The Scarlet Letter*, *The House of the Seven Gables*, and *The Marble Faun*.

The tales are among the first Hawthorne wrote: they appeared in the 1832 number of the *Token*. The earliest story we may have of Hawthorne, "The Hollow of the Three Hills," introduces the atmosphere of time and place found in the following tales: we are in "those strange old times, when fantastic dreams and madmen's reveries were realized among the actual circumstances of life." The other stories also have a historical setting, and Hawthorne explains why it attracts him: "Such scenes as this (so gray tradition tells) were once the resort of the Power of Evil and his plighted subjects." The setting in the other stories is similarly marked by some kind of crisis, violence, or evil visitation which brings the elemental forces of good and evil into focus. In "The Gentle Boy" and "My Kinsman, Major Molineux" the climax lies in the very aggressive violence and the physical intensity of the world, the community: "His persecutors beat him down, trampled upon him." "On they went, in counterfeited pomp, in senseless uproar, in frenzied merriment, trampling all on an old man's heart." There is both physical and spiritual violence, and violation of the spirit. "Roger Malvin's Burial" deals with the effect of war and "battle . . . so fatal to those who fought"; the spiritual degradation of Reuben Bourne stems from the conflict both spiritual and physical as it reveals itself in him at the point of departure from the dying Roger Malvin.[94]

One of the tales, "The Wives of the Dead," is characterized not by violence but by a certain numbness of sorrow, which in the end is turned into pure joy. Hawthorne's introductory lines are an understatement which amounts to an excuse for writing the tale: "The following story, the simple and domestic incidents of which may be deemed scarcely worth relating, after such a lapse of time, awakened some degree of interest, a hundred years ago, in a principal sea-port of the Bay Province."[95] The words "scarcely worth relating" (and the putting of the commas as well) are of central importance in this connection. Hawthorne guards himself against didacticism and antiquarianism by way of an obvious understatement and rationalization; after all the story was of some interest, "a hundred years ago." The implication is, however, that the reader has not grasped anything if he does not see what is "worth relating," namely, that in some way the past must be sensed before one is able to feel and grasp the present in its fulness.

"The Wives of the Dead" deals with "peculiar sorrows" as well as "delightful thoughts."[96] To begin with the happiness of the sisters is only a memory and belongs to the past; this, in turn, makes the present sorrow the more overwhelming. Sorrow and happiness accentuate one another; the intensity and depth of feeling are dependent upon what has been. The opening of the tale is an attempt to lead the reader to a distinction between the trifling fact of the past and its significance to those involved. What is "scarcely worth relating" because it happened "a hundred years ago" — these two phrases are not used to minimize those events in importance, but to make the reader know, identify with, and accept those events and — as we shall see — also that past. In the other early tales Hawthorne's rationalization is more subtle and deliberate, but its effect is to appeal to the reader and place him in the story and its history.

In "The Gentle Boy" the history grows out of the persecution of the Quakers in 1659. It has been pointed out that in the early version of the tale, published in the *Token* in 1832, Hawthorne emphasizes Puritan guilt "by rationalizing Puritan persecution of Quakers in such a way as to suggest that the reader too would have acted Puritanically in the same situation." But the revised version is more suitable for our purpose since it underlines the *mutual* guilt stemming from the historical conflict.[97] Instead of a particular and overt example of evil action we are confronted with a basic fact of existence. The rationalizing arguments in the first three paragraphs balance the two conflicting forces. "Quakers, led, as they professed, by the inward movement of the spirit" are set against the Puritan notion of them "as holders of mystic and pernicious principles." The careful balance is even more worked out: "The Quakers, esteeming persecution as a divine call to the post of danger, laid claim to a holy courage, unknown to the Puritans themselves, who had shunned the cross, by providing for the peaceable exercise of their religion in a distant wilderness."

The rationalization which is intended to draw the reader into the story's history, is equally balanced. The Puritans may be justified in rejecting the Quakers as "it was the singular fact, that every nation of the earth rejected the wandering enthusiasts." The fanatical enthusiasm of the Quakers was such that it "abstractedly considered, well deserved the moderate chastisement of the rod." However, after these limited allowances have been made, Hawthorne ends with a final verdict: "An indelible stain of blood is upon the hands of all who consented to this act." But this verdict is again modified and interpreted by an earlier statement; "all," that is, both Puritans and Quakers "produced actions contrary to the rules of decency."

A "large share of the awful responsibility" rests upon the governor, but so it does upon the following generations of Quakers because of their "revengeful feelings" and "bitter mockery," feelings which also nurtured the original crime. The two evils, abstract guilt and unreasonable retribution, are carefully balanced. The story itself is about Catherine's fanaticism, leading her away from a mother's obligations, and a Puritan community's cold rigidity and severity.[98]

"Roger Malvin's Burial" serves also to demonstrate the immediate and peculiar human implications and possibilities which are inherent in Hawthorne's imputation of guilt and reconciliation to a historical event, traditionally regarded as glorious. Indirectly he states the relevance of his version of Lowell's Fight in the first paragraph of the tale by way of rationalization. He says that there is "much to admire" of "heroism" and "chivalry" and "valor," when disregarding "certain circumstances" of human baseness and cruelty always accompanying a war. And on one level of meaning Hawthorne admits that the "battle, though so fatal to those who fought, was not unfortunate in its consequences to the country; for it . . . conduced to the peace which subsisted during several ensuing years." But "fatal" has a double meaning in the light of Reuben Bourne's fate and points also to his *internal* guilt and defeat growing out of the war. The minute recordings of history and tradition tell everything glorious, but not the defeat of a soul. Hawthorne seems to ask whether the readers will recognize the implication of guilt and evil, which is the spiritual aspect of the dubious circumstances cast "judicially into the shade."[99] The rationalization of a fatal struggle in the light of the ensuing peace is not used to minimize the importance of the negative aspects but as a means of reconciling and taking responsibility for the past in its totality.

Hawthorne returns to the underlying idea of the introductory paragraph later in the tale. After describing Reuben's agonizing departure from the dying Roger Malvin he looks at the conflict from the vantage-point of the reader who is not yet sufficiently identified with Reuben's dilemma: "Death . . . must have been Reuben's own fate had he tarried another sunset; and who shall impute blame to him if he shrink from so useless a sacrifice?"[100] Moreover, one cannot disregard the good, the peace, which grows out of the struggle and belongs to following generations. The reader is in the same position as Reuben, who seems to be in possession of all the good that can be extracted from his dilemma, if he does not make a useless "sacrifice." In other words, while all the good extracted from the events and all subsequent events like it, is still with us, we may, according to Hawthorne's rationalizing argument, live through a "fatal" event and forget it. However, the rest of the tale is there to present the historical event and all its human implications in such a way that it is impossible to forget it, with all its circumstances of heroism and human baseness, of guilt, loss, and reconciliation. Identifying with Reuben the reader goes through an experience in many ways similar to one described by Hawthorne in *The American Note-Books*: "A man, virtuous in his general conduct, but committing habitually some monstrous crime, — as murder, — and doing this without the sense of guilt, but with a peaceful conscience, — habit, probably, reconciling him to it; but something (for instance, discovery) occurs to make him sensible of his enormity. His horror then."[101] Experience teaches Hawthorne that life's criminals generally and their descendants rationalize their actions and do not regard themselves as especially sinful.

We have already pointed to Hawthorne's effort to bring out the mutual responsibility in "The Gentle Boy," so that the implications of the story outlast the particular and remote revelation of evil forces. The ending of the story also makes it clear that though the actual persecution is over, the infirmity of the heart which causes the tragedy is an elemental factor in life in spite of the fact that in the end Catherine, the Quakeress, is "a subject of not deep, but general, interest; a being on whom the otherwise superfluous sympathies of all might be bestowed."[102] The "deep" fact yet remains: "There is evil in every human heart, which may remain latent, perhaps, through the whole of life; but circumstances may rouse it to activity."[103] The final reconciliation, after tragic loss, grows out of two extremes, the self-sufficient rational metaphysics of the Puritans and the emotional fanaticism of the Quakers, merely tempered by the practical charity of Dorothy Pearson. The eventual good grows out of an entangled mixture of good and evil.

The extraordinary balance of two evils in "The Gentle Boy" is effected chiefly, but not entirely, by exposition; the scene in the church illustrates how the fierceness of the persecutors is balanced with Catherine's neglect of her "duty."[104] This balance draws the reader into the story and its history with its commonness of guilt and responsibility. If the reader identifies with and subscribes to the central progression in the story, as in the case of Reuben Bourne, he may, after the actual persecution (truth) and the children's beating of Ilbrahim (fiction), have attained to a sense of the past. Hawthorne does not think of these historical characters as examples of insight. But the relevant point is that they have met basic evil in their lives in one way or another, and that the reader, if he discovers Hawthorne's intention, also discovers a condition in history which belongs to his own age and history. "Roger Malvin's Burial" is a study in the psychology of a guilty man and deals with the inner conflict in one character. But the introduction is such that Reuben Bourne's fate is just one of many less obvious "circumstances."[105] His story is representative, not singular.

To sum up: in all the stories mentioned we witness in one way or another an all-inclusive crisis involving violence and defeat. The whole community is involved, all the characters act and are acted upon. All are entangled in a conflict of evil and good and subsequent guilt and responsibility. The reader is drawn into the story's history by the author's careful weighing of the rationalizing argument, often with direct appeal to the reader's common sense or conscience. Hawthorne points out the elemental condition of evil and guilt *through* history.

As to reconciliation and the feeling of responsibility for history, "The Wives of the Dead" shows that the moment of crisis must be resolved. And we pointed out in connection with "The Gentle Boy" that the reconciliation grows out of two opposing extremes, while the norm, the plea for righteousness, has all the time been present in Dorothy Pearson. Yet the discords remain unresolved; good and evil persist, as does the struggle between the head and the heart. It is Dorothy's merit that she can live in this mystery without withdrawing from it; when she meets evil and recognizes it she shows "a firm endurance" in spite of "a thousand sorrows."[106] She commits herself entirely to the victims, Ilbrahim, her husband, and Catherine, sensing that charity counts most, without asking too many questions.

However, these tales also contain distorted and disrupted personalities. Pearce has shown that Hawthorne, in "My Kinsman, Major Molineux," links and identifies a pre-revolutionary leader of mob activities in Boston, a William Molineux, with the tar-and-feathered Old Tory in Hawthorne's story in the sense that both are mutually involved in an action stemming from a "temporary inflammation of the popular mind."

Artistically the two Molineuxs are one through Robin in the sense that if the reader identifies with Robin he will also identify with the mob leader Molineux and the Tory Molineux; that is, he will identify not only with the perpetrator's principles but also with their consequences. But this identification will mean an inner loss. Robin sees his kinsman at last, helps to drive him away and trample upon him, and therefore also turns against himself, for "what he inevitably helps destroy and drive away is himself, or part of himself."[107]

"The Gentle Boy" has a greater tragic impact than "My Kinsman, Major Molineux"; Tobias Pearson and Ilbrahim are at the mercy of forces stronger than themselves. Hawthorne makes it clear that any rationale for their excesses is abstract and that any plea for historical necessity is insufficient. And involved with and behind these excesses lies Catherine's giving up her son, a part of herself, and the distortion of Tobias's character. Again Catherine and Tobias are representative figures and point to the flaw in the communal conscience which cannot be "abstractedly considered,"[108] but only sensed by the reader as it exists in the tale.

In "Roger Malvin's Burial" Reuben Bourne finally drives away his son by killing him. This is the final outcome of the process which started at the point of departure from Roger Malvin. Guilt and final reconciliation through expiation are, as frequently in Hawthorne, expressed through disconnected relations between kinsmen. Like Robin in "My Kinsman, Major Molineux" Reuben must destroy something in himself in order to become more than he is. But then it is impossible to forget what is destroyed or driven away. Ilbrahim knows intuitively, as it were, what is lost, namely his natural innocence and capability for fellowship. Pearce suggests that to Hawthorne something like "Original Sin becomes the prime fact of our political and social history." In the final procession in "My Kinsman, Major Molineux" the fiendish-looking man leading the parade is acting the part of the devil. Added to evil personified is the central image of laughter which has cumulative effect and reaches its climax when Robin joins it.[109] At this point the "temporary inflammation" is at its highest. Yet the recognition does not take place till Robin sees his kinsman.

Hawthorne has already stated the terms involved when he made the friendly visitor ask: " 'May not a man have several voices, Robin, as well as two complexions?' "[110] The reader who identifies his consciousness with Robin's, must accordingly, as this argument runs, answer together with Robin. This answer is not found through conceptual understanding, but by "living" in the imaginary world of Hawthorne's recaptured past where truth and fiction can meet. The implicit meaning in the gentleman's statement is that Robin must accept reality, and rise above the guilt, which must be faced and accepted for what it is. One can gain freedom and live in the present only if the ambiguous and guilty past has been accepted.

Thus Hawthorne has consciously given a historical background in these tales which the protagonists, Hawthorne, and the readers have in common. There is a living tradition which he can draw from and regard as a common heritage. Robin and his kinsman are one through the mob leader by the name of Molineux, Reuben and his wife and son are one through an action of guilt, and Catherine, the Pearsons and the sympathizing Puritans are one in the days after the persecution over "Ilbrahim's green and sunken grave."[111] And through the history the readers have in common with them, or Hawthorne will *make* them have in common, they are one with them too.

In all these tales Hawthorne relies upon the reader's identifying his consciousness with that of the protagonists. If he does so, the reader enters dramatically into the story, and as Robin and Reuben he has to partake in the historical responsibility, which by means of the story's intention and development is not only the protagonists', but the reader's. All the happy and good consequences cannot be severed from the evil circumstances which accompany a violent change. The argument is that if one enjoys the good in a state of righteousness one is also guilty of the evil. Only by recognizing his responsibility for history can man reach that state of human freedom which he is trying to attain. For the problem of the meaning of history is always the problem of the meaning of life itself. Man is a historic creature who is to some extent involved in the march of ages, but always involved in a false understanding of his own predicament. Viewing life and history from his own limited perspective he either denies the meaning of history or he completes it falsely. Only by recognizing the human situation of sinfulness can man reach his destiny in history.

### The Romances.

The imputation of guilt and reconciliation through history is not *the* major theme in Hawthorne's works. It seems that in *Twice-Told Tales* Hawthorne has moved away from it into something which is more typical of him. Instead of tracing the eternal verities through history and deliberately aiming at a historical sense he is chiefly concerned with the disclosure, recognition and acceptance of guilt and redemption in the *present*. In "Wakefield," "Young Goodman Brown," *The Scarlet Letter*, *The Blithedale Romance*, and *The Marble Faun* the protagonists see themselves as they really are when acting or when acted upon, and consequently they come to know themselves. Here Hawthorne is concerned with the discovery of self. In these stories and romances history is a subject in which the present is seen through the past in the sense that human nature is thought of as universally the same in all ages and places and therefore universally present.

Harry Levin and F. O. Matthiessen may join in saying that *The Scarlet Letter* with its past setting is the only romance where the past is not a problem: "Not sin, but its consequence for human lives is Hawthorne's major theme."[112] But the major theme calls for the development of our historical theme too. Pearl, "a creature that had nothing in common with a bygone and buried generation, nor owned herself akin to it," and who plays on the graves, is brought into historical reality at the end of the book. Her future grows out of Hester's history. Yet Pearl's history is not revealed to us (apart from the fact that she becomes quite prosperous). We do not know if she will grasp Dimmesdale's discovery, namely to be aware of "the worst," evil in all its complexity and ambiguity. A central thought in *The House of the Seven Gables* is echoed here: the curse of sin and guilt is transmitted from one generation to another. Nor is Pearl without a "heritage." Her extreme and dubious gaiety is transmitted from Hester's violent energy in fighting her sorrows. But Pearl is also Hester's history. As the offspring of an illegitimate union termed sinful by the chorus in the book, she marks Hester and places her in the present among "her realities." And since the letter and Pearl point to Hester's sin and guilt they connect her "forever with the race and descent of mortals." However, this is Hester's position from the beginning and Hawthorne is not out to ascribe it to her, but to make her discover it herself. Dimmesdale is not only a study in the psychology of a man ridden with concealed guilt. He exemplifies also how his religious conviction keeps the historical sense alive. Guilt and final resolution through confession are spiritual "facts," operating in history. When Hester says, " 'The past is gone! Wherefore should we linger upon it now?'," Dimmesdale can agree only if he breaks with his faith. The letter is always present in history, even if Hester throws it away.[113]

Dimmesdale, Hester, Chillingworth, and the Puritan community are all involved in the movement of history, and the guilt is all-inclusive. Chillingworth has married Hester without love, and Hester him because she has admired him. His subsequent fall into the shape of a monstrous devil is also the result of Hester's adultery. And Dimmesdale's fate is a product of the secret between Hester and Chillingworth. The final resolution, Hester's and Dimmesdale's new stature, Chillingworth's complete obsession and the shifting cruelty and forbearance of the Puritan women and the government are part of the same dynamic, ambiguous, collective history of mankind in whose guilt all are involved to a degree that cannot be stated abstractly. Hawthorne addresses "the whole human brotherhood in the heart's native language."[114]

Yet there is no redemptive love as in "The Gentle Boy" or "Egotism; or, The Bosom Serpent," or as less fortunately suggested at the end of *The House of the Seven Gables*. In *The Scarlet Letter* as in "Alice Doane's Appeal" there "is a vision of history containing judgment but not mercy, condemnation but not forgiveness, sin and suffering but no remission." This vision is brought across by three significant rationalizing arguments. First it is Hawthorne's contention that *The Scarlet Letter* contains a truth which even "our modern incredulity may be inclined to admit." And in the chapter, "A Flood of Sunshine," the returning beauty of Hester proves that the past is not "irrevocable." Hester's contention that the past is gone is not only contradictory; it reduces her own womanhood and love for Dimmesdale, which had reached its consummation in the past, to nothingness. She cannot eat her cake and have it. When Hawthorne for the third time turns more directly to the reader, he is concerned with the proper interaction of natural gaiety and gloomy experience in the world of sin. The next generation were Calvinists who "wore the blackest shade of Puritanism, and so darkened the national visage with it, that all the subsequent years have not sufficed to clear it up." History imaginatively recalled, so far as Hester's world is directly historical, shows that a complete experience of history includes the remembrance both of the gloom and of the spiritual joy. The first Puritans had known, on many occasions, the now "forgotten art of gaiety."[115]

The historical theme is more at the centre when the whole community is involved in the action. Thus the significance of the Election Sermon is more general and representative than personal and singular. But Hawthorne is anxious to modify and throw ambiguous light on the interpretation of the Sermon. The community ascribes Dimmesdale's pathos to his sense of imminent dying and sadness at leaving his beloved congregation and takes a naive view of his saintliness. After the confession new light is thrown upon the sermon. For Dimmesdale's prophecy about "a high and glorious destiny for the newly gathered people of the Lord"[116] is based upon the constant interchange and movement between the pulpit and the pillory, sanctity and sin, in which both Dimmesdale and Hester share. ". . . thus can he [Hawthorne] cut through conventional appearances, and come into possession of what Eliot has called 'a sense of his own age'."[117] If the reader identifies with Dimmesdale's point of view, and Hawthorne intends him to, the "glorious destiny" of which he may be a part does not grow out of the people's notion of sanctity and perfection and justice, but of a personal recognition of mankind's common guilt and its need for reconciliation. This is the lesson, the "shower of golden truths," "at once a shadow and a splendor," which Dimmesdale leaves behind for the future to whom it will all be history. Sin takes place in history, both "in the view of Infinite Purity" and in the view "of a this-world order," the latter of which Hester is primarily aware.[118]

In *The House of the Seven Gables*, Hawthorne gives the most deliberate and extensive treatment of the historical theme. The theme of guilt and reconciliation through history is here most ambitiously aimed at. Even if Hawthorne intended a more realistic novel, this is obscured by his treatment of time and by his assuming the point of view of the romance, "the attempt to connect a bygone time with the very present that is flitting away from us. It is a legend prolonging itself . . . down into our own broad daylight." This goes against any attempt to limit the temporal pattern to the temporal present. The shadow of the past is always there in the present. ". . . this visionary and impalpable Now, . . . if you once look closely at it, is nothing."[119]

Hawthorne repeatedly states the "moral purpose" which deals with the interdependence and interaction of past and present. He will show "that the wrong-doing of one generation lives into the successive ones, and . . . becomes a pure and uncontrollable mischief." In the opening of the first chapter a similar overt, rather abstracted thesis is set forth. Hawthorne wants "to illustrate how much of old material goes to make up the freshest novelty of human life . . . the act of the passing generation is the germ which may and must produce good or evil fruit in a far-distant time."[120]

There are other more integrated references to the historical theme throughout the story. The Pyncheons' doubt about their moral right to possess their house leads to the question "whether each inheritor of the property — conscious of wrong, and failing to rectify it — did not commit anew the great guilt of his ancestor, and incur all its original responsibilities." Later in the story when Judge Pyncheon meets Phoebe, and she recoils from his attempt to kiss her, his real temper is disclosed and Hawthorne asks: ". . . was it hereditary in him, and transmitted down, as a precious heirloom . . . ? . . . It implied that the weaknesses and defects, the bad passions, the mean tendencies, and the moral diseases which lead to crime are handed down from one generation to another, by a far surer process of transmission than human law has been able to establish in respect to the riches and honors which it seeks to entail upon posterity."

This quotation throws light upon another concern of Hawthorne's in the first part of the book: ". . . would it not be a far truer mode of expression to say of the Pyncheon family, that they inherited a great misfortune, than the reverse?"[121] The statement is ambiguous because the "misfortune" is not merely the original guilt of Colonel Pyncheon and the subsequent curse of Maule which have descended from these two ancestors, nor the hereditary position, and the gold, but the elemental basic condition of the human heart, in this novel represented as inherited traits of character. Out of the history of the Pyncheons and the Maules develops the central idea about the evil and guilt and curse which the Pyncheons have gone on heaping upon themselves.

The "misfortune" consists also in the decline of the aristocratic class and the rise of a plebeian one, which "is one of the truest points of melancholy interest that occur in ordinary life." Hawthorne makes it clear that what we witness in Hepzibah is the ultimate decline of aristocracy in New England. Throughout the book the Pyncheons, the aristocratic family line, are really about to disappear. Hawthorne accepts these changes as part of the movement of history. "The tragedy is enacted with as continual a repetition as that of a popular drama on a holiday."[122]

However, it is not only a question of overturning an old social order, and letting the plebeian one take over in order to set the misfortune right. The ambiguity in the reference to the "great misfortune" left it to the reader to form his judgment. Now Hawthorne confronts him with his sense of Hepzibah's fate. He rationalizes in such a way as to make his answer indirectly obvious: Hepzibah, once in the cent-shop and in the new democratic economy and intercourse, confronts the reader with the particular, individual and moral implications of the change, and draws the reader into the answer by way of rhetorical rationalizations. While Judge Pyncheon represents and reenacts the original crime, under the cover of democratic expediency, Hepzibah stands for the obsessive withdrawal into the faded past peopled with dead characters like Jaffrey Pyncheon or the recessive aesthetic deformity of her brother Clifford. She gains a pathetic stature in all her suffering and insight into the moral and religious implications.[123] She sees that their utter degradation implies doom and spiritual defeat as well.

To Hepzibah and Clifford the world is dead in the widest sense. The doom is ever-present in the portrait and gaze of Colonel Pyncheon and cannot be removed. The past has contaminated this world, the present has killed it, or attempts to, through a social development fatally inimical to it. There is, however, a deeper intuition in Clifford of a broken chain of humanity which ought to be restored; his and Hepzibah's flight from the house, leaving the whole past and the dead

Judge behind, are attempts to join humanity and escape from the guilt and "the responsibilities." But the modern world is hostile and also alien to the aristocratic downfall. The manifestation of guilt and defeat is without significance to it, only the rise and fall of "temporal welfare."[124]

However, *The House of the Seven Gables* is not to be Hepzibah's and Clifford's tragedy exclusively. It is Hawthorne's general intention that all men share in "the wrong-doing of one generation" in history,[125] so that somehow, all men, both Maules and Pyncheons, must be involved in this tragedy and must finally get an equal share of the reconciliation and triumph which will grow out of it. Thus thematically and according to its reiterated intention the book centers on Phoebe, and Holgrave who is a Maule. They must share guilt and reconciliation, but also attain a sense of triumph. The forced happy ending does not bring this about, but the fact that it is intended to, is the missed possibility of the book! Hawthorne attempts a reconciliation of the values of the past and the present, but the ending is too much about "the temporal welfare" of the characters, less about the moral implications and the significance of history.

For the history of the Pyncheons does not come to an end. It starts again at the end of the book. Though Maule's curse is seemingly hovering over the head of the Pyncheons for the last time, a new history starts, as in "Alice Doane's Appeal" and "My Kinsman, Major Molineux," when the guilt and evil is faced, accepted and understood for what it is, and when the isolation is broken and brotherhood reestablished. Therefore Phoebe and Holgrave are the central characters in the book, as we approach its end. They become so not only because they represent youth and the future, but because they experience an increasing insight into the connection with the past. Phoebe has "'grown a great deal older'." In the end Holgrave calls himself a "conservative." Actually he has always been aware of the inherited curse in the Pyncheon family, which will dispossess and destroy them.[126] Thus the union between Phoebe and Holgrave seems to bring about the perfect recognition of what the past is like and a new hope through its acceptance and the responsibilities imposed by it.

The new insight into life which history has given them is well brought out in Phoebe's remark after having listened to Holgrave's story about Alice Pyncheon: "'I have been happier than I am now; at least, much gayer.'"[127] Phoebe's and Holgrave's new hope for the

10

future should be based upon their recognition of the weight of *their* past and their initiation and their entrance into the variegated life of the present. Their union should express both Hawthorne's sense of the heavy significance of history and the hope for human fellowship in spite of, or rather just because of this significance. It is the *return* to historical reality, which should grow out of a comprehensive conception of the historical theme.

The rationale, as I have pointed out, is clear in *The House of the Seven Gables*. The guilt of history is an "uncontrollable mischief" also in the present and remains so. Hawthorne repeats it to illustrate Clifford's situation towards the end of the book in a passage strongly reminiscent of a central idea in *The Scarlet Letter*: "It is a truth . . . that no great mistake, whether acted or endured, in our mortal sphere, is ever really set right." However, Holgrave and Phoebe are hastily brought together in a sorrowless union and receive all the gold of the doomed Pyncheons, which had created such misery and crime in the past. ". . . Hawthorne overlooked the fact that he was sowing all over again the same seeds of evil."[128] If Hawthorne's provision of an artificial happy ending is to have any meaning for our investigation, it can only be an ironical and symbolical one. What seems at first sight a bliss of fate, may at closer scrutiny turn out to be only partially so, or the symbol for the continuance of the mischief, its effect dependent on the degree of historical insight and responsibility felt by the two lovers.

The bequest of wealth becomes then a symbol for the enduring curse in history; or rather, the lust for it represents the ever-lasting and fatal "infirmity" of the human heart. The lust for it is clearly manifested in the chorus, the town characters, which under the new democratic system have a greater chance to realize their lust for wealth. The organ-grinder's monkey stretches out its hand covetously and Hawthorne comments: "Doubtless, more than one New-Englander . . . passed by, and threw a look at the monkey, and went on, without imagining how nearly his own moral condition was here exemplified." In the same way the puppets of the show-man are base images of modern covetousness "by their haste to toil, to enjoy, to accumulate gold, and to become wise." In accordance with this line of argument Holgrave's and Phoebe's newly acquired property *is* their future and therefore the test of whether they have gained insight into themselves by viewing themselves in the light of history. And therefore the future lies open as Hawthorne suggests towards the end: "Maule's well, all this time, though left in solitude, was throwing up a succession of kaleidoscopic pictures, in which a *gifted eye* might have seen foreshadowed the coming fortunes of Hepzibah and Clifford, and the descendant of the legendary wizard, and the village maiden, over whom he had thrown Love's web of sorcery. The Pyncheon Elm, moreover, . . . whispered unintelligible prophecies."[129]

Here the tone is not jubilant, not merely because of the vague "prophecies," but mostly because of the word "sorcery," which is a craft assisted by evil spirits, or black magic as such. And that love involves its victims in the fallen world is no strange idea in Hawthorne. If the ending is viewed in this way, and we submit that it is in tune with Hawthorne's repeated intention, then the uncomfortable discrepancy lies between this very significance and the characters' pure rejoicing and feeling of happiness. They are close to losing our total sympathy. When Holgrave asserts ambiguously that he wants a house of stone, that is, of "permanence," [130] this can be read as an indication of his wish to establish permanent wealth as well. Also the Judge had wanted a house of stone. If Hawthorne wants to contrast Phoebe's and Holgrave's blurred insight into history with a true sense of responsibility for history, he destroys the hero and heroine completely for the reader and thereby as carriers of significant truths.

Since I am concerned with Hawthorne's imputation of guilt and reconciliation through history, the failure to portray Phoebe and Holgrave convincingly does not destroy my argument. It only appears that in this romance there is a disquieting gap between intention and achievement. The two lovers are not related to their society. Thus they do not discover the burden of guilt in which they take part; they have no real need and sense of community and finally, no sense of the past. Phoebe and Holgrave do not identify with their world; original and repeated guilt, imputed to all men, is not theirs.

The weak ending is even more evident because Hawthorne involves the reader by alluding to the inheritance from the past in the chapter concerning Alice Pyncheon, and through ironical rationalizations. After the unpleasant ending of the puppet-show, which represents the present confusion and moral condition, Hawthorne says: "But, rather than swallow this last too acrid ingredient, we reject the whole moral of the show."[131]

History as seen here is a continuum, joining character, reader, and also author. As the historical theme reveals a quality of life that exists at any time in that continuum, it also throws light on the mutual involvement and responsibility of the reader, the character, and the author in that historical continuum. Hawthorne achieves this effect by portraying a historical episode which has an enduring significance and by connecting the character with that episode, and making him recognize his relationship to it. Thus the theme can be either universalized or made contemporary. The historical element gives distance and objectivity to what is contemporary, and the contemporary element gives current significance to the historical situation. Hawthorne makes the reader aware both of his relationship to the historical event and to its present equivalent. Finally he creates a direct relationship between the reader and the protagonists in order to bring about an awareness of the reader's responsible involvement in their destiny. When Hepzibah sees the resemblance between the Colonel and the Judge and fears a new curse, Hawthorne comments ironically that she "did . . . bewilder herself with . . . fantasies of the old time," but she is actually close to the author's vision. She *needs* a walk "along the noonday street to keep her sane"; she needs to enter the community, but the book exists to tell us that she cannot make it without the "moral and religious" implications.[132] Hawthorne may wonder if the reader will see those.

He is at least prepared for the conclusion that the struggle between history and the present is not quite one-sided. Holgrave becomes a conservative; evil remains, but so does Phoebe's charity. And while the pride and covetous lust of the Pyncheons are denounced, the reader is left thinking that mortal life will always contain the enduring germs of evil and guilt. History gives this verdict.

The ending of *The House of the Seven Gables* blurs the historical theme, and leaves it to a great extent unresolved and unrealized. It is not realized later either; in fact it passed away. Hawthorne "could no longer be vitally interested in old moral themes in a new Civil War and . . . he had grown too old really to care about the impulses which once moved his creatures of imagination."[133] He ceased to be concerned with the complex origin of guilt and how it involves all men through history in a union of fellowship.

As Edward Davidson has shown, Hawthorne's failure is seen in the unfinished romances. They all deal with Americans who on going to England find that what they have inherited is only the evil consequences of decaying estates and persecution. After this recognition the young American turns away from his old home and the past, confident that the past has nothing in store for him. He confronts the world as a new man to whom the past means nothing morally speaking; thus the theme of history's moral significance is non-existent.

The theme of earthly immortality made possible by the elixir of life in *Septimus Felton* reflects the inner contradiction of Hawthorne's approach. Septimus Felton wants to live through all the phases of history in order to experience history as present and learn from it, so that he can become a benefactor of his fellow-beings. But then he cannot escape the earthiness of the Wandering Jew who is never released from his mortal frame, while that in him which demands release is not satisfied. Finally Septimus fails, unconvincingly, because the suppositions on which he acts are antithetical and inconsistent. And history is no longer a medium for discovering or imputing eternal verities in man's existence.[134]

Hawthorne seems unable to conceive of America any more: "No really integrated principles can be made out of his varying reflections on his social and economic milieu."[135] And when he turns to Europe, the historical theme is also non-existent. He cannot describe significantly an American's search for roots in England, which in the end seems to have no other purpose than to see a far-away past and for the final time to find it irrelevant. The seekers gain no new insight or recognition of their involvement in the chain of humanity, except that the past is no clue to the understanding of self-hood. They do not see themselves as the past has made them, nor their responsibility for the spiritual implications of history. Redclyffe in *Dr. Grimshawe's Secret* appreciates that he is not affected by the past in any way. To him it is fortunate that one has no responsibility for the past.[136] So the loss of social and cultural continuity between England and America is less important; more damaging to Hawthorne is his failure to establish thematic continuity: " 'Let the past alone: do not seek to renew it; . . . be assured that the right way can never be that which leads you back to the identical shapes that you long ago left behind'."[137] Therefore romances are no longer a possible literary form for a writer who depends upon a significant past.

*The English Notebooks* and the unfinished romances reveal Hawthorne's "confidence in the present and future greatness of America." At the same time, as an imaginative author, he felt drawn to England because of its landscape, historical associations and scenes, its literary tradition, and above all its ancestral character of being the old home.[138] In other words, England attracted the imaginative artist and repelled the American patriot; the result was a mental cleavage and one of several reasons for Hawthorne's unhappiness during the last years of his life. In his prime Hawthorne goes against a melancholy and anti- quarian love for the past. But he ends on the same note of chagrin for a lost home, or, by an effort of will, he throws it away as a true patriot.

Marius Bewley in discussing the opposition in Hawthorne between the Old World and the New and that between the past and the present, says that the problem grew increasingly unmanageable; he points to Hawthorne's sense of crime and guilt which isolated him because the general climate of opinion ignored it. For a while the Puritan past remained a proper frame of reference; Hawthorne was ironical about contemporary beliefs and attempted, as we have seen, to create a sense of responsibility toward history and its lesson of enduring evil and guilt. This attitude involved, however, that as an artist he did not "adjust himself . . . to the society that, as an American, he wished to believe in." This artistic isolation was bearable as long as it did not throw doubt upon his patriotism. But when he came to associate Europe with a decayed ruin, and with isolation and guilt, Hawthorne as an American distrusted that association even if it was a prerequisite for a meaningful function as an artist, and attracted his deepest sympa- thies.[139] Hence the mental cleavage, the unproductive wavering be- tween a sense of the past and championship of the present and bright future, and the unresolved and uncomfortable portrayal of Kenyon and Hilda in *The Marble Faun*.

Within a Puritan frame of reference Dimmesdale, Hester, the listeners in "Alice Doane's Appeal," and Edith and Edgar in "The May-pole of Merry Mount" will all make a meaningful return to society; for them the facts of existence and the meaning of history are one. The "modern" characters, Holgrave, Coverdale in *The Blithedale Romance*, and Hilda in *The Marble Faun*, do more or less return to their earlier way of life even if they have gained a sense of the modern dilemma. It seems that when Hawthorne finds images or pieces of them in Colonial history, he can treat the problem of his own day intelligibly and directly, without being hampered by patriotic lean- ings. When he turns to Europe, however, the opposition is intractable. When the contemporary scene is depicted, the cultural dichotomy between Europe and America enters into his work at the expense of his sense of the enduring values in human life. Just as Hawthorne makes separate choices in the two cultures without stepping into either, Kenyon and Hilda define the moral in *The Marble Faun* without relating it to themselves.

I have frequently referred to *The Blithedale Romance* and *The Marble Faun*. Neither contains primarily the historical theme: they deal with the discovery of the self in the present, and with the way in which the characters come to discover their entanglement in evil and guilt. But Miriam and Donatello come also to see their involvement in a mythological, theological, and historical perspective through the metaphor of Rome which is "of all time, and of all the world,"[140] and brings to them the experience of evil, and the need for confession and repentance.

*The Blithedale Romance*, which has been called an "analysis of the meaning of history,"[141] is Hawthorne's attempt to project a contemporary milieu into an Arcadian setting in order to see how and where man went astray. Therefore his characters break with historical reality and time, and live in a "vast, undefined space."[142] The experiment makes them violate the values of moral, sex, and tradition, and reject a sense of history and a sense of continuity or of time. It also distorts their natural need and capability for common fellowship.

In the following final part *The Marble Faun* will be used to illustrate the timeless and eternal aspect of the historical theme. Since I am now more concerned with the significant values as such and not with the deliberate attempt to create a sense of responsibility and identification with history, *The Marble Faun* serves well for this purpose. For the intense concern with historical time is connected also with the idea of eternal verities or the sense of an eternal essence in the realm of mortals. This was especially relevant in Hawthorne's own age which seemed to have lost the dimension of eternity.

The setting in *The Marble Faun* points to the main theme. Donatello is plunged into all time in Rome, is confronted with it and "the prototype of evil"[143] and, eventually, with the means of return to a meaningful world of history. For Rome is beyond and outside physical time too. The experience of *all* history condensed and its moral significance concentrated into one single symbol, cannot be related to any objective structure of history. "It is a vague sense of ponderous remembrances; a perception of such weight and density in a by-gone life, of which this spot was the centre, that the present moment is pressed down or crowded out, and our individual affairs and interests are but half as real here as elsewhere. Viewed through this medium, our narrative . . . may seem not widely different from the texture of all our lives."

Rome escapes any ordinary formula of explanation, and can only be sensed by the historical imagination. At times Hawthorne tries to preserve the sense of confused time and even of place, so that the reader will not return to the present. The timeless atmosphere is first effective in bringing out a plausible significance of the mythological faun, and in making such old symbols as the serpent, the dove, and the child clasping the dove as relevant in the "now" as they have been for the last two thousand years.[144]

The recognition of the moral significance of Rome's "historic" "dust" is timeless in two ways: it may take place at any time and penetrate into the human consciousness as it does in Miriam's case when she sees her likeness to Beatrice in Guido's picture. Miriam's recognition suggests the unavoidable involvement in a criminal past and equally the basic moral destiny which history imparts metaphorically. Secondly, recognized and accepted for what it is, Rome's history as a metaphor for the recognition of evil belongs to the same dimension of timelessness. Guido's picture of Beatrice tells Miriam that there is a timeless, enduring element in history, and it is her very sense of her own likeness to Beatrice which constitutes that enduring element of evil and guilt, which as a historical creature in "the massiveness" of Rome's history she cannot escape.[145] However, this sense of Rome's timeless essence is still dependent upon the character's memory and degree of insight which, as Miriam and Donatello find out on their return to Rome, must work in historical reality. And Hawthorne does not think that the sense of involvement in evil and guilt within the dimension of history will go beyond mortality. He thinks rather of death as a release from the sense of timeless sorrows and care in history.

Similarly the imputation of guilt and redemption to the characters through their sense of history points to an aspect of timelessness in the self. By retelling the Fall of Man in the figure of Donatello, or by chronicling the decline and fall of the Pyncheons, Hawthorne shows how man can come to know himself by merging his history, present, and future. The new insight is, however, not a certainty and a universal human experience, but only a human possibility as long as man senses history and becomes responsible for it. In a way this is the kind of historical "redemption" which releases Donatello and Miriam, and Holgrave and Phoebe from the chronological order of time, despite the earthly roots. They possess enduring moral qualities which make them belong also outside the scope of time, of the limited "now," or past.

Hawthorne's conscious attempt to search out and recapture the past, and let modern daylight in on marks and associations which seem to be lost, leads to his insight into the timeless and enduring elements found in history. Hawthorne's almost empirical approach conditions the recognition of timeless morals. Among the many things Hawthorne describes and criticizes in the fanatical Quakers, Dimmesdale, Clifford, "The Man of Adamant," Wakefield, Donatello, Miriam, and his contemporaries is not only that they want to be liberated from the chronological order of historical time, but that they also try to escape the lasting element in history which characterizes life and gives man responsibility and the strength of brotherhood. For the escape is ultimately a sign of spiritual pride and an unwillingness to recognize sin, one's own or others', which involves man in history. Donatello is only slightly conscious of antiquity or time before he has sinned. When he *is* conscious, he is first overwhelmed by the gloom and guilt of history. Then his and Miriam's murder secures them a kind of brotherhood. It "melts into the great mass of human crime, and makes us, — who dreamed only of our own little separate sin, — makes us guilty of the whole. And thus Miriam and her lover were not an insulated pair, but members of an innumerable confraternity of guilty ones, all shuddering at each other."[146] Their crime is in this sense also timeless.

The righteousness, the light, which so often in Hawthorne's fiction is love, kindles a new spirit in Donatello after their meeting in Perugia. Hawthorne writes of his own love that it moved him from shadow and unreality into life and eternity. It takes both guilt and love to make up the new historical reality, the new Eden which can only be properly viewed "through the transparency of that gloom which has been brooding over those haunts of innocence ever since the fall. Adam saw it in a brighter sunshine, but never knew the shade of pensive beauty which Eden won from his expulsion." Donatello's transformation is presented historically, with two cut-backs into the Golden Age "before mankind was burdened with sin and sorrow, and before pleasure had been darkened with those shadows that bring it into high relief, and make it happiness." His struggle is *typical* and representative of the struggle of the human race and has therefore a timeless quality. Kenyon sees Donatello as natural man upset by modern history and civilization. Thus Donatello's experience is a universal experience, the Fall is repeated. Its pattern is timelessly valid and only assumes new forms to exemplify it in the present. Therefore the past is the

present. And when Miriam sees Beatrice she knows that the present
is the past.[147]

The eternal historical cycle has only made a turn. Donatello
" 'has travelled in a circle, as all things heavenly and earthly do, and
now comes back to his original self, with an inestimable treasure
of improvement won from an experience of pain'."[148] History is, in
other words, a realm of endless possibilities of renewal and rebirth.
The chain of evil is not an absolute historical fate.

Hawthorne is not consistently philosophical on the direction of
human history. But he points to the fact that the irrevocable movement
of historical time is toward death. On the social and political level,
as in "The Legends of the Province House," "My Kinsman, Major
Molineux," and *The House of the Seven Gables* we witness the ultimate
decay and defeat of one social class or political movement and the
rise of another. This movement is also immediately felt in one's individual life. In Hawthorne's works there is a constant awareness of the
transitoriness of human existence. And Hawthorne's frame of reference
is often the progression from life to death in history, as we see it in the
history of the Pyncheons, in Donatello's loss of innocence, and in the
approaching downfall of Blithedale. Everywhere in history transience
is most strongly experienced.

*The Blithedale Romance* can in a general way throw light upon the
meaning of history, especially with regard to its direction and final
end. The believers in a New Eden planted away from the modern
world think of the mere present as the dimension in which a creative,
productive element is at work and can be revealed. The rebirth or new
achievement takes place in time, and time and space engender *all*
growth and *all* things. The people at Blithedale will show "mankind the
example of a life governed by other than the false and cruel principles
on which human society has all along been based." There are no
limitations imposed upon man in time: ". . . we had divorced ourselves from pride." Viewed in this way history is not merely about the
futility of effort and about works and things crumbling into dust.
Man's happiness on earth is "an object to be hopefully striven for,
and probably attained." But as the worldly-wise and sceptical Coverdale points out, the reformers do not distinguish between material
achievement and moral growth, when they believe that pride as
well as the fetters of conventional society can be thrown away.
As Hawthorne had already pointed out in "Earth's Holocaust"
and now in *The Blithedale Romance*, progress in human knowledge and

in the improvement of goods, as evidenced by history, is one thing, moral improvement and perfection is quite another. Still the direction of history is the condition under which the search for moral identity can be realized. The reformists at Blithedale live in space and fail completely. To them "everything in nature and human existence was fluid . . . it was a day of crisis, and . . . we ourselves were in the critical vortex. Our great globe floated in the atmosphere of infinite space like an unsubstantial bubble." Consequently they are frustrated when they try to achieve "rebirth without roots."[149] For moral birth and rebirth takes place within history's cycles of life and death, and this is another positive aspect of historical time. History testifies to and contains the possibility of redemption.

Yet Hawthorne is ambiguous about a complete acceptance of and reliance upon time in this life. Rome confirms the vanity of striving and of schemes. The attainment of moral recognition is not a matter of mere rejoicing, but rather a matter of gloom. Donatello goes to prison, Miriam to a nunnery, both separated for ever. The bleak consequences of the transience and gloom of history on the present in spite of accompanying moral insight, is contrasted with the hope of salvation not through a complete resolution and a perfect union of the lovers in this life, but through entrance into a heaven of eternity beyond time.[150]

Hawthorne's ambiguity towards the positive and negative aspects of history is also connected with his critique of the significance attached to time on account of the social changes in his own century. Time came, through the transition from a domestic to a capitalistic economy, to be viewed positively. Time became money, and man was evaluated according to his striving and achievement in this world. Man was less and less measured according to his inner ethic. And it is characteristic that the reformists at Blithedale try to forget history, its negative implications, and its direction towards death, through ceaseless striving and activity: ". . . it was dizzy work." They live in space without history and future, in a "spick-and-span novelty."[151] Hawthorne is equally pessimistic about the fate of a possible great work which the ceaseless striving can produce. History is evidence of objects' transitoriness.

If Hawthorne comes close to a complete philosophical theory of history, it is the theoretical projection into history of the pattern or cycles of birth, growth, decline, and death. The repeated changing cycles of birth and death can be said to be the permanent and timeless law of history; to human experience this is another way of seeing a timeless dimension beyond the chronological order of time. The cyclical view enables Hawthorne to resolve objectively his ambiguity about the positive and negative aspects of history's march. Thus he can be concerned with the temporal manifestations of this cyclical return, and point to the presence of good and evil in it. Hawthorne recognizes that history is always a source of both good and evil, though he is by no means morally neutral as between good and evil.[152] God is above history, and Man has his destiny beyond present time and its fashions. History *per se* does not solve the enigma of history; still, there are glimpses of meaning in it, which transcend the march of the ages, bear the whole project of history, and suggest how life can be renewed collectively as well as individually. By seeing oneself in a historical pattern containing the prelapsarian state of innocence as well as the Fall and the tragedy of struggle, death, and subsequent hope of reconciliation, one can also accept the same limitations upon the human condition in the present. As Zenobia finally sees: " 'There are no new truths, much as we have prided ourselves on finding some.' "[153]

## NOTES

[1] Two unpublished dissertations I have not had access to, namely Edward Dawson, "Hawthorne's Knowledge and Use of New England History: A Study of Sources" (Vanderbilt University, 1938), and Delmer Rodobaugh, "Hawthorne's Use of the English and Italian Past" (Minnesota, 1951).

[2] *Journal of English Literary History*, XXI (December 1954), 328–349. Since this paper was accepted for publication, Roy Harvey Pearce, "Romance and the Study of History" has appeared in *Hawthorne Centenary Essays* (Columbus, Ohio, 1964), pp. 221–244. Pearce's study centers on Hawthorne's symbolism from the point of view of "existential historicism" (p. 230), and does not make a detailed examination of the historical

theme as it appears in Hawthorne's works. So there should be room for both articles.

[3] Julian Hawthorne, quoted by Charles Ryskamp, "The New England Sources of *The Scarlet Letter*," *American Literature*, XXXI (November 1959), 272.

[4] III, 15. All citations to Hawthorne's writings refer to *The Works of Nathaniel Hawthorne*, ed. George P. Lathrop (Boston, 1882–83), 13 vols.

[5] I, 293. Hawthorne makes this reservation quite frequently. See "Howe's Masquerade," I, 276; "Roger Malvin's Burial," II, 381; "The Custom House," V, 52; preface to *The House of the Seven Gables*, III, 13.

[6] Richard Harter Fogle, *Hawthorne's Fiction; The Light and the Dark* (Norman, Okla., 1952), p. 115.

7 "The Custom House," V, 52. See also the introductory paragraph to "The May-pole of Merry Mount," I, 70.

8 III, 13. On the characteristics of the romance, see Brander Matthews, "Romance against Romanticism," *The Historical Novel and Other Essays* (New York, 1901), pp. 31–48. According to Matthews romance "is always in accord with the essential truth of life" (p. 38). It deals with absolutely all time. ". . . it takes no account . . . of the accidental accompaniments of human existence" (pp. 40–41).

9 Cf. also *The American Note-Books*, IX, 224: "Let us content ourselves to be earthly creatures, and hold communion of spirit in such modes as are ordained to us."

10 "The Old Manse," II, 30.

11 *The House of the Seven Gables*, III, 15.

12 Cf. T. S. Eliot, "The Hawthorne Aspect," *The Shock of Recognition*, ed. Edmund Wilson (New York, 1943), p. 861: "His erudition in the small field of American colonial history was extensive, and he made most fortunate use of it."

13 Norman Holmes Pearson, ed. *The Complete Novels and Selected Tales of Nathaniel Hawthorne* (New York, 1937), pp. ix-x.

14 Hawthorne's sister, Elizabeth, said that he "was not very fond of history in general." Quoted by Ryskamp, 272.

15 "Old Ticonderoga: A Picture of the Past," III, 592.

16 Quoted by Ryskamp, 272.

17 IV, 430.

18 V, 26 and 24.

19 V, 26 and 43. See also "The Hall of Fantasy," II, 207; "Edward Randolph's Portrait," I, 297–298.

20 "Howe's Masquerade," I, 290.

21 "The Old Manse," II, 30–31.

22 See Benjamin T. Spencer, *The Quest for Nationality* (Syracuse University Press, 1957), p. 310.

23 In his youth, Hawthorne was, like Irving, Emerson, and Longfellow, also much interested in creating a national literature for its *own* sake, based upon native material. See Hyatt H. Waggoner, *Hawthorne: A Critical Study* (Cambridge, Mass., 1955), p. 36.

24 I, 26. See also *The House of the Seven Gables*, III, 31 and 150.

25 III, 31.

26 Hawthorne refers to this himself in the preface to *The Marble Faun*, VI, 15.

27 I, 127 and 142. See Richard Chase, *The American Novel and Its Tradition* (New York, 1957), p. 76.

28 Perry Miller & Thomas H. Johnson, ed. *The Puritans* (New York, 1938), p. 85.

29 III, 215; II, 228.

30 III, 148 ff.

31 Quoted by R. W. B. Lewis, *The American Adam: Innocence, Tragedy, and Tradition in the Nineteenth Century* (Chicago, 1955), p. 160.

32 *Septimus Felton*, XI, 407–409. The reformers in *The Blithedale Romance* live in a "vast, undefined space" (V. 360), seemingly outside history; yet their purpose is to improve life on *earth* (341–342).

33 Roy A. Male, *Hawthorne's Tragic Vision* (Austin, Tex., 1957), p. 76.

34 Lewis, p. 161 and 21.

35 Austin Warren, ed. *Representative Selections of Hawthorne* (New York, 1934), p. xlv.

36 "A Virtuoso's Collection," II, 551–552.

37 See Male, pp. 119–120.

38 Quoted by Joseph Schwartz, "Nathaniel Hawthorne, 1804–1864, God and Man in New England," *American Classics Reconsidered*, ed. Harold

C. Gardiner (New York, 1958), p. 139.

[39] "P's Correspondence," II, 416.

[40] Miller & Johnson, p. 83.

[41] See the introductory paragraph to "The May-pole of Merry Mount," I, 70; "Edward Randolph's Portrait," I, 293.

[42] III, 219, 442, 303–316.

[43] II, 203; I, 333 and 336.

[44] Cf. "The Hall of Fantasy," II, 204–205; *The House of the Seven Gables,* III, 216 and 219. When something will not serve a needful purpose, it will decay and wither away of itself.

[45] Warren, p. xxvii.

[46] Male, pp. 134–135.

[47] Lewis, p. 117.

[48] II, 295. See also *The House of the Seven Gables,* III, 196–197; *The Blithedale Romance,* V, 341–342.

[49] Quoted by Male, p. 128.

[50] III, 268–284 and 333. Cf. Male, pp. 134–135.

[51] XII, 280–281.

[52] XII, 280.

[53] V, 60.

[54] "The Custom House," V, 24, 27, 25.

[55] I, 293.

[56] III, 447, and Kenneth B. Murdock, *Literature and Theology in Colonial New England* (Cambridge, Mass., 1949), p. 77.

[57] Miller & Johnson, p. 84.

[58] III, 13.

[59] III, 13.

[60] *The American Note-Books,* IX, 226.

[61] "Edward Randolph's Portrait," I, 293.

[62] Fogle, p. 9.

[63] See Male, p. 4. He sees Hawthorne as one who opposed various efforts to achieve "rebirth without roots and Christianity without the crucifixion."

[64] V, 132.

[65] II, 107.

[66] Murdock, p. 87.

[67] I, 70.

[68] See *The Scarlet Letter,* V, 227–255, and *The Blithedale Romance,* V, 385–397.

[69] V, 55. Charles Feidelson Jr., *Symbolism and American Literature* (Chicago, 1953), p. 9 and 12.

[70] *The Marble Faun,* VI, 134. See also Lewis, pp. 114 ff.

[71] "The May-pole of Merry Mount," I, 72; V, 256–269.

[72] I,75; VI, 135.

[73] "The Haunted Mind," I, 345; "Egotism; or, The Bosom Serpent," II, 321.

[74] See preface to *The House of the Seven Gables,* III, 13; V, 164.

[75] See Male, pp. 158–159.

[76] III, 473. Again it is illustrative to see the similarity with Puritan ideas about the writing of history. Perry Miller says about the characteristics of Puritan historiography that it is concrete, episodic, and anecdotal. ". . . the Puritan has no hesitancy in sifting his material, placing emphases, omitting facts, generalizing upon any single piece of evidence, interpreting every action by one explicit standard." Miller & Johnson, p. 84.

[77] III, 224–251 and V, 527–539.

[78] Cf. *The American Note-Books,* IX, 27: "To have one event operate in several places, — as, for example, if a man's head were to be cut off in one town, men's heads to drop off in several towns."

[79] "Time's Portraiture," XII, 129.

[80] III, 18.

[81] VI, 124; II, 19; V, 18. According to *The American Note-Books,* IX, 27, even the subjective experience of irreversibility, another temporal time-factor, is highly ambivalent.

[82] XII, 280. In "Alice Doane's Appeal," *The House of the Seven Gables,* and *The Scarlet Letter* interpretations

of crucial events reflect the position of the observer and fuse the sense of the fact and the sense of a more or less *enduring* moral meaning.

83 "The Custom House," V, 57.
84 *The Blithedale Romance*, V, 394.
85 Preface to *The Marble Faun*, VI, 15.
86 III, 475 and V, 322.
87 Henry James, quoted by Male, p. 141.
88 V, 60 and 50.
89 V, 64–66, 50, 53, 25.
90 V, 65 and 66.
91 XII, 295, 280, 289, 292. Waggoner, p. 45.
92 XII, 295 and 294 (italics added). Waggoner, p. 45.
93 Pearce, "Hawthorne and the Sense of the Past or, The Immortality of Major Molineux," 339.
94 See Randall Stewart, *Nathaniel Hawthorne* (New Haven, 1948), pp. 29–30. I, 288; I, 122; III, 640; II, 381.
95 III, 598.
96 III, 598 and 603.
97 Pearce, op. cit., 335–336. See Seymour L. Gross, "Hawthorne's Revision of 'The Gentle Boy'," *American Literature*, XXVI (May 1954), 208.
98 See I, 85–87.
99 II, 381.
100 II, 390–391.
101 IX, 273.
102 I, 126.
103 *The American Note-Books*, IX, 43.
104 I, 103.
105 II, 381. See "The Custom House," V, 55.
106 I, 115.
107 "My Kinsman, Major Molineux," quoted by Pearce, op. cit., 329. And Pearce, 329.
108 I, 86.
109 Pearce, op. cit., 330. Cf. "Young Goodman Brown," II, 99, where laughter also represents evil.
110 III, 636.
111 I, 126.

112 Harry Levin, *The Power of Blackness* (New York, 1958), p. 78. F. O. Matthiessen, *American Renaissance* (New York, 1941), p. 343.
113 Quotations from V, 164, 310, 307, 80, 113, 242.
114 V, 173.
115 Waggoner, p. 148. And quotations from V, 112, 243, 277.
116 V, 294 ff. Note that Dimmesdale is aware of misinterpretations of his sermons. See 174–175.
117 Matthiessen, p. 193. Cf. V, 293.
118 V, 295 and 306. See John C. Gerber, "Introduction," *The Scarlet Letter*, (New York, 1950), p. xxxi.
119 III, 14 and 181.
120 III, 14 and 18.
121 III, 34, 146–147, 34.
122 III, 55 f.
123 III, 75.
124 III, 75, 138, 199–201, 300 ff., 75.
125 III, 14.
126 III, 256 and 219–223.
127 III, 255–256.
128 III, 14 and 371. And Matthiessen, p. 332.
129 III, 198, 197, 377–378 (italics added).
130 See Male, p. 8: "As 'love stories,' Hawthorne's romances are centered upon the Original Sin. For it seems clear that he interpreted the Original Sin as the mutual love of man and woman." And III, 372.
131 III, 197.
132 III, 80 and 75.
133 Edward H. Davidson, *Hawthorne's Last Phase* (New Haven, 1949), p. 157. See also Davidson, "The Unfinished Romances," *Hawthorne Centenary Essays*, pp. 141–163.
134 *Septimus Felton*, XI, 407–409. Randall Stewart, ed. *The American Notebooks* (New Haven, 1932), p. lxxxvi. And see "A Virtuoso's Collection," II, 558.
135 Matthiessen, p. 361.
136 XIII, 230.

137 *The Ancestral Footstep*, XI, 488–489.
138 Randall Stewart, ed. *The English Notebooks*, (New York, 1941), p. xxxiii ff.
139 *The Complex Fate*, (London, 1952), p. 57 f.
140 VI, 135.
141 Waggoner, p. 174.
142 V, 360.
143 Male, p. 158.
144 VI, 20 and 124. Cf. Henry Adams, "Rome," *The Education of Henry Adams* (Boston, 1918), esp. pp. 90–95. And Waggoner, pp. 207–213.
145 VI, 124, 83–84, 21.
146 VI, 208.
147 VI, 318–319, 104, 263. See Stewart, ed. *The American Notebooks*, p. lxx.
148 VI, 491.
149 V, 342, 341, 480. Male, p. 142.
150 See *The Scarlet Letter*, V. 304. Note also Miriam's and Donatello's separation, and the thwarted love in *The Blithedale Romance*. Cf. "The Wedding Knell," I, 51.
151 V, 479 and 468.
152 Cf. Waggoner, p. 260, and Schwartz in *American Classics Reconsidered*, pp. 135–136.
153 V, 573.

# HARTVIG NISSEN
# AND AMERICAN EDUCATIONAL REFORM

## By Einar Boyesen

The close connection, political and otherwise, with the English-speaking nations that is typical of modern Norway, is a relatively late development. And nowhere does this hold more true than in the field of education.

To the Norse vikings and colonists of the early Middle Ages, who extended their forays even to the Western Hemisphere, the North Sea was an inland lake. There was also a cultural "give and take"; Christianity came to Norway from England together with the first formal education, later quite a few Norwegians went to French universities. But from the fourteenth century onward Norway drifted into the orbit of the Danish realm, which was closely tied to Germany. The change of orientation was symbolized by the forcible introduction into Norway of the Reformation. Even Norwegian schools took their models predominantly from the German educational system with its mixture of authoritarianism, Lutheranism, and Latin.

In the sixteenth and seventeenth centuries growing Norwegian shipping and commerce again turned the eyes of the country westward, a development which also had cultural repercussions. The change was further accentuated by the impact of French and English enlightened and revolutionary thought, which also brought America into the picture as the testing ground of new political ideas. But in cultural life German influences remained predominant. Even after the revolution of 1814, when Norway broke away from Denmark and gave itself an extremely democratic constitution, the efforts to establish a school system in accordance with the new ideals largely sought their inspirations in Denmark and Germany.

It was only toward the middle of the nineteenth century that Norway began paying more attention to the great Anglo-Saxon democracies across the ocean, even in its educational thinking. In part, this reorientation was connected with general changes, noticeable in many fields of Norwegian life. But the strongest influence in the new direction was due to the activity of one man, Hartvig Nissen (1815—74), the leading Norwegian school reformer of the century.

More than any of his contemporaries Hartvig Nissen combined a deep personal allegiance to Norwegian political and cultural traditions with a broad international orientation. Holding several high administrative positions within the school system he was able to make most of his reforming ideas materialize. And by his widespread and tireless efforts as a publicist, expressing his views in books, pamphlets, government reports, and articles in newspapers and journals, he managed to establish his reforms and plant their leading principles firmly in public opinion.[1]

It was in the 1840's that new ideas began to take shape in Hartvig Nissen's mind, a deep conviction that education was all-important to the sound development of democratic society. Like many of his fellow-countrymen he was deeply worried by the revolutions of 1830 and 1848. The violent upheavals of the masses in nations great and small made him realize that it was now mandatory to pay attention to the needs of the common man. He believed that the development of broad popular education adapted to the conditions of his time was the most efficient means of ensuring a peaceful and balanced social growth. But it is typical of the initial orientation both of Nissen and of his contemporaries that their early educational projects show little or no trace of Western influence. They are wholly based on Scandinavian, and to some extent German, sources. And this one-sided orientation prevailed far into the 1840's.

Nissen's isolation from the ideas gaining currency in the United States is brought out by one striking detail. Up to 1850 he was largely occupied with the problems of the secondary school, in which he himself was working at the time. One of his main concerns was the creation of a reasonable standard of higher education for the neglected half of the potential school population, the girls. This idea, of course, was also one of the tenets of contemporary American reformers; in particular they emphasized the natural ability of women as teachers. In 1839 the leading figure in the American school world, Horace Mann, had proudly declared at the dedication of the Lexington Teachers' College for women: "We believe it will be the first normal school, properly so called, in the world, exclusively dedicated to the female sex".[2] During the late 1840's Hartvig Nissen worked in the same direction. In 1849 he presented the program of a progressive school for young girls, an institution which he eventually came to head himself. But he made no reference to his American counterpart and *his* plans, although these parallel efforts would have strongly supported his own cause if he had known about them.

Thus, it was not till after 1850 that American education came to influence Nissen's thinking. The reasons for his new orientation may be several. Beginning in 1825, Norwegian emigration to the United States in the 1840's took on proportions which caused widespread concern. The ensuing discussion gradually touched upon many general aspects, good and bad, of American civilization itself. But Nissen's interest also had a more direct source. The Swedish educationist and politician P. A. Siljeström visited England in 1848, the United States in 1849—50, and England a second time in 1854. One of the results of his studies was a two-volume work, *Resa i Förenta Staterna* (Journey in the United States, Stockholm, 1849—50), apparently the first large-scale survey of the American school system to be published in Europe. Hartvig Nissen was closely following Scandinavian educational discussion at the time. It is extremely probable that he studied Siljeström's work at its appearance, and that this reading drew American education into the circle of his interests.

The most striking personality he was to become acquainted with from the very beginning of his introduction to the American school system was Horace Mann. It is of course possible that Nissen had heard about Mann's work already in the 1840's, even if the interest of the American in female education was not known to him. In any case Nissen almost certainly had read about him in Siljeström's great book, where Mann is an important source of inspiration and is often referred to as the leading light in American educational reform. Mann's dominant position had recently been emphasized by his great activity as Secretary to the Board of Education in the state of Massachusetts 1837—49, a contribution that was characterized by his fresh and far-sighted initiative, his eminent administrative ability, and his rare power of persuasion equally effective with school commissions and legislatures. His annual Reports soon gained renown as a storehouse of pedagogical information, presented with sound practical judgment and model objectivity. The Reports carried Mann's name far beyond the borders of the United States. They became indispensable reference works, a treasury of knowledge and encouragement also to the progressive educational movements in Europe.

It is probable that Nissen was impressed at an early stage by Mann's general views, which were later to influence him so deeply. However, his first reference to American school reform was not directly connected with Mann. It had to do with Nissen's nascent propaganda for a reform of the Norwegian elementary school, which for years was to be one of his main tasks.

After the establishment of Norway's independence in 1814 both the municipalities and the Government had taken steps to develop primary education. In particular, a law of 1827 increased the number of permanent schools and teaching positions, and improved the teachers' salaries. The Government gave special support to these reforms in less wealthy regions. A number of new teachers' colleges insured a better recruitment of staff. But Nissen's ideas went beyond the fulfilment of such basic demands. In a little book from 1851 he outlined his ideas about a complete reorganization of elementary schools in the countryside — Norway at the time being overwhelmingly rural. But even more than administrative reforms he advocated a review of the general aims of the schools, in order to make them an instrument of education for citizenship, an idea that was familiar also to many American school reformers. So far, he wrote, the country had lacked "a teaching which is geared to life as it really is and its real needs, a teaching which gives the mind a *universal* development, which educates all *those* powers in man through which he could and should be able to make his active contribution within the framework of the rich and comprehensive life of our time".[3]

In its further development this program was to play a great part in Norway in the struggle for a better elementary education. But to the practically minded Nissen no less important than the program itself was the possible means of realizing it. In particular he felt that it would be decisive to the success of a possible reform to have placed in key positions within the educational system competent and open-minded specialists, who would be able to guide and control the work. In his plan from 1851 this idea was one of the basic points. As an example Nissen in his book referred to a recent Danish law according to which a trained pedagogue should thereafter be a permanent member of the school commission in the city of Copenhagen. But now he also referred to laws of 1841 and 1843 in the American state of New York, according to which a salaried superintendent of schools was to be appointed in each county, — two, if the number of schools in the district exceeded 150. These superintendents were supposed to visit the schools as frequently as possible, to investigate everything regarding the schools with the local inspectors, to examine and express their opinion about applicants for teaching positions, to report regularly to the highest school authorities of the state, and by all available means "promote a good education, raise the character and ability of the teachers, and serve the interests of the schools".[4]

Nissen's source for this information was a pamphlet by James Henry, *An Address upon Education and Common Schools* (Albany, 1843). Nissen's own plan for a similar arrangement in Norwegian elementary schools was based on Henry's material. The main expense of the new positions Nissen suggested should be covered from the interest on "Oplysningsvæsenets Fond", a public foundation whose capital originated from the sale of land placed at the disposal of the church (compare the American "land grants").[5] Both the suggested system of general inspectors and the way of financing the innovation became salient points in the battle over the new school law of 1860. The established positions (in the Norwegian law called "School Directors", originally six in number, now seventeen) have proved, through more than a century, to be as important to Norwegian education as Nissen expected them to be.

This direct American influence was largely confined to an administrative detail. Much more decisive to Nissen's reorientation was his sojourn in Scotland at public expense, from April to October 1852, in order to study the elementary education of that country. His travel report of almost 500 pages was published by the Norwegian Government.[6]

This long stay in Scotland became an important factor in Nissen's development as an educator. His studies widened his view: to his thorough knowledge of education on the continent he now added a keen understanding of the British school system, studied in one of its most characteristic manifestations. But in our connection it is no less important that his months in Scotland also came to increase his interest and knowledge in the field of American education, in particular as reflected in the ideas of Horace Mann. Even from this point of view Nissen's book is one of the most interesting documents in the history of Norwegian schools.

In his Preface Nissen emphasized the special difficulty involved in describing the Scottish educational system, since there was no predecessor to build on. "To be sure", he continued, "the American Horace Mann, well known as educator and statesman, in a book, *Report of an Educational Tour in Germany, France, Holland and Parts of Great Britain and Ireland* (1843), has reported no little about the schools of Scotland. But he has limited himself to making some remarks about what he saw and heard during a rather short visit of the Scottish school world, even if these remarks are interesting and informative".[7]

This note of reserve was fully justified. Horace Mann's chapter on Scotland was only a minor and not too essential part of an extensive report, in which the great nations on the European continent were bound to predominate. In comparison, Nissen spent much more time in the country. Both before and during his visit he was able to study extensive printed matter, and to discuss it on a journey of several weeks in the company of one of Her Majesty's inspectors.

But this better preparation did not make the Report of his only predecessor less interesting to him; he studied it critically and carefully. And there is reason to believe that he read with equal interest the other parts of Mann's report, where his general ideas on education are expressed most clearly, and where his own American background is often brought out, implicitly or explicitly. In addition we know that Nissen in Scotland met other American school men who visited the country for the same purpose, and may have been able to add to his knowledge.[8]

The Mann and Nissen reports were not only different as regards thoroughness, but also in scope. Mann was largely interested in the general conditions of the Scottish schools. Nissen concentrated his observations on the elementary schools, and was also much concerned with practical and administrative details, which he reported on minutely. Moreover, much had happened since Mann's visit almost ten years before, and Nissen knew these recent developments well.

Sometimes, he was therefore able to correct or supplement Mann's information. In other cases he just expressed his reservations. For our concern these particulars are not too important. And the same holds true of many details where the two educators agree in their observations, — for instance, about the education of Scottish teachers, their methods and their contact with their classes, the work and attitude of the pupils, and the entire school milieu with its buzzing energy and vivacity. Some of the problems under discussion were of permanent concern to Nissen, like the hygienic working conditions in the schools, the importance of modern teachers' colleges, and the need for competent inspection and leadership. But even if Mann is mentioned, his American background is rarely referred to.

Another aspect is the general educational program which gradually emerges from Nissen's discussion of the Scottish schools. For the first time the great reformer here sees his own ideas clearly and completely, both the fundamental principles and the practical means of realizing them.

Basic to Nissen's thinking was the idea that the task of the school is to serve the entire nation. At this early stage he had already presented the first tentative outline of that "unified" school which in Norway was not to materialize completely until the 1930's. A contemporary Norwegian educator had seen society as being sharply divided into four orders, and expressed his hope that the schools could be arranged in accordance with these different needs.[9] Nissen protested against such attitudes. On the contrary, he maintained, education at the elementary stage should be uniform for all social classes. The fellowship that is thus created should not be broken before professional specialization makes a differentiation necessary. Through this unified school the isolation of the broad masses would be countered, and the higher culture of the upper classes would be allowed to percolate all through society.

Equally important to Nissen was the fellowship of shared interests to be created by the unified school. "We can not be confident that society will not misunderstand its own interest, and forget its duty toward the school and itself, until those classes of the nation which contribute most to the maintenance of the elementary school, and through men from their midst have an essential part in the direction and surveillance of it, themselves use it for their own children and thus become directly interested in all that pertains to it".

To Nissen, such ideas were not just educational. They were part of a general democratic philosophy, and he did not mince words about it. "It may be regarded as peculiar to our era, that it becomes more and more concious of the truth that the well-being of the common people and the lower classes generally is a necessary condition for the well-being of the higher classes and of the entire society". To a certain extent all members of society "share the responsibility" for the moral and physical existence of the individuals and the free and successful development of all the social powers. And "among all the means available to society in that direction, the school holds high rank".[10]

This pedagogical philosophy Nissen did not derive from Horace Mann. It was the logical outcome of the growth of his own nation, and the development of his own thought from his early youth onward. But if in his Scottish report the program was expressed with clarity and with awareness of its democratic implications, it may have something to do with the strong impressions he received both from his own observation of Scottish schools and from the parallel attitude which he now came to meet more extensively in the writings of Horace Mann. In their ideas about the political and social background of a democratic school there was complete agreement between the two educators; and Mann's attitude was brought out unmistakeably in his Report. To him, "education and democracy were . . . . correlatives". The free common school, "one and the same for both rich and poor", was "the greatest discovery ever made by man", a privilege that should be as free to the people as "breathing the common air, or enjoying the warmth of the unappropriable sun", the supreme guarantee of national and social unity.[11]

Such American ideals were not fully realized in Scotland, in spite of the relative political democracy of the country. But like Nissen Mann enjoyed observing how the Scottish schools had nevertheless gained the love of the entire population down into the lowest layers of society, and how there was a general willingness to support the school by voluntary contributions, the result of a long and valuable tradition.

In other parts of his report Mann was not afraid to point to countries where the general background was different. Not least did he emphasize the negative influence of German authoritarianism on education. To Mann the wonderfully efficient Prussian schools did not seem to create the broadly educated general population one would expect. The reason was political: life outside of the school walls lacked the inspiration of a free society, and offered the pupils little opportunity of using the knowledge they had acquired. Nissen expressed his explicit agreement with Mann's reasoning on this point.[12]

It must have been a great inspiration to Nissen to find his own deepest conviction thus confirmed by a colleague of Mann's authority. And the result is manifest. Whatever the relationship of their ideas in detail — and it would often be impossible to ascertain, — hardly a single one of the great European school reformers of the period comes as close in his constructive thinking to Horace Mann's essential ideas as does the Norwegian Hartvig Nissen.

Still, these were largely general impressions as far as American education was concerned. But they were soon to gain more substance through Nissen's visit to the International Exhibition in London in 1854.

In its general impact this sojourn could not be compared to the five months spent in Scotland two years earlier. Nissen stayed in London for five weeks only. He did not come for study, but as a government representative, responsible for the Norwegian section and the Norwegian pedagogical information service at the Exhibition. Notwithstanding, the visit came to give Nissen American contacts which he otherwise might have missed.

One of these contacts was actually Scandinavian: the Swedish reformer P. A. Siljeström. Nissen doubtless knew his work before. Now he met him personally at the Exhibition, where Siljeström was Nissen's Swedish counterpart, and the friendship of the two men became strong and personal. It came to pass that for many years they cooperated at home in Scandinavia in educational efforts of which, for both of them, American ideas formed an integral part.

No less important was Nissen's encounter in London with the American pedagogue Henry Barnard (1811—1900). Here Nissen made the personal acquaintance of one of the educational leaders of contemporary USA, a collaborator, friend and great admirer of Horace Mann; the two are often mentioned together. As superintendent and school principal Barnard had been active in educational reform work in Connecticut. Among his books was *School Architecture* (1839), which strongly influenced P. A. Siljeström's book on the same subject (1856). Later (1855—81) Barnard was to be editor of the *American Journal of Education*, and from 1867 to 1870 was the first US Commissioner of Education, the real founder of the federal Bureau of Education.

Nissen had a special reason for approaching Henry Barnard. After a year of studies in Europe the latter had published in 1851 a book on the European education of teachers, where the single page devoted to Norwegian conditions was not too satisfactory. Nissen therefore invited his "un-usually attractive" colleague to Norway, in order to make him bring his book more up to date on this point, and it is quite possible that the visit actually took place.[13] But most important was, of course, the personal contact established in London, and the conversation of the two men there, in connection with the American section at the Exhibition.

The years that followed were crucial to Nissen's career. It was in the late 1850's that he turned his educational ideas into a political program, and gradually gained that support which insured his victories in the 1860's. In the incessant fight by word of mouth and pen for his many reform projects Nissen obviously had to choose his main arguments in accordance with the immediate needs of his own nation. But it is striking that when, in support of his views, he referred to foreign models and parallels, English and American materials and authorities now played a much more important part than had been the case before. For practical reasons it is difficult to follow Nissen's English and American reading in detail during this period. But it was continuous and extensive, quite apart from the indirect impulses he received in his cooperation with other American-influenced educators like P. A. Siljeström. Nissen's reasoning was often strongly marked by the ideas he absorbed from these new sources. And his very strategy with its continuous effort to win broad popular support for the new school was clearly connected with the democratic ideals of that educational world that by now had become a part of his own thinking.

As mentioned above, Nissen in the 1850's concentrated his powers on the great reform of the elementary school. As Consultant to the Ministry from 1850 to 1854 he was able to influence developments directly. The result of his efforts was a law which was passed in 1860, and which proved to be epochal in the history of Norwegian popular education.

In the 1860's Nissen followed up this victory with a similar great reform of secondary education. For several decades the secondary schools had been the center of heated debates in Norway. The reformers wanted to break the predominance of Greek and Latin, open the schools to Modern Languages and Science, and generally make them serve the current needs, national and social, of the entire people. In a number of weighty and clear-sighted articles in the 1860's, published in the daily and professional press, Nissen crystallized the results of this debate and suggested practical and pedagogically acceptable solutions. He created a strong opinion in favor of his ideas, and also convinced many of the political leaders. In 1865 the Government appointed him Permanent Under-Secretary to the Ministry of Education, the top administrative position in the school system of the country; he remained Under-Secretary until 1872, the year before he died. At the same time he was appointed Chairman of a Government committee charged with the task of formulating the draft of a new law about the organization of the secondary schools. The law was passed in 1869, largely in accordance with Nissen's suggestions. The details of the law are not important here, but the general ideas behind them are. Instead of the "learned" (Latin) schools and the more modest "middle" and "city" schools ("Borgerskoler") the new law introduced a secondary education consisting of three preparatory years, six "middle" years, and a "gymnasium" of three years divided into a Latin and a Science side. The new "middle" school was intended to satisfy the growing demands for a more extensive general education, including foreign languages, in new layers of the population, and to prepare for the many new professions and positions below the academic level which were typical of the new society. But indirectly the reform was also intended to strengthen the position of elementary education within the school system as a whole. To the greatest possible extent the three preparatory years were to equal in subjects and material the three lowest classes of the existing elementary school. This arrangement actually represented the first step toward the creation of that unified elementary school for the entire people which was to materialize in the next century, a school which gives all higher education a common foundation and definitely does away with the system of parallel and separate schools for the upper classes and for the broad layers of population. Thus, without actually proclaiming it, the reform in reality decided that also Norway from now on intended to build its elementary school on that democratic principle which had long been recognized as the foundation of popular education in America.

This contact in the 1850's and 1860's with American educational thought moreover became a link in a Nordic cooperation which forms an interesting chapter in the history of the American impact.

We have already touched upon the American background of the Swedish reformer P. A. Siljeström, his influence on Nissen's development, and their collaboration along parallel lines. In Sweden's Eastern neighboring state, Finland, Siljeström maintained similar relations with the educational leader, Uno Cygnäus (1810—88). While most of the teaching career of Cygnäus belonged to Russia and Finland, he shared the international outlook of his two Nordic colleagues. When in 1858—59 he studied the educational systems of Sweden, Denmark, various German states, Switzerland and Holland, he was prevented by illness from including England and Norway in his itinerary. But in his youth he had spent the years 1840—45 as a Lutheran clergyman in Finno-Swedish and German congregations in the colonies of the Russian-American Trading Company in Alaska (Novo Archangelsk), and also gathered some pedagogical experience there. While he never visited the United States itself he obviously received strong impressions from the American school world. And his friendship and frequent discussions with P. A. Siljeström, outstanding European authority on American education and key man in the field in Scandinavia, gave him additional impulses in the same direction.

In Cygnäus' own work for the improvement of elementary education in Finland there are many points of similarity to the ideas which we know already from his Swedish and Norwegian counterparts: education for citizenship (Swedish: "medborgarlighet"); the elementary school as "the general educational institution of the entire nation" (in Siljeström's formulation: "a basic school common to all classes" making state supported private schools on the same levels superfluous); a common education of women and men for the teaching profession; increased use of women in the schools; better salaries for teachers; more competent inspection; a certain municipal self-government in educational matters by elected school commissions; and a pedagogically competent Ministry of Education.

This parallel in aims and means was emphasized by an innovation which was to prove of considerable importance to the schools of the North. From July 28 to 30, 1868 a national conference of Swedish elementary school teachers was held at Örebro. The executive committee of this meeting for the first time also invited representative educationists from the other Nordic countries. This meeting thus became the first in the series of Nordic School Conferences, which since 1870 have regularly gathered Scandinavian teachers from all types of schools for discussion of the pedagogical problems of the day. But in our study it is of special importance that at the meeting in 1868 the committee brought together the three leading Nordic school reformers of American inspiration: Siljeström, now a member of the Swedish parliament and the guiding spirit within Swedish educational reform; Cygnäus, Chief Inspector of Finnish elementary education and teachers' colleges; Nissen, the administrative leader of Norwegian education. And one of the striking features of the meeting was the presentation for the first time before a Nordic educational audience of the reforming ideas within the American and Anglo-Saxon school worlds. It was Hartvig Nissen who at the meeting referred directly to this American background. The subject of his opening paper was the elementary schools of his own country. But in many ways the statement was a tribute to the ideas of Horace Mann, who had died in 1859.

Nissen began by outlining the development of Norwegian elementary education, from the first attempts at organization in 1739 down to that law of 1860 which to a considerable extent was Nissen's own work. But in his paper he went on to demonstrate that this law could only mean a modest step toward much more ambitious goals. Because of his own democratic ideals Nissen desisted from any comparison with the educational systems of the authoritarian monarchies of his day. Instead, he chose to make a comparison with Canton Zürich in Switzerland and the state of Massachusetts in the USA, and made the two exemplify in factual detail the strong demands which face the schools in democratic societies, and the willingness to sacrifice which such demands require from the population.

Nissen's discussion clearly brought out that in his opinion the school authorities ought to be given more power than was the case in Zürich and Massachusetts at this time. But he made the additional remark that "in a country where the people through its representatives play a significant part in the making of laws, it should be taken for granted that liberty and power of decision are left as unrestricted as is in any possible way compatible with the general aims of the school".

In comparing the Norwegian educational laws with those of the two other countries with pronouncedly democratic constitutions Nissen made it clear that the school legislation of Zürich and Massachusetts expected a much heavier contribution from individuals and municipalities than was the case in Norway. This was only possible, Nissen admitted, because in these two states the people had developed a more mature understanding of popular education, its importance, aims and means, than had his own nation. Nissen informed his Nordic audience about this situation with his accustomed sober and disinterested objectivity. But indirectly his own ideals stood out unmistakeably. And to the reader of his paper today, it is striking how powerfully the ideas of Horace Mann were still an active element in Nissen's mind.

The second leading paper at the Örebro meeting was read by Uno Cygnäus. He described the reform movement in the Finnish elementary schools much along the lines advocated by his Swedish and Norwegian colleagues.

Nissen's paper at Örebro was given considerable publicity in Norway both in the daily and the professional press. But much more important in all respects was the publication, a few months after the meeting, of his book about the school system of Massachusetts.[14]

It is a book which evokes interest both for its timing and for its tone. It is not primarily concerned with polemics: the first battles were already won. But in consolidating his gains, and strengthening his position for a new advance, the author confirmed the value of his aims by placing them within the general movement of educational progress. Sixteen years before he had described the education of Scotland with the same purpose. Now, without laboring the parallels, he described in similar detail another modern educational system of recognized importance, in one of the most progressive of the United States, as he had already done in brief outline in Örebro. The book shows how thoroughly Nissen now knew the American education he referred to. Indirectly it also demonstrates how much the American model and its prestige may have meant to him even during his years of preparation and struggle.

The book was printed at Government expense. In the Introduction (which of course was also written by Nissen) the Ministry of Education declared that in handling matters connected with the schools it was important to the Ministry "to have as exact knowledge as possible of those principles on which the school system is founded in other countries, to know the ways in which the principles are being applied under varied and diversified conditions, and the effects that are observed and the experiences that are noted with regard to the operation of the school under its different systems of arrangement. Among those countries which demand recognition for the entire mode of dealing with this important social question, the republics of North America retain a high position. There the willingness to make sacrifices for the improvement of the school has to a remarkable degree penetrated into the attitude of the nation. As a consequence, the development and the progress of the school have taken place with amazing speed, and older descriptions of the schools in these states therefore no longer give a faithful picture of their present condition. Acknowledging these facts the Undersecretary for Education has prepared an account of the school system of Massachusetts, based on the most recent sources, and also on older works, previously known in our country".

"Supposedly", the Ministry continued, "the distribution of the information contained in this book may prove useful even in wider circles by strengthening the interest in these matters and clarifying the ideas". The Ministry therefore suggested that the book be issued as a Government publication, "to be distributed among those who by their position are able to exert influence on the development of our schools or who presumably harbor a special interest in it, in particular the school boards and municipal councils of the country, school teachers, the administrative authorities of the schools, and members of parliament".[15] Behind the somewhat dated flourishes of ministerial style the substance of this statement is clear enough. It was published in the daily press, and also in its entirety in *Almueskoletidende*, the journal of the elementary school.

The book gives a broad analysis against an historical background, beginning with the settlement of New England, the first enthusiastic establishment of schools, and the relative slackening of interest following the War of Independence. But the book concentrates mainly on the period from the 1830's onward, when democratic principles were more generally accepted in America and the dangers inherent in the development of modern civilization were more clearly realized. From then on, Nissen says, "in all of America, and not least in Massachusetts, the home of the free school, work has been going on incessantly toward the development and perfection of the schools, with an insight and a self-sacrifice which has caught the attention of the European nations. The position of the church in America, and notably the absence of a state church, the strong democratic spirit and the municipal selfgovernment that springs from it, naturally give that country's efforts for the development of the schools an individual character and a special form in many respects".[16]

In his discussion of this form Nissen often displays a somewhat professional or technical interest in the divergence of the two school systems, and the reasons for it. For instance, he points to the different part played by legislature versus administration in the two countries, the deep-going divergence in the field of administrative organization, the special difficulties created in Massachusetts by immigration, and the consequences to religious instruction of the lack of an established church in the USA.

Sometimes Nissen's attitude toward such American peculiarities is critical. This holds good especially when it comes to the lack of tenure in the elementary teaching profession in America, a condition which seemed to Nissen to prevent the development of a stable and self-respecting order of teachers in the country: if the same system were transferred to Norway, the lack of security would "break down the operation of the school for generations". In other cases Nissen's attitude is more ambiguous, for example in his discussion of the position of the secondary schools. He carefully reports that Mann much preferred the state-supported schools to any form of private academy, as "the education most appropriate to our conditions, character and needs as a free people". But Hartvig Nissen was himself the former principal of an important private progressive school. Thus, he understandably reserves his judgement on this point.

In other matters, however, his opinion is strongly expressed, and it is extremely positive. Parts of his survey of the schools of Massachusetts should justly be seen against the background of the great school reform in which Nissen was himself engaged, and the tactical considerations which his position demanded. Often the American example adds prestige to what had now also been done in Norway. In other cases the Americans had found better forms or formulations, and Nissen likes to stress these. The American measures might point to lacunae that still remained within the Norwegian reform work, and demands which had originally been overlooked. Among the more or less disguised allusions of this kind are Nissen's description of the organization he aspired to emulate the Massachusetts system of inspectors, his reference to the competent staff of professional advisers attached to the Massachusetts Ministry of Education, and to the Massachusetts system of special financial support of schools in sparsely populated municipalities, arrangements which Nissen coveted at home, and was partly successful in establishing.

In particular, Nissen was impressed by the broad popular support of the school reforms in Massachusetts. He admired the way in which the American school authorities had been able to interest the common man in what they were doing, and make him feel education as his personal concern. Nissen ended his book with extracts from the annual reports of the Massachusetts school-commissions, reports which were widely distributed in the local districts and created a lively contact between school and home. Public opinion in educational matters is clearly expressed in these documents, says Nissen; after reading a few of them, he noted, "it is as if one had listened to the entire nation expressing its views on these matters". Behind such words is Nissen's own desire to make the people participate in the long-range development of the school, and to prepare it for the continued sacrifice that is necessary, a conviction that motivated the writing of his own book.

In his work and his writing Nissen was primarily concerned with facts. His style is rarely colored by emotion. In the introductory pages of his book, however, a few sentences reveal how strongly the subject was connected with the deepest motive forces of his personality. To study the American schools is not only extremely interesting, he says. "It strengthens and elevates the mind of the educator to see a nation which has made its institutions a clear and complete expression of its own thought and volition, work in all great essentials so steadfastly, unceasingly and persistently through the centuries for that great idea: a better and more complete education of the growing generation. By observing the life and the movements within the American school world I have myself gained strength in my conviction about the importance of the school for the individual and for society and my hope of its progressive development at home. In a similar way I have believed that those among my fellow-countrymen who share my opinion about the importance of the school, and who wish for its uninterrupted development toward greater perfection, may appreciate more complete and reliable information about the schools of America".[17]

One can hardly say that this American impact was decisive to Hartvig Nissen's work. In its main features his contribution was formed by his own personality, and in a larger sense by great historical forces, in Norway itself and in Europe. But the American example became an important factor in bringing his ideas into shape during his most creative period. The work of his American counterparts strengthened his own courage and corroborated his conviction at times when it may well have been needed. Among the many who have moulded the school of modern Norway the country also owes a distant debt of gratitude to Horace Mann and his colleagues.

In his own way Nissen thus presents an interesting personal aspect of the general Norwegian attitude in the nineteenth century toward the great republic across the Atlantic. All through the period in question a heated debate was going on in Norway for or against America. The dissension reflected a general development which is typical of European opinion in the century under consideration, from the theorizing idealization of past generations to the more realistic understanding of the present. Doubtless Hartvig Nissen was well aware of the less attractive sides of American life. At the time when he wrote his book they had been sufficiently revealed to the world by the

Civil War. It is interesting to note that in spite of such qualifications of his enthusiasm Nissen unerringly maintained his faith in the basic qualities of American democracy. He became the Norwegian herald of one of the strongest manifestations of American idealism, the faith in democratic education. And he thus made it a factor in the parallel development of his own nation.

Few individuals have left their mark more strongly on Norwegian education in the nineteenth century, than did Hartvig Nissen. And even his orientation toward the United States was not lost on the following generations. The roads he pointed to, soon became main-thoroughfares. Only a few decades were to pass before American personalities and places like John Dewey, Dalton and Winnetka were household words to Norwegian educators. To the generation after 1945 reference to American educational psychology and American educational debate became a matter of course. The exchange of educational information across the ocean, by textbooks, travelling, publications and fellowships, has developed continuously and extensively in a way that would have staggered Hartvig Nissen and his contemporaries. Norwegian educators made independent contributions to the discussion of the American school system, with a scholarly thoroughness and an access to primary material which make the reports of a hundred years ago appear modest. But it has all grown by a natural development from those first contacts with the American educational world that were established from the 1850's on by the intellectual curiosity and youthful enthusiasm of Hartvig Nissen.

## NOTES

[1] For H. Nissen's life and work, see E. Boyesen, *Hartvig Nissen og det norske skolevesens reform*, I—II (Oslo, 1947). The materials for the third volume of this work were lost by enemy action during the war 1940—45. When finished, the volume will discuss in detail the American relationship of Nissen, which can only be outlined in this brief article.

[2] E. I. F. Williams, *Horace Mann; Educational Statesman* (New York, 1937), p. 203.

[3] H. Nissen, *Grundtræk af en Plan for Omdannelsen af Almueskolen paa Landet* (Christiania, 1851), p. 4.

[4] H. Nissen, *Grundtræk*, pp. 74—76.

[5] H. Nissen, *Grundtræk*, pp. 8 f.

[6] *Beskrivelse over Skotlands Almueskolevæsen tilligemed Forslag til forskjellige Foranstaltninger til en videre Udvikling af det norske Almueskolevæsen* (Christiania, 1854).

[7] H. Nissen, *Beskrivelse*, p. IV; other direct references pp. 13, 53, 62, 65—67 and 173. Mann's work is printed

among his *Annual Reports on Education* (Boston, 1868), as Report No. 7, pp. 230—418. It is broadly discussed in E. I. F. Williams, *Horace Mann*, pp. 245—274.

[8] H. Nissen, *Beskrivelse*, p. 146.

[9] F. M. Bugge, *Det offentlige Skolevæsens Forfatning i adskillige tydske Stater*, III (Christiania, 1839), 5—8.

[10] H. Nissen, *Beskrivelse*, 271—274.

[11] H. Mann, *Report of an Educational*

*Tour*, p. 287. Compare E. I. F. Williams, *Horace Mann*, p. 249.

[12] H. Nissen, *Beskrivelse*, p. 173, note.

[13] Letter from H. Nissen to his wife, July 13, 1854 (unpublished); compare E. Boyesen, *H. Nissen*, II, 332.

[14] H. Nissen, *Skolevæsenets Ordning i Massachusetts fremstillet af H. N.* (Christiania, 1868, IV, 92 pp.).

[15] H. Nissen, *Skolevæsenets Ordning*, p. III.

[16] H. Nissen, *Skolevæsenets Ordning*, p. 2.

[17] H. Nissen, *Skolevæsenets Ordning*, p. 3.

# BARTLEBY THE INSCRUTABLE: NOTES ON A MELVILLE MOTIF

## By Otto Reinert

In the continuing Melville revival,[1] "Bartleby the Scrivener" is becoming a central item in the canon. It marks a wryly defeatist retreat from the expansive, symphonic, poly-generic form of the great allegorical journeys.[2] It levels and disciplines their pseudo-Elizabethan garrulity, barbarian or magniloquent, with a gain, very often, in stylistic relevance. As a quietist postscript to Melville's Promethean phase it is an index to larger issues, both in Melville and in the proliferating Melville literature. Its contemporary appeal is evident in the frequency with which Gogol, Dostoevsky, Kafka, and Camus figure in recent comments.

## I

"Bartleby" first appeared, anonymously, in the November and December issues of *Putnam's Monthly Magazine* for 1853. By then Melville had published seven novels in as many years, but nothing since *Pierre*, in August, 1852. In early October of that year he received a letter from G. P. Putnam soliciting contributions to a new monthly,[3] but at the time he seems to have been trying to give literary shape to the story of Agatha Robertson, the patient, long-suffering sailor wife, with which a Nantucket acquaintance had furnished him.[4] Elizabeth Melville reported in her memoirs that by the spring of 1853 her husband's new work was "nearly ready for the press," but in the end the project proved abortive. That spring, Melville's family, worrying about "the strain on his health," brought about by "the constant in-door confinement" and "constant working of the brain, & excitement of the imagination,"[5] tried, unsuccessfully, to get him a consular appointment abroad. When, sometime in the summer or fall of 1853, he decided to try to make a living by writing for *Putnam's*, the Agatha theme of patient endurance, his wearying writing efforts of the previous winter and spring, his dilemma as writer after the relative public failure of *Moby Dick* and the absolute one of *Pierre*, and his concerned family's attempts to find him more rewarding employment, all seem to have gone into the making of the story of the pale, enigmatic, and unemployable scrivener.

Biography has largely been superseded by metaphysics in recent "Bartleby" criticism. The current "Bartleby" boom owes a debt to the existentialist vogue. As early as 1941, F. O. Matthiessen called the story "a tragedy of utter negation,"[6] and in 1950 Newton Arvin took the Wall Street setting as an image of "the cosmic madhouse" and Bartleby himself as a dramatization "not [of] the pathos of dementia praecox but [of] the bitter metaphysical pathos of the human situation itself."[7] Four intensive studies of "Bartleby" have appeared since Arvin's book on Melville. Although two of them[8] read it as a parable on the plight of the modern writer, they are only incidentally concerned with the extent to which Melville may have allegorized a crisis of audience alienation in his own career. Like the other two,[9] they search the story for a comment on the human predicament.[10]

In Bartleby's preference for "dead-wall revery" (pp. 34, 38),[11] rather than "copying," Leo Marx sees a parallel to Melville's preference for a philosophical novel like *Moby Dick* rather than the reportorial semifiction of one like *Typee*. But Marx reads the story not as Melville's endorsement of his scrivener self but as a "counter-statement to the large and ever-growing canon of 'ordealist' interpretations of the modern writer." The story says that if the writer "forgets humanity, as Bartleby did, his art will die and so will he." The social commitment of art is the burden also of John Gardner's interpretation, but he finds the prototypal artist not in Bartleby but in the lawyer-narrator, whose compassionate and understanding account of his clerk reconciles the conflicting pulls of self and society, imagination and rational judgment. The story amounts to an apotheosis of art in an age that is without religious faith. Richard H. Fogle decries the artist parable and sees in Bartleby "representative man." Like Gardner, Fogle speaks of a "narrator-god," but Fogle's narrator, unlike Gardner's, is unable to rescue Bartleby from his "predestinated woe." Bartleby is a passive, "melancholy Thoreau," perverted to passivity before the story begins.

For all their differences of approach and interpretation, Marx, Gardner, and Fogle all regard the title character as the victim of some kind of psychological blight or paralyzing distortion of vision. Marx ascribes Bartleby's withdrawal from human fellowship to his fatal delusion that man-made walls are as impenetrable as the wall of human mortality, Gardner to his vision of a dead letter world, and Fogle to some obscure hurt he has sustained at the hands of Wall Street society. In the sense that they all three assume or imply some ideal, or norm, or sane compromise, of attitude to experience, from which Bartleby, for some reason or other, has strayed, all three read the story as a document of ultimate affirmation.

But for Kingsley Widmer "Bartleby" affirms nothing but the paradox of the clerk's "rebellious negation." Widmer sees the story as a "comedy-of-the-absurd" or as a piece of "Kafkaesque-metaphysical-expressionism," in which the failure of the "liberal rationalist" in a "grotesque universe" is sardonically pointed up by Bartleby, "the ultimate passive resistor," who "*is* humanity," both as "forlorn negation and as the obsession of the benevolent rationalist's consciousness."[12] Widmer, I think, over-emphasizes the comical aspects of the narrator's position at the expense of its other facets. The value of his study is his recognition of the employer-Bartleby relationship as the story's core and his definition of that relationship as absurd deadlock. Widmer's thesis invites a closer consideration of action and imagery in "Bartleby" in the context of Melville's other works of existential protest. Such an approach can illuminate both those other works and "Bartleby" itself — not as parts of a single, compound statement of philosophy but as autonomous fictions on related themes and of similar imagistic method and texture. An awareness of an element of the absurd in the tragic experience and its traditional forms of literary expression obviates the charge that an existentialist approach to the heart of the Melville canon is unhistorical.

## II

Interpreting "Bartleby" is a precarious business. The story is open and inclusive, its form a system of ambiguities in check and balance, too fine and fragile for singleminded rigor of explication. Its meaning is the total pattern yielded by the formal and substantive facts of the narrative, and criticism can achieve no synonym. The oddity of the events is set off by the commonplace setting in which they occur and by the commonplace character who narrates them. The disparity insinuates allegory. But transliteration into a coherent system of abstracts has so far neither succeeded in fully accounting for facts and imagery or for all significant aspects of tone and structure nor to some extent avoided violating their collective integrity. Gardner, for example, reads "Bartleby" as a story about the redemption of life by engaged art and finds it pervaded by Christian symbolism. But his conclusion, "... there will be, after life, art. The artist rolls the stone away — that is the narrator's creative act — and man escapes from the Tombs," represents an attempt to find an Easter or resurrection motif in the account of Bartleby's death that lacks support in the narrative and imagistic facts.

As the lawyer's monologue, "Bartleby" is drama. A private memory is being made public, and the speech manner reveals the speaker's character. When Hoffman holds that the penultimate paragraph on the dead letter office is "anticlimactic" and "out of tone with the rest of the story, a pun rather than a symbol," he overlooks its function in characterizing the baffled lawyer who conscientiously gives his audience every scrap of evidence (including, ironically, hearsay) that may conceivably help to explain the phenomenon of Bartleby. The pun is the lawyer's, not Melville's, and the lawyer's eager seizure of it betrays his rationalist limitations. Gardner, similarly, ignores dramatic convention when he accounts for Bartleby's perversity by assuming a conditioning dead letter office in his past. He infers a fact from what the employer, as anxious as anyone to "explain" Bartleby, only dares to call a "vague report." The inference is a piece of plausible irrelevance. Only as a fact not of Bartleby's past but of the narrator's performance does the dead letter office function fully both as an image of the failure in communication that is Bartleby's psychological climate and as a tonal element that marks a move away from the terse dignity of language in the death episode to something like the circumstantiality and pontification of the lawyer's opening, autobiographical remarks. As such it is both a framing and a distancing device.

The story of the lawyer and his difficult clerk poses a subtler antithesis than one of savior and saved, or of clown and martyr, or of exploiter and exploited, though all of these are in part relevant. Its theme is an impasse of being between, as Widmer has it, rational benevolence on the one hand and a will of absolute denial, including denial of all self-interest, on the other. One corollary is the tension between the "form" of the self-explaining lawyer's modulations of voice and narrative manner and the "matter" of Bartleby's nearly mute impenetrability. Another is a disparity that raises a problem of interpretive strategy. Bartleby's preposterous behavior and his employer's tolerance of it need to be reconciled with the realistic decorum of the surface "story of Wall Street" (as the original publication in *Putnam's* subtitled it). At times, narrative details effortlessly assume symbolic power in the existential allegory in which alone the incongruous Bartleby seems to belong. The office keys are an example. Three keys are accounted for, but the fourth, the lawyer tells us, he "knew not who had" (p. 31). One Sunday morning he finds an inside key in the office door and Bartleby within. The extraliteral meaning of the episode is best left indefinite, but in context the facts surely generate some such meaning around the images of "lost key," "secret access," and insidious "taking possession." But at other times Bartleby intrudes, like some pathetic ghost, upon the foreground of a plausible and solidly delineated genre picture. It is, of course, very much part of Melville's larger, controlling irony that the business lawyer's anecdote is too small for the whole meaning of the story about Bartleby, but the decorum of anecdote strains whenever the excess, for lack of any other narrative vehicle, issues in allegory. Where ulterior meanings have not been embodied, "interpretation" marks the only significant line of coherence.

There is (for example) the scene in which Bartleby, evicted from the office by its new tenant, sits upon the banister and keeps turning down every one of his employer's offers of jobs while claiming not to be "particular" in his choice of occupation (pp. 48–50). As an item in the larger ironic pattern of action the episode offers no special difficulty. It is just about the only scene in which Bartleby volunteers speech beyond his one fixed reply, and it comes to an end when the remonstrating, cajoling lawyer runs away without a word. And although part farce and part nightmare, its integrity as narrative sequence is never in doubt, because its decorum of realism can absorb Bartleby's fantastic behavior: the lawyer's headlong, speechless flight is proof that common sense recognizes it *as* fantastic. Given the lawyer's normal decency and prudence, his escape, under the circumstances, seems a likely reaction. And because it does, the scene can allegorize a larger meaning: in the face of irrational non-response rationality has no choice but self-preserving flight.

But Bartleby's "I am not particular" perplexes not just the lawyer but anyone who tries to "understand" the clerk. The lawyer despairs and runs because he can see no rational connection between Bartleby's claim and the fact of his repeated rejection of job offers. By the norms of common sense, ordinary semantics, and prudent self-interest — Wall Street norms — there is no connection. But because the compelling power of the Bartleby figure and the combination of obtuseness and candor in the employer's report on him have by now alerted us to implications of values beyond Wall Street's in what Bartleby says, *we* require his words to make significant sense. Aside from the fact that crude, insolent jeering on Bartleby's part would be pointless, there is nothing in his opaque psychology to support the assumption that he is simply making fun of his employer. To assume that Bartleby is mad and his words a schizophrenic's gibberish would be to irretrievably collapse any subterranean meaning and hence to trivialize the whole story and leave the lawyer's obsession with Bartleby and his final respect for his wisdom of mystical negation unexplained and inexplicable. And to take "madness" as an ironic synonym for "wisdom" leaves an awkward hiatus between surface meaning and deep meaning and reduces rich ironies to a cheap verbal trick.

But if Bartleby is neither a psychopath nor an ironist, his words must mean what they seem to say. The point is precisely that Bartleby's and Wall Street's worlds of discourse are not only different but discrete. The lawyer hears in Bartleby's claim that he is "not particular" only a statement at patent variance with the facts and hence mad. But if taken to apply to qualities not of immediate but of ultimate human action, the words become an affirmation of guiltlessness in the face of suffering. Bartleby is ironical only in the limited sense that he does not disclose the pertinence of his assertion. Faced with offers of a variety of jobs — as store clerk, bartender, and traveling tutor — he quietly insinuates a metaphysical syllogism. It is perfectly true that he is not particular: he will accept any employment that is "stationary," "definite," and does not entail "too much confinement" (p. 49). Since he rejects all the ordinary occupations in the service of business, pleasure, and learning that the lawyer suggests to him, the inference is that he regards the common labors of men as confinement among indefinite unstables. In an existence of which "nothing is ascertainable," "copying" is absurd, and for a "being" whose known "original sources" are "very small" (these are the first things we are told about Bartleby [p. 16]), verification of copy must seem manifestly impossible. He will not go home with his employer, because he refuses to acknowledge any home in a prison existence, but the qualified form of his refusal — "at present I would prefer not to make any change at all" (p. 50) — suggests that in an indefinite world of flux even an assertion of absolute inertia can have temporary validity only. Nevertheless, he remains till the end in passive contemplation of stone walls, as if in silent, mocking imitation of the stationariness which the world's futile employments fail to provide.

In the absence of terms of control in the facts of the narrative, one cannot insist on the accuracy of this or any other single, precise formulation of what the lawyer in another scene refers to as Bartleby's "paramount consideration" (p. 26). But the structural and narrative function of the episode is too important for any serious interpretation of "Bartleby" to ignore it. It divides the Wall Street part of the story from the Tombs part. Office cedes to prison and tomb, bustling, successful lawyer to cadaverous, catatonic prisoner. It presents Bartleby's final refusal to accommodate himself to the lawyer's kind of world. As narrative, there is nothing indefinite about any of this.

The implications of the staircase episode suggest Bartleby's ambivalence. Rejecting Wall Street, he also rejects the Wall Street lawyer's proffered benevolence. To refuse to share his home is to deny the "bond of common humanity" (p. 33) which the lawyer recognizes between Bartleby and himself. Bartleby's solitary way leads only to the Tombs. The absolutist is not fit for life. Self-disqualified for the human condition, he is, simultaneously, the hero of an existentialist tragedy and the Bergsonian "mechanical man," the rigid humorist, of comedy.

The generic ambivalence of the story of the conflict between Bartleby and Wall Street appears as well in the two applications of the story's master image. As Bartleby faces walls, his employer faces Bartleby. On the one hand, we follow the developing one-way dialogue between utilitarian, adaptable World and unchangeable, intransigent Self. In the encounter of employer and employee, the former's role is at first that of a fussy philistine, the pompously benevolent authoritarian who becomes ridiculous in his helplessness as Bartleby's perversity frustrates his pursuit of "the easiest way of life" (p. 16). Bartleby, the pallid young proletarian of business bureaucracy, who will neither co-operate nor depart, puts the "elderly" lawyer of "snug business," "cool tranquillity," and certified "prudence" and "method" (pp. 16–17), through an erratic sequence of strong emotions: surprise, anger, perplexity, pity, revulsion, entreaty, pride, betrayal, flight, contrition. His isolation keeps the churchgoer out of church and turns the business lawyer into a melancholy sentimentalist. The sameness of his denial elicits a variety of persuasive strategies, and its mildness covers severity of will. Inert himself, he compels his employer to abandon his "snug retreat," in which — paradox becoming irony — all the usurping Wall Street clerk does is contemplate walls. Oxymora, the rhetorical figure for paradox, immediately come to mind in any attempt to describe Bartleby. He is meekly insubordinate, forlornly purposeful. His silence is eloquent, his pride pitiful.

But in the lawyer's account of the odd relationship between Bartleby and himself, we trace, on the other hand, also a movement from talkative complacency, naively giving itself away, to sparse narrative, involvement, and awe. Since the story is told retrospectively, the movement adds a dimension of irony to the narrator's self-exposure at the beginning. When Bartleby dies in the Tombs, the narrator has reached a point beyond vacillating between a sense of brotherhood based on the vulnerable conviction that "both I and Bartleby were sons of Adam" (p. 33) and a too ready sense of kinship with "the old Adam of resentment" (p. 43). He is beyond the comfortable conviction that prudence and Christian charity are one and the same and beyond the calm resignation to the disposition of a mysterious Providence that comes from reading "Edwards on the will" and "Priestley on necessity" (p. 44). He has moved beyond, even, the transfixing moment when Bartleby's unexpected presence in the office had seemed to strike him as the treacherous bolt from the blue had struck and killed the placid Virginian "at his own warm open window ... upon the dreamy afternoon" (p. 41). His relation to the dying Bartleby has become something like the Portuguese sea captain Don Pedro's relationship to Gulliver on the return voyage from Houyhnhnmland: tireless benevolence tirelessly rejected.

In Melville, however, the antithesis is less clear-cut than in Swift; that, one is tempted to say, is its point. There is an element of responsibility and guilt in the employer's attitude, as there is not in Don Pedro's spontaneous and unperturbed goodness. While Bartleby is still with him, he is "touched" by the thought that the scrivener may have "temporarily impaired his vision" (p. 38) in his service. And Bartleby is not an obvious misanthrope like Gulliver; hence, he is less grotesque, more pathetic. He is not quite immune to his would-be benefactor's efforts to establish rapport. While he reiterates his negative preference in the face of a bust of Cicero, "his countenance," his empoyer tells us, "remained immovable, only there was the faintest conceivable tremor of the white attenuated mouth" (p. 36). The monotone of his negation paradoxically triumphs over the stilled

Ciceronian oratory, but the twitching mouth — attenuated, as it were, both by fasting and by silence — betrays his touched, living humanity.

Comedy and tragedy, anecdote and parable, balance and inter-penetrate in "ambiguous equilibrium."[13] Characters are complemen-tary foils. The comical antithesis of the two Dickensian clerks Turkey and Nippers is a simple parallel to the complex lawyer-Bartleby rela-tionship. Between the white and black walls that enclose the office on either side, they perform, with unerring regularity of rhythm, their daily interchange of sobriety and inebriation, obeisance and insolence, effectiveness and ineffectiveness. Between them, the law business gets done. The phrase "nip and tuck," which their names call up, suggests, not so much competitiveness (as Leo Marx says), as critical equi-librium, a precariously shifting but never overturned balance, "a close thing," in the *Oxford Dictionary* definition of the phrase. Together, they are man alive in measured flux between light and dark, and their employer's fatherly indulgence with their antics represents, perhaps, less a god-like quality than an easy-going pragmatist's compromise with complementary instabilities.

In one sense, Bartleby is in obvious contrast to his two mercurial fellow clerks. He is always the same; "motionless" (p. 23) is the first adjective applied to him when he appears in the office. Turkey and Nippers take turns storming at his idle scrutiny of "no view at all" (p. 23). He is repeatedly "cadaverous," "a very ghost," "an appari-tion." Turkey drinks too much and Nippers suffers from indigestion; Bartleby is never seen either to drink or to eat. But in the sense that Bartleby's dead-level sameness and non-engagement in ordinary living represent a kind of existential zero, Turkey and Nippers, in the con-stancy of their mutual balance of opposite ways and moods, are, jointly, more like an image of Bartleby than his foil. Turkey is a florid Englishman, Nippers a sallow American; Bartleby, of no known origin, is "a bit of wreck in the mid Atlantic" (p. 39). The wall outside his window is nondescript, neither black nor white. His career in the law office begins in diligence and ends in idleness. The impertinence of his "passive resistance" (p. 28) is set off by the mildness of the formula by which he asserts it: in the uncertainty of existence a refusal to co-operate can be a matter of preference only, not of conviction. His colleagues' assertiveness is blustery but intermittent. His stillness comprises their lability, his death their life.

Bartleby's inertia usurping the law office is a paradox that points up the ambiguity of the lawyer's position. When he finds himself, like

Turkey and Nippers, automatically using Bartleby's favorite verb, he fears "what further aberration" may follow from his continued "contact with the scrivener" (p. 37). The reference to Bartleby's impassive diffidence as some kind of spreading psychological infection makes sense on Wall Street terms, and events justify the lawyer's fears. Gradually, Turkey and Nippers and Ginger Nut disappear from the narrative, as if legal business were coming to an end. Then the lawyer abandons his chambers — clearly a move which Wall Street, if it knew the facts, would regard as an "aberration." The lawyer's early, ponderous pun on Ginger Nut's name and favorite food is now seen to have been an ironic anticipation of the failure of the legal profession in a world inhabited by Bartleby: "Indeed, to this quick-witted youth, the whole noble science of the law was contained in a nut-shell" (p. 22). But the kernels are gone from the shells in Ginger Nut's desk, and so what the lawyer meant to be a witty image of a concentrate of learning in small space suggests instead the way in which Bartleby's passive negation has extended the emptiness of his "hermitage" (*passim*) through all the lawyer's crowded and busy chambers. The agent of justice capitulates to his servant's great denial. The full significance of the irony, however, is evident only in the lawyer's final cry. The surface meaning of "Ah, Bartleby! Ah, humanity!"is the lawyer's awareness, at the end, of Bartleby as suffering mankind incarnate, but Bartleby's negation and the echo of the comically inept nutshell image from the earlier passage suggest as well that quintessential man is null. The implication of the ambiguity is that the lawyer in his final exclamation is both Wall Street's facile and pompous-sentimental moralist and the saintly Bartleby's sympathetic chronicler who in the involvement of his "fellow-feeling" (p. 19) is no longer "Master in Chancery."

The ambivalent stimulus of Bartleby evokes ambivalent responses in his employer. Bartleby draws from the latter images now of bathos ("a bit of Windsor soap" [p. 28]), now of pathos (" a pale form . . . laid out, among uncaring strangers, in its shivering winding sheet" [p. 33]). The encounter with Bartleby shatters the lawyer's safe complacency and engages the irrational depths of his being. He solicits the scrivener's insubordination in order to relish his own just anger: he "burn[s] to be rebelled against" (p. 29). The object of pity and patience, the human pretext for "delicious self-approval" (p. 28), becomes a near-provocation to murder (p.43). When the lawyer abandons Bartleby out of concern for his professional reputation, he finds that he must tear himself away "from him I had so longed to get rid of" (p. 47), and when Bartleby has been removed to the Tombs, the lawyer haunts the prison himself. When he finds Bartleby's earnings tied up in an old handkerchief in the deepest recesses of his desk, it is as if the realization that Bartleby's money is as idle in its retirement as Bartleby himself proves too much for his tolerant humanity. Confronted with such depths of forlornness, the guardian of "rich men's bonds and mortgages" (p. 16) finds his "melancholy" becoming "fear," his "pity" "repulsion" (p. 35).

These instabilities of feeling prove the accuracy of the lawyer's description of himself as "a human creature, with the common infirmities of our nature" (p. 31). There are overtones of psychological allegory in the fact that he is Turkey's and Nippers's employer. And Bartleby's ambivalent hold on him derives from his sense of sharing a common humanity with his scrivener. This is not quite to say that Bartleby is his employer's psychological double; an allegory of identity is too small and tenuous to cover all the narrative facts. But it is to suggest that the lawyer, no less than Bartleby, though in a different way, is "representative man." Bartleby represents man's refusal to accept his condition and engage his will and effort in pursuit of action. He will not compromise with the whimsical malignancy or indifference that appears to rule his existence. The lawyer is the compromising, indulgent, adjustable *honnête homme*. His very tolerance of his impossible clerk for so long is evidence. The "aberration" into which Bartleby causes him to lapse is a doubly ironic description of what happens to him. The inner action of the story is the lawyer's achievement of awareness, but his awareness of Bartleby's plight is also, as the inclusive reference of his final cry shows, an awareness of self. It is true that his narrative manner throughout is that of a man puzzled as much by his own reaction to Bartleby as by Bartleby himself. But his failure to grasp the full import of the story he has told does not prove that Bartleby has left him essentially unchanged. It is an item of psychological realism that checks the incipient sentimentality of the story. At the time of the telling of the story the lawyer is still calmly and competently performing the functions of his profession. He could hardly do so had he been the kind of man who could admit his devastating insight into the case of Bartleby to full consciousness. No more can he articulate it completely. He remains a safe and prudent man of property still. But his epitaph on Bartleby is not that of a man who is still convinced that "the easiest way of life is the best" (p. 16). If *he*

— successful, adjustable, limited — at the end suspects that it is the forlorn and wilful martyr of self-enclosed selfhood and not Wall Street that possesses the ultimate wisdom, then the point of the story about Bartleby is not the exhibition of victimized Everyman in his retreat from action and fellowship as perverse, but the sense on the part of Everyman's other, worldly self that what the world calls perversity or madness is really recognition. Bartleby "knows" where he is and can therefore "want nothing to say" to the world's emissary who has come to tell him that he is not in the Tombs in "so bad a place as one might think" (p. 51). And the emissary ends by abandoning his mission and instead admitting Bartleby to the timeless company of "kings and counselors" (p. 53), a Job asleep beyond the further reach of God's scourge. He does not comment on the grub-man's guess that Bartleby is a "forger" (p. 52), but in the spirit in which he contemplates the dead Bartleby the grub-man's choice of word must strike him as being about as wrong as it could possibly be.

In the lawyer's epitaph on Bartleby, the ambivalences of the story come to a paradoxical climax but are not resolved. The impasse remains: both the lawyer and Bartleby are both protagonist and antagonist, both victim and victimizer. But the effect of Bartleby's quiet passion of withdrawal on the lawyer is the engagement of his fellow feeling in an "over-powering stinging melancholy" (p. 33) with the human condition itself and his awareness of passive endurance as crowned wisdom. It is an action that enforces the latent symbolism of an earlier scene: the lost, last key is Bartleby's.

## III

"Bartleby," as far as we know, was the first piece of fiction Melville completed after *Moby-Dick* and *Pierre*. Between the novels and the short story Melville's fictional treatment of the existential problem underwent an obvious reduction in size of both hero and fable. For Prometheans, we get a white-collar anti-hero; for *King Lear* and *Hamlet*, *Bleak House* and *Notes from the Underground*; for assumptions, preferences; for Ahab's and Pierre's home-forsaking quests, Bartleby's uterine retreat;[14] for the violence of the whale and the intolerance of Pierre's conventional society, Bartleby's mild-mannered apathy; for poetry and rant, a fixed word formula and silence. The works that followed "Bartleby" also deal with passive suffering and nonheroics in a mode of irony: most of the other *Piazza Tales* (1856) and the two novels that preceded the thirty-four year silence and *Billy Budd* (1891) : *Israel Potter* (1855) and *The Confidence Man* (1857). But the changes are more obvious than basic. Where Ahab and Pierre lunge, Bartleby withdraws, but his polite *non serviam* is no less absolute than theirs. If there is "naught beyond" the shifting ambiguities of experience (*Moby-Dick*, p. 162) and if "silence is the only voice of our God" (*Pierre*, p. 239), then Bartleby's taciturn passivity before a dimly lighted nothing defines man's only available form of metaphysical non-acceptance, and if the lawyer's growing obsession with his scrivener is a gradual perception of self, then "Bartleby," like *Moby-Dick* and *Pierre*, moves centripetally. And both heroic myth and office parable deal with the theme of existential ambivalence — with that human nature which, as Melville says in *The Confidence Man* (p. 77), like the divine nature, "is past finding out." Like *The Confidence Man* and *Billy Budd*, they adumbrate an antinomic ethic.

The questing Promethean hero is ambivalent in his double role of scapegoat savior and impious rebel. Already Taji in *Mardi* is both slayer and rescuer, both Hautia's and Yillah's, both pursuer and pursued. He commits himself enthusiastically to the "bold quest" of his "chartless voyage," but the ending of *Mardi* is at best inconclusive. Ahab is both the captain of a whaling ship and a monomaniac cripple seeking private revenge on "a dumb brute" (p. 161). His ship belongs both to the fair-minded Captain Peleg and to the hypocritical skinflint Captain Bildad. The ostensible purpose of the *Pequod's* voyage represents a burgeoning economic enterprise, a heroic harvesting of the sea's bounty, an extension of mid-century American empire-building — *and* an acquisitive culture's brutal raid on innocent nature. Moby Dick's whiteness, Ishmael tells us, symbolizes holiness and innocence but also death and, as "colorless all-color" (p. 193), a metaphysical inscrutability that may mask a void. Ishmael is drawn both to the "green, gentle, and most docile earth," the soul's "insular Tahiti" (p. 274), and to the brave Bulkington vision of the "landlessness" in which "alone resides highest truth, shoreless, indefinite as God." "Better," he says, "to perish in that howling infinite, than be ingloriously dashed upon the lee, even if that were safety!" (p. 105). His voice mingles with the shouts that implicate all of the *Pequod's* crew in Ahab's blasphemous enterprise. It is he, not Ahab, who says that "unless you own the whale, you are but a provincial and sentimentalist in Truth" (p. 336). And yet, Ishmael is the sole survivor of the *Pequod's* wreck.

Pierre is both Hamlet and Manfred as he brings suffering and death to everyone in his sacrifice of everything for a girl who may or may not be his sister and who is and is not his wife. The agony of his entrapment between a "not wholly earth-emancipated mood" and a "sky-assaulting one" (p. 408) issues in his dream of the titan Enceladus, the child of an incestuous union of earth and heaven, shackled by the one, defying the other. Like Ishmael's commitment to the "howling infinite," the authorial comment on Enceladus-Pierre favors the titanic gesture of revolt: ". . . whoso storms the sky gives best proof he came from thither! But whoso crawls contented before the crystal fort, shows it was born within that slime, and there forever will abide" (p. 408). But no more than in *Mardi* does the plot outcome in *Moby-Dick* and *Pierre* unequivocally endorse the heroic raid on the infinite. Prometheus may not be guilty in any eyes but heaven's, but suffering is inevitably his self-inflicted doom in Melville. In the penultimate chapter of *The Confidence Man* Melville pretty clearly defines the larger dimensions of his satirical river boat allegory by associating his scamp hero with Hamlet, Don Quixote, and Milton's Satan. There is a crucial pun in the designation "confidence man." As by imagery he is both "lamblike" and reptilian and by action both masker and unmasker, so is the confidence man quite literally both "charlatan" and "man of trust." It is a measure of the complexity of the novel that his name, "Frank Goodman," cannot be taken to be wholly ironic.

Moby-Dick enrages Ahab because he discerns "inscrutable malice" (p. 162) behind the maiming force of its white, "battering ram" front, its "dead, blind wall," its "dead, impregnable, uninjurable wall" (pp. 334–336), its "pasteboard mask" (p. 161). "If man will strike," Ahab cries, "strike through the mask! How can the prisoner reach outside except by thrusting through the wall? To me, the white whale is that wall, shoved near to me" (pp. 161–162). Pierre faces "the wall of the thick darkness of the mystery of Isabel" (p. 200). When he cannot reconcile his "two grand resolutions" of publicly acknowledging Isabel as his sister and withholding knowledge of her identity from his mother, he dashes himself "in blind fury and swift madness against the wall" (p. 201). He says that "if the uttermost virtue, after all, prove but a betraying pander to the monstrousest vice — then close in and crush me, ye stony walls, and into one gulf let all things tumble together!" (p. 321). He thinks of "all the ambiguities which hemmed him in" as "stony walls all round that he could not overleap" (p. 396). In his dream, the stone giant Enceladus bat-

13

ters impotently "at the precipice's unresounding wall" (p. 407). He
dies within prison walls. The episode in *Israel Potter* in which Israel is
confined and, by the death of his employer, abandoned in a narrow
cell inside the stone walls of the house at Brentford, suggests the way
in which adverse chance circumstance condemns Israel, the faithful
underling, to a lifetime of imprisonment and exile. His lot comprises
both alienation and claustrophobia.

The wall imagery in the novels has become ubiquitous in "Bartleby."
Bartleby himself literally faces walls throughout the story, but there
are also the recurrent confrontations of him and his employer, in
which the man of safe and sane moderation batters as vainly at the
scrivener's massive non-co-operation as Ahab's and Pierre's outraged
idealism assaults the unanswering universe. Bartleby, that is, is not
only a blighted idealist whose eyesight, like Pierre's as he wrestles
with the transcendentalist mysteries of his novels (and like Melville's
own), fails from endless wall scrutiny. He is also, like Moby Dick,
Pierre's "ambiguities," and Enceladus' mountain opponent, an inscrutable, riddling antagonist. He is both an inert Prometheus, and the
rock on which Prometheus is tortured. He is both martyr and sphinx,
both "king" and "incubus" (p. 45).

In the Tombs, Bartleby looks neither at the grass at the foot of the
prison wall, nor at the sky above. Like Pierre, he is engaged in a
"duel in which all seconds are forbid" (p. 411), including nature's
earth and heaven. Only "the eyes of murderers and thieves" (p. 51)
peer down upon his stubborn stance. But his wilful isolation in a fallen
world is as fatally monomaniac as it is heroic. The lawyer calls his
prison death a sleep "in the heart of the eternal pyramids" (p. 53),
but the image of royalty eternally and splendidly entombed is still
an image of death. Between the thick and gloomy walls of "Egyptian
... masonry," Bartleby will not acknowledge his fellowship with the
green grass, the "soft imprisoned turf ... under foot" (p. 53). Denying
his bond with nature as with man, he dies, insisting till the end on the
solitariness of his imprisonment — literally, an imprisonment for life.
Similar imagery of pyramid, prison, and grave in *Moby-Dick* and
*Pierre* is tied to the idea that the center of life is a void. Ahab's "Egyptian chest" (p. 182) is obsessively held by the whale's "pyramidical
white hump" (p. 180), although he feels there may be "naught beyond" its mask-wall. "I do not think that any sensation lurks in it"
(p. 335), says Ishmael of Moby Dick's head. The Mount of the Titans
in *Pierre* — the Delectable Mountain no more — is "the Cheopian

pyramid itself," fronting "disordered rows of broken Sphinxes" (p. 404). In another compendious image in *Pierre*, the core of a world that consists of nothing but "superinduced superficies" and the heart of man coalesce in the "central room" of the "pyramid": "with joy we espy the sarcophagus; but we lift the lid — and no body is there! — appallingly vacant as vast is the soul of a man" (p. 335).

The encounter of man and whale in *Moby-Dick* is a clash of active forces, but in *Pierre* and "Bartleby" the analogous images are of deadlock or stalemate: rock facing mountain, a prisoner facing walls. The questing hero of *Moby-Dick*, quiet in "Bartleby," is already quiescent in *Pierre*. Perplexed by ambiguity, Pierre, self-styled "fool of Truth, fool of Virtue, fool of Fate" (p. 422), ends by disavowing both Lucy and Isabel: "Away! — Good Angel and Bad Angel both, — for Pierre is neuter now!" (p. 425). The melodramatic rhetoric cannot obscure the imagistic connection between the novel and the shorter fictions that followed, in which quiescence has become stasis (cf. Israel Potter's "fifty years of exile" and the structure of repetition in *The Confidence Man*), and language states and implies rather than gestures heroically. Incommunicative, inert, passive, without attachments, desires, or ambition, Bartleby is the completely asocial individual. He has no personality, if by personality we mean the form in which the self offers itself to other selves. Bartleby's repudiation of the sociality which alone makes successful enterprise possible is the main point of the story to the extent that it offers a critical comment on Melville's contemporary America. In "The Encantadas," the ten descriptive sketches of the Galapagos Islands that was the second piece Melville published in *Putnam's Monthly* and which presumably followed "Bartleby" in composition, the islands are the human neuter rendered geographically, Bartleby metamorphosed:

... But the special curse, as one may call it, of the Encantadas, that which exalts them in desolation above Idumea and the Pole, is, that to them change never comes; neither the change of seasons nor of sorrows. Cut by the Equator, they know not autumn, and they know not spring; while already reduced to the lees of fire, ruin itself can work little more upon them. ... However varying their place may seem by reason of the currents, they themselves, at least to one upon the shore, appear invariably the same: fixed, cast, glued into the very body of cadaverous death. ... In no world but a fallen one could such lands exist. ... (pp. 150,151).

Not just the wasteland image of clinkers and lava set in a vast and changing sea, but one of the narrative sketches as well relates to the castaway figures in *Moby-Dick*, *Pierre*, and "Bartleby." Hunilla, the brave Creole widow, alone on Norfolk Island after the death of her husband and her brother,[15] belongs with Pip, Ahab's overthrown humanity; with Ishmael, the shipwrecked outcast; with Bartleby, the derelict in mid Atlantic; and with Israel Potter, accidentally left alone aboard an enemy ship at sea. All are "exalted" in their "desolation," and all are passive sufferers in the "appalling ocean" that Ishmael says surrounds man's soul (p. 274). Etymology connects his phrase with the pallor which Bartleby has in common with Vivia, the seeker-hero of Pierre's abortive, autobiographical novel (p. 356). Like Moby Dick's, their colorlessness suggests nothingness. "The palsied universe lies before us a leper," says Ismael (p. 194). "Appalling is the soul of man!" cries the author of *Pierre* in another echo of *Moby-Dick*. "Better might one be pushed off into the material spaces beyond the uttermost orbit of the sun, than once feel himself fairly afloat in himself!" (p. 335). The image is of man forlorn in a blank ocean vastness, the empty microcosm of his own consciousness. It is an image of fearful solipsism: reality is in the deep stretches of the mind.

Light-darkness antitheses link *Pierre*, "Bartleby," and "The Encantadas" in a sequence of responses to ambivalence. In this sequence Bartleby's neutrality marks a dead center between moral polarities. The possibility that vice and virtue are indistinguishable or even one is intolerable to Pierre. Neuter, the idealist turns nihilist. The author of "The Encantadas," on the other hand, sees in the two-sided Galapagos tortoise an emblem of dualism: "... even the tortoise, dark and melancholy as it is upon the back, still possesses a bright side; its calipee or breastplate being sometimes of a faint yellowish or golden tinge" (p. 154). Although in its "natural position" its "livelier aspect" is hidden and its "darker" exposed, there is a lesson for man in its two-sidedness. "Consider the vacillations of a man," the reader is admonished in another sketch. The Buccaneers who "robbed and murdered one day, revelled the next, and rested themselves by turning meditative philosophers, rural poets, and seat-builders on the third" (p. 174). Between Pierre and the Encantadas traveller there is Bartleby, who neither rages in exasperation against, nor, serene and mordant, philosophizes about, man's various, multitudinous soul. And no tortoise lesson can benefit the employer in his dealings with the monadic clerk, whose singlemindedness is a protest against the ambiguous variousness of being. The pivotal figure in the office enclosed by white and black walls and run by the Turkey-Nippers see-saw is forever neuter. The victim of blank inscrutability is himself blankly inscrutable. Ambivalent, he occupies, as it were, both sides of the antithesis of man and (in Ishmael's phrase) "the heartless voids and immensities of the universe" (p. 193).

Rage or acceptance? Ahab or Starbuck? The choice would be easier if there were not a Bulkington side to Ahab's quest and if Starbuck's submission to Christian orthodoxy were not touched — like the lawyer's in "Bartleby" — with unheroic prudence and compromise, and if Starbuck himself, by virtue of his position on board, were not associated with the complacent equanimity and insensitive materialism of his fellow mates, Stubb and Flask, respectively. A detail of recurrent imagery illuminates the contrast. Stubb and Ahab are both pipe-smokers, but while Stubb remains one till the end, Ahab, on a day early in the quest, flings his still lighted pipe into the sea in a gesture of serenity repudiated. "Thunderstruck" once by Bartleby's unexpected presence in the office, the lawyer recalls the hapless Virginian, another pipe-smoker, and, like Ahab, victim of a sudden, searing encounter with the absolute (p. 41).

To remain unaware of life's riddles, like Flask, or to ignore them, like Stubb, or to resign oneself to them in pious acceptance, like Starbuck, is in all cases to earn a measure of serenity in the midst of mortal peril but at the price of truth. To challenge inscrutability is either to pursue truth even unto damnation only to realize, like Pierre, its "everlasting elusiveness" (p. 399), or, like Bartleby, to retire, silent and unseeing, within walls that provoke, isolate, and imprison. In the Tombs, the green of the screen that separates Bartleby from the others in the office has become the "gloom" of brick walls. This statement of man's antinomic dilemma does not make room for the ambiguities of the lawyer-narrator's position in "Bartleby" or for those of Ishmael's in *Moby-Dick* (his loyalty to Ahab, his friendship with Queequeg, his final sea rescue by the bereft *Rachel*). But it will serve to suggest the values that are in critical equilibrium in Ishmael's two linked equations. There are, he says, a "wisdom that is woe" and a "woe that is madness" (p. 423). In *Moby-Dick*, the issue is between land and ocean. In *Pierre*, the same issue is symbolized by the two flowers that grow on the mountainside near Saddle Meadows: "the catnip and the amaranth! — man's earthly household peace, the ever-encroaching appetite for God" (p. 405). Pierre himself defines it as "the possible reconcilement of this world with our souls" (p. 244) — a reconcilement which his ambiguous career proves *im*possible. In "The Encantadas," the "crowning curse" of the tortoise is its "drudging impulse to straightforwardness in a belittered world" (p. 156). There is grim irony in the fact that the animal's hopeless impulse can be checked only by rendering it immobile, in effect, consigning it to starve: it is only when it is turned over on its back that the tortoise exposes its bright side. The streets of London, "the City of Dis," in which Israel Potter for years ekes out a miserable existence, are likened to "the vitreous rocks in the cursed Galapagos, over which the convict tortoises crawl."[16] Bartleby is Wall Street's drudge, but, like the Encantadas tortoise's, his drudgery "crowns" him: in death he is asleep with kings. His employer's practical dilemma is that he is caught between irreconcilables: belittered Wall Street and straightforward scrivener.

But the most explicit passage in all Melville on the ethics of existential antinomy is the Plinlimmon pamphlet in *Pierre* on chronometrical and horological time. Pierre happens to find the pamphlet in the seat of the coach that carries him and Isabel from Saddle Meadows to New York. He reads it while they pass through "an almost unploughed and uninhabited region," in order — the irony is obtrusive — "to force his mind away from the dark realities of things" (p. 243). Plinlimmon's argument, in brief, is that a conduct of life by the imperative absolutes of chronometrical time amounts to "a sort of suicide as to the practical things of the world" (p. 250), and that so far from straying from Christ's teaching, the "virtuous expediency" (p. 252) of the worldly moralist who prudently trims his sails to the changing winds proves that the chronometrical man has not sufficiently heeded the Savior's warning to us horologicals that His kingdom is not of this world. In heaven, only, can man "freely turn the left cheek, because there the right cheek will never be smitten" (p. 252).

The acidity of that last sentence justifies Lawrance Thompson's scorn for commentators who have taken Plinlimmon to be Melville's spokesman in saying that Christ's message is to condemn man's "appetite for God." But Thompson himself misses the point of the pamphlet when he sees in it only a parody of "the shallow Christian doctrine of Mrs. Glendinning and Mr. Falsgrave."[17]

Plinlimmon himself is described as part Apollo, part "old Saturn." The "something latently visible" which repels in his visage "may best be described as non-Benevolence. Non-Benevolence seems the best word, for it was neither Malice nor Ill-Will; but something passive. To crown all, a certain floating atmosphere seemed to invest and go along with the man. That atmosphere seems only renderable in words by the term Inscrutableness" (p. 341). Plinlimmon — neutral, passive, crowned, afloat, inscrutable, emanating non-benevolence — is an early Bartleby, Bartleby in the role of callous philosopher. The title of his pamphlet is the Greek word for "if" ("EI"), and "if" is the word on which the fragment teasingly ends. His first name, Plotinus, suggests an idealist non-corporeality that is amusingly incongruous with his second name, that of a Welsh mountain. In Thomas Gray's Pindaric ode, "The Bard," the title character recalls "Modred, whose magic song/ Made huge Plinlimmon bow his cloud-topped head." The allusion is ironic. Unlike his mountain namesake in the poem, Plotinus Plinlimmon, also "cloud-topped," as far as Pierre is concerned, in the Olympian inscrutability of both his appearance and his philosophy, no more bows to the sky-assaulting Pierre than the Mount of the Titans bows to Enceladus in Pierre's autobiographical dream. *Pierre* is dedicated to Mt. Greylock, and in "The Piazza," the relativist fable that Melville put at the beginning of the *Piazza Tales*, Greylock is both the scene and the instrument of the narrator's and the girl Marianna's mutual illusion.

It would seem as if Melville in the early 1850's repeatedly cast his protagonists in the role of ineffectual bards whose quests for ultimates are defeated by walls of flesh or stone: Ahab's poetic bent and powers are manifest, Pierre and Bartleby's employer are both authors of narrative prose, and Bartleby himself is a "scrivener." Ahab "piled" "all the general rage and hate felt by his whole race from Adam down" upon Moby-Dick, the incarnation, to him, of "all that most maddens and torments: all that stirs up the lees of things; all truth with malice in it; all that cracks the sinews and cakes the brain; all the subtle demonisms of life and thought; all evil" (p. 181). Their quests alienate Ahab and Pierre from conventional Christianity and finally from all human fellowship. In their frustration they turn to murderous rage. Once, at least, Bartleby's employer is almost of their company. On a certain occasion, "in a solitary office, up stairs of a building entirely unhallowed by humanizing domestic associations," he is restrained only by the Christian injunction of neighborly love from laying hands on the exasperating Bartleby and perhaps killing him, as "the unfortunate Colt" had killed "the unfortunate Adam" (p. 43). To reject pity is to reject human kind, and the stronger the pity proffered, the more intolerable the rejection. It is precisely in the man of "fellow feeling" that absolute non-response prompts violence.

The philosophical relativism with which Plinlimmon's inscrutability is made synonymous cannot be readily identified with the abstracts imaged by Moby Dick's whiteness (leprous or blank or holy or innocent), with Pierre's "ambiguities," or with Bartleby's non-response. Rather, the double standard of the Plinlimmonian ethic is a descant, part mocking, part stoically prudent, on the wisdom-woe-madness triad in *Moby Dick*; it expounds the theory to which the impossible plot of *Pierre* failed to give adequate fictional substance; and it offers a clue to "Bartleby" as the tragi-comedy of a chronometrical individual in a horological world. At the end of the story, the lawyer-narrator's worldly, horological wisdom shares in the woe of Bartleby's mad, chronometrical isolation. We find a similar antinomy in the later fictions. The two-sided Galapagos tortoise, "both black and bright" (p. 155), is an image of dualism. Captain Delano, another good-natured, limited Everyman, cannot in the end rescue Benito Cereno from the blighting, chronometrical memory of "the Negro." The confidence man's professions of charity, the greatest of chronometrical virtues, is a cozening device against an April Fool's crowd of horologicals of "no trust." The moment Billy Budd has felled Claggart, Captain Vere knows: "Struck dead by the angel of God. Yet the angel must hang!" White-Jacket's resignation to the fact of brutal injustice on board a man-of-war has in Vere become tragic wisdom, woe beyond madness. At "the last Assizes" Billy will be acquitted, but "how here?" "We proceed," Vere reminds the drum court that hears Billy's case, "under the law of the Mutiny Act."

## IV

In his heroic phase, Melville plotted Promethean assaults on a universe which, keeping its secrets, provoked high-minded idealists of truth and justice to rebellion or despair. In the *Piazza Tales*,[18] rebellion, with one exception, has become passive suffering. The exception is the last of the tales, the Hawthornian "The Bell-Tower," in which the "unblest foundling" Bannadonna, for whom "common sense was theurgy; machinery, miracle; Prometheus, the heroic name for machinist; man, the true God" (p. 220), is killed by his creature, the shrouded robot Talus, whose name is that of Artegall's iron instrument of justice in *The Fairie Queene*, V. Bannadonna is an arrogant technician and rationalist, a forerunner of an industrial civilization. His *hubris* lacks Ahab's and Pierre's metaphysical context and their nobility of aim. His fate, consequently, is hardly felt to be ambivalent. In the other *Piazza Tales*, not assault but illusion is the main narrative image. The human problem is that of being in a world of seeming: Pierre's provocation without his response, gullible and helpless man victimized by the eternal cheat's universal masquerade. The *Piazza Tales* points forward to Melville's next book, *The Confidence Man*.

In "The Piazza," the allusions to Eve, Una, and Titania turn the narrator's ascent to Marianna's hut into an excursion to a fairyland of lost innocence, elusive truth, and enchantment. The girl is named after the ambiguously fated girl in *Measure for Measure*, and the disillusioned narrator leaves her in the company of fleeting shadows, still undeceived about the drab reality of life below. Bartleby retires from a world of uncertain flux to contemplate the only stable reality: walls that confine and conceal. In the shadow of his negative absolutism, his employer discerns the bedrock of human misery that the world's gay glitter hides from view (p. 33). In hardly admitted unease, he vaguely probes the apparent substance of his own existence by way of telling the story of his strange clerk. Behind the surface black-and-white ambiguity of "Benito Cereno" is the bitter irony that Captain Delano is able to liberate Cereno and to save himself only because his open and trusting nature fails to suspect the true state of affairs on board the *San Dominick*. A single gesture betraying suspicion on his part would have been fatal. And his rescue of Cereno is only physical. In "The Lightning-Rod Man," the narrator's fearless stoicism under the threat of the Jovian thunderbolt is in dignified contrast to the craven and superstitious folly of the seller of lightning-rods, who relies on a mechanical device to ward off the visitation from the ultimate powers. Most of the epigraphs for the ten Encantadas sketches are taken from the Cave of Despair and Bower of Acrasia episodes in *The Fairie Queene* (I, 9; II, 12) — properly enough, since despair and guile are recurrent motifs in "The Encantadas." The Galapagos are the *enchanted* islands. Ocean currents deceive sailors as to their true position. There is a ship in these waters said to sail "full of wind in a calm" (p. 171). From afar, Rock Rodondo presents the appearance of a friendly, white sail, but on approach it is found to be a barren, burnt-out land. But here is illusion within illusion. For on these seemingly uninhabitable shores the strangest human dramas have been enacted: Hunilla's brave and pitiful endurance, the anarchy

of the thieves' republic, the depraved and treacherous evil of the Cali-
ban-like hermit Oberlus, the manifold activities of the Buccaneers.
Both man and his lot are various. The tortoise is both black and bright.
As a literary whole, the *Piazza Tales* represents a lessening of creative
energy after *Moby-Dick* and even *Pierre*. For such a small collection,
the pieces are surprisingly — and somewhat unpleasantly — heterogeneous. There are signs of fatigue: a note of relaxation and improvisa-
tion ("The Piazza," "The Lightning-Rod Man"), of imitation ("The
Bell-Tower"), of failure to sustain a narrative scheme ("Benito
Cereno," "The Encantadas"), of jaunty journalese ("The Piazza,"
"The Encantadas"). The very slightness of the whole, however, makes
the connections in theme and imagery between the individual tales
and Melville's previous, major fiction all the more significant. They
reinforce the impression of consistency in all Melville's mature work.

Of the three major tales, only "Bartleby" is successful fiction. The
narrative material in "Benito Cereno" has been awkwardly deployed,
and "The Encantadas," although a work of richer and denser structure than "Benito Cereno" and of frequent beauty and subtlety of
detail, is, by design, discursive travelogue rather than coherent narrative or single symbolic image. The tortoise symbol is its main relevance
to a discussion of antinomy in Melville. The author's attitude to the
tortoise is complex but fixed, a spatial variant of the lawyer's shifting
attitudes to Bartleby's inverted *hubris*. Together, tortoise and scrivener,
both ambivalent, the one as image, the other by the narrator's response to his negation, mark a stage of ironic detachment in Melville's
continuing treatment of man's existential dilemma. From Ahab's
and Pierre's destructive fury against cosmic riddles he moves in
delicate balance between numinous negation and worldly affirmation
in "Bartleby" and between cynicism and faith in *The Confidence Man*
to the tragic quiet in which Billy Budd unquestioningly accepts, and
Captain Vere argues his tortured submission to, the martial law imposed upon man's mutinous existence.

In "Bartleby" Melville deals with the theme of antinomy in terms
of one of the sustaining relationships of a commercial civilization. The
employer is a well-intentioned and prudent bourgeois, representing a
system of law instituted for the protection of property. The employee
is without other social ties than the transient, impersonal, economic one
that he breaks. When the clerk becomes an obsession of the lawyer's
mind, the inversion of the normal order of dependence suggests a variant
of successful romantic rebellion (the lawyer once, in unconscious irony,

contrasts Bartleby and Byron) against a materialist culture whose spirit is only precariously and inadequately nourished by accepted orthodoxies. But the prototypal, two-phased romantic action of alienation and usurpation occurs in a realistic setting. Melville's fable was given him by the socio-economic fact that a single menial of the money society is without power to effect any change in the system that exploits him. By withdrawing, Bartleby personifies the doubts about his pursuits that insinuate themselves into the mind of the new economic man in an officially Christian society. To the extent that the fable of Bartleby and his employer is one of Kant imposing himself upon Locke, it ramifies to involve the whole nineteenth-century crisis of faith.

As artifact, the story is an understatement of the Promethean myth: *Moby-Dick* contracted and de-rhapsodized; *Pierre* divested of the inflated grandeur of plot and rhetoric which Melville's (by then) almost compulsive cynicism continually had embarrassed with mock-heroics. Because the narrator is a distinct, consistently engaged and participating character, as Ishmael fails to be during long stretches of *Moby-Dick* and as the intrusive, overwrought authorial voice of *Pierre* never is, "Bartleby" is a work in which art can be felt to control whatever private agony or anger moved Melville to write. That the smaller compass obviously made such control easier to achieve in the short story than in the novels does not alter the fact of the story's greater integrity of achievement. Grotesque patterns of speech and action emerge from the clash of the inert human isolate with a narrative substance that reflects the busy commonplaces of an acquisitive culture and which is conveyed in a comically self-revealing voice. It is, characteristically, an age of "the absurd" in art and literature that has rediscovered "Bartleby." Behind the innocent surface of a tale of a weird clerk Melville still queries the terms on which man holds life. In "Bartleby," too, he is of the party of the great myth-making pessimists of our tradition: Cervantes, Swift, Flaubert, Ibsen, Kafka.

## NOTES

[1] According to the *PMLA* bibliography, in every year for the last seven, the number of new publications on Melville has either equalled or exceeded 38, the previous peak, reached in 1951 (the year of the *Moby-Dick* centennial).

[2] For the view that *Pierre*, like *Mardi* and *Moby-Dick*, is built around a symbolical journey motif, see Nathalia Wright, "*Pierre*: Herman Melville's *Inferno*," *American Literature*, XXXII (1960), 167–181. In "The Shorter

Fiction of Herman Melville," *South Atlantic Quarterly*, LII (1953), 414–430, Charles G. Hoffman suggests that it was Melville's realization, after *Pierre*, of the structural failure of his novels that caused him to turn to shorter fiction.

3 Jay Leyda, *The Melville Log* (New York, 1951), I, 461.

4 *Ibid.*, pp. 451–542, 454, 457, 461–462, 464.

5 *Ibid.*, pp. 468, 469.

6 *American Renaissance* (New York, 1941), p. 493.

7 *Herman Melville* (Am. Men of Letters series, 1950), pp. 242–243.

8 Leo Marx, "Melville's Parable of the Walls," *Sewanee Review*, LXI (1953), 602–627. John Gardner, " 'Bartleby': Art and Social Commitment," *Philological Quarterly*, XLIII (1964), 87–98.

9 Richard Harter Fogle, "Melville's 'Bartleby': Absolutism, Predestination, and Free Will," *Tulane Studies in English*, IV (1954), 125–135. Kingsley Widmer, "The Affirmative Negation: Melville's 'Bartleby,' " *Modern Fiction Studies*, VIII (1962), 276–286. — Imputing autobiographical intent to Melville, says Fogle, is to make him "guilty of a puerile irony and an elaborate trick," and Widmer huffs that "equating Bartleby with Melville reduces the novella to a trivial and elaborately obscure personal document." This seems excessively puristic. That criticism may dispense with biography is not to say it is adulterated or disgraced by it or that a pluralist approach may not enrich a reading. Widmer's own provocative existentialist view of "Bartleby" neither cancels nor is cancelled by Arvin's version of the biographical view that Lewis Mumford advanced in *Herman Melville* in 1929. In "Bartleby," says Arvin, Melville "announced to those who could understand him

that he would no longer willingly be misemployed" (p. 211).

10 Widmer's and Gardner's essays appeared after Marvin Felheim's brief survey of the "Bartleby" bibliography in "Meaning and Structure in 'Bartleby,' " *College English*, XXIII (1962), 369–370, 375–376. But Felheim's categories were already obsolete. He distinguished among "traditional kinds of treatment in which literary historians search for actual identities [other than Melville himself]" (e.g., Bartleby is a satirical portrait of Thoreau), identifications of Bartleby with Melville himself ("scrivener" equals writer), and — rather unhelpfully — "aesthetic" approaches.

11 All references for quotations from Melville in this article are to the Hendricks House editions: *Piazza Tales*, ed. Egbert S. Oliver (New York, 1948); *Pierre*, ed. Henry A. Murray (New York, 1949); *Moby Dick*, eds. Luther S. Mansfield and Howard P. Vincent (New York, 1952); *The Confidence Man*, ed. Elizabeth S. Foster (New York, 1954).

12 Widmer refers with approval to Mordecai Marcus's note, "Melville's Bartleby as Psychological Double," in *College English*, XXIII (1962), 365–368.

13 Edward H. Rosenberry, *Melville and the Comic Spirit* (Cambridge [Mass.], 1955), p. 145.

14 Though the *Pequod* is perhaps a womb symbol.

15 In Hunilla, says Leon Howard, Melville appears to have laid to rest the ghost of Agatha Robertson (see p. 180, above) (*Herman Melville. A Biography* [Berkeley and Los Angeles, 1951], pp. 210–211). But the motif of innocent and patient endurance of physical hardship and psychological pain is prominent also in *Israel Potter*.

16 *Israel Potter; His Fifty Years of Exile* (London, 1923 [Constable ed.]), p. 212.

17 Lawrance Thompson, *Melville's Quarrel with God* (Princeton, 1952), p. 275.

18 Except for the first tale, "The Piazza," which was written specifically to introduce the collection, the Piazza tales had all first appeared in *Putnam's Monthly*. The dates of their original publication are: "Bartleby," Nov.–Dec., 1853; "The Encantadas," March–May, 1854; "The Lightning-Rod Man," Aug., 1854; "The Bell-Tower," Aug., 1855; "Benito Cereno," Oct.–Dec., 1855. Melville put them in the following order in the collected volume: "The Piazza," "Bartleby," "Benito Cereno," "The Lightning-Rod Man," "The Encantadas," "The Bell-Tower." See Egbert S. Oliver's "Explanatory Notes" in his ed. of the *Piazza Tales*, pp. 225 ff.

This article went to press before the appearance of Norman Springer's "Bartleby and the Terror of Limitation," *PMLA*, LXXX (September, 1965), 410—418; and Herbert F. Smith's "Melville's Master in Chancery and His Recalcitrant Clerk," *American Quarterly*, XVII (Winter, 1965), 734—741. — Springer locates the "terror" of the story in the failure of the narrator's Christian charity to breach the wall of Bartleby's "preference for no thing" and the clue to its artistic control in the reader's awareness of the narrator's limited perception. With this I have no serious quarrel. I only query his suggestion that Melville's story — unlike the lawyer's — intimates an explanation of, or answer to, or remedy for, Bartleby's condition. Smith finds allegorical implications in the legal terminology, particularly in the distinction, connoted by "chancery" (originally a royal court), between 'equity' ("the ideal application of justice") and 'common law' (written law of precedence, relative justice). This is useful, though I don't know why Smith ignores the fact — surely all the more relevant in view of his findings — that the lawyer-narrator is no longer Master in Chancery at the time he tells the story of Bartleby.

# HJALMAR HJORTH BOYESEN:
## OUTER SUCCESS, INNER FAILURE

### By Per E. Seyersted

Modern man experiences many forms of migration. In the course of his journey from youth to old age, he may move from country to town, climb on the social scale, advance through stages of technical development, and drift away from religion. Migratory man is made increasingly aware of his need for roots and continuity and for the sense of belonging to an organic whole. He needs to establish his identity, to define his attitudes towards his environment, and to work out his rôle in life.

Hjalmar Hjorth Boyesen was one of the more than half-million Norwegians who experienced the profound change involved in migration to the United States. In *Giants in the Earth*, O. E. Rølvaag has pointed out two antipodal immigrant types personified by Beret and Per Hansa. While she suffers and dies a spiritual death, he thrives under the alien conditions, and even if he does not escape what Oscar Handlin has called the "shock of alienation," he is a successful builder of an empire. While she is like a "small boat" which should never have left the protection of its native shore, he is a "big boat" that can conquer any unknown sea.

When Boyesen landed in New York in 1869 at the age of twenty, he looked upon himself as a "big boat" destined for success, and, indeed, even though he had to go through nearly all of modern man's migrations, he seemed to strike new roots, to find his identity, and to achieve his aspired goals. At twenty-three he had his first novel accepted by Howells who praised his English. At twenty-five he was made a professor at Cornell. He won the friendship of such Americans as Longfellow, Mark Twain, Howells, and President Cleveland, and of Europeans such as Bjørnstjerne Bjørnson and Turgenev. He published twenty-four books and hundreds of articles before he died in 1895, and achieved considerable fame. He helped make his new countrymen acquainted with Norwegian culture and European realism. He took part in American politics. He married an American. In short, he appeared to have found his rôle and played it well, and to have successfully incorporated his old Norwegian self into his hyphenated American identity.

In his recent biography of Boyesen, Professor Clarence A. Glasrud treats of the author's youth in Norway, his ambition to become a writer in America, and, particularly, his subsequent life there. Examining Boyesen's career and writings in the light of his life and times, the biographer shows that the author was inescapably exposed to certain of the difficulties and drawbacks that face the immigrant. On the whole, however, he represents Boyesen as a person who successfully fused his Norwegian past with his American present and who never "found fault with his father's advice to emigrate."[1]

In respect to Boyesen's authorship, Mr. Glasrud shows how his ambition to become a writer dictated a number of his actions, such as his emigration and his use of English as his only language. What still remains to be done, it seems to the present writer, is to show that Boyesen's vision of his rôle as a poet, which he thought nature had destined him for, shaped not only his actions, but also to a large degree his attitudes. Furthermore, that it was Bjørnson who served as his most important model and touchstone. Finally, that certain events in 1885 and 1891 on the one hand forced Boyesen to realize that he had lost not only his Norwegian roots, but even his identity, and on the other, made him feel that, in spite of his outer success, he had failed to reach the goals he had set up for himself.

Mainly using newly uncovered material, and concentrating on certain crucial events in Boyesen's life, we shall try to support these contentions, and at the same time we shall try, also, to fill in some of the "regrettable omissions" (as Mr. Glasrud calls them) in our knowledge of Boyesen and shed new light on certain of the "unanswered questions" regarding important aspects of his development.

In turning first to the reasons that made Boyesen go to America in 1869, his biographer is mistaken in stating flatly that Boyesen admired his father, Captain Sarolf Boyesen, and that in his childhood and early youth he had been "sheltered from the harsher realities of life."[2] Mrs. Asora Koch, a Norwegian relative of Boyesen who spent some years with Ingolf, his Chicago brother, has been able to put many things in a new light, by information which our two previous informants, Boyesen and his half-sister Austa, for obvious reasons kept to themselves.

The years in Kongsberg were very hard on the whole family after Boyesen's father, then a Lieutenant, had become a Swedenborgian, thereby exposing even his children to ridicule from intolerant neighbors. His wife had to console them and to try to make ends meet, while Sarolf, an idealist and escapist, was largely living in a dream world, constantly visiting Heaven. No wonder that Hjalmar loved his mother who had "balm in her words, healing in her touch," and who "gave and gave, without thought of demanding anything in return," and that he was ambivalent towards his father, feeling ashamed of his irresponsibility, perhaps also his nonconformity, even if, at the same time, he was proud of his stand against Norwegian intolerance.

In 1854 Sarolf sought refuge for a year in America after having sent his family to Judge Hjorth, his wife's adoptive father, at Systrand on the Sognefjord. In the United States the Lieutenant found both the religious and the political freedom of which he had been deprived in Norway; and Hjalmar may in a way have felt that this was a vindication of his father's stand. When the Lieutenant returned to Norway, he re-entered the Army. His wife, meanwhile, knowing that he was less of a support than a burden to his family, decided not to rejoin him.[3]

When children go through a period of rôle-playing, giving free rein to their vivid, romantic imagination and acting out a succession of parts, this is a phase in their normal development. When we see, however, the intensity with which Hjalmar at Systrand imagined that he was destined to play a great part in life, and the fervor with which he worshipped and identified himself with the heroes he saw as models for this rôle, it is difficult not to regard it as in part a compensation for the shame he felt his father had brought on the proud family name. Hjalmar's tutor and Snorre's Norse Royal Sagas had convinced the boy that the descendants of the heroic Vikings were destined to lead the world. "Never shall I forget the thrill of patriotic pride which rippled through me at the consciousness that I belonged to this select and favored race," he told later, and on another occasion added: "I had from the time I was old enough to think at all cast myself for an heroic part in life."[4] His reading and his tutor had also taught him that the gift of song was the greatest and noblest which the gods could

bestow upon man, and from now on his aspiration was to become a
modern skald.[5] When he started to write, he was encouraged by the
blind Mrs. Hjorth who herself had literary ambitions and often made
Hjalmar's sister Christine take dictation in the middle of the night.[6]

At Systrand, Hjalmar acquired "a sense of kinship and closeness
to the soil" and absorbed the local folklore.[7] He was furthermore
influenced by Old Norse literature and by Tegnér's *Frithiofs Saga*.
After Bjørnson's peasant tales began to appear in 1857, however, they
soon became the most important influence of all. A poem in one of
them (*Arne*, 1858) voices the restlessness not uncommon in those
living on the narrow Norwegian fjords:

> Up, heart, up! and away, away!
> Over the mountains high,
> For my courage is young, and my soul will be gay,
> If no longer bound straitly and fettered I stay,
> But seeking yon summit to gain,
> No more beat my wings here in vain.

Boyesen tells us how as a boy he "walked up and down the beach at
Sognefjord, and now murmured, now whispered and now again shouted
this proud verse to the mountains. The world always seemed so
beautiful on the other side."[8] So intensely did Hjalmar identify with the
heroes of the fiction he read that, as he later observed, he regarded life
through the medium of literature, a statement he once elaborated in
this way: "All the things I looked at (girls included) were subject to
some kind of romantic embellishment and glorification... My fancy
played mischief with me and made me honestly see things as they were
not... I 'worked up' the incident..., transposed it into a more effective key. And I did this quite unconsciously."[9]

Some years after the death of his mother in 1859, Hjalmar confided
to his father (who had now become a Captain) the "glorious secret"
that he was a poet. Telling him that Norway was too small to make
authorship profitable and that his writings were nothing beyond the
ordinary anyway, the Captain robbed the boy of his belief that he should
succeed as a poet. "I took the matter deeply to heart," Boyesen later
said. "It was desperately hard to come down from the pedestal of my
fancied greatness and take my place in the ranks of ordinary humanity
... and the chagrin... of being consigned to the crowd of 'citizens'
who shout as the hero goes by was more poignant than any emotion
I have ever experienced... In spite of my discouragement, however,

14

I could not keep from writing. . . I no longer fancied I was producing masterpieces, but was merely seeking relief for an overburdened heart." What burdened him was the gulf between ambition and achievement. Part of him could not give up the idea that he was destined to become a great skald. And the Captain had added something which could only fire the boy's ambition while making the rôle even more impossible to fill. "A poet," his father said, "must be inspired by the consciousness of addressing a large number of his fellow-men, if he would rise above the petty concerns of the hour and really speak what would have a high human worth, a resonance that should come down through the succeeding ages."[10]

Around the time when Hjalmar began his studies at the University of Christiania (1867), it became evident that a brother-in-law of Sarolf had so completely mismanaged Hovin, the large family estate to which Sarolf was a co-heir, that it would have to be sold at auction.[11] This was a hard blow to the Boyesens. There would be no inheritance, and "the family name would no longer stand for pre-eminence. . ." This is Boyesen's expression about another family whose members, in somewhat similar circumstances, chose to emigrate to the United States rather than face the loss of prestige.[12] Such drastic measures were not uncommon at the time. For instance, in 1886 Boyesen's patrician friend, the Norwegian author Alexander Kielland, who was just experiencing the effects of a financial debacle, told him that he would rather go to America than stay at home under such degrading circumstances.[13] As for Hjalmar, a photograph of him taken at this time gives the impression, as we would expect, of a sensitive and ambitious young man. However, his face also shows something dissatisfied and defiant, something supercilious and insecure, qualities that also seem to have characterized him when he occasionally took part in student discussions.[14]

If the Hovin disaster gave Hjalmar the first incentive to emigrate to America, the second certainly was his father's remarks when in 1868 they again discussed the literary aspirations of his son. The Captain once more questioned whether the young poet would have anything to say worth listening to. But then he went on to suggest that Hjalmar should break loose from small and intolerant Norway while he was still young and capable of adapting himself to changed conditions, and that before settling down he should see America where the Captain had deposited some money and where there was "a far greater future" in store for a man with Hjalmar's education and talents.

The Captain ended with these words: "If, then, you prove yourself strong enough to conquer a new language, and make it so perfectly your own that you can mold and bend it to your will, then I shall believe in your literary aspirations, and not until then." Just as Hjalmar's attitude towards his father was still ambivalent, the Captain's reactions to his literary aspirations were once more two-sided. While on the one hand he again shook his son's belief that he was destined to become a great poet, he on the other made him envisage the rôle of someone speaking to a world audience. His statement, as Boyesen has told us, remained with him ever after.[15]

Hjalmar had just then obtained his General Education (or *Examen Philosophicum*) degree, and he now had to decide whether or not to go on for graduate studies. It therefore seems very probable that the decision to go to the United States was taken at this time. Apparently neither the Captain nor his son heeded the advice of A. T. Boyesen, Sarolf's brother, a Swedenborgian minister who had worked in America. In a guide-book for Norwegian emigrants to the United States, published in 1868, this relative stated that adaptation to foreign conditions demanded a considerable effort, and that those who lived under reasonably favorable conditions in Norway undoubtedly were better off staying in their native country.[16]

We know that in 1869 a scandal erupted in the Boyesen family: according to Mrs. Koch, the Captain lived with his housekeeper and did not bother to marry her until some time after she had born their first child, and as a result he was dishonorably discharged from the Army.[17] Norway was a small country, and the news became common gossip. When we consider that Hjalmar was the epitome of correctness (perhaps in an effort to offset a tendency at times to be irresponsible), we are not surprised that he, as Mrs. Koch informs us, was ashamed of his father, felt contempt for him and described him to Ingolf as unfit "for every occupation & use in this life."[18] And yet he was loyal, too. When the ex-Captain after eight very lean years descended with his rapidly growing family upon Hjalmar in America, the kind son bought a farm for them.

This information no longer allows us to consider Hjalmar's emigration to have been entirely voluntary. To be sure, the main reason behind his going to America was his desire to try out the idea the Captain had instilled in him of learning English and adressing a world audience. But it is equally certain that he was unhappy about the shame and loss of prestige that had been brought on his family.

This situation probably made him see emigration as the only course out of uncomfortable conditions, and subconsciously to envisage a possible success in America as a vindication of Norwegian setbacks. It also made him think less favorably of Norway while "working up" America as a contrast, with its religious and political freedom and social and economic opportunities. Seen in this light, Boyesen would appear to have had more than the average immigrant's share of reasons to speak well of his new country and to justify his emigration.

Boyesen started on his literary career in America the year after he arrived. Intending to use Norwegian literature as a vehicle for his ambition, he always carried with him some of its best specimens. He made it the subject of his 1872 Urbana Commencement Address, and his novel *Gunnar* was so heavily indebted to Bjørnson that, as Boyesen later confessed to him, it "would not exist had you never written."[19] At the same time he turned away from all contact with his countrymen and every use of his native language. "It was clear to me," he wrote, "that if I were ever to use English with that finer sense of the color and individuality of the language I would have to cease to be bilingual. I would ... substitute it for my mother tongue; I would make it the natural medium of my speech and thoughts."[20] Driven by an ambition which kept him "awake night after night like a fine melody that haunts your ear," he pursued this program with vigor in spite of homesickness and poor health (his sleepless nights had begun to tell).[21]

Initially, he suffered inevitable literary frustrations. The editor Howells very often had to turn his writings down; such defeats reminded Boyesen of the uncomfortable gulf between his ambition and his performance and made him vacillate painfully between dejection and great aspirations and dreams.[22] But his "trust in Providence," as he termed it to Ingolf, was rewarded in March, 1873, when Longfellow praised his poems and Howells assured him that his "power" and "genius" made his American future certain.[23] This Boyesen saw as a confirmation of his idea that he was really destined to play a great rôle. It made him forget whatever thoughts he may have harbored of giving up the fight against heavy American odds and swallowing the bitter pill of returning to Norway.

His soaring ambition soon became apparent. Boyesen's motive for making a trip to Europe in 1873 was not, as Mr. Glasrud suggests, to visit his family. The journey turned out the way it was planned, that is, as a literary pilgrimage. When he had been appointed a professor at Cornell in April, 1873, and had obtained a half year's leave of absence, ostensibly to study in Germany, he lost no time in preparing for the real purpose of his trip which was to gather material for his literary activities in a wider field. His decision to spend a year abroad was made prior to the Cornell appointment: "My whole future depends ... upon this European trip," he had then told Ingolf.[24] He planned to make notes of people and places, much in the way he had done during his 1867 walking tour of Norway. Furthermore, he intended to advertise American literature in the Old World. But above all, he wanted to meet the literary great of Europe. Among the letters of introduction he solicited was one to Bjørnson, whom he characterized as "Norway's greatest man in the 19th century."[25]

Many would agree with this evaluation by Boyesen. As a poet, novelist, and dramatist, Bjørnson was in his time as highly regarded as the contemporary Ibsen. Being furthermore Norway's foremost fighter for political and religious freedom, he was, in fact, a modern skald, the very personification of everything Hjalmar admired in the Viking heritage. Thus he was bound to become the special hero with whom the aspiring author wanted to identify himself. It was Bjørnson's poem that as a boy he declaimed to the mountains. It was Bjørnson's tales that served as a model for *Gunnar;* and it was Bjørnson's gospel that he preached to Howells (as the latter has told us). Bjørnson is "the man I most truly love and revere," Boyesen wrote to R. B. Anderson on May 29, 1873. He had met his idol briefly while a student in Christiania. Now he looked forward to meeting him as a fellow author.[26]

Bjørnson was a man who demanded much of his friends: they had to understand, revere, support and obey him, and they had to be outstanding in their field. On his side, he could develop an overwhelming enthusiasm for someone he liked (only to drop the person later).[27] Boyesen met these requirements on all points. He had for years identified himself with both the man and his writings. He was an enthusiast who was longing to render homage to his hero. And the master, it turned out, had followed and been impressed by his own doings in America. When we add these facts to our general knowledge of Bjørnson, we may safely assume that Boyesen did not exaggerate when he told Ingolf that Bjørnson hailed him as a brother poet and treated him accordingly.[28]

Boyesen's 1873 diary has recently come to light, but unfortunately, the part which probably covered his meeting with Bjørnson is lost.

From other sources, however, we can make out that the two men spent five days in each other's company. They met in Christiania on August 18, 1873, and went together the following day to Bø in Gausdal, a valley in the Gudbrandsdal region, where Bjørnson invited Boyesen to join him as a speaker at a "grand Republican meeting" on the 21st.[29] In a letter to Howells, Boyesen tells how, during those days, he became "very intimately acquainted with Bjørnson," who gave him the monopoly of translating him into English with these flattering words: "You are the first translator or critic who has ever rendered & understood the spirit of my writings!"

After they had "made a kind of covenant of life long friendship," Bjørnson added: "When you shall be betrothed, then ask your beloved if she will come & stay with me & my family for half a year or as long as she may wish. I want the privilege of giving her the great impression of our Norse life." Thinking of "what significance such an acquaintance & the daily intercourse with such a man must have been to [him]," Boyesen said that from a "literary point of view" the experience had been "invaluable."[30]

This reference to the literary significance of the meeting with Bjørnson leads us to the question: to what degree are Boyesen's writings autobiographical? He once stated that it was impossible for him to write without having a real topography in his mind.[31] We saw that he contemplated the world through literature and often made literature of his life. He turned most of his meetings with great authors into articles. Many of the personal incidents and reflections in his 1873 diary are lifted almost bodily into his fiction.

It was therefore likely that Boyesen would use his momentous meeting with Bjørnson in his imaginative writing. And in the story "A Child of the Age" he does precisely that. The Norwegian Herluf Gamborg, the son of a conservative judge, is inspired by a republican speech given by the visiting Bjørnson; and what had been his "vague, youthful enthusiasm for great, but half-comprehended ideas" is now turned towards "definite purposes rationally conceived." He joins Bjørnson on the platform: "And [as] Herluf spoke ... his ... thoughts ... tumbled forward ... and the world, as it lay shimmering at his feet, seemed an ocean of light." "He felt, what had been a mere empty phrase to him before, that he was a Norseman. He walked about with Bjørnson, and talked with him as he had never talked with any man before; for he had never before known the happiness of being completely understood. He laid his soul bare before him, and went away with a new strength and thrust throbbing through his being. He knew now a man cast in the heroic mold — a poet, a prophet, a warrior."[32]

We have, unfortunately, no comments from the great Norwegian on this meeting with Boyesen. If we judge from Bjørnson's recorded praise of him after their next encounter, however, there is every reason to believe that Boyesen's accounts of their meeting in 1873 are basically true, and that Bjørnson took to him just as warmly as Howells had done and Turgenev was to do. Such an overwelming reception might have turned the head of any aspiring author. Like Herluf Gamborg Boyesen probably bared his soul to Bjørnson and confided to him his hopes and aspirations, which his older and more realistic colleague helped turn from a "vague enthusiasm" towards more "definite purposes rationally conceived." Boyesen thus described his friend to Howells: "There is something so grand & so overpowering in the whole man, — he is a living Saga." To Ingolf he was much more outspoken: "I have never in my life met a man who has impressed me as being greater than Bjørnson. He is a Poet in all his life & there is no more glorious calling under the sun than that of a Poet, when he understands & fills his office like him," — and this included, in Boyesen's words, being a leader of men and a great citizen deeply interested in all public concerns.[33]

There can be little doubt that Bjørnson emerged from these five days as Boyesen's ideal of a modern skald. When Mr. Glasrud states that "after Boyesen's meeting with Turgenev, other events of the European tour faded into the background," he underrates the importance and lasting effects of the encounter with Bjørnson.[34] We should not be deceived by the fact that Boyesen was more ready to acknowledge publicly his indebtedness to Turgenev than that to Bjørnson (except in the case of *Gunnar*). His relationship with Turgenev, like that with Howells, was happy and quiet; there was nothing to hide. The faithful Russian never denied him his friendship and encouragement, and Boyesen repaid it with warm admiration of both the man and his creed and writings. The connection with the unreliable Bjørnson was different. It turned out to be a stormy one, in which Boyesen on a few occasions was met with extreme warmth only to be left in the cold for most of the time. As his letters show, he nevertheless continued to worship his unpredictable hero, whom he imagined had blessed his American venture, and to hunger for the least sign of his friendship and encouragement. But the relationship remained tense and delicate. It was too important to Boyesen, too intimately connected with his secret ambitions, and too fragile to be manifested to the public with his usual openness.

The overwhelming Bjørnson — Europe's first orator and an irresistable chieftain, as Boyesen described him — on the one hand fired his dreams and ambitions to their highest pitch and awakened him to what he thought were his potentialities. On the other he presented to him a model and touchstone for his future activities.[35] Boyesen could now see before him the rôle of a Norwegian-American skald and how he was to embody its poet-prophet-warrior aspects. As a poet, he would go on singing of his beautiful Norway. As a prophet, he would bring Norway's incomparable culture, particularly the works of his hero, to the knowledge of the United States, where they could marry with the incomparable opportunities of that country. And through his children he would let America benefit from his select Viking blood. As a warrior, he would fight for freedom and progress, and particularly win American support for Norway in its struggle for political and religious liberty.

We do not know what Bjørnson thought of Boyesen's literary potentialities. But it is very likely that he expected him to be useful both as a translator of his own works and as an unofficial ambassador of Norway who, together with R. B. Anderson, would explain to the Americans the country's desire to diminish the Swedish influence in their land. (The official ambassador of the two sister-countries was usually a Swede). Boyesen, for his part, was convinced that the master who had received him so warmly shared his belief in a great future; and he felt more justified than ever in his views on Norway, America and emigration. Norway, beautiful but backward, afforded no scope for his gifts, while America, the country of freedom and opportunities, would yield him the success due to him. Covering the period from August 22 to September 23, the last part of the 1873 diary shows Boyesen to be reassured that he is on the road to greatness. Seeing a parsonage on his way to the Hjorths (who now lived in Christiansand) and recalling that some of his fellow students at home had aspired to become parsons, he comments: "Ah, what an humble lot, what modest aspirations! No, where happiness should thrive, there the pulsebeats of the great life of the world must be felt, & one must be conscious that one's life & deeds exert their influence in wide & ever widening circles."

Even though Norway could not give him the great life, there were sides of it that appealed to him: "Ah beautiful is Norway & it is a great gift of heaven to be a Norseman! ... Among these mountains I have found back [sic] my old self, such as it was in the days long gone by. I am almost a boy again & feel an absurd inclination to do & say boyish things." To this he added: "And still I am grave too, & happy in thinking of the fair future which God has unfolded before me." Norway's most important function was to provide him with literary material: "It is so strange to be looking upon Norway in this, as it were, outside way as a mere observer who is to make use of his experiences in the future ... [with the] expectation of gain." The diary shows him indeed mostly as a rather unfeeling foreigner in quest of literary material. Sensing, however, that this attitude was a little callous, he immediately adds: "But I am a patriot nevertheless & the future shall prove it."

The love bestowed upon him by the Hjorths made him realize for a moment that he might feel homesickness in America: "There is nothing like home. Ah, if I could but take it & transplant it bodily [sic] on American soil." And in a rare show of humility he added: "All the past bursts upon me ... My voluntary exile [lets me] feel the value of what in my youthful arrogance [I have] thrown away." But the moment he recalled the great part he was to play, such thoughts vanished, and declaring himself an American, he returned to an unfeeling and somewhat condescending attitude. After reporting the Judge's farewell speech for his grandson whom he feared he would never see again, Boyesen comments: "Would do admirably in a story." The diary quotes his reply to this speech: "I do not regret my choice ... There are those things in life that to a man are more precious than love and domestic happiness." As we see, he thought he could do without his Norwegian roots, and when he boarded the steamer for Denmark on September 6, he felt a sense of relief through being "once more free & roaming about the world at pleasure."

Though Boyesen wrote so self-confidently about his Norse patriotism, it nevertheless represented a problem. Having visited St. John's College in Cambridge in July, 1873, he wrote in his diary: "Wished for a moment that I had been born in England and had passed my college years in the shade of these venerable Gothic buildings, but in the next moment, felt the more strongly my pride as a *Norseman* and felt ashamed of my wish." And on his return from Europe he wrote to R. B. Anderson: "My stay in France and Germany made me feel quite cosmopolitan and I was half inclined to repudiate my nationality. Now I have happily got over this disagreeable state and I am once more myself. You know it would be a misfortune to me in more than one respect, if I should lose the national stamp which nature has pressed upon my heart and upon my forehead. It would dissipate my energies which are now all concentrated on one thing and it would probably put a stop to my literary career."[36]

In such words we realize that Boyesen saw his literary career as largely dependent upon his being a Norwegian and introducing to his American readers a country that was new to them. But it is hard to believe in the depth and genuineness of his Norse feelings when in the course of half a year he could be thus affected by three different countries. It would seem that the cosmopolitan Boyesen's deepest loyalty, or patriotism, was reserved for the dream of his own greatness, and that he would have put on any national mask and "worked up" any patriotism that appeared to serve his self-aggrandizement and promise him success. A statement in a letter he wrote from Leipzig to Professor Willard Fiske suggests the interdependence of his literary ambitions and his Americanism: "I am ... yearning for the resumption of my literary efforts. I never ... felt more passionately American than I do at present."[37]

In another respect, also, did he look forward to his future ties with America. While on his way to Christiansand he had imagined himself the hero of a poem where "some indefinite, ideal American girl ... was with [him] & understood [him] and could share the charm of the hour." In Leipzig he penned this sigh: "[I am] still as lonely as I was ever: & have not even a distant prospect of marriage. I confess I would give anything in my possession to find a woman whom I could love, as I wish to love; even if the love was unreturned, I should not regret it; for it warms one up [sic], it makes one generous, unselfish & warm-hearted, & I am dreadfully afraid that I am in a good way to lose that *immediateness* (or primitivity) of feeling which has always been my best treasure."[38]

Upon his return to America, Boyesen was to write *A Norseman's Pilgrimage* where we meet an example of such an ideal American girl. Olaf Varberg, a successful Norwegian-American author, spends a summer back home with his Norwegian grandparents together with Ruth Copley, his American girl-friend, whom he compares to the Norwegian Thora Haraldson. To Olaf, the blue-eyed, child-like and insignificant Thora represents the "peaceful, simple life of the North, with its small aims and cares, its domestic virtues, and its calm, idyllic beauty. Love to her means duty and a gentle submissiveness." Ruth, on the other hand, is a dark-eyed, brilliant and magnificent beauty whom it somehow seems a privilege to be allowed to worship. In her "bosom lives a world of slumbering tumult, a host of glorious possibilities, which ... will one day ... develop all the emotional wealth and grandeur of perfect womanhood." "She is the flower of a larger and intenser civilization," Olaf tells himself, "and it is my own future which I love in her".

Much more in this novel is taken from Boyesen's life than the first chapter which he himself owned to be autobiographical. The Margaret and Faust-episode, for instance, is copied from a Leipzig incident described in his diary. It is fairly certain, therefore, that Olaf stands for Boyesen himself when it is said of him that his head was constantly filled with possible plots for novels and that he felt an "irresponsible ... desire to ... act out the plot, and carry out the illusion to its last consequences."[39] When the young author shortly thereafter met Turgenev in Paris, the effect of the meeting was not so much to make him a realist (Turgenev later termed him an incurable romantic), but rather to make him want even more to act out the romantic plot of the great part he thought was his.[40] Turgenev unwittingly pushed him in this direction by receiving him warmly, by presenting to him an example of a successful author in voluntary exile, and by confirming Boyesen's belief in American possibilities for success when he said that to him the charm of American institutions had "always been in the fact that they offer the widest scope for individual development."[41]

On his return to America, Boyesen received letters from Howells and Turgenev with statements which seemed to justify his high ambitions. "I shall expect high things from you," Howells wrote to him in January, 1874, and the next year even: "I believe you have the genius of Bjørnson." "I will follow with great interest every step of yours in the literary career now opening before you," Turgenev wrote a month later.[42] Bjørnson was the only one of his mentors to remain silent, but he did send *Redaktøren*, a drama he was just bringing out. On August 28, 1874, Boyesen wrote him that he had tried to find a publisher for the play he was now translating, and he added: "It was a great moment in my life when I met you, and your words, printed or spoken, contain a force which lifts and fills me ... And your drama ... filled me once more with the same fiery aspiration which I felt that memorable day in Gudbrandsdal, a yearning for a more active life, a longing to step forward into the foremost battle-line and speak my piece." He ended with these words: "Thanking you for what you gave, and hoping for a closer association in the future, I remain, your friend Hjalmar H. Boyesen."

Bjørnson answered a month later, and the letter must have been most unexpected. Bjørnson expressed his irritation that Boyesen had tried to have his play published. All he had wanted was to have it translated. And for this piece of work the young Norwegian, whom Howells was to term a "philological genius," was now ordered to seek the aid of a native American. Moreover, Bjørnson did not deign to comment upon *Gunnar*, which Boyesen had recently sent him in book-form.

This cold letter from a man who in Boyesen's imagination loved him warmly, must have been a terrible disappointment to him. Even though it could not diminish his own love for his hero, he did not dare approach him again until November 20, 1876. Writing to him then on behalf of *Scribner's* who wanted a contribution, he added these personal remarks: "I have written a number of reviews of your books in American magazines, but because of your silence I did not feel sure you would want to see them ... Your strong words at our last meeting still live in my memory, and even reconcile me with the thought that our personal friendship perhaps has been broken. But I hope you will forgive me if I have in any way offended you. You can never efface the impression your strong personality and your powerful voice have made on me, and I am therefore confident in the hope that we will meet once more as friends. Your ever grateful countryman Hjalmar H. Boyesen."

The fact that Bjørnson did not answer this letter and never sent him any further books for translation could only increase Boyesen's desire to step into a real "battle-line," such as New York or Boston, where he could prove that his own high hopes and Bjørnson's praise of him in 1873 had been warranted. "I feel that there are possibilities within me which must in time bloom forth into a larger & freer reality, into some achievement which shall show that my aspirations have been something more than a youthful delusion," he wrote to Longfellow when in 1877 he had heard the rumor of a Harvard vacancy and was enlisting the poet's help. "From my early boyhood I have had but one hope, one passion ... [to be] a man of letters." He looked forward, he said, to a possible sabbatical year abroad which would enable him to indulge in "the happiness of devoting myself exclusively to the work for which, I believe, Nature intended me." "If you knew how I have hungered for a larger life," he exclaimed, adding that "the intellectual solitude" of Ithaca crippled his strength and threatened to "fossilize" him.[43] Such words were characteristic of Boyesen. He felt himself called to do great things and worked vigorously towards them, all the while suspecting, however, that they might never be realized. He would then blame his set-back on some outer condition, so that he could go on believing in his own greatness and try even harder to give proof of it.

Let us pause for a moment to look, for the sake of comparison, at Paul Knaplund (1885–1964), another gifted Norwegian who like Boyesen came to the United States at the age of twenty and went on to become a professor at a well-known American university. Crossing the sea as a "small boat," with no knowledge of English and of America, Knaplund's only certainty was that he would miss his old home and country, that he would be a stranger and feel lonely and desolate, and that he would meet with defeats and disappointments. With no belief in his greatness and his ability to conquer the unknown, he was grateful for every small step forward. Guided by the image of the beloved parents he had left in Norway, and starting out as a farmhand in a Norwegian-American community, he did not force his Americanization. It was a more gradual process, helped on first by a "mystical allegiance" with the soil he tilled, and then by a sense of community with fellow Norwegian-Americans, on the farm and later at school. Only when he was ready for it did he move on to the all-American world and to an identification with America and Americans in general.[44]

When Boyesen, on the other hand, insisted that he had felt at home from the day he arrived in the United States, he was probably to a certain degree flattering his new countrymen. Even so we may take it that he really believed that he could do without a sense of continuity with his Norwegian beginnings and at will grow organically into America and become an American. In his diary after he had followed his Margaret through Leipzig we find this comment: "It is strange how perfectly irresponsible one feels when abroad. I can very [well] imagine myself doing the most absurd things in a merely aesthetical way, without thinking to ask whether any moral law was involved." Now it is clear from the context that at this time he really considered America his second home and not as "abroad." But when after a year the ambitious Boyesen found out that he did not want to belong in Ithaca, he observed in the same vein, in connection with Ralph, the hero of a story, that it was "a more serious thing than he had imagined, to cut the cable which binds one to the land of one's birth. There, a hundred subtle influences, the existence of which no one suspects until the moment they are withdrawn, unite to keep one in the straight path of rectitude ...; the opinion of his fellow-men had been the one force to which he implicitly deferred ... To such a man the isolation ... among strangers was tenfold more dangerous."[45]

This is the same Boyesen speaking who once owned to G. W. Cable that he was "almost totally devoid of principles."[46] Not that he ever deviated from the path of rectitude. But he lacked the inner guide which immigrants like Paul Knaplund, Beret and Per Hansa had in their attachment to God, their parents, or the soil, and also the outer guide they had in their fellow Norwegian-Americans. Boyesen's only real beacon was his dream of greatness, and everything and everyone was to serve this ambition. God was not a master to him (as He was to Beret), but more an ally in his search for greatness. When Boyesen embraced the new theory of the survival of the fittest, and kept on stressing the pre-eminence of the Vikings, it was because it seemed to guarantee his success, particularly in the United States with its "widest scope for individual development." Norwegians in America certainly ought to keep their deepest national traits, he said. But in order not to live in vain they should "first of all be Americans" and assert their influence in that country. And he declared that those who criticized America — its politics, for instance — should rather have stayed in Norway.[47]

Boyesen did not regret, he stated in 1877, that he had lost his own tongue in the same degree that he had gained another. And his Americanization was to be crowned by his marrying an American girl.[48] His attitude was no doubt Olaf's: "It is my own future which I love in her." And she should further serve him by helping him to keep "that immediateness" which he regarded as his "best treasure." Although he had told Ingolf that experience had taught him to form his estimate of women according to better standards than the "external beauty" which previously had been all he cared for, he particularly stressed how "divinely beautiful" Lillie Keene was when finally in 1878 he won his ideal American girl.[49] Boyesen had met her first in Mark Twain's Hartford circle, probably early in 1876, and he evidently saw her beauty and her social standing as visible proofs of his success and a symbol of that American greatness which she would help him turn into a reality.[50]

In Paris in 1879 the couple saw a good deal of Mark Twain and his wife, and Olivia Clemens has given this description of them: "Mr. Boyesen ... is evidently as proud of her beauty as ever — he spoke of Mr. Auerbach's calling on them frequently and saying to him, 'Mr. Boyesen if you will just let me come and sit and look at your wife' — but I should feel annoyed if Mr. Clemens felt that the dainties of life were as essential to me as he evidently feels they are for his wife — he said she needed everything dainty around her."[51]

With disarming naiveté Boyesen thus gave a perfect description of their relationship: he who had wanted Lillie to serve him in his self-aggrandizement now found that she had changed their rôles. Having been brought up as a millionaire's daughter, she was very much a "victim of false education and standards."[52] A friend of Boyesen's oldest son has stated that Lillie was a social climber. She married the author solely because she thought she could manage him to her own purpose, which was to get the best of everything by means of Boyesen's increasing fame and earning capacity.[53] Mrs. Koch has quoted Ingolf as stating in 1895 that Boyesen had been driven to his death by Lillie. To this statement she added her own observations that Lillie was exceedingly demanding, always occupied with herself, and never interested in creating a real home for her husband and sons, and that Boyesen, although he continued to keep up appearances and to be proud of Lillie's beauty, was certainly not devoted to her, at least not during his later years, as Mr. Glasrud states.[54]

That Boyesen saw the truth about Lillie and yet did not want to see it is suggested by the sonnets he wrote to her shortly after their marriage, where he tries to make himself believe that he loves her in spite of her faults, and by "Mabel and I (A Philosophical Fairy Tale)," which was apparently written shortly after their first meeting. In this story the hero wants to see things as they are and not as they seem, and a pair of spectacles obtained from an "Old World sprite" helps him see, for example, that his prospective father-in-law is a parrot. He then wants to know whether his beloved Mabel is really as good and beautiful as she appears to be, or whether this is only a delusion. But he decides not to use the glasses after all: "What good would it do me if I found out that she too was a parrot,"[he says to himself]. "The fairest hope would go out of my life, and I should have little or nothing left worth living for." Finally, however, he looks at a small girl who, strangely enough, is not transformed like the others. "Here, then, was really a creature that was neither more nor less than it seemed. For some inconceivable reason the tears started to my eyes."[55]

Seen in this light, the story forms an illustration of Boyesen's basic dilemma. Besides suggesting his interest in evolution, it shows how he was magically drawn not only by his dreams of American fame, but also by his idealistic conceptions of women and of conditions generally in the New World. When he suspected they were all delusions, he hesitated to use his Old-World, realistic glasses. Should one of his dreams unexpectedly prove to represent a reality and not merely a chimera, he was moved to grateful tears.

The move to New York in 1880 gave Boyesen the opportunity he had desired to observe and, in the manner of an American Bjørnson, step into the battle-line of American public affairs. But here, too, the final result was disillusionment.

Very shortly the man who had advised his fellow Norwegian-Americans not to criticize American politics did the same thing himself, complaining vehemently to R. B. Anderson of the vast corruption he saw in New York City.[56] He now realized with regret that American *laissez-faire* created opportunities not only for the strong and honest, but even more for the vigorously dishonest. Such experiences inspired him to write "A Dangerous Virtue," the story of Anders Rustad, a blue-eyed newcomer from Norway who is robbed of his money by a smart bank-president in New York, and sues him, feeling "a sort of fierce satisfaction amid all his misery that now at last he saw things as they actually were." The exposure to hard realities wears him down, however, and he dies.[57] The story may also have been inspired by Bjørnson, who in Boston in 1880 discussed with his American admirer how he had turned from his previous idyllic novels to "practical sermons" dealing with "the great questions of life." One of these was the question of "commercial honor" which Bjørnson had recently treated in his drama *En Fallit*.[58]

The new personal encounter with Bjørnson during his American tour 1880–81 temporarily revived the friendship of the two men. While in Boston, Boyesen took Bjørnson to a meeting of the Papyros Club. When the Norwegian heard the applause which greeted Boyesen there, and when he realized how highly he was regarded as an author and scholar by such men as Howells and Longfellow, he was so impressed that he restored Boyesen completely to his previous position of favor. The great Bjørnson wrote his wife that Boyesen had developed tremendously, and in a long article on him in the Christiania newspaper *Dagbladet* described him as a very capable, true-hearted, courageous, and progressive Norwegian in an American setting, a man to whom the Norwegians ought for their own sakes to offer a university chair.[59]

This new warmth naturally had its effect on Boyesen. Just after Bjørnson had left America, Boyesen wrote him a letter with this telling statement: "Lillie says you are the first and only to make her jealous, the only to compete with her for a place in my heart." That the Norwegian poet again represented a powerful lure to his admirer is evident from Boyesen's comments in a letter to Bjørnson three months later upon reading some of his speeches in Norway: "My blood runs quicker when I think that such things can now be said openly at home. If it had been like this in my days, I would hardly now have been an American ... But don't get me wrong," he hastened to add: "I would scarcely wish my fate to have been different."[60]

In his answer of August 29, 1881, Bjørnson first congratulated his friend on his new position at Columbia University, and then added: "I can't stand it that you live a literary life half on show. So many others can do that. No, write something now and then out of your full heart." At the end of the letter Bjørnson spoke of Lillie, whom he had met a couple of times just before he left: "How beautiful she was, the first as the last evening! I was so scared that she should have other interests than you and sit there empty ... and too much have that relationship to you which is satisfied if vanity is satisfied, and tired if that is not the case. Frankly, you are dear to me. But you comforted me once. Can you do it again? I need it, because I am not sure. A man who is in public life and who is brave and true must have a wife who can die for him ... Give her my best regards if she is the one who smiles in your life, comforts you in the evening and encourages you in the morning. Your true friend, Bj. Bjørnson."

Bjørnson's visit and this letter were of great importance to Boyesen. The great skald loved him again, believed in him and encouraged him to give his best, in poetry, scholarship and public life, and he even implied that Boyesen was important enough to deserve a wife who could die for him. All this fitted exactly with Boyesen's own vision of his rôle and his still unrealized potentialities. As for Bjørnson's almost direct statement that Lillie was empty and vain and no wife for Boyesen, the latter had evidently stood up for her; yet in his heart of hearts he was ready to put on the realistic glasses which the Old-World sprite was offering him. Now that Boyesen's own sense of importance was so

15

formidably inflated by his hero, it was not so dangerous for him to destroy his illusion about Lillie, since he would have a great deal left to live for anyhow. Bjørnson's encouragement of Boyesen in 1881 was a strong support for him when in the following years he had to see further illusions fall by the wayside. As late as 1890 he wrote to his idol: "It would be impossible for me to pay my great debt of gratitude to you."[61]

Seeing himself in this hopeful light, Boyesen made the most of the opportunities which New York afforded him to plunge into that kind of American life he so long had wanted. In innumerable newspaper-articles he brought the Norwegian case against Sweden before the American public.[62] He also wrote speeches for President Cleveland whom he apparently knew quite well.[63] He was active in a number of clubs where he spoke "as an American citizen ... deeply attached to the country and its institutions."[64] He may also occasionally have taken part when Lillie entertained her fashionable guests, some of whom, one of his sons has told us, "had the semblance rather than the substance of culture."[65]

But his home was not a real home to him, as we know from Mrs. Koch. To Paul Knaplund, who also married an American girl, his home became "a shrine, a holy place" and his wife "a partner;" America became his country "largely because it was the land of his wife and children."[66] Boyesen, meanwhile, did everything to make his marriage seem a success, as he did with his career, putting himself in the limelight whenever he could. But he found that it demanded concessions. Not only was he forced to see the truth of Howells' statement that New York is a "mart" where "money counts for more and goes for less than in any other city." But he also felt that there was no real freedom in America.[67] Evidently bowing to the pressure of conformity, he overcame his rather critical attitude towards the various churches and joined the Episcopalians, whom he had recently derided to Bjørnson.[68]

Then suddenly something happened which marked a turning point in Boyesen's life and views. Having slapped a boy who had long pestered one of his sons, Boyesen was ordered by a court, in May, 1885, to pay damages for the boy's deafness, even though Boyesen's witnesses seem to have proved that the defect was caused by other factors than the slapping.[69] This financial setback must have seemed to him the result of American legal injustice. More important, it also meant a loss of prestige to the up-and-coming author; and it gave him a feeling of having been censured, or even rejected, by America, besides reminding him of a sore point in his Norwegian past. The event resulted in a growing disaffection towards America, and the rebirth of a powerful longing for Norway.

The latter was the first to become visible. In June, 1885, Boyesen jumped at a publisher's suggestion that he write a history of his native country. This indirect contact with Norway was more important to him than were his own sons, he said in an unguarded moment (Mrs. Koch has confirmed that there was no closeness between Boyesen and his sons when she knew him), and he hoped the work on the book would be a matter of years. In July he suddenly told R. B. Anderson that he would give one year of his life to be in Norway again and five to see Bjørnson and hear his voice.[70] This was also the time when he relived in memory his glorious days of 1873 with Bjørnson through writing "A Child of the Age." The story ends in a reconciliation between the conservative Judge and the radical Herluf, who returns to Norway for good from his American exile.

On November 3, 1885, Boyesen wrote to Anderson: "... financial troubles incident upon that dastardly suit have made me sleepless and miserable and a most incomprehensible, overwhelming longing for Norway has come over me. It seems to me now that if I do not go to Norway next summer I shall go mad." The letter ends with these words: "[Bjørnson] seems to have abandoned me of late, in spite of all my love for him." The master had indeed abandoned him (Boyesen did not hear from him until 1890), but the reason he would never know. In 1883 Henrik Ibsen had told Bjørnson that he had a much lower opinion of Boyesen than that expressed in Bjørnson's article in *Dagbladet*. This statement evidently caused the impressionable Bjørnson to forget all the American praise of his friend.[71]

Boyesen may have thought that he lost the lawsuit because he was born abroad. In any case, the incident altered his views on America and emigration. When Alexander Kielland wrote him in January, 1886, that he wanted to emigrate, Boyesen seems to have replied that there was no freedom and no equality in the United States, and that he felt the pain of emigration in his roots. While he earlier had criticized the immigrants for their slow adaptation, he now blamed the Americans for not accepting the newcomers.

That he gradually came to see America and the Americans as blocking his road to greatness would seem to be a major reason behind what Professor Marc Ratner has termed Boyesen's change in these

years from the position of an evolutionary optimist who believed in
the status quo to that of a reformer who believed in aiding the evolutionary process.[72] In spite of his disaffection towards America, he
intensified his work for reform, and in the end he even moved towards
what might be called a near-socialistic backing of the rights of the
masses.

He realized that as an immigrant he would always be a hyphenated,
handicapped American. Consequently, he now also began to move
closer to his fellow Norwegian-Americans, evidently feeling that they
ought to work together. Addressing such an audience, for once in his
native language, he said: "Nature here is not our nature — the social
order is not our social order. It may in many respects be better, but
however much you grow into it, it will never become ours. That is the
lot of the exile ... [and] we will never succeed ... in getting rid of
this feeling of being a foreigner which robs us of the real pleasure in
our work."[73]

The incident in 1885 brought into sharp focus the resentment that
had gradually built up in Boyesen. Granville Hicks has observed of
him that his best quality was his "power of indignation," but it seems
to the present writer that the prime motive for the attacks he launched,
particularly after 1885, on American social phenomena, was his anger
at being stopped, as he saw it, in his progress towards fame.[74] When
we consider how devastating the clash must have been between his
exceedingly lofty dreams and the hard American realities, it is not
surprising that his indignation clouded his vision and that he now,
as Howells observed, was "some times of a wandering and uncertain
touch."[75] Boyesen's friend went on: "There are certain stories of
his which I cannot read without a painful sense of their inequality
not only to his talent, but to his knowledge of human nature, and
of American character."

He now came out with particular strength against the two main
factors which he saw as responsible for his own dangerous expectations: romantic literature and the American dream of success. In
articles he lauded the new European literature for dealing with vital
realities rather than with the impossible dreams of the romantics.
In his own fiction he told, for instance, of a disillusioned Norwegian
immigrant who resented the influence of the poets "which had come
near ruining his life." The unlimited ambition encouraged by the
American dream of success is dangerous, Boyesen wrote, because it
has every chance of being thwarted; and the result may be "discontent

and disaffection toward the state which fails to satisfy the expectations it has aided in arousing."[76] In addition he attacked the harsh American realities he had awakened to. And with the same "fierce satisfaction" of disillusionment which he once had described in Anders Rustad he now lashed out particularly against the American woman. His novel *The Mammon of Unrighteousness* was started at this time. Intended to be "true to the logic of reality," this book describes how Kate van Schaak (who according to Austa Boyesen was modeled on Lillie) completely out-schemes her ambitious husband.[77]

That this new, "personal" realism went hand in hand with a new, equally personal romanticism is not so paradoxical as it might seem. Unlike his hero Anders Rustad, Boyesen did not die from seeing the realities. But he often felt the need to seek refuge from reality in stories that enabled him to dwell on his romantic, prelapsarian life and mood. Norway and Bjørnson drew him more and more as the years went by. Having in a sense "lost" America, he felt more truly Norwegian than ever and longed for that feeling of being at home which he supposed he would experience in Norway. How strongly he pined for Bjørnson's encouragement is suggested by the fact that once the otherwise very honest Boyesen lied (as his own letters prove) to Howells about having received a letter from Bjørnson. And at one point Howells evidently felt it necessary to send his friend this encouragement: "tell [Bjørnson] that, put together, you and I are as big as he is."[78]

When Boyesen finally heard from Bjørnson in 1890, he answered: "If I had had you near me all these years, how much richer my life would have been ... O dear Bjørn, you can't imagine how much I look forward to seeing you this summer! ... I have so much to tell you that I feel dizzy when I think of it."[79] When the trip had to be cancelled, Boyesen wrote to a friend that he was "heart-broken" at losing the sight of Bjørnson, and he added: "I have ceased to hope for anything. Fate always defeats my plans with a ruthless disregard of my feelings. The family obligation (rigidly interpreted) is a terrific one, depriving man of all his independence as an individual. He can no longer shape his action with reference to his own pleasure or benefit."[80]

When Boyesen finally crossed the Atlantic in 1891, his delight in seeing Norway and Bjørnson again was marred by sharp disappointments. That he was now taken for a foreigner by his compatriots could only strengthen that feeling of being a stranger in his own country which came to him almost the moment he landed. He felt out of step with the "self-assertive modernness" of a nation that was now culturally more progressive than were the Americans. The ideal, submissive Norwegian wife of his memory twenty years ago was being replaced, as he later said, by the progressive young woman who adored Zola and declared Bjørnson old-fashioned. With "an indefinable regret" he saw that Norway had lost a certain sweet, pastoral tranquility and that it was "an idyl no more, but a *fin de siècle*, realistic novel."[81] Evidently he wanted the idyllic and not the realistic. In any case, he never desired to visit Norway again, and what had been his homesickness turned into homelessness as he saw that even his Norsedom was hyphenated.[82]

When he went to see Bjørnson, he did have "much to tell" him. He had worked hard and written much, and he had just published *Mammon*, his most important attempt at realism. No wonder that he felt "dizzy" when thinking of all he had to report to the Norwegian! The visit started well enough with Bjørnson raising the Stars and Stripes to welcome him. But the master's new coolness soon became apparent, and this may have made Boyesen's Norwegian language even more halting than would otherwise have been the case. "Every now and then ... I had to resort to English," he wrote in a later article about the two-days' encounter.[83] Bjørnson then showed impatience: " 'Why, speak your mother-tongue, man,' he said; ... Well, I accepted his advice, but made during the next half-hour the humiliating experience that I had partly forgotten my mother-tongue ... My conversation therefore flagged, and for the first time in my life I felt ill at ease in Bjørnson's presence ... I had an acute sense of my shortcomings; and I gave up the attempt to pour forth the full flood of thought that rose and overbrimmed my mind at each of my host's questions."

Boyesen's pain is also evident in the letter he wrote to Bjørnson on November 3, 1891: "I regret ... that I misrepresented myself, giving you, through my lack of practice in using my mother tongue, the impression of a much poorer mind than mine really is ... I saw, too, that you had a somewhat lower opinion of me than when we met this side of the ocean. There was something very strange about the whole trip; I felt both pleased and punished because of my voluntary exile. It showed me what I lost when I abandoned my native country."

What a difference between these words and his almost identical statement of 1873! Only now did he fully realize what it was that in his youthful arrogance he had thrown away, as he had put it then. His last four years show him digesting his 1891 losses, and there can be little doubt that on the whole he now regretted his emigration. When Paul Knaplund likewise revisited Norway in his later life, it made him feel thoroughly American and particularly happy with his New World family circle and obligations. When Boyesen saw Norway and his relatives in 1891, it reminded him painfully of what it meant to have a real home.

Boyesen's affection for America was not increased when on his return he found a review of *Mammon* stating that the book was unpatriotic and asking why the author had not remained in Norway if he did not like America as it was.[84] But Norway was not his any more. He had lost his sense of continuity, and he no longer felt a real Norseman. While the spiritually "unusually self-contained" Knaplund had kept his Norwegian past "within himself [as] a retreat, a secret garden with flowers and greensward which could not be trampled upon and crushed by callous intruders,"[85] Boyesen had worn *his* past as a mask which should earn him money from his public. His last Norwegian trip made him see how empty was the soul behind it.

A result of Boyesen's visit was his realization that he had lost his identity. Decades before Rølvaag he observed that the immigrant brings "a fatally detached and incomplete self" to America as "all the finest tendrils of the torn roots of his being remain in the old soil," and that "after the transplantation, he loses . . . his distinctness of . . . individuality."[86] Furthermore, the individuality is split in two. Boyesen had been haunted by "a sort of somnambulistic confusion of identity" during his visit to Norway, he said in the essay "My Lost Self."[87] His "lost Norse self" met his American self when he arrived in the Old Country, making him feel as if he consisted of "a Norwegian Jekyll and an American Hyde."

Boyesen probably developed the same theme in his essay "My Lost Rip van Winklehood;" we know it was written in 1894, but it has never come to light.[88] He may have quoted Irving's description of the hen-pecked Rip looking at a statue of himself of twenty years earlier: "He doubted his own identity, and whether he was himself or another man." In the former essay, Boyesen's American counterpart posed the question of whether it was not his lost youth more than his lost self he was regretting. But Boyesen himself could only end with these words: "Suffering, as I do, from the old confusion of identity, I shall have to leave the question unanswered."

What particularly "punished" Boyesen in Norway was that Bjørnson had lost faith in him and thus seemingly no longer blessed his American venture. Boyesen now withdrew from his hero, apparently feeling that he had lost him forever. In the few letters he later wrote to him, he added practically nothing personal, and after 1891 he never heard from his hero again. That Bjørnson, his foremost model and touchstone, now had a lower opinion of him made him largely feel a failure in his rôle and doubt his ability to fill it. It was at this time that Boyesen recalled how his father had once taken him down from the pedestal of fancied, clandestine greatness, a greatness, he said, "than which I know no more delightful sensation."[89]

That the blow in 1891 was hard is suggested by the fact that Boyesen tried to soften it by blaming it on his hitherto unregretted loss of the Norwegian language. (Howells later said that "to the last, I suppose, when he was fagged, ... English ... must have been a serious ... unconscious strain on him.") He may now have recalled Turgenev's statements that the Russian language was what sustained him in exile and that "nothing great is accomplished outside nationality." Rølvaag was later to echo this when he said that the native language is the medium in which "one's emotional life can move ... freely and naturally," and that acquiring a new language requires a superhuman "re-making of soul."[90]

But Boyesen could not altogether give up his self-dramatization, his idea that nature had intended him for a great destiny, a belief which constituted the only real continuity in his life. In order not to break down mentally he had further to rationalize his set-backs. He would undoubtedly have agreed with Howells who later said of him that he "could have won even wider fame ... if he had remained in Norway; ... [there] the name of Boyesen would have been set with the names of Bjørnson, of Ibsen ..."[91] In an article Boyesen summed up his views on "The Emigrant's Unhappy Predicament:" "It is this chilling sense of difference between him and the natives which dooms the immigrant to failure or to a success below the utmost reach of his powers." And he continued: "It constitutes a discount, and a heavy one, which is charged by the land of his adoption on his life's capital. Of that margin of superioty which determines survival and dominance, he is obliged to sacrifice much, if not all, in the mere effort at adaption to new conditions ... He is ... apt to have a tormenting sense ... of having fallen short of high achievement, even when he is most vociferously applauded." Growing even more personal, Boyesen added:

"If he be a poet he can but murmur in broken syllables (like a musician playing upon an untuned instrument) the song that in his native tongue would have burst clear and melodious from his breast."[92]

The friendship with the faithful Howells now became even more important to Boyesen. Howells on his side has owned that the "chief pleasure of [his] winters" had been Boyesen's "coming every week for a full evening of such talk as only old friends, long agreed about life and art, can have."[93] What further supported Boyesen during these last years was his outwardly successful activities. He wrote feverishly, he made speeches, he lived in the style of a man of the world, he went horse-riding: "in the saddle ... for once, the world is at my feet," he said.[94] He loved success, and the Americans gave him a fair share of it. His international fame was reflected by a French literary dictionary which gave him as much space as it did Bjørnson.[95]

But at the same time Boyesen sought refuge in reminiscences about his Systrand years, the only period of his life in which his dreams of greatness had been spared destructive confrontations with reality. During that glorious time he had formed an organic part of his environment and his experiencing self had been one and undivided. All the environmental elements had supported his self-aggrandizement: nature, folklore, history, family and social order. Now we find him trying to evoke his past, for instance by writing autobiographical articles and by occupying himself with the Vikings; thus he spoke at the reception of the Viking ship that came over in 1893, and he worked on Viking literature the last months of his life.[96] When in 1893 he read Arne Garborg's book on Jonas Lie, he "for the first time forgot [his] lecture at the university," as he wrote to Garborg, and later on the podium he "could scarcely talk sense ... [as he] heard the bogy hooting as he had heard him ... at Systrand."[97]

What perhaps helped Boyesen most to keep a certain balance of mind even during these last years of his life was his work in the garden at "The Moorlands," his home on Long Island, where he grew vegetables and mowed grass. In contact with the soil he finally reached a certain detachment and experienced something, at least, of that sense of reality which such occupation had given his fellow countrymen Per Hansa and Paul Knaplund, and which previously had been denied to him because of his dreams and his frustrations. Like the hero of one of his earliest stories he had once aspired at going

beyond the sun. Now he felt with a new sense of resignation that
he had carried his illusions to their last consequences. He may have
recalled the continuation of his childhood poem from *Arne*:[98]

> Once I thought that I really might grow to be great.
> In afar in the world I might grapple with fate;
> For the voice of Ambition cried loudly 'Arise,
> Yong spirit! and struggle thy best for the prize.'
> But the maiden she taught me (with never a word)
> That the dearest of things God can give
> Is not to be famous, renowned or great,
> But perfect in manhood to live.

The Norwegian original of the last line — "menneske ret at blive" —
suggests the idea of becoming a harmonious man, more than does the
translation.

At "The Moorlands," "Nature . . . [afforded him a] miraculous
clearness in the brain" which finally also seems to have enabled him
to see the folly of chasing American fame. "Nothing can persuade
me that this fever . . . of competition which is now consuming the
heart and brain of humanity is wholesome," he wrote. "In order to
become sane again and tranquilly contented, we shall have to return
to the soil . . . [I feel its] vitalizing and rejuvenating touch . . . every
day among my flowers and beans and cabbages." The last poem
Boyesen wrote, the posthumous "Pollen," also suggests this healthy
occupation with the organically creative. As for America, a statement
just before his death shows that here he saw the possibility of a new
contact even with his adopted country: "[With a] close and intimate
acquaintance with a bit of earth which you can call your own . . .
your patriotism somehow strikes root and becomes a solid and tangible
thing. You become wedded to the soil of your country, and your
affection . . . grows and spreads, until you may securely rest in its
shadows."[99]

This relaxation and sense of detachment gave Boyesen a little relief
and rest from his lifelong rôle of wearing a mask. Behind such a mask
in man we sometimes find — in the words of the Norwegian psycho-
logist Ragnar Rommetveit — a place, a mood, a mother, a bit of
the self which in the earliest youth had been whole.[100] Boyesen,
the gentle, simple-hearted enthusiast, restless and rootless, tired of a
task he could not master, nostalgically evoked them all.

## NOTES

[1] Cl. A. Glasrud, *Hjalmar Hjorth Boyesen* (Northfield, Minn., 1963), p. 18.

[2] Ibid., pp. 3, 6.

[3] The information in these paragraphs is derived from *Norges Statskalender* (Christiania, 1843 et seq.), and from statements made to the present writer in 1962 and 1964 by Mrs. Asora Koch, Oslo. The quotation is from Boyesen, "The Scandinavian Wife," *North American Review*, CLXI (October, 1895), 435.

[4] "My Lost Self," *Literary and Social Silhouettes* (New York, 1894), p. 198. "Boyesen's First Book," Indianapolis *News*, September 30, 1893, p. 9.

[5] "Retrospect," an autobiographical chapter in *A Norseman's Pilgrimage* (New York, 1875), p. 17.

[6] Statement made to the present writer in 1962 by Mrs. Sofie Hall, Oslo, the daughter of Christine Boyesen. It is possible that Mrs. Hjorth started writing only after Boyesen left Systrand.

[7] "Outdoor Life in Norway," *Monthly Illustrator*, V (July, 1895), 16.

[8] *Arne*, translation by Walter Low (London, 1895), p. 183. Boyesen's "Speech at the opening of the Norwegian-American Seamen's Association's Bazar, March 31, 1891," Columbiana Collection, Columbia University. Quoted by permission.

[9] "The Mother of Ivan Tourgueneff," *Century*, XLVIII (June, 1894), 450. "A Youthful Reminiscence," *Lippincott's Magazine*, LV (March, 1895), 418.

[10] "Boyesen's First Book." Frank E. Heath, "Hjalmar Hjorth Boyesen," *Scribner's Monthly*, XIV (October, 1877), 777.

[11] Statement by Mrs. Koch. Henning Sollied, *Akersgårder* (Oslo, 1947), p.

216, reports that the auction took place in 1871.

[12] "The Modern Migration of Nations," *Chautauquan*, IX (February, 1889), 282.

[13] For this and later references to the Kielland-Boyesen correspondence, see Per E. Seyersted, "Dengang H. H. Boyesen kurerte Kiellands Amerikafeber," *Edda*, LXV (July-August, 1965), 208–224.

[14] See *Studentene fra 1867* (Kristiania, 1917), and "Forhandlingsprotokol for Det Norske Studentersamfund," Universitetsbiblioteket, Oslo.

[15] "Boyesen's First Book."

[16] *Udvandrerens Veileder og Raadgiver* (Christiania, 1868), pp. 1–4, 130, 131.

[17] The last issue of *Norges Statskalender* to list the Captain is that of 1869. The official documents that would have proved the discharge to have been dishonorable are no longer in existence. If the Captain did have a pension (as Boyesen stated to Cable), it might indicate that the discharge was not dishonorable.

[18] This, and Boyesen's further letters to Ingolf are in the possesion of Mr. Stephen Rowan, New York. The present letter is dated November 13, 1872. Quoted by permission.

[19] See letter to Professor L. Dietrichson, [July?], 1872. Letter to Bjørnson, August 28, 1874. These letters, and all other Boyesen–letters to Bjørnson, are in Universitetsbiblioteket, Oslo. Quoted by permission. Most of this article's Boyesen–Bjørnson material is taken from Per E. Seyersted, "Bjørnsons ukjente vennskap og brevveksling med Hjalmar Hjorth Boyesen," *Edda*, LXIV (January–March, 1964), 18–48. All the Bjørnson letters to Boyesen are in the

H. H. Boyesen Collection in the Clifton Waller Barrett Library of the University of Virginia Library. Quoted by permission.

²⁰ "Boyesen's First Book."

²¹ Letter to George W. Cable, January 20, 1878, quoted in Arlin Turner, "A Novelist Discovers a Novelist: The Correspondence of H. H. Boyesen and George W. Cable," *Western Humanities Review*, V (Autumn, 1951), 353. Boyesen writes about his health in a letter to Ingolf, February 12, 1873.

²² See letter to Howells, December 21, 1872. Boyesen's letters to Howells are in the Houghton Library, Harvard University. Quoted by permission. Part of the two men's correspondence is published in Marc Ratner, "Howells and Boyesen: Two Views of Realism," *The New England Quarterly*, XXXV (September, 1962), 377–90.

²³ Letter to Ingolf, November 22, 1872. See letter from Howells, March 27, 1873. The Howells letters to Boyesen are in the University of Virginia Library (see note 19). Quoted by permission.

²⁴ Letter to Ingolf, February 2, 1873.

²⁵ "Lecture on Bjørnstjerne Bjørnson. First delivered December 6, 1892." MS, Columbiana Collection, Columbia University. Quoted by permission.

²⁶ See W. D. Howells, "Hjalmar Hjorth Boyesen," *Harper's Bazar*, January 25, 1896, pp. 70–71. This obituary (which the editor of the *Cosmopolitan* ordered from Howells only to reject it as not being what he wished to publish), contains certain frank statements which Howells left out in his later version of it in *Literary Friends and Acquaintance* (New York, 1900). All Boyesen's letters to R. B. Anderson are in the State Historical

Society of Wisconsin, Madison. Quoted by permission. A discussion of Bjørnson's influence on Howells, by Berit Spilhaug Johns, will appear in the next vol. of this series.

²⁷ See Seyersted, "Bjørnsons ukjente vennskap..."

²⁸ See letter to Howells, September 27, 1873. Letter to Ingolf, September 4, 1873.

²⁹ The diary is owned by the present writer. The quotation is from the letter to Ingolf, September 4, 1873.

³⁰ Letter to Howells, September 27, 1873.

³¹ See Preface to *The Mammon of Unrighteousness* (New York, 1891).

³² *Vagabond Tales* (Boston, 1889), pp. 71–75.

³³ Letters to Howells, September 27, 1873, and to Ingolf, September 4, 1873. The definition is from "Norwegian Painters," *Scribner's Magazine*, XII (December, 1892), 760.

³⁴ Glasrud, *H. H. Boyesen*, p. 35.

³⁵ See "Lecture on Bjørnson...."

³⁶ Letter of April 18, 1874.

³⁷ Letter of November 30, 1873. Fiske Collection, Cornell University Library. Quoted by permission.

³⁸ Diary.

³⁹ *Pilgrimage*, pp. 266, 237.

⁴⁰ See New York *Daily Tribune*, July 29, 1889, p. 6.

⁴¹ "A Visit to Tourgueneff," *Galaxy*, XVII (April, 1874), 460.

⁴² Letters from Howells, January 24, 1874, and November 4, 1875. Letter from Turgenev, February 24, 1874. Cornell University Library. The letter is quoted in full in Per. E. Seyersted, "Turgenev's Interest in America as Seen in His Contacts with H. H. Boyesen, W. D. Howells and Other American Authors," *Scando-Slavica*, XI (1965), 25-39.

⁴³ Letter of December 16, 1877. Houghton Library, Harvard University. Quoted by permission.

44 See Paul Knaplund, *Moorings Old and New. Entries in an Immigrant's Log* (Madison, Wisc., 1963), pp. 14, 15, 117, 134–135, 189, 222.

45 "A Good-for-nothing," *Scribner's Monthly*, X (July, 1875), 365.

46 Letter of February 17, 1878, quoted in Turner, "A Novelist Discovers a Novelist," p. 356.

47 See Heath, "H. H. Boyesen," *Falconberg* (New York, 1879), pp. 134–35, and "Norsk-amerikansk Literatur og Kritik," *Dagbladet* (Christiania), October 18, 1879.

48 See Heath, "H. H. Boyesen."

49 Letter to Ingolf, February 2, 1873. Letter to Howells, March 10, 1878.

50 See Kenneth R. Andrews, *Nook Farm. Mark Twain's Hartford Circle* (Cambridge, Mass., 1950), p. 91.

51 Letter to Olivia Clemens' mother, March 16, 1879. Mark Twain Papers, University of California, Berkeley. Quoted by permission.

52 Letter from Austa Boyesen to Laurence M. Larson, December 6, 1936. Record Series 15/13/24 in the University of Illinois Archives. Quoted by permission.

53 Statement to the present writer by Mr. Cortland Smith, New York, 1963.

54 See Glasrud, *H. H. Boyesen*, p. 219.

55 See sonnets "To Lillie," *Idyls of Norway* (New York, 1882). The story was first published in *St. Nicolas*, IV (January, 1877), 206–214.

56 Letter of February 27, 1881.

57 *Scribner's Monthly*, XXI (March, 1881), 745–759.

58 "Lecture on ... Bjørnson."

59 Bjørnson's letter to his wife and his article, both dated November 8, 1880, are quoted in Seyersted, "Bjørnsons ukjente vennskap ..."

60 Letters dated April 21, and August 8, 1881.

61 Letter dated April 14, 1890.

62 See letter to Bjørnson of September 4, 1882.

63 Information derived from Bayard Boyesen, "Autographical Fragment." This undated MS belongs to the present writer.

64 "New Reasons for Restricting Immigration," *Our Day*, III (February, 1889), 128.

65 Bayard Boyesen, "Autobiographical Fragment."

66 Knaplund, *Moorings Old and New*, pp. 128, 129, 266.

67 Howells, "H. H. Boyesen."

68 See letter to Bjørnson, August 8, 1881.

69 See New York *Times*, May 6 and 8, 1885.

70 Letters to R. B. Anderson, July 5 and November 3, 1885.

71 See Seyersted, "Bjørnsons ukjente vennskap ..."

72 Marc Ratner, "Hjalmar Hjorth Boyesen: Critic of Literature and Society." Doctoral dissertation, New York University, 1959, p. 11.

73 "Speech ... 1891."

74 Granville Hicks, *The Great Tradition* (New York, 1933), p. 158.

75 Howells, "H. H. Boyesen."

76 "Wild Oats," *Our Continent*, I (February 22, 1882). "What Shall the Public Schools Teach," *Forum*, VI (September, 1888), 95.

77 Preface to *Mammon*.

78 Boyesen to Bjørnson, May 10, 1891: "I wrote to you a year ago ... but had no reply from you." Boyesen to Howells, September 23, 1890: "Bjørnson sends all manner of affectionate greetings to you." This one letter from Howells is owned by Mr. Stephen Rowan.

79 Letter of April 14, 1890.

80 Letter to W. M. Paine, June 25, 1890. The Newberry Library, Chicago. Quoted by permission.

81 "Another Day in Norway," *Century*, LIV (August, 1897), 552.

[82] W. H. Carpenter, "In Memoriam: Hjalmar Hjorth Boyesen," *Columbia University Bulletin*, December, 1895.

[83] "Conversations with Bjørnstjerne Bjørnson," *Cosmopolitan*, XV (August, 1893), 418.

[84] Boyesen's Preface to *The Golden Calf* (Meadville, 1892).

[85] Knaplund, *Moorings Old and New*, p. 15.

[86] "The Emigrant's Unhappy Predicament," *Chautauquan*, XV (August, 1892), 608.

[87] *Silhouettes*, pp. 194–204.

[88] See letter to S. Pritchard Mason, December 27, 1894. New York Public Library.

[89] Philadelphia *Inquirer*, October 1, 1893.

[90] Howells, "H. H. Boyesen." Turgenev as quoted by Howells, *Atlantic Monthly*, XXXIII (March, 1874), 369. Theodore Jorgenson and Nora A. Solum, *Ole Edvart Rölvaag; A Bi-*

*ography* (New York, 1939), pp. 168–169.

[91] Howells, "H. H. Boyesen."

[92] "Emigrant's . . . Predicament."

[93] Howells, "H. H. Boyesen."

[94] "Authors on the Wheel," *Critic*, October 12, 1895, p. 227.

[95] *Dictionnaire International des Ecrivains du Jour* (Florence, 1891).

[96] See Magnus Andersen, *Vikingefærden* (Kristiania, 1895) and *Verdens Gang* (Kristiania), October 21, 1895.

[97] Letter to Garborg, December 31, 1893. Universitetsbiblioteket, Oslo. Quoted by permission.

[98] "The Norse Emigrant," *Galaxy*, XV (Febr., 1873), 199–203. *Arne*, p. 210.

[99] "My Rural Experiences," *Lippincott's*, LVIII (July, 1896), 123. "Pollen," New York *Telegram*, October 29, 1895.

[100] Ragnar Rommetveit, "Kven er eg?" *Den frie talerstol* (Oslo, 1963), pp. 127–132.

# THE IMPRESSIONISM OF STEPHEN CRANE: A STUDY IN STYLE AND TECHNIQUE

By Orm Øverland

## 1
### *Introductory*

The critics of Stephen Crane — his contemporary reviewers as well as present day scholars — have from time to time used the term impressionism to describe his art, their statements ranging from his contemporary Edward Garnett's "He is the chief impressionist of our day ..." to R.W. Stallman's "... there is a close parallelism between Crane's impressionistic prose and impressionistic painting." For Joseph Conrad this seems to have been the most striking aspect of his friend's art: "He certainly is *the* impressionist and his temperament is curiously unique. His thought is concise, connected, never very deep — yet often startling. He is *the only* impressionist and *only* an impressionist."[1] But although colleagues and critics have thus labelled Crane, little has been done in detail to justify the description. Edward Garnett's essay is useful, but sketchy, and Stallman's analysis is mainly restricted to a discussion of what he calls Crane's "prose pointilism" and the analogy "between Crane's use of color and the method employed by the impressionists and the neo-impressionists."[2]

Much, therefore, remains to be done in clarifying this aspect of Crane's art. Impressionism is not a mere technical manipulation of modes of expression, but is a way of perceiving the surrounding world, based on fundamental attitudes which will set their unmistakable stamp on an author's work at all levels — not only, or even mainly, his more overt manipulations of color, but his language, his choice of words, his syntax, and the larger structural patterns of his work as well. The technique of any writer cannot be conceived of as merely a manner of or a device for expressing something; the meaning of a statement cannot be isolated from its form. Indeed, as Susanne K. Langer remarks, " 'Seeing' is itself a process of formulation" and not a passive process.[3] Thus the study of an author's "way of saying something" should prove a possible approach to both the total meaning of a work of art and the writer's *Weltanschauung*.

A fairly large bibliography exists on the subject of impressionism in literature. This scholarship, however, is largely concerned with Danish, French, German, and Spanish impressionism and thus will not necessarily apply to literature in the English language in all details. For stylistic features in one language need not be expressive of the same quality in another, and hallmarks of impressionism in German may perfectly well be common usage in English.[4] In English criticism, although impressionism is a term frequently used to describe an author's manner of writing, the term still remains a rather vague one when applied to literature. Few attempts at a closer description of what the term may imply have been made. When such descriptions or definitions have been offered, moreover, they as a rule deal only with certain (and not always essential) aspects, and, what is worse, the definitions are often not only inadequate, but misleading.

It will therefore be necessary to attempt a general discussion of impressionism before we approach the impressionism of Stephen Crane. We will then classify and discuss significant stylistic traits from Crane's work, trying to determine whether they express, may be found compatible with, or seem to refute an impressionistic attitude. As "significant" I regard such traits that are more expressive and burdened with meaning than others or stand out because of their frequency or strike one as deviating from common usage.

Most critics seem to agree that there is a close connection between naturalism and impressionism. German scholars in particular have formulated a system of *Stilentwicklung* where the development naturalism — impressionism — expressionism is depicted as a series of steps following one another in a thoroughly logical manner. The first, they say, is dominated by the outer world, the second by the meeting of the outer world and the inner Ego, and the third is wholly dominated by the inner Ego.[5]

In many schools of fiction, among them both naturalists and impressionists, it has been an ideal that the novelist give his work an objective effect by withdrawing from his novel: "Le grand art est scientifique et impersonnel." It is not for the author to moralize or explain. He renders reality, and the reader is left to draw his own conclusions without the aid of a commenting middleman.

There is, nevertheless, an important difference between naturalists and impressionists in their approach to their material. The former firmly believed that reality *could* be seized upon, while the impressionists went one step further toward "realism" and "objectivity." Even though one holds the sensory impressions to represent all that is tangible and concrete different attitudes may still result. You may — like the naturalist — consider these impressions to be *actual images of things* and reproduce them as accurately and completely as possible through an analytic process, or you may — like the impressionist — regard your impressions as *being reality, not representing it,* and therefore rest satisfied with receiving these impressions as a passive medium and reproducing them as they appear to you.[6]

To the susceptible mind of the impressionist the surrounding world viewed at large is not simple and well ordered, but an indistinct and obscure picture made up of an irresistible flood of confused and ever changing sense impressions.[7] Only through an analytical process of judging and classifying do they finally emerge as a coherent and comprehensible picture. To the impressionist this analysis introduces order where there is none, and interprets reality instead of rendering it. Consequently, the impressionist will avoid such an analysis and content himself with the rendering of impressions.

In his discussion of impressionism in *The Foreground of American Fiction* Harry Hartwick wrongly maintains that impressionism is based on the principle of "analysis, or the refraction of large units into smaller ones for the purpose of study and classification." Further on he states that impressionism insists on experience being "broken into fragments, each fragment to be respected for its own sake, each passing moment or passion to be welcomed individually and squeezed dry before it can escape us."[8]

Contrary to this interpretation, the fundamental view of impressionism is that experience *consists* of fragments, therefore *is* these fragments and appears to the author as such. On the other hand, the impressionist's basic attitude does not necessarily result in a succession of fragmentary impressions. His first image of a scene may as well be a vague and indistinct impression of the whole. It would then be this impression he tries to convey to his reader. In either instance it is left to the reader to create a coherent and meaningful picture. In the words of Hamlin Garland: " . . . the impressionist does not mix his paints upon his palette. He paints with nature's colors, — red, blue, and yellow; and he places them fearlessly on the canvas side by side, leaving the eye to mix them, as in nature."[9]

Impressionistic technique, with its assumed objectivity, is also a means of creating an illusion — "the illusion that the reader is participating in the events, scenes or actions described."[10] In his attempts to be as "realistic" as possible the impressionist tries to present the consciousness of his characters as it functions by rendering only its undeveloped impressions and associations, thereby letting the reader share in the very process of perception. And the impressionist tries to make the reader even more a direct partaker of his experience by concentrating not on the object or scene itself but on the atmosphere which surrounds it and the feelings or sensations which are evoked. A still further effect of his efforts toward "realism" is the elimination of all beyond the actual sensations of impressions of his characters: what cannot be sensed does not exist for the impressionist.

All this may technically be an expression of aloofness and objectivity, but in its effect on the reader it is highly suggestive and subjective. Garland, too, was aware of this subjectivistic aspect of impressionism, its rhetoric, so to speak: "It must never be forgotten that they are not delineating a scene; they are painting a personal impression of a scene, which is vastly different."[11] At the same time, the impressionists apparently remained convinced that their sensations or impressions, when described in language, are capable of rousing the same sensations in the reader as those roused in the author on receiving them. If such were not the case the rendering of experience in terms of effects only would be well nigh impossible.[12]

Charles C. Walcutt remarks that impressionistic technique springs from the "belief that reality is illusory and phantasmagoric."[13] Our impressions of the surrounding world are to a large extent determined by circumstances; color, for instance, is no exact quantity, but the result of a certain intensity of light or shade. Our condition of mind at any given moment must also be taken into consideration. These factors are beyond our power to influence; therefore the impressionist's passive recording of an illusory reality. His mind is acted upon by certain forces, and rendering his reactions to these stimuli as truthfully as he can is his sole responsibility. Here we are back again with naturalism and its view of man at the mercy of natural forces. This passive attitude is basic not only to the impressionist's art but to his entire *Weltanschauung.*

The impressionists in painting, it has been said, "owed as much to Zola as to any painter," and Zola himself recognized their work as a further development of his own naturalism.[14] There are many points of resemblance in the technique applied by impressionist painters and writers. Because of these parallels it is tempting to draw comparisons between the two arts. This has often been done, and if literary realities are not lost sight of a comparison may be useful.[15] Obviously, Crane is influenced by contemporary impressionism, both in art and writing. But while much has been written on the subject, answers remain vague.

We have little information as to what he read. Although in a letter he confesses having read "a great deal," he liked to pose as the ignorant young writer who knew neither "Balzac and Dostoywhat'shisname" nor "De Maupassant, Zola, Loti and the bloke who wrote — I forget the book."[16] Some critics have stressed his desultory reading to the point where he appears as virtually illiterate.

This notwithstanding, Crane seems to have had a fairly good knowledge of the literature of his time and of the contemporary literary debate. Early in his career he came in close contact with William Dean Howells and Hamlin Garland, two American writers of his time who were well informed about European literary movements and were extremely willing to hand their information and their ideas down to a promising young recruit in the "battle for realism."[17] Crane's biographers also have mentioned that he associated with the young artists in the studios of New York.[18] This, we will see, had definite effects on his literary theories and his technique. There is perhaps scant evidence of direct contact with many of the movements, authors or artists with whom we may find Crane's art to be related. But such evidence is not strictly necessary. The new ideas in literature and art were in the air of New York. One might rather ask how Crane could escape being influenced by them?

## 2
### *Credo*

Unlike many of his contemporaries Stephen Crane was not an intellectual critic and has not written at any length on his theories of literature. What comments he has made on the art of writing must be gathered together from many sources — letters, statements as remembered by friends, and occasional passages in his fiction. No wonder if these fragments, when put together, do not form a coherent picture on all points.

Nevertheless, Crane regarded art as a serious undertaking and not, as has been said, as "a matter of no great moment... a natural function."[19] This one might expect from a writer who published his first book at his own expense rather than making any concession to what he regarded as dishonesty. When the following year (1894) Crane at last succeeded in finding a publisher for *The Black Riders*, he again refused to omit anything that to him was important. Art was important to Crane and it was also of some importance that others believed in his sincerity.[20]

Another aspect of this attitude is expressed in Crane's often repeated view that art is "an effort born of pain — despair, almost."[21] Again and again in his correspondence we find his thoughts circling around the problems of expression and communication, with phrases like "child of pain," "child of suffering," and "great deal of labor." "When I express an opinion in writing I am in the habit of considering a long time and then formulating it with a great deal of care," he wrote to Nellie Crouse. Earlier he had told her, "Script is an infernally bad vehicle for thoughts. I know that, at least."[22]

There is a close connection between such statements and the way in which Stephen Crane actually worked. A short book like *Maggie* was rewritten at least four times in the course of two years before Crane thought it fit for publishing. After writing a story Crane "would put it away for two or three weeks, and work on something else until his mind was thoroughly clear for a fresh consideration of it. When the story was taken out for revision it would be turned over to his friends for criticism, and Crane would argue with them about the objections they would make."[23] How is this picture of Crane to be reconciled with our picture of an impressionist "simply setting forth in his own way his own impressions," as on one occasion he is reported to have characterized himself?[24] In most cases this "setting forth" is no simple matter as Crane so modestly stated. We must distinguish between the aim of a work of art and how this aim is accomplished. Creating, and through this creation invoking in others the spontaneous impression may as often as not be the result of hard labor.

Stephen Crane justly wrote that he was giving form to his work "with a great deal of care": he was writing with other purposes in mind than merely to entertain, and therefore he always wanted "to be unmistakable." This statement is clarified and explained in a letter to John Hilliard where he writes: "And my chiefest desire was to write plainly and unmistakably, so that all men (and some women) might read and understand. That to my mind is good writing." In a later letter to Hilliard he again stresses this point: "... I endeavored to express myself in the simplest and most concise way. If I failed, the fault is not mine." But by being unmistakable Crane does not mean imposing a didactic moral on a story. He is first of all concerned with literature as art: "I have been very careful not to let any theories or pet ideas of my own creep into my work. Preaching is fatal to art in literature. I try to give to readers a slice out of life; and if there is any moral or lesson in it, I do not try to point it out. I let the reader find it for himself. The result is more satisfactory to both the reader and myself."[25]

Crane's expression " a slice out of life" clearly stems from Zola and his theories of the naturalistic novel. Other formulas from the naturalistic stock of ideas are to be found in his letters too. The one best known is probably the inscription he wrote across the cover of several copies of *Maggie :* the book "tries to show that environment is a tremendous thing in the world and frequently shapes lives regardless."[26] Is naturalism pessimistic or optimistic? Some critics find it to be based on desperate, pessimistic determinism, while others see in it an optimistic affirmation of man's freedom and progress. But both answers are equally correct; behind them is a dualism embodied in naturalistic literature.[27] In a letter to Nellie Crouse Crane touches upon this problem and offers an answer hardly to be expected by the author of, for instance, "The Blue Hotel": "I don't like to make wise remarks on the aspect of life ... The final wall of the wise man's thought however is Human Kindness of course. If the road of disappointment, grief, pessimism, is followed far enough, it will arrive there. Pessimism itself is only a little, little way, and moreover it is ridiculously cheap."

Another letter from Crane illustrates a similar dichotomy between a deterministic view and an emphasis on the importance of man's own will — a dichotomy also found in his fiction: "I do not think that much can be done with the Bowery as long as the [word blurred] are in their present state of conceit ... In a story of mine called 'An Experiment in Misery' I tried to make plain that the root of Bowery life is a sort of cowardice. Perhaps I mean a lack of ambition or to willingly be knocked flat and accept the licking."[28] In other words, even a change of environment would not be of any real help as long as "the root" was a certain state of mind and depended on man's will. But such seemingly non-naturalistic statements should not bring confusion to our idea of Crane as a naturalistic determinist. As Walcutt has shown, this dualism is found in many writers in the movement. Even in this respect Crane may thus be said to be a typical representative of naturalism.

Like other naturalists Crane often stressed the importance of the author's personal experience.[29] His view is clearly expressed in the answer he gave C. K. Linson on being asked why he had exposed himself to the cold when doing observations for his story "The Men in the Storm": "How could I know how those poor devils felt if I was warm myself?"[30] Now this is a rather remarkable statement from the man who wrote a great novel of war before seeing warfare and who started writing *Maggie* before leaving college. But the discrepancy is in no way unique. Recent investigations into Zola's method of writing have revealed a similar discrepancy between his own theory of the importance of documentation and careful gathering of material and the actual creative process.

In an often quoted letter, Crane puts on paper his "little creed of art": ". . . art is man's substitute for nature and we are the most successful in art when we approach the nearest to nature and truth. . . ."[31] Nature, life, truth are all expressions for what Crane strove to get at, and, as he himself acknowledged, his was no easy goal to reach. In *War Memories* one of the characters, a war correspondent like the author, cries out: "But to get to the real thing! . . . It seems impossible! It is because war is neither magnificent nor squalid; it is simply life, and an expression of life can always evade us. We can never tell life, one to another, although sometimes we think we can" (IX, 201).[32] What was "the real thing" to Crane, and what was it he wanted to communicate to his readers?

It is on answering this question that Crane reveals the difference between his theory of art and that held by those known as realists or naturalists. The only thing a writer honestly could strive to express was his personal vision or impression of "reality" — reality as it *seemed* to him and what he *felt* about it: "for I understand that a man is born into the world with his own pair of eyes, and he is not at all responsible for his vision — he is merely responsible for his quality of personal honesty. To keep close to this personal honesty is my supreme ambition . . . I, however, do not say that I am honest. I merely say that I am as nearly honest as a weak mental machinery will allow."[33]

We have seen Crane using the phrase "slice out of life" and claiming that this was what he wanted to give his readers. Clearly this statement can only be understood as meaning life *as he saw it* — his personal impression of this life. Crane wrote that *Maggie* "tries to show that environment is a tremendous thing in this world." But he also spoke quite differently about his purpose in writing this novel of the New York slums. Concluding a letter to a lady who had written to him about the book he says: "I had no other purpose in writing 'Maggie' than to show people to people as they seem to me."[34] Crane could never have said "as they *are*." All that was possible was to show them as he personally perceived them, as they "seemed" to him. This is impressionism, or at least an important criterion of impressionism.

The impressionist is reluctant to analyze his impressions intellectually and is first of all concerned with recreating them as they appear to him at a given moment. Thus he will tend to emphasize the subjective and emotional aspect of what he describes. Crane is also recorded to have expressed himself to this effect. One of his friends relates the following episode from Crane's college days. On the beach he asked Crane for advice on how to "get the real thing." Stephen scooped up a handful of sand and tossed it to the sea breezes: "Treat your notions like that," he said. "Forget what you think about it and tell what you feel about it . . ." In other words, you get closer to the real thing by writing down your spontaneous and personal impression than by analyzing it. Linson remembers a similar remark Crane once made when reading "The Battles and Leaders of the Civil War," then appearing in *Century*, on a cot in Linson's studio: "I wonder that *some* of these fellows don't tell how they *felt* in those scraps! They spout eternally of what they *did*, but they are as emotionless as rocks."[35]

The immediate suggestion which a scene evoked in his mind, the lightning flash of the impression, depending both upon his own state of mind and the different components of outer reality coming into his vision, was the reality which Crane tried to put into writing. In *War Memories* we find him giving us such an impression, explaining first how it came into his mind and then telling us what he has done or tried to do with it in writing — a rare and lucid illustration of his literary theory and method:

> The interior of the church was too cave-like in its gloom for the eyes of the operating surgeons, so they had had the altar-table carried to the doorway, where there was a bright light. Framed then in the black archway was the altar-table with the figure of a man upon it. He was naked save for a breech-clout, and so close, so clear was the ecclesiastic suggestion that one's mind leaped to a fantasy that this thin, pale figure had just been torn down from a cross. The flash of the impression was like light, and for this instant it illumined all the dark recesses of one's remotest

idea of sacrilege, ghastly and wanton. I bring this to you merely
as an effect, an effect of mental light and shade, if you like; something done in thought similar to that which the French impressionists do in colour; something meaningless and at the same time
overwhelming, crushing, monstrous. (IX, 245–46)

In Crane's work there are several instances where he refers to the
French impressionists as models. The following lines from *The Third
Violet* illustrate the impressionist theory of color being only the result
of light upon form, changing from moment to moment with the
character of the light in which it is seen: "Later in the day he made a
sketch, choosing an hour when the atmosphere was of a dark blue,
like powder-smoke in the shade of trees, and the western sky was
burning in strips of red."

A discussion on color between Hollanden and Hawker in the same
novel also reveals another aspect of Crane's impressionism: fidelity to
one's personal vision:

> "Say, does that shadow look pure purple to you?"
> "Certainly it does, or I wouldn't paint it so ..."
> "Well, if that shadow is pure purple, my eyes are liars. It looks
> a kind of slate colour to me. Lord! if what you fellows say in your
> pictures is true, the whole earth must be blazing and burning and
> glowing and —"
> Hawker went into a rage. "Oh, you don't know anything about
> colour, Hollie." (III, 172–73)

Crane's use of color on many points bears close resemblance to the
technique of the impressionist painters. But of course there is a great
difference between literature and painting in this respect. The painter
shows us the color, while the writer can only suggest it in language.
It is therefore interesting to see Crane describing a specific shade of
color by referring directly to impressionist painting in the opening
lines of *George's Mother*: "In the swirling rain that came at dusk the
broad avenue glistened with that deep bluish tint which is so widely
condemned when it is put into pictures" (X, 19). And again in "Horses
— One Dash": "Above them, the sky was of that marvellous tone of
green — like still sun-shot water — which people denounce in pictures" (XII, 203).

A similar attitude is also expressed in a remark he made to one of
his brothers: "Will, isn't that cloud green? ... But they wouldn't
believe it if I put it in a book."[36] Here Crane seems to identify himself with those painters whose colors were "so widely condemned,"

and to foresee people denouncing his own similar use of color in his writing. Like the impressionist painters Crane does not believe that anything has an objective color, a color which belongs to it in all situations and under any conditions. The color of any object is the color it seems to have to any observer at any special moment. Clouds are not green, but a particular cloud may be green under certain conditions and to a certain observer.

"L'épithète rare, voila la marque de l'écrivain," said the brothers Goncourt. And for the impressionist who tries to render a transitory impression it is necessary to avoid ordinary and well used words and to choose words and phrases that have preserved their freshness.[37] The impression is in itself unique, determined by conditions which are not likely to coincide in exactly the same manner at any other time. Thus it is self evident that the impressionist writer cannot put his impressions on paper through the clichés of conventional language. Crane's opinion of such means of expression was expressed one day he was reading in Linson's studio "when suddenly the magazine hurtled to the floor. 'Any writer who will use such a mildewed phrase as "from time immemorial" ought to have his brain sluiced! These mutts ... who write with a phrase dictionary in their eye should be digging sewers. Their English is cast iron.' "[38]

The impressionist, then, chooses the rare word or expression, often by introducing usual words in new and unexpected surroundings or by taking into use words from dialect, slang or foreign languages, and Beer relates that Crane already as a boy "had a passion for outlandish words."[39] Another aspect of this attitude is illustrated by a quotation from Emerson which Crane copied into his notebook: "Congratulate yourselves if you have done something strange and extravagant and have broken the monotony of a decorous age."[40]

Several of Stephen Crane's critical remarks are concerned with the structure of the novel, and his opinions on this question are also related to impressionistic theory. The reader's illusion of participation is more easily maintained in a short piece of fiction than in a novel that, in Crane's words, "goes on and on like Texas." Length may thus be an important criterion in criticism from an impressionist's point of view. Crane is at his best in his short stories and shorter novels — he criticized even *The Red Badge* for being too long — and one of the most common objections he has to other authors' works — authors he otherwise admired — is to the length of novels like *War and Peace, Anna Karenina,* and *Salammbô*.[41]

A writer who tries to render the momentary impression of reality is not interested in enumerating detail after detail in the manner of a Zola or a Norris. The impressionist's technique must necessarily be quite different. So Crane acknowledged that Zola was a "sincere writer" but doubted if he were much good: "He hangs one thing to another and his story goes along but I find him pretty tiresome."[42] How, then, is the novel to be constructed? As usual Crane's answer is scant. But in his definition of a novel as a "succession of sharply-outlined pictures, which pass before the reader like a panorama, leaving each its definite impression," he makes the point clearly enough.[43] This is what Crane meant a novel should be and what his best fiction is.

Stephen Crane never showed any interest in systematizing his theories and opinions and some of the more or less casual remarks we have discussed in our reconstruction of his literary credo may seem to contradict one another in some respects. Again, we may find some of his theories contradicted by his fiction and in such cases we must, of course, rely on how he actually wrote. But these qualifications taken into consideration, the material certainly points toward the conclusion that what literary theories Crane had were based on impressionism or ran closely parallel to it. And, what is more, Crane is recorded to have said that this was so: "Impressionism was his faith. Impressionism, he said, was truth, and no man could be great who was not an impressionist, for greatness consisted in knowing truth. He said he did not expect to be great himself, but he hoped to get near the truth."[44]

3
*Style*

> Behind the lines these two were acting
> a little isolated scene. (I, 67)

Through an objective technique the impressionist seeks to create the illusion of participation in the reader. In order to achieve this effect certain elements in fiction may be repressed in favor of others. By eliminating the narrative the author avoids intruding on the reader's conscience through the persona of an explaining and describing narrator who stands between the reader and the world of the novel. In the extreme this would lead to a novel written in the form of a play with a structure scenic rather than narrative. In his best work Stephen Crane was true to his conception of the novel as a "succession of sharply-outlined pictures, which pass before the reader like a panorama," and as a result he has been criticized for lacking "the architectonic touch, a larger sense of the whole; he did not know how to build up connective tissues. Consequently," continues Harry Hartwick, "his work is a mass of fragments ..."[45] Few critics would today agree that *Maggie* or *The Red Badge of Courage* lack an "architectonic touch," but our concern here is to discuss whether Crane made use of such an episodic technique and eliminated the narrative with artistic purpose.

Any part of *The Red Badge* may serve as an illustration. After the opening paragraph of the first chapter we are in the midst of a heated argument among the soldiers. Then we are introduced to a "youthful private" and given a close description of his hut. The central part of the chapter presents an indirect version of the youth's thoughts, through which we learn about his background and his great problem: would he run or no; and the chapter concludes with a discussion among the youth and two comrades. These scenes again consist of several fragmentary pictures, incidents, and details: glimpses of groups of soldiers and fragments of discussion which make us spectators on a scene, not an audience being told about it. The episodic flashback on the youth's life gives no coherent description of his previous experience. We are not told where he came from or what his name is; but various incidents are made vivid and his thoughts, as he lies on his bunk, are presented.

This technique is applied throughout the novel: details and fragments are juxtaposed to form scenes. An examination of the structure of chapter four, to take one more example, brings out that it consists of impressions of the following scenes or episodes: (1) The brigade halts, and through the smoke the soldiers see running men. (2) A discussion among the soldiers is rendered by reporting only the different remarks as heard, stripped of all descriptive comment. Each speech is thus a detail which together with the others form the impression of a conversation. (3) The battle din brings the debate to a conclusion. (4) Scattered glimpses of the action in front as seen by the soldiers: a flag amidst blurred forms of troops; a running stream of men; a battery changing position. (5) The explosion of a shell. (6) The enemy starts firing at the brigade. Glimpses are given of the effect on both nature and the soldiers. (7) The lieutenant is wounded. The regiment laughs nervously at his swearing. There are detailed observations of the actions of the lieutenant, and the captain binds his wound with a handkerchief. (8) Again there are scattered glimpses of action in front. Soldiers are seen to retreat in disorder. (9) The veterans and the new regiment show different reactions. (10) The youth is seen. He looks at the rabble and remembers a vivid detail. (11) Further detailed impressions of the retreating soldiers and the officers trying to stop them. (12) The impression this "mad current" makes on the youth and what he resolves to do.

The structural pattern is a simple succession of fragmentary episodes. H. E. Mencken was correct in noting that Crane had "no literary smalltalk." But when he criticised him for inability in "passage work" he did not understand what the author attempted to do.[46] Through "passage work" the author intrudes into the story and this is something the impressionist above all strives to avoid. The linking of the various incidents is left to the reader.

Similarly, *Maggie* and *George's Mother* are episodic in structure. As in *The Red Badge*, the development of the characters is revealed through their behavior in seemingly isolated scenes or episodes and explicit explanations are avoided.

> A thousand details of colour and form
> surged in his mind. (I, 62)

If, to the impressionist, experience consists of unrelated fragments, we should expect to find this expressed in the structure of his fiction's episodes and scenes down to their smallest components, the single detail. Although both naturalists and impressionists may pay much attention to detail there is a radical difference in their use of it. Where the naturalist tends to be complete and comprehensive in his description, Crane, the impressionist, is highly selective. Where the naturalist tends to give equal emphasis to a great number of details, Crane singles out the first detail that catches the eye, the main impression at this one occasion, and lets it completely dominate the scene.[47]

The one detail selected to convey the impression of the rendered scene often seems insignificant and inconsequential compared with the momentousness of the action. In the quiet following the red explosion of a shell we are made aware of one detail only: "There was a little shower of pine needles" (I, 58). Similarly, in the middle of the description of a volley of fire, "Twigs and leaves came sailing down" (I, 59). There is no attempt to provide an elaborate background: when the "bullets began to whistle" the falling twigs and leaves are perceived on a par with the men's constant dodging and ducking, and both observations are passed on to the reader without discrimination as to relative significance.

A detail may frequently be used to create a contrast. The youth lies in his tent wrestling with his ever-returning problem — how will he behave when the ordeal comes: "And as he sweated with the pain of these thoughts, he could hear low serene sentences. 'I'll bid five.' 'Make it six.' 'Seven.' 'Seven goes' " (I, 45). In his own eyes the youth "was a moral outcast," and the voices of the seemingly unaffected fellow soldiers playing cards underline this self-condemnation better than would a long explanation on behalf of the author. By presenting impressions rather than explaining he gives the reader an illusion of seeing for himself. Earlier in the novel the youth stands waiting in the dark of an early morning together with his regiment. To his impatient and uneasy mind all thoughts and impressions are distorted. The gloom is "mystic," the distance "ominous" and the campfires seemed to advance "as the orbs of a row of dragons": "He turned toward the colonel and saw him lift his gigantic arm and calmly stroke his moustache" (I, 38). The calm motion of the colonel sets off the youth's troubled speculations.

Sometimes details do not only seem insignificant, but apparently have no specific meaning or function whatsoever: "As the horseman wheeled his animal and galloped away he turned to shout over his shoulder. 'Don't forget that box of cigars!' The colonel mumbled in reply. The youth wondered what a box of cigars had to do with war" (I, 38). And so, in fact, do we. No more is ever heard of a box of cigars. Why then put it into the book? As in all these instances of Crane's use of detail we here see the impressionist's attitude to experience as a succession of detached and momentary impressions. The author does not introduce order where there is only confusion.

> ... the scene was a wild blur. (I, 164)

This attitude also finds expression in the technique of rendering scenes vaguely or indistinctly or even giving the reader a distorted view of what is actually taking place. Both techniques should be regarded as different aspects of what we have termed reluctance against analysis.[48] Thus an impression consisting of several mixed or blended components which are conceived as a whole will by the impressionist be presented unanalyzed, and, accordingly, indistinct or blurred. On the other hand, momentary, fragmented impressions, which gradually might be formed into a meaningful whole by the reflecting mind, will be rendered by the impressionist as they originally appeared.

The two aspects are not necessarily isolated in different scenes or episodes. A certain detail may catch the eye and stamp itself clearly on the mind while the surroundings are conceived more or less indistinctly: "As the smoke slowly eddied away, the youth saw that the charge had been repulsed. The enemy were scattered into reluctant groups. He saw a man climb to the top of the fence, straddle the rail, and fire a parting shot. The waves had receded, leaving bits of dark débris upon the ground" (I, 68). Against the vaguely conceived foreground is seen the sharply outlined figure of the retreating rebel.

Often the actual objects viewed are not described at all. The author may render the impression or sensation only and refrain from any representation of the thing itself: "The flaming opposition in their front grew with their advance until it seemed that all forward ways were barred by the thin leaping tongues, and off to the right an ominous demonstration could sometimes be dimly discerned" (I, 162). Similarly, the image "cantering cluster" (I, 74) is a vague, undetailed, but none the less vivid impression of a group of soldiers.

Closely related to this technique is Crane's frequent and peculiar use of words like "figure" or "form."[49] It is as if the author is reluctant to state that the forms he discerns are, in fact, human beings: "He discerned forms begin to swell in masses out of a distant wood" (I, 72). "Through the clouded dust or steam one could see the thin figure dealing mighty blows" (George's Mother, X, 24). The forms and figures are, experience tells us, human beings, but the impressionist tries to render his impressions unadulterated by former experience and logical conclusions. It is the fleeting moment of the first look he wishes to put on paper. Of course a second look may help clear things up: "In front of the gruesome doorway he met a lurching figure. It was his father ... "(Maggie, X, 173).

Our impression of a scene may change gradually until we realize what we actually are seeing or hearing. A second glance may give us a wholly different impression than did the first one. But both impressions are equally valid, since it is only our impression of reality that counts — that in fact is reality. This attitude is reflected in the following passages from The Red Badge: "And thereafter [the brigade] lay stretched in the distance behind a long grey wall, that one was obliged to look twice at to make sure that it was smoke" (I, 56). "Wild yells came from behind the walls of smoke. A sketch in grey and red dissolved into a mob-like body of men who galloped like wild horses" (I, 59). At first the smoke seemed to be a wall and as long as this was his impression it was as true as any other fact. The reader, too, is "obliged to look twice" before realizing that it actually was smoke. There is an important difference between this mode of expression and saying that "the brigades lay stretched behind a screen of smoke which at first glance appeared to be a long grey wall." Similarly, the indistinct "sketch of grey and red" dissolves into its component parts as we observe it.

In the previous examples the causes of the changing impressions and the uncertainty as to what actually is taking place are wholly external. Equally important are instances where it is the fictional character's state of mind — his emotions and fancies — that, so to speak, tricks him and gives him a distorted impression of reality. Again, of course, one impression is as valid or true as the other. Crane remarks on this phenomenon in "The Blue Hotel" when he says, "Any room can present a tragic front; any room can be comic" (X, 112). And in *The Red Badge* we see how a landscape changes in significance when the youth sees it a second time: "Absurd ideas took hold upon him. He thought that he did not relish the landscape. It threatened him ... A house standing placidly in distant fields had to him an ominous look. The shadows of the woods were formidable. He was certain that in this vista there lurked fierce-eyed hosts" (I, 50–51). But later he returns to the same scene: "In the afternoon the regiment went out over the same ground it had taken in the morning. The landscape then ceased to threaten the youth. He had been close to it and become familiar with it" (I, 55).

A similar experience is repeated toward the end of the book when the soldiers find time to "regard the ground over which they had charged" after again having retreated to their former positions. The youth "wondered at the number of emotions and events that had been crowded into such little spaces. Elfin thoughts must have exaggerated and enlarged everything, he said" (I, 175–76).

Perhaps the best example of how "any room can present a tragic front" is found in *George's Mother*:

> To Kelcey there was a million voices ... he followed his mother up the centre aisle of the little chapel. To him there was a riot of lights that made him transparent. The multitudinous pairs of eyes that turned toward him were implacable in their cool valuations.
> – – –

> When from the mists of his shame and humiliation the scene
> came before his vision, he was surprised to find that all eyes
> were not fastened upon his face. The leader of the meeting seemed
> to be the only one who saw him . . .
> A man . . . began to sing . . . Others, scattered sparsely
> throughout the innumerable light-wood chairs, joined him as
> they caught the air . . . The chandelier in the centre was the
> only one lighted . . . (X, 66–67)

Obviously the author is not primarily interested in the objects on
which the several impressions are based. The function of his technique
is to reveal the character's state of mind through direct presentation,
by showing how his impressions are colored or distorted.

> From their position as they again faced
> toward the place of the fighting, they
> could of course comprehend a greater
> amount of the battle than when their
> visions had been blurred by the hurling
> smoke of the line. (I, 153)

Limiting himself to the personal view, the impressionist will only
describe what is actually in sight or within hearing and how these
things appear to him. Throughout *The Red Badge* (except in the
first paragraph where, as it were, the "camera eye" settles down
on the camp and the youth, and the concluding one where it again
recedes) we in our imagined roles as spectators never have a larger
view of the field than has the main character. So conscious is Crane
of the point of view he has established for the novel that before he
lets us have a larger view of the battlefield through the eyes of the
youth and his comrade, he is careful to explain that they now "could
of course comprehend a greater amount of the battle" than before.

One consequence of this technique with regards to Crane's style is
the predominance of verbs of perception. Things are constantly
"seen," "heard," and "felt": they become real through the act of
perception. Also when a scene is rendered independently of the point
of view of a specific character it is often explicitly stated, nevertheless,
that it "could be seen." Before the description of the army camp in the
opening paragraphs of the novel it is "revealed" by "the retiring fogs."
Of the "hostile camp-fires" across the river it is not enough for Crane
merely to state that they were there, but that "one could see" them.

This insistence on describing what is actually experienced only is
perhaps seen most clearly where Crane explicitly distinguishes between

the impression of an object, or what is visible of it, and what is actually known about this object through experience or logic: "His eyesight was shaken and dazzled by the tension of thought and muscle. He did not see anything excepting the mist of smoke gashed by the little knives of fire, but he knew that in it lay the aged fence of a vanished farmer, protecting the snuggled bodies of the grey men" (I, 189–90).

Another example may be taken from "The Open Boat": "The sun swung steadily up the sky, and they knew it was broad day because the colour of the sea changed from slate to emerald green streaked with amber lights, and the foam was like tumbling snow. They were aware only of this effect upon the colour of the waves that rolled toward them" (XII, 31). Crane describes what the boat crew did see and tells us that on these facts they based their knowledge of the change from night to day. Then, as if to underline their restricted vision, he goes on to stress the fact that they did not know the actual "process of the breaking day" and again repeats that they were only aware of "this effect upon the colour of the waves."

As the view of the fictional characters is restricted to what at any given moment they are able to grasp through their senses, so the author is confined to relating what it is possible for these senses to reveal. The opening lines of the same short story are illustrative of this technique: "None of them knew the colour of the sky. Their eyes glanced level, and were fastened upon the waves that swept toward them. These waves were of the hue of slate, save for the tops which were of foaming white, and all of the men knew the colours of the sea" (X, 29). Here Crane limits himself to describing only what his characters are alleged to see, and if on any occasion he should feel obliged to tell us something that in all probability could not have been seen, he is careful not to violate his point of view: "In the wan light the faces of the men must have been grey. Their eyes must have glinted in strange ways as they gazed steadily astern" (X, 31). Since it could not be observed how, exactly, their faces were or their eyes glinted Crane evades the difficulty by indicating how they "must have been."

By making use of such a technique the author pretends not to be omniscient and thus gives his readers a greater illusion of being spectators to what is being described. And this, we have said, is one of the main aims of the impressionist writer (although, needless to say, the strict use of a physical point of view is not restricted to impressionism alone).

17

It could be seen that a great thought
was within her. (*George's Mother*, X, 29)

In his study of the technique of the novel Staffan Björck points
out that the naturalists and impressionists were especially interested
in interpreting movements of an individual's body as an indication
of what is going on in that person's mind.[50] In the latter part of the
19th century all the answers to the problems of psychology were by
many thought to be found in physiology, and this may be one reason
why naturalistic writers show such an interest in physiological appearances. Crane's habit of seeing physiological appearances as indications of a character's thoughts and feelings, however, is also an aspect
of his restricted point of view.[51]

When the youth in *The Red Badge* is asked by the tattered soldier:
"Where yeh hit?" we *see* his embarrassment; we are not told about it:
"He turned away suddenly and slid through the crowd. His brow was
heavily flushed, and his fingers were picking nervously at one of
his buttons. He bent his head and fastened his eyes studiously upon
the button as if it were a little problem" (I, 91). Crane does not venture
to say what was going on behind the "heavily flushed" brow. He shows
us the youth with all the outward signs of not feeling too comfortable
nor over-confident, but the conclusions are left for the reader to draw
as a participating observer on the scene.

The following two passages from *The Red Badge* may serve as further
illustrations of the same technique: "In the regiment there was a
peculiar kind of hesitation denoted in the attitudes of the men"
(I, 145). "Into the youth's eyes there came a look that one can see in
the orbs of a jaded horse. His neck was quivering with nervous weakness, and the muscles of his arms felt numb and bloodless. His hands,
too, seemed large and awkward, as if he was wearing invisible mittens.
And there was a great uncertainty about his knee joints" (I, 73).
Exactly what the peculiar kind of hesitation was like the reader must
judge himself from what he sees of "the attitudes of the men." As for
the youth, there is no attempt at any explicit interpretation at all
except, perhaps, the noting of a similarity between the look in his
eyes and in those of "a jaded horse." Otherwise his physiological
reactions are described.

This technique is not restricted to *The Red Badge* but is found
throughout Crane's work, so frequently, indeed, that it comes close
to being a mannerism. The following examples are from *George's
Mother*:

He regarded himself in the mirror . . . He should have seen a grinning face with a rather pink nose. His derby was perched carelessly on the back part of his head. Two wisps of hair straggled down over his hollow temples. There was something very worldly and wise about him. Life did not seem to confuse him. Evidently he understood its complications. His hand thrust into his trousers pocket, expressed a young man of vast knowledge. (X, 21) Still it could be seen that she even then was planning skirmishes, charges, campaigns. (X, 25)

It is interesting to note the reservation implied in the expression "should have seen" in the first example. Seemingly, Crane insists on his being the objective recorder of appearances by professing that he has no way of knowing what Jones actually did see in the mirror. (It is evident, too, that this particular manner of description is remarkably well adapted to bringing out the ironic quality that permeates Crane's work.)

After the shipwreck prior to the happenings related in "The Open Boat" the "captain had on him the stern impression of a scene in the greys of dawn of seven turned faces, and later a stump of a top-mast with a white ball on it, that slashed to and fro at the waves, went lower and lower down." This wreck has wrought a great change in the captain, but we are made aware of this change only through certain observations on the change of his voice: "Thereafter there was something strange in his voice. Although steady, it was deep with mourning, and of a quality beyond oration or tears" (XII, 30). Similarly in "The Blue Hotel," where the Swede, before joining in on the game of cards, "remained near the window, aloof, but with a countenance that showed signs of an inexplicable excitement" (X, 97). Crane does not tell us that the Swede *was* excited. He is the objective observer and with him we are allowed to see that the Swede's countenance "showed signs" of such a state.

> There was a youthful private . . .
> (I, 23)

One of the most conspicuous traits of style in *The Red Badge* is the anonymity of the novel's characters. Not once does Crane use a proper name in his narrative. Only in the dialogue do we learn the names of some of the persons. In order to define a character Crane selects a single epithet, often the first adjective used to describe him. Thus Jim Conklin is presented to us as "a certain tall soldier" (I, 21), and although his first name is revealed on p. 23 ("What's up, Jim?") and his surname on p. 43 ("Well, Jim Conklin says we'll get a plenty of fighting this time."), his name is never mentioned in the narrative sections of the novel. When we meet Jim Conklin among the wounded men walking away from the front lines, we see that "he stalked like the spectre of a soldier" (p. 88). On the following pages he is called "the spectral soldier" until the youth recognizes him and cries out, "Gawd! Jim Conklin!" (p. 93) after which he is again referred to as "the tall soldier." As before our vision is restricted to what the observers see or understand.

This technique is no unprecedented feature in Crane's writing. In his very first work of fiction, *The Sullivan County Sketches*, it is applied quite consistently. Although names are used in Maggie, in narrative as well as in dialogue, we know that Crane had first written a draft of the novel without any names at all.[52] In the final version of *Maggie*, and in the novel succeeding *The Red Badge, George's Mother*, this usage is somewhat modified. Thus George Kelcey is merely a "brown young man" until we hear an old friend of his call out, "Hello, Kelcey, ol' boy!" (X, 20) After his name has been "revealed" in this manner, it is freely used by the author in the narrative.

> And at last his eyes seemed to open to
> some new ways. (I, 199)

The wholly objective observer, however, is a fiction if we are to believe what Stephen Crane himself has said on honesty and the truthful rendering of reality. A writer cannot say how things *are*, but only how they seem or appear to *him*, how they are according to his "own pair of eyes." This was not merely a theory that Crane expressed when writing about fiction, but an attitude embodied in his style and technique. The world of Stephen Crane is a world of appearances.

The following passage from *The Red Badge* describing Jim Conklin as seen by Henry Fleming in the procession of wounded men may serve to show how such an attitude towards reality effects the author's style: "The shadows of his face were deepening, and his tight lips seemed holding in check the moan of great despair. There could be seen a certain stiffness in the movements of his body, as if he were taking infinite care not to arouse the passion of his wounds. As he went on, he seemed always looking for a place, like one who goes to choose a grave" (I, 92–93). There seems to be no reason to suspect that the soldier's tight lips were not withholding a moan of despair, nor that the reason for his moving carefully actually was "not to arouse the passion of his wounds." Also we eventually learn that he really was "looking for a place" and that he was going "to choose a grave." But Crane merely shows us what he sees and gives us his impressions of it, and lets the reader decide what final conclusions, if any, may be drawn.

Of course there is nothing remarkable in occasionally using the word "seem." But when it occurs 82 times in the course of a novel's 180 pages we may safely consider it to be of some significance — especially when it is only one of the many means used to express this same attitude: "The body seemed to bounce a little way from the earth" (I, 98). "He seemed about to deliver a philippic" (I, 98). "This instant's hesitation seemed to fill him with a tremendous, fantastic contempt. ..." (I, 152). The same effect is arrived at through the use of similar words and expressions: "The greater part of the untested men appeared quiet and absorbed" (I, 51). "These troops had apparently been going forward with caution ..." (I, 171).

Another expression of the same attitude is the use of "as if." Generally this figure of speech serves to introduce a comparison. Frequently, however, it merely serves the same function as the adverb "apparently": "... there was a sudden halt, as if they feared to go near" (I, 152). "They looked wild-eyed, as if amazed at this furious disturbance they had stirred" (I, 162). "He strode toward the men nervously, as if he expected to be assaulted" ("The Blue Hotel," X, 97). In such instances no actual comparison is, strictly speaking, being made. The effect of what formally is a comparison is here merely to express how these characters appeared to behave themselves. In Møller Kristensen's words: by assuming the appearance of being merely the objective spectator the author leaves to the reader, also a spectator, to find the logical relations between the different impressions himself.[53]

> He went as near as he dared, trying to overhear words. Perhaps the general, unable to comprehend chaos, might call upon him for information. And he could tell him. He knew all concerning it. Of a surety the force was in a fix, and any fool could see that if they did not retreat while they had the opportunity — why — (I, 77–78)

It must be admitted, however, that the author, and through him the reader, of *The Red Badge* is not merely an ordinary spectator. The point of view is dual: we are both spectators on a scene where the main character is one of the actors, and we experience the same scene, to a large extent, through this main character. We do not only see him in action; we have access to his innermost thoughts and feelings. Clearly the author must at times penetrate surfaces and appearances. The passage quoted above is a good example of the manner in which Crane frequently does this — a technique which has been termed "substitutionary speech."[54]

In direct speech we have what is supposed to be an exact replica of the words or thoughts uttered. In indirect speech only the forms of verbs and pronouns are changed to the extent made necessary by the use of the third person; otherwise it is assumed that the words used are those of the speaker. A third way of representing what a character says or thinks is a narrative where the author speaks on his own behalf giving information of the contents of a character's speech withouth pretending to reproduce the words of the character in question. A combination of the two latter methods is the special form of substitutionary speech where "the reporter [is] experiencing the actor's speech, speaking in the actor's name, substituting his own voice for the actor's although still aware that he is the first person and the actor the third. So it is partly the actor speaking through the reporter and partly the reporter speaking through the actor."[55] And, it will be remembered, this midway area between external facts and the author's personality is the special domain of impressionism.

Before we discuss this technique in detail it is convenient to give some further examples of its application by Crane:

> There was the law, he said. Nature had given him a sign. The squirrel, immediately upon recognizing danger, had taken to his legs without ado. He did not stand stolidly baring his furry belly to the missile, and die with an upward glance at the sympathetic heavens ... The youth wended, feeling that Nature was of his mind. She reinforced his arguments with proofs that lived where the sun shone. (I, 82–83)
> He would die; he would go to some place where he would be understood. It was useless to expect appreciation of his profound and fine senses from such men as the lieutenant. He must look to the grave for comprehension. (I, 55)

In both these passages we are given an impression of the working of the youth's mind without the use of those verbs of utterance usually found in connection with direct or indirect rendering (exception made for "said" and "feeling" in the beginning and end of the first example).

The result is to give the reader an illusion of having direct access to the character's thoughts without interfering elements of narrative.

In substitutionary speech the actual act of thinking or speaking tends to slip into the background. It is of minor importance to be aware of the speaker or the thinking person *qua* speaker or thinker, says Luise Thon.[56] Speech and thought are of importance as experienced phenomena only, especially thought in its most instinctive forms. The impressionist is not, that is, primarily interested in how — or even that — these thoughts or words are created. His main concern is the impression of these manifestations themselves: "This sight also filled him with wonder. The brigade was hurrying briskly to be gulped into the infernal mouths of the war god. What manner of men were they, anyhow? Ah, it was some wondrous breed! Or else they didn't comprehend — the fools" (I, 77). Here the youth's thoughts are rendered in such a way as to acquire an almost independent status.

Luise Thon also stresses that in substitutionary speech there is no clear distinction between it and the narrative.[57] Thus it serves to break down the artificial and imposed distinctions by which man organizes his impressions into well-ordered units: "A corporal began to swear before the assemblage. He had just put a costly board floor in his house, he said. During the early spring he had refrained from adding extensively to the comfort of his environment because he had felt that the army might start on the march at any moment. Of late, however, he had been impressed that they were in a sort of eternal camp" (I, 22). First we have pure description as our interest centers on one of the several groups which together make up our impression of the army camp in the opening chapter of the novel. Then we have the corporal speaking, as made clear by the here necessary "he said." Thereafter, however, his monologue is rendered in substitutionary speech: the words used are evidently not those of the corporal. The act of speaking glides into the background and our interest is concentrated on the impression of what is said. Or *is* this said: no clear distinction is made between what is uttered or thought and what may be a report of past happenings. Thus substitutionary speech serves to express the impressionist's world of confused sense impressions.

In the following passage, where a description of the scene, Henry Fleming's actions, his thoughts, attitudes, and feelings, are all intermingled, creating a single consecutive flood of impressions, this effect of the impressionist's use of substitutionary speech is quite clear:

The shadows of the woods were formidable. He was certain that in this vista there lurked fierce-eyed hosts. The swift thought came to him that the generals did not know what they were about. It was all a trap. Suddenly those close forests would bristle with rifle barrels. Iron-like brigades would appear in the rear. They were all going to be sacrificed. The generals were stupids. The enemy would presently swallow the whole command. He glared about him, expecting to see the stealthy approach of his death.

He thought that he must break from the ranks and harangue his comrades. They must not be killed like pigs ... (etc., I, 51)

Although substitutionary speech has been said to be one of the hallmarks of impressionism,[58] in one respect it is obviously in contrast with a general trend in impressionistic technique: the withdrawal of the author from the novel. Throughout these passages from *The Red Badge* the ironic and personal tone of the author is evident; the author is commenting on his characters, albeit somewhat more subtly than in the traditional 19th century novel. Substitutionary speech is exceedingly convenient as a means of giving a description this ironic quality.[59]

> The houses of the village glided past in a moment ... ("Horses – One Dash," XII, 213)

One aspect of the impressionist's reluctance to analyze is a tendency to veil or neglect causal relations between objects, actions or phenomena described.[60] The immediate impressions we receive of phenomena through our senses are often quite different from what we finally realize them to be. Only by applying logic and relying on experience can we make them fit into the laws of cause and effect and other terms through which the surrounding world is meaningful to us. Sometimes the interval between the perception and the realization of its meaning may be quite noticeable — as when one of two trains at a station slowly begins to move and the passengers are at first at a loss to determine which of the trains is actually on its way. But as a rule our interpretation of our impressions is, for all practical purposes, instantaneous. Thus, when Stephen Crane describes houses as gliding past a man on horseback, he is recording a primary impression and rejecting logic.

In another passage from the same short story the wilful neglect of logical nexus is even more pronounced: "Suddenly some low houses appeared squatting amid the bushes. The horseman rode into a hollow until the houses rose against the sombre sundown sky, and then up a small hillock, causing these habitations to sink like boats in the sea of shadow" (XII, 204). By riding up the hillock the horseman *causes* the houses to "sink like boats in the sea of shadow." In this case a causal relation is stated, but in a way that *ipso facto* negates all logic and experience. As we have seen, Crane has a tendency to use "seem" about phenomena which, to all appearance, are factual. In passages like the one quoted above, on the contrary, he states a purely imaginative fact as if it were real, thus further stressing the importance of the individual impression of reality.

Instead of imposing a wholly illogical cause, as above, the impressionist may overlook the cause altogether and render its effect alone: "A beam of red firelight fell across the trail. Richardson sat sleepily on his horse while the servant quarreled with somebody — a mere voice in the gloom — over the price of bed and board" (ibid., 204). Out in the dark we know that such a beam of light *means* that a door has been opened. But we see only the light; accordingly Crane gives us this effect and lets the reader deduce the cause as he must in real life.

A more frequent expression of this aspect of the impressionist's passive attitude is the use of figures (more or less related to the synecdoche) where impressions of details are rendered without giving their wider relations, or where such impressions only gradually gain in meaning.[61] In the passage quoted above we see the germ of such a technique. We are told that "the servant quarrelled with somebody." But as this "somebody" is only inferred from "a mere voice in the gloom," it would perhaps be more "correct," according to impressionist theory, to let us hear the voice only, or let us hear the voice and then reveal that this is a "somebody." And this is what Crane repeatedly does. So often do such figures occur in his writing that they strike one as a mannerism:[62] "From one of these [fires] near by there came sudden sharp voices in a row" (I, 131). "He was recalled by a hoarse laugh and a sentence that came to his ears in a voice of contempt and amazement" (I, 149). "A pessimistic voice asked ..." ("Twelve O'Clock," XII, 106).

In none of these cases are we told anything about whom the voice or voices may have belonged to. They seem to exist independently of any owner. Such a primary impression may develop until it also includes the person or persons from whom these various utterances have come:

"From the window at which the man raged came the sound of an old voice, singing . . . A little old woman was the owner of the voice" (*George's Mother*, X, 24). " 'What's wrong wi'che?' said a voice in the gathered gloom, and Jimmie came forward" (*Maggie*, X, 174). As the result of a second look or thought the impressions of these voices grow to encompass the "owner" as well. In the latter example this is brought about by external circumstances while in the first the new information is added as an afterthought: first that the "old voice" was singing; then that it belonged to "a little old woman."

Another effect of this technique is evident in the following examples from *Maggie*, where the members of the body which are singled out strike one as having a peculiarly autonomous quality, even more than was the case in the previous examples: "On an upper hall a door was opened and a collection of heads peered curiously out, watching her" (X, 174). "Through the open doors curious eyes stared in at Maggie" (X, 202). ". . . she went before open doors framing more eyes strangely microscopic, and sending broad beams of inquisitive light into the darkness of her path" (X, 203–04). The eyes and heads peer or turn quite independently of any will or body.

This technique is very effective in the description of a bar: "An odour of grasping, begrimed hands and munching mouths pervaded all" (X, 182). And a bartender is — in the eyes of little Jimmie — reduced to a pair of hands: "Straining on his toes he raised the pail and pennies as high as his arms would let him. He saw two hands thrust down to take them. Directly the same hands let down the filled pail, and he left" (X, 147). The technique here serves a realistic purpose since Jimmie is too small to see more of the man behind the bar than his hands. Typically, Crane the impressionist does not go out of his way to indicate that the hands do belong to anybody.

Synecdoche is often used in connection with descriptions of crowds or other foregatherings of people: "But he was amid wounds" (I, 92). "Many heads surged to and fro, floating upon a pale sea of smoke" (I, 185). Also here the heads are independent objects which do not merely seem to float but are actually "floating." In the following passage the impression may develop differently from what we have now become used to, but the effect is the same: "The sidewalks became tossing seas of umbrellas" (*Maggie*, X, 208). What we realize to be a sidewalk changes into "seas of umbrellas." Again we would normally expect "seemed to become."

> He was welded into a common perso-
> nality which was dominated by a single
> desire. (I, 64)

Along with Crane's use of detail we also found an opposite technique of neglecting all detail and giving only a vague and sweeping impression of a scene. In the following we are again confronted with a technique that may seem to contradict what has just been said above: " 'Whoop!' said the Rum Alley tenement house. The hall filled with interested spectators ... The Rum Alley tenement swore disappointedly and retired" (*Maggie*, X, 175). "Whole brigades grinned in unison and regiments laughed" (I, 40). "Presently the army again sat down to think" (I, 47).

We have seen how a single detail like a pair of hands, a head or a voice may be substituted for an individual, or a group of such details for a group of individuals. In these examples, however, the individual has disappeared altogether and has become merely an undistinguishable part of a whole.[63] The explanation of such a dichotomy in technique is similar to that applied in the previous case: where the main impression is that of a group each individual is an insignificant detail that may safely be neglected. The sense of unity is so strong that the group is visualized as a living entity. The Rum Alley tenement whoops and swears, the army thinks, and regiments laugh. In "The mob of men was bleeding" (I, 92), this effect is emphasized by the use of the third person singular of the copula.

Often this sense of the group as a living entity is so strong that it prevails even after the group itself is dissolved: "At nightfall the column broke into regimental pieces, and the fragments went into the fields to camp" (I, 41). "The line, broken into moving fragments by the ground, went calmly on through fields and woods" (I, 51). "The group of urchins burst instantly asunder and its individual fragments were spread in a wide respectable half-circle ... " (*Maggie*, X, 173). The individuals that formed it are still conceived in terms of the group as its parts or fragments.

> He finally concluded that the only way
> to prove himself was to go into the blaze,
> and then figuratively to watch his legs
> to discover their merits and faults. (I, 35)

In some of the synecdochal figures discussed above parts or functions of the human body, the voice for instance, are conceived as wholly independent objects: "Presently the latter heard a voice talking softly near his shoulders. Turning, he saw that it belonged to the tattered soldier" (I, 95). At first the tattered soldier is conceived only as a voice. But even after the realization of who was talking, the voice still seems to be considered as an object belonging to the tattered soldier.

In this way the individual is often regarded not as an entity, but as consisting of several more or less independent parts that function like so many pieces of machinery. To be able to prove himself the youth has to "watch his legs to discover their merits and faults" and to experiment with his own body in the manner of a chemist, using "blaze, blood, and danger" as reagents, and study the resulting reactions. Behind such a technique we may again find a profoundly objective and passive attitude toward the surrounding world — objective in its insistence on recording only what is perceived by the senses, and passive in its view of man as a conglomerate of various parts and forces over which he has no real control.

In *George's Mother* Mrs. Kelcey is first shown to us cleaning her kitchen: "She splashed about, the dwindled muscles working to and fro under the loose skin of her arms" (X, 24). This is the image of a mere puppet where "dwindled muscles" serve as strings. Advancing on the battlefield Henry Fleming is preoccupied with his new experience and "his forgotten feet were constantly knocking against stones or getting entangled in briers" (I, 49). In cases of high tension, as in battle, it is natural that one's selfcontrol is somewhat diminished.

In the following examples the youth has no will of his own at all to direct or restrict what appear as physiological reflexes: "Before he was ready to begin — before he had announced to himself that he was about to fight — he threw the obedient, well-balanced rifle into position and fired a first wild shot. Directly he was working at his rifle like an automatic affair" (I, 64). "Within him something bade to cry out. He had the impulse to make a rallying speech, to sing a battle hymn, but he could only get his tongue to call into the air: 'Why — why — what — what's th' matter?' " (I, 112–13). Although war emphasizes man's helplessness when confronted with the forces of nature and society, this view (also shared by naturalistic writers) of man unable to govern his own thoughts and actions fits into the prevalent impressionism of Crane's work.

The body of a human being is sometimes visualized as something separate from the human being himself — as something, so to speak, moved about by its owner: "He lifted himself upon his toes and looked in the direction of the fight" (I, 80). "They moved their stiffened bodies slowly, and watched in sullen mood the frantic approach of the enemy" (I, 72). These soldiers may move themselves "mechanically, dully" (I, 67), but they at least move themselves. In other cases they often find themselves being moved about more or less like tin soldiers: "They were marched from place to place with apparent aimlessness" (I, 53). "... before he was entirely awake, he found himself running down a wood road in the midst of men ..." (I, 48). The youth himself has apparently had nothing to do with his own action: he just finds himself running.

Tongues are sometimes conceived as quite independent objects that act on their own accord: "The men of the new regiment watched and listened eagerly, while their tongues ran on in gossip of the battle" (I, 57). In *Maggie* such a conception of different parts of the body is quite common, and some examples have been discussed previously in connection with synecdoche. Sometimes they are nothing else; but often they also express this more extreme view: "Her hair straggled, giving her red features a look of insanity. Her great fists quivered as she shook them madly in the air" (X, 174). In this passage the straggling hair and the quivering fists are both conceived on the same level: there is an impression of both as separate and unruly parts of the body. Some lines further down, "Her cursing trebles brought heads from all doors save the one she threatened. Her eyes glared in every direction. The air was full of her tossing fists." While in the former example the fists have a passive character, here the cursing trebles, glaring eyes, and tossing fists all play an active role. *She* does not bring heads from all doors by cursing, it is the cursing trebles themselves that do this. She does not glare — her eyes do; and her tossing fists have acquired a peculiar detached quality.

Crane often makes use of conspicuous stylistic devices in order to give various parts of the body this detached quality: "He passed over his brow a hand that trembled" (I, 170). The use of the indefinite article in this case emphasizes the impression of this hand as a separate object independent of the person moving it.[64] The logical phrase might be: "He passed his trembling hand over his brow."

Adjectives may serve the same stylistic function: "The youth put forth anxious arms to assist him ..." (I, 93). "Of a sudden he felt a heavy and sad hand laid upon his shoulder" (I, 56). "Women shrugged impatient shoulders ..." (*Maggie*, X, 208). "The youth turned quick eyes upon the field" (I, 72). Clearly it is the youth who is anxious and not the arms he puts forward, and the same is the case with the "sad hand" and the "impatient shoulders." "Quick eyes" is decidedly more vivid and impressive than the same idea expressed with the adverb "quickly." By using adjectives in this manner Crane also succeeds in connecting a rather abstract notion of for instance anxiety or sadness with a concrete sense impression. Another result of his using adjectives instead of adverbs in these cases is that our attention is directed to the arms or hands themselves and not to the action performed with them.

Even facial expressions are endowed with this independent quality. Thus an expression is often perceived as something "worn": "His lean features wore an expression of awe and admiration" (I, 89). "He wore a look of watchfulness" (*Maggie*, X, 182). The implications of such a stylistic trait may be best demonstrated by comparing two passages: "A scowl of mortification and rage was upon his face" (I, 167), "Dust and stains were upon his face" (I, 124). Both the scowl and the dust and stains are conceived as having essentially the same qualities, being, to the objective eye, something on the surface of a face. There is nothing to indicate that expressions thus worn originate within the persons themselves.

> A flurry of fast questions was in the air. (I, 192)

This characteristic of Crane's style is also present in his treatment of speech and utterances: "A little group of soldiers surrounded the two youths. 'Are we, sure 'nough? Well, I'll be derned! Charge? What fer? What at? Wilson, you're lyin'' " (I, 156). By omitting all verbs of utterance and not referring to any person in particular as articulating these questions and remarks, the author has made the utterances themselves independent of those who spoke them. Thus eliminating the narrator the impressionist again withdraws from his work, and the scene is conveyed directly to the reader by letting him hear fragments of conversation. In addition Crane succeeds in giving us the impression of several people speaking all at once — an effect achieved both by omitting all verbs of utterance and by placing all the ejaculations within one set of quotation marks.[65]

The independent quality of utterances may be accentuated not only through what is omitted but by what is affirmed:

> Meanwhile, the soldier who had fetched the rumour bustled about with much importance. He was continually assailed by questions.

"What's up Jim?"
"Th' army's goin' t' move."
" Ah, what yeh talkin' about? ..." (I, 23)

Here the assailing questions themselves have acquired an active status and are still further removed from the domain of those who — supposedly — ask them than in the passages hitherto discussed.

A similar conception is expressed in the following examples: "A low, tittering laugh went among his fellows" (I, 39). "But, of a sudden, cries of amazement broke out along the ranks of the new regiment" (I, 72). In either case it is the laugh or cries that demand our interest, not how they are made. This active quality of utterances is most frequently expressed by the verb "to go." When "broke out" is used the cries are active to the degree that they, so to speak, make themselves. The impression is still dominated by the cries independent of the act of crying, and this fact is accentuated by the wholly passive role attributed to those who perform it.

This manner of perception is carried still further in the following passages: "There was heard the cushioned sound of blows, and of a curse squeezing out from between the tight teeth of one" ("The Blue Hotel," X, 117). "From his lips came a black procession of curious oaths" (I, 66). The image of oaths coming in a "black procession" is visual (synaesthesia), and the oaths have thereby reached the point of becoming concrete and tangible. From here there is only a short step to the conception of utterances as objects: "There were crows and catcalls showered upon him ..." (I, 41). "Immediately canteens were showered upon him" (I, 153). There is no difference in quality between the calls and the canteens as for their materialness or tangibility in these two sentences, and similar passages bear evidence of the same attitude: "A slim youth on a fine chestnut horse caught these swift words from the mouth of his superior" (I, 78). "He now hurled a strange mass of language at the head of his son" ("The Blue Hotel," X, 109).

Sven Møller Kristensen finds it to be characteristic of impressionism that all phenomena are conceived as things or objects. Sensations, living entities and their manifestations of life are described in terms that in normal usage are reserved for descriptions of concrete matter.[66] This is what we have seen Crane doing in many of the examples discussed above. As Møller Kristensen affirms, this technique is to a large extent an echo of the naturalist's scientific and mechanistic view of life. But it also accentuates the passive role of man in an otherwise active universe: he is governed or controlled by his sensations and other manifestations and not vice versa.

A battery spoke. (I, 55)

The prevalent passive tone in Crane's style as far as human beings are concerned becomes even more conspicuous when contrasted with the active tone of his language in connection with environment or lifeless matter. While Crane's men are "marched from place to place with apparent aimlessness" and the youth has no control over his own tongue or actions, his batteries speak as a matter of course.

In the following examples the active tone conveyed by the verbs and adjectives is evident: "From a position in the rear of the grove a battery was throwing shells over it" (I, 68). "The guns squatted in a row like savage chiefs. They argued with abrupt violence ... Their busy servants ran hither and thither" (I, 69). Not only arms, but other equipment as well, are in this manner imbued with an active quality often denied human beings: "A flag, tilted forward, sped near the front" (I, 63). "The white-topped wagons strained and stumbled in their exertions like fat sheep" (I, 104). Man's prostration is perhaps nowhere demonstrated more strikingly than in his conflicts with an active and wilful surrounding nature: "Sometimes the brambles formed chains and tried to hold him back. Trees, confronting him, stretched out their arms and forbade him to pass" (I, 86).

In many of the metaphors and similes of these examples we recognize the language of animation or personification. Up to this point Crane's use of animation seems to comply with our pattern of impressionism. But throughout his work he also uses this artistic device in a manner that may hardly be explained along such lines: "The mournful current moved slowly on, and from the water, shaded black, some white bubble eyes looked at the men" (I, 49). "Smoke clouds went slowly and insolently across the fields like observant phantoms" (I, 55–56). "At first the grey lights of dawn came timidly into the room, remaining near the windows, afraid to approach certain sinister corners" (*George's Mother*, X, 58).

Here the pathetic fallacy becomes, perhaps, a little too strained. Such passages impress us primarily as being whimsical and might even be taken to indicate a romantic, fairy-tale-view of nature. But such an assumption would likely lead us into a blind alley. Luise Thon finds this technique to be characteristic of the German impressionists, and she sees it as motivated by the impressionist's attempt to make the reader partake of his own experience by getting as close as possible to the actual impression. For such a purpose, "was liegt ihm näher als das Verhalten und Tun des eigenen Wesens."[67]

Be this as it may, Crane's metaphors of this type sometimes tend to have an expressive rather than an impressive effect. In this connection it is useful to recall the view held by many scholars that expressionism may be regarded as a further development of impressionism: "They made toward a little glass-fronted saloon that sat blinking jovially at the crowds. It engulfed them with a gleeful motion of its two widely smiling lips" (*George's Mother*, X, 20). "In a dark street the little chapel sat humbly between two towering apartment-houses" (ibid., 65). In these passages the main purport of the metaphors is no longer to give vivid impressions, but to characterize the qualities of two different influences at work on George's life. It seems evident that in such instances Crane's style has taken a step beyond impressionism. In the present study, however, we will refrain from pursuing that path, well aware that the trend toward symbolism is a necessary aspect of any complete picture of Stephen Crane.

> The red sun was pasted in the sky like a wafer. (I, 98)

A comprehensive analysis of Crane's imagery would doubtlessly throw interesting sidelights on his work, but would carry us far beyond our present scope. Here we shall look into those aspects of his imagery which will add to the picture of his impressionism.

His similes, being the figure of speech most often found in Crane and in impressionistic writing in general, are of greatest interest.[68] As we repeatedly have noticed, the attempt to get as close as possible to the actual impression is one of the main forces in the making of Crane's style and technique. It is this aim that Luise Thon sums up in her characterization of impressionism as "die Kunst des Treffens" — the art, that is, of getting at the most strikingly adequate expression of the author's impression of reality.[69] This important feature is perhaps seen more graphically in Crane's imagery than in any other aspect of his work.

Whether he is describing an action, an object, or the sensations and feelings of a character, Crane will almost invariably resort to a comparison of some kind. Since the personal impression of any experience is of greater importance to the impressionist than any accurate

18

description of "reality," and since such impressions often come to us surrounded by sudden intuitions and vague or striking associations, the prevalence of such figures in an author's style may also be an indication of his attitude to reality.

Toward the end of *George's Mother* George is sitting at his mother's deathbed: "Kelcey began to stare at the wall paper. The pattern was clusters of brown roses. He felt them like hideous crabs crawling upon his brain" (X, 90). This image is by itself arresting and connotative. But on closer thought it gives us no actual information of Kelcey's emotions while watching his mother die. It is merely a vague and (seemingly) sudden impression of a feeling which the author is unable to articulate adequately, and which he therefore suggests through a comparison.[70] Technically the image is quite objective: this is how Kelcey feels, and no intruding author steps in to explain his emotions. But again we see that this objectivity is illusory. In the very use of such a striking image we are made aware of the author as artist. It is quite evident from what we know of George that the image is foreign to his imagination.

The passage above shows several of the characteristics of Crane's imagery: 1) Through an unexpected, rare, or even bizarre, image he seeks to arrest the reader so that the impression will strike home. 2) Description of what is seen or felt is sacrificed to an association or comparison that may let the reader partake in the author's impression of what is experienced. 3) The image creates an illusion of objectivety although we become aware of the author in the manner in which this illusion is created.

A great number of Crane's similes begin with "it was as if." Instead of telling us what something is, he tells what it reminds him of and what associations it brings to the mind of the character in question. Of a brigade going into action he says: "It was as if it had exploded" (I, 56), and when the bullets began to nip at the trees: "It was as if a thousand axes, wee and invisible, were being wielded" (I, 59). A regiment is preparing for an attack: "It was as if seven hundred new bonnets were being tried on" (I, 62), and when the "crimson roar" of battle reaches the youth, "It was as if worlds were being rended" (I, 85).

Throughout *The Red Badge* things happen and things are seen as if they were something else: "As if by agreement, the leaders began to slacken their speed" (I, 160). ". . . the colour-sergeant flinched suddenly, as if struck by a bludgeon" (I, 164). These images are conventional and their primary function is to throw light on the object or action itself. As isolated features they would hardly indicate an impressionistic attitude. But their profusion bears evidence of a writer who easily resorts to the more or less spontaneous associations invoked by the impression of a scene, instead of analyzing it and arriving at a more accurate description.

There is no sharp division between these "conventional" similes and those that are more typical of impressionism. But there is nevertheless a difference in effect between the instances above and the following ones: "He waited as if he expected the enemy to suddenly stop, apologize, and retire bowing" (I, 73). "The artillery were assembling as if for a conference" (I, 115). ". . . the men trudged with sudden heaviness, as if they bore upon their bended shoulders the coffin of their honour" (I, 175). In the first group the comparisons are purely descriptive, while in the latter the function of the comparison is primarily that of qualifying the personal impression of what is seen. This difference, however, is obviously one of degree and not of a fundamental character. The constant use of the figure "as if" gives Crane's descriptions a vague and unreal quality, reminding us of the impressionist's attitude to reality: he cannot reveal "reality" to the reader, only his personal impression of it.

When we read in *Maggie* that, "The forlorn woman had a peculiar face. Her smile was no smile. But when in repose her features had a shadowy look that was like a sardonic grin, as if some one had sketched with cruel forefinger indelible lines about her mouth" (X, 201), the description becomes shadowy as well as her features. The "shadowy look" is compared with a "sardonic grin" which is compared with the effect of a certain action. When this "forlorn woman" accosts Jimmie, he answers "with the savageness of a man whose life is pestered," and the woman follows him "along the sidewalk in somewhat the manner of a suppliant." It is evident that an author who writes like this is not attempting to give any accurate description of what these people are doing or look like, but is trying to convey the impression of a scene. Therefore there is no need for exact comparison either, and Crane finds it sufficient to state that the woman acted "in *somewhat* the manner of" someone.

Seeking an expression for an ever changing and transitory appearance the impressionist's images naturally tend to be particular and personal rather than general and universal. They do not profess to reveal about the objects or situations described any deep and hidden truth which will be valid for all time. The aim is merely to convey the immediate impression evoked by a certain set of circumstances, the interplay of which would most probably occur only on that one and unique occasion. Often this makes Crane's images seem rather far-fetched as in the following passages: "Tents sprang up like strange plants. Camp-fires, like red, peculiar blossoms, dotted the night" (I, 41). "... shifting forms which ... had been growing larger and larger like puppets under a magician's hand" (I, 66). "... the general beamed upon the earth like a sun" (I, 79). It is the extraordinary and unusual image that is most apt to strike the reader's eye and give him the impression of partaking in a unique experience.

In order to make an impression as real as possible to his reader by evoking sensations common to human experience, Crane, we have seen, applies adjectives and verbs normally used in connection with human actions and reactions. He also tries to achieve this aim by comparing sensations or impressions to the most common and every-day experiences. In some cases the use of this technique may bring about a striking contrast between the thing seen and the image evoked to describe its impression: "In the eastern sky there was a yellow patch like a rug laid before the feet of the coming sun ..." (I, 37). "The men dropped here and there like bundles" (I, 67). "One of the wounded men had a shoeful of blood. He hopped like a schoolboy in a game" (I, 88).

This inclination to find a striking or original image may at times have an effect probably not intended. Instead of giving the reader the illusion of partaking in a unique experience, it may merely make him aware of reading a clever author. The similes in the following passages all have a tendency to turn our attention away from the impression itself to its vehicle: "He had the appearance of a business man whose market is swinging up and down" (I, 77). "He was like a listener in a country store to wondrous tales told among the sugar barrels" (I, 89). "The babe sat on the floor watching the scene, his face in contortions like that of a woman at a tragedy" (*Maggie*, X, 143).

At times Crane's images attain an almost independent status. The vehicle becomes, as it were, the object itself: "... one could see across [the stream] the red, eye-like gleam of hostile camp-fires set in the low brows of distant hills" (I, 21). "Staring once at the red eyes across the river, he conceived them to be growing larger, as the orbs of a row of dragons advancing" (I, 38). When we first see the confederate camp-fires they have a "red, eye-like gleam" and the image of them as eyes is further developed in the metaphor "set in the low brows of distant hills." When the same fires are shown to us some pages later, the first impression of them as something "eye-like" has become strengthened. What was previously referred to as the gleam of camp fires now appears merely as "the red eyes," and these are in their turn the tenor of a new comparison.

We have hitherto chiefly discussed Crane's imagery from a technical point of view. But a consideration of content may also throw some light upon our subject. Like so many of his other stylistic traits, Crane's animal imagery tends "to reinforce the determinism of [*The Red Badge*] and to deflate man's pretensions to heroic conduct":[71] "[Veterans] were digging at the ground like terriers" (I, 53). "The man was blubbering and staring with sheep-like eyes at the lieutenant ... " (I, 67). "He ran like a rabbit" (I, 74).

In the following passage from *George's Mother* the final statement about the condition of people in the slums of New York follows as a natural conclusion after this series of images: "She looked out at chimneys growing thickly on the roofs. A man at work on one seemed like a bee. In the intricate yards below, vine-like lines had strange leaves of cloth. To her ears there came the howl of the man with the red, mottled face. He was engaged in a furious altercation with the youth who had called attention to his poor aim. They were like animals in a jungle" (I, 25). But man's passive condition and inability to cope with external forces stronger than himself is also expressed in other types of imagery: "For a moment he felt in the face of his great trial like a babe ..." (I, 48). "Here and there were officers carried along the stream like exasperated chips" (I, 60). "The regiment, like a cart involved in mud and muddle, started unevenly with many jerks and jolts" (I, 162).

> ... they fastened upon each other
> various strange epithets. (I, 33)

In order to arrest the reader and make him more receptive to the impression Crane may use an unexpected, rare or even bizarre image. Similarly he will frequently use words "of a connotation particularly unusual in the context":[72] "The regiment was fed and caressed ..." (I, 28). "The regiment slid down a bank and wallowed across a little stream" (I, 49). "The dimensions of their howls were extraordinary. They expended their lungs with prodigal wills" (I, 66). Commenting on this aspect of Crane's language in the famous concluding sentence of chapter nine in *The Red Badge* Phillip Rahv writes that "as a stylist he was above all concerned with getting away from the morbidly genteel narrative language of his time; the daring colloquialism 'pasted in the sky' must have appealed to him on the well-known avantgarde principle of 'make it new.' "[73]

The impressionist often uses words which are suggestive by their very sound in order to attain the most striking and appropriate rendering of acoustic impressions.[74] Such onomatopoeia are very frequent in Crane's style: ". . . the clatter of a horse's galloping hoofs . . . The exiting clickety-click . . ." (I, 38). ". . . from behind also came the tinkle of equipments . . ." (I, 39). "[The regiment] wheezed and banged with a mighty power" (I, 64). "The steel ramrods clanked and clanged with incessant din . . ." (I, 66).

A peculiarity in Crane's use of adjectives is his habit of connecting an adjective and a substantive where a strictly logical consideration would require a connection between the corresponding adverb and the verb: "The loud soldier blew a thoughtful cloud of smoke from his pipe" (I, 43). Obviously the soldier, not the smoke, is thoughtful. *The Red Badge* abounds in such juxtapositions: "To his attentive audience he drew a loud and elaborate plan of a very brilliant campaign" (I, 22). "The latter with calm faith began a heavy explanation . . ." (I, 53). "A bird flew on lighthearted wing" (I, 82). Again we see that it is the impression of an act *per se* that the impressionist is primarily interested in, not the action as expressed by the verb. By using an adjective instead of an adverb he forces the reader to pay attention to the object of the sentence rather than the verb. Consequently the reader's awareness is weakened both of the actual performance of an action and of the fact that the impression associated with the object in the final analysis must be related to the subject.

The same attitude may be traced in expressions like: "He breathed a deep breath of humble admiration" (I, 90). Here the manner in which the tattered man breathed becomes a quality belonging to the breath and is made to appear as almost independent of the subject of the sentence. It is still more obvious in phrases where a prepositional adjunct is substituted for the adverb: ". . . the army. . . began to tremble with eagerness . . ." (I, 21).

Several scholars have remarked on the frequency of nominal construction in impressionistic writers, and Luise Thon finds this tendency to be evident in cases where the impressionist substitutes a substantive (often with a qualifying adjective) and the preposition "with" for an adverb.[75] In Crane this usage is so frequent that it must be taken into account: "There was a youthful private who listened with eager ears. ..." (I, 33). "... began the loud soldier with scorn" (I, 33). "... said the other with cold judgment" (I, 33). "... companions cried with emphasis ..." (I, 39). "Some ardour of the air which was causing the veteran commands to move with glee — almost with song ..." (I, 40). "... they were routed out with early energy ..." (I, 46). The effect in all these cases is to weaken the sense of action described by the verb.

> There was rustling and muttering among
> the men. (I, 62)

The passive *Weltgefühl* of the impressionist probably appears most clearly in his particular use of the verb and its forms.[76] Several aspects of Crane's usage have above been shown to express this basic attitude: a weakening of the verb through a substitution of adjectives and prepositional phrases for adverbs; a predominance of verbs of perception throughout his work; a frequent use of verbs like "to seem" and "to appear;" and the passive quality of verbs when applied to man, and a corresponding active quality in their application to environment and lifeless matter.

One of the most prominent features of impressionistic style is the avoidance of the active forms of verbs in favor of the verb's substantival forms.[77] In *The Red Badge* there are many examples of such usage: "From off in the darkness came the trampling of feet" (I, 37). "From the road came creakings and grumblings as some surly guns were dragged away" (I, 38–39). "Then, upon this stillness, there suddenly broke a tremendous clangour of sounds. A crimson roar came from the distance" (I, 85). In these passages the verb (usually "to be" or "to come") is not the bearer of action and our interest is not centered on actions, but on their effects. In the second example the "creakings and grumblings" are not even logically connected with the guns: it is merely stated that these sounds were heard as the guns were dragged away.

The many instances where Crane's characters "give" shrieks or "make" announcements have a similar effect: "The youth gave a shriek ..." (I, 84). "He made a gesture" (I, 97). "Then he made a calm announcement" (I, 101). "He now gave a cry of exasperation and made a furious motion with his hand" (I, 102). The verbs have merely a syntactical function in the sentence, as it were, and do not have the same stylistic prominence as the nouns denoting action. The result is a description of the effects of an action rather than of the performing of it.

Perhaps one of the most conspicuous traits in Crane's style is the profusion of constructions with "there was" and a verbal noun. In his book on English stylistics Max Deutschbein finds this language typical of the language of impressionism.[78] It is typical of Crane's: "There was much scoffing at the latter. ..." (I, 35). "There was an occasional flash and glimmer of steel. ..." (I, 38). "There was a subdued debate" (I, 39). "There was a vigorous discussion" (I, 39). "There was perspiration and grumblings" (I, 46). Again the sense of action otherwise conveyed by verbs is weakened by the use of nouns, and again our interest is focused more on our impression of the effect of an action than on the performance itself.

> You are a complete impressionist.[79]
> Joseph Conrad

This study has not been concerned with a general analysis of the prose style of Stephen Crane. In that case our approach would have had to be much wider, and to include other features not necessarily indicative of any particular "ism."

But I hope to have demonstrated that the characteristics selected for discussion represent essential aspects of Crane's style and technique, that they taken together form a meaningful pattern, and that impressionism is the one term which best describes them. It should also have been made clear that Crane's impressionism is not accidental but the result of a conscious effort by the author and probably influenced by the ideas of impressionism current in the early 1890's. Crane's literary theory — if such we may call his scattered remarks on writing — is a clear and explicit statement of an impressionist credo.

By concluding that Stephen Crane was an impressionist this paper may not have come up with sensational news. But I hope that, besides showing how and why Crane, indeed, was as impressionist, it has also contributed to making impressionism a somewhat more precise, useful, and meaningful term in the stylistic analysis of American prose fiction.

The investigation was based on the expressed belief that the study of an author's style and technique is a fruitful approach to the total meaning of his art. I have not been concerned with a close analysis of the meaning of any specific work by Stephen Crane. Rather, I have tried to arrive at conclusions which have validity for his writing considered as a whole by throwing light on some aspects of the writer's personality and his fundamental attitudes toward the world he is describing. For although an author's individual works are separate entities, the personality of their maker, which is ever present in his style, is a least common denominator in the light of which these works may and should be studied.[80]

## NOTES

[1] E. Garnett, "Stephen Crane and his Work," *Friday Nights* (London, 1922), p. 209; *Stephen Crane: an Omnibus* (London, 1954), pp. 184–85; Stephen Crane, *Letters*, ed. R. W. Stallman and Lillian Gilkes (New York, 1960), p. 155.

[2] *Omnibus*, p. 185.

[3] *Philosophy in a New Key* (New York: Mentor Edition, 1948), p. 84.

[4] A convient example is the use of the possessive pronoun which, in cases where it is obligatory in English, in German has a marked impressionistic effect. See Luise Thon, *Die Sprache des deutschen Impressionismus* (Munich, 1929), pp. 16–17.

[5] See, e. g., Thon, *Die Sprache d. d. Impressionismus*, pp. 5–6, and Eva Weidner, *Impressionismus und Expressionismus in den Romanen Virginia Woolfs* (Greifswald, 1934), pp. 20–21.

[6] See Sven Møller Kristensen, *Impressionismen i dansk prosa, 1870–1900* (Copenhagen, 1955), p. 21. It is interesting to note that Arne Garborg, a Norwegian poet and novelist of the period who had been through both these stages, has it that *naturalists* who inclined toward this latter attitude *called* themselves *impressionists*. "Den idealistiske reaktion," *Tankar og utsyn* (Oslo, 1950), p. 104.

[7] See Thon, *Die Sprache d. d. Impressionismus*, p. 7.

[8] (New York, 1934), pp. 38, 41.

[9] H. Garland, *Crumbling Idols* (Chicago, 1894), pp. 126–27.

[10] Herbert Read, *English Prose Style* (New York, 1925), p. 155.

[11] Garland, *Crumbling Idols*, p. 133.

[12] For a survey of the critical debate on this question see Sigmund Skard, "The Use of Color in Literature," *Proceedings of the Am. Philos. Soc.*, XC (1946), 170–72. It is known that Stephen Crane was acquainted with Goethe's theory of color and that he was especially impressed by Goethe's analysis of "the effect which the several colors have on the human mind" (*Letters*, p. 336). For a discussion of a possible relationship between Crane's art and Goethe's *Farbenlehre* see Robert L. Hough, "Crane and Goethe: a Forgotten Relationship," *Nineteenth Century Fiction*, XVII (1962), 135–48.

[13] Ch. Walcutt, *American Literary Naturalism, a Divided Stream* (Minneapolis, 1956), p. 236.

[14] Anthony Bertram, *A Century of British Painting, 1851–1951* (London and New York, 1951), p. 64. See F. W. J. Hemmings, "Zola, Manet, and the Impressionists," *PMLA*, LXXIII (1958), 410.

[15] See Skard, "The Use of Color," pp. 181, 202.

[16] *Letters*, pp. 78, 160.

[17] As a reporter for the New York *Tribune* Crane wrote about Garland's

lecture on "Americanism in the Novel: William Dean Howells and Henry James" in his series of *Lecture-Studies in American Literature and Expressive Art* in 1891, and in Crane's report Garland recognized "unusual precision of expression and set about establishing a more intimate relationship." Garland quoted his definitions of realism from Howells' *Criticism & Fiction,* and we may presume that Crane was familiar with this volume published the preceding spring. At any rate we know that *Maggie,* begun at Syracuse University in the spring of 1891, was rewritten twice during the following winter, and Stallman is assured that it was the literary creed of Howells and Garland that influenced Crane towards this reconstruction. See Lars Åhnebrink, *The Beginnings of Naturalism in American Fiction* (Uppsala, 1950), p. 442; Garland, *Roadside Meetings* (New York, 1930), p. 189; Howells, *Criticism & Fiction and Other Essays,* ed. Clara M. Kirk and Rudolf Kirk (New York, 1959), p. 270; and *Letters,* p. 16n.

18 Joseph J. Kwiat, "Stephen Crane and Painting," *American Quarterly,* IV (1952), 331–38, shows that Crane was associated with art and painting even before he made friends with the young painters in the Art Students League. Many contemporary critics noted a resemblance between Crane's technique and that of the impressionist painters: e.g., H. G. Wells, "Stephen Crane from an English Standpoint," reprinted in *The Shock of Recognition,* ed. Edmund Wilson (London, 1954), pp. 662–63; Garnett, "Stephen Crane and his work," p. 215; and John D. Barry, "A Note on Stephen Crane," *Bookman,* XIII (1901), 148. But according to Hough, "Crane and Goethe," p. 148, "much of the argument over whether or not

Crane is indebted to the impressionists is primarily academic. He did know Goethe, and this accounts for many of his color techniques." And, knowing Goethe, "he knew something about impressionism before he knew the impressionists."

19 Jean E. Whitehead, "The Art of Stephen Crane," unpubl. diss. (1944), quoted in *Omnibus,* pp. xxxi–xxxii.

20 See *Letters,* pp. 39–40. In a letter to John N. Hilliard, Jan. 1896, he writes: "The one thing that pleases me in my literary life... is the fact that men of sense believe me to be sincere" (*Letters,* p. 109). Later he seems partly to have lost this integrity and he wrote pot boilers like *Active Service, The O'Ruddy,* and *Great Battles of the World* in futile attempts to raise money. In 1899 "he made to some visitor a remark behind which one hears with pain the lifelong conscience of an artist dying: 'I get a little tired of saying, Is this true?' " John Berryman, *Stephen Crane* (New York, 1950), p. 247.

21 See the almost identically phrased passages in *Letters,* pp. 78–79 (to an editor of *Leslie's Weekly,* Nov. 1895), and p. 159 (to Hilliard, 1897?). The same view is expressed in a letter to Clarence L. Peaslee in Feb. 1895, *Letters,* p. 52.

22 *Letters,* p. 116 (Feb. 1896), and p. 86 (Dec. 1895).

23 Quoted in *Omnibus,* p. 7.

24 Berryman, *Stephen Crane,* p. 124.

25 *Letters,* p. 52 (to Peaslee, Feb. 1895), p. 109 (Jan. 1896), and p. 158 (1897?). Cf. his comment on Tolstoy quoted in *Omnibus,* p. 182.

26 *Letters,* p. 14.

27 On this "divided stream" of literary naturalism see Walcutt, *American Literary Naturalism,* p. 3 and passim.

28 *Letters,* p. 99 (Jan. 1896), and p. 133 (to Catherine Harris, Nov. 1896).

29 "... the cut-and-dried curriculum of the college did not appeal to me. Humanity was a much more interesting study. When I ought to have been at recitations I was studying faces on the streets, and when I ought to have been studying my next days lessons I was watching the trains roll in and out of the Central Station." *Letters*, p. 109 (to Hilliard, Jan. 1896?).

30 Corwin K. Linson, *My Stephen Crane*, ed. Edwin H. Cady (Syracuse, N.Y., 1958), p. 58.

31 *Letters*, p. 31 (to Lily Brandon Munroe, March 1894?).

32 Volume and page here and in the following refer to *The Work of Stephen Crane*, ed. Wilson Follett (12 vols. New York, 1925–1927).

33 *Letters*, p. 110 (to Hilliard, Jan. 1896?).

34 *Letters*, p. 133 (to Catherine Harris, Nov. 1896).

35 Berryman, *Stephen Crane*, p. 25 (also *Omnibus*, p. xxxiv), and Linson, *My Stephen Crane*, p. 37.

36 Berryman, *Stephen Crane*, p. 143.

37 See Thon, *Die Sprache d. d.Impressionismus*, pp. 10, 12–15, and 21, and Møller Kristensen, *Impressionismen*, pp. 80–81.

38 Linson, *My Stephen Crane*, p. 30.

39 Thomas Beer, *Stephen Crane: a Study in American Letters* (New York, 1927), p. 51.

40 Berryman, *Stephen Crane*, pp. 267–68.

41 *Omnibus*, pp. 181–82.

42 Beer, *Stephen Crane*, p. 148.

43 *Omnibus*, p. 190.

44 Berryman, *Stephen Crane*, p. 73.

45 Hartwick, *The Foreground of American Fiction*, p. 42. This judgment echoes Mencken's in his "Introduction," *Work*, X. Garnett had a closer sympathy with Crane's aims: "[*The Red Badge*] was a series of episodic scenes, all melting naturally into one another and forming a just whole; but it was

not constructed, in any sense of the word" (p. 209).

46 Mencken, "Introduction," pp. xi-xii.

47 There are, of course, exceptions to this rule in Crane's writing. One of the most conspicuous is perhaps the description of the interior of the youth's hut on p. 23 of *The Red Badge*.

48 See Thon, *Die Sprache d. d. Impressionismus*, pp. 126–27.

49 Compare Møller Kristensen, *Impressionismen*, p. 124 on the use of *"skikkelse"* in Danish impressionistic prose.

50 Björck, *Romanens formvärld* (Stockholm, 1954), p. 150.

51 Compare Garnett, "Stephen Crane and his Work," p. 205: "We would define him by saying he is the perfect artist and interpreter of the surface of life;" p. 206: "The rare thing about Mr. Crane's art is that he keeps closer to the surface than any living writer, and, like the great portrait-painters, to a great extent makes the surface betray the depths."

52 Beer, *Stephen Crane*, p. 81.

53 Møller Kristensen, *Impressionismen*, p. 148. Compare Thon, *Die Sprache d. d. Impressionismus*, pp. 160–61.

54 Some scholars prefer to use the German *erlebte Rede* or the French *style indirect libre* also in an English context.

55 Bernhard Fehr, "Substitutionary Narration and Description: a Chapter in Stylistics," *English Studies*, XX (1938), 97.

56 Thon, *Die Sprache d. d. Impressionismus*, p. 96.

57 ibid.

58 Max Deutschbein and Walther Azzalino, *Einführung in die englische Stilistik* (Leipzig, 1936), p. 83.

59 Compare Møller Kristensen, *Impressionismen*, p. 47, who says that the tendency to give descriptions a touch of irony is common among im-

pressionists. Irony permeates Crane's work. This has been evident in many of the passages chosen to show other stylistic traits, and especially in those showing his tendency to interpret physiological appearances as indications of a character's thoughts and feelings.

⁶⁰ Compare Møller Kristensen, *Impressionismen*, p. 119.

⁶¹ Compare Thon, *Die Sprache d. d. Impressionismus*, p. 158.

⁶² Ford Madox Ford, "Techniques," *The Southern Review*, I (July, 1935), 31–32, has made the following observation: "But it was perhaps Crane of all that school or gang... who most observed that canon of Impressionism: 'You must render: never report.' You must never, that is to say, write: 'He saw a man aim a gat at him;' you must put it: 'He saw a steel ring directed at him.' Later you must get in that, in his subconsciousness, he recognized that the steel ring was the polished muzzle of a revolver. So Crane rendered it in *Three White Mice* which is one of the major short stories of the world. That is Impressionism! "— Which of course it is. Although Crane has written a story called *"Five* White Mice," however, the incident Ford describes does not exist — neither in that story nor in any other by Crane.

⁶³ Compare Møller Kristensen, *Impressionismen*, p. 133.

⁶⁴ Compare ibid., pp. 127–28, and Thon, *Die Sprache d. d. Impressionismus*, pp. 156–57.

⁶⁵ This latter effect may also be brought about by the use of repetition: "Now the men turned at the woeful complaints of him upon the ground. 'Who is it? Who is it?' 'It's Jimmie Rogers, Jimmie Rogers'" (I, 152).

⁶⁶ Møller Kristensen, *Impressionismen*, p. 126.

⁶⁷ Thon, *Die Sprache d. d. Impressionismus*, p. 39. Compare Møller Kristensen, *Impressionismen*, pp. 158–62.

⁶⁸ Møller Kristensen, ibid., p. 147. Garnett, "Stephen Crane and his Work," p. 208, speaks of "the gift peculiar to the author of using some odd simile which cunningly condenses the feeling of the situation."

⁶⁹ Thon, *Die Sprache d. d. Impressionismus*, passim.

⁷⁰ Compare Møller Kristensen, *Impressionismen*, p. 148.

⁷¹ Stanley B. Greenfield, "The Unmistakable Stephen Crane," *PMLA*, LXXIII (1958), 568.

⁷² Harold C. Martin, "The Development of Style in Nineteenth-Century American Fiction," *Style in Prose Fiction*, ed. Harold C. Martin (New York, 1959), p. 133. This technique has several times been noticed in connection with "The Open Boat." Conrad writes of the "inspired audacity of epithet which was one of Crane's gifts that gave me most delight." "Stephen Crane," *Late Essays* (London, 1926), p. 149.

⁷³ "Fiction and the Criticism of Fiction," *Kenyon Review*, XVIII (1956), 284.

⁷⁴ Thon, *Die Sprache, d. d. Impressionismus*, pp. 7–8.

⁷⁵ Thon, ibid., p. 77.

⁷⁶ "Das Verbum, das vor allen andern Wortformen imstande ist, Aktivität und Passivität auszudrücken, kann fast allein schon zeigen, wie das Weltgefühl einer Kunst beschaffen ist." Thon, ibid., p. 42.

⁷⁷ Max Deutschbein, *Neuenglische Stilistik* (Leipzig, 1932), p. 132.

⁷⁸ Deutschbein, ibid., pp. 132, 157.

⁷⁹ Conrad in *Letters*, p. 154 (to Crane, Dec. 1, 1897).

⁸⁰ A longer version of this paper was submitted to the University of Oslo in partial fulfilment of the require-

ments for the degree *cand. philol.* in 1962. It is impossible to record in full my debt to professor Sigmund Skard, who originally suggested I undertake this study and who in his help and advice in the process of revising it for publication, has gone far beyond the duties of a teacher and editor. Besides the editors of this volume, professor R. W. B. Lewis, and professor Jay Martin have kindly read the manuscript.

# E. A. ROBINSON: "EROS TURANNOS"
## A CRITICAL SURVEY

### By Sigmund Skard

Since its appearance in 1914 "Eros Turannos" has been commented upon in critical analyses of unusual brilliance. The poem has steadily gained in stature, until it now ranks at the top of Robinson's production. But interpretation has been divergent, and there is still something to be added. In the following survey an attempt is made to bring together as far as possible all critical contributions (they are listed in a bibliography at the end of the article), and to coordinate their results in a general discussion.[1]

### 1. *The Text.*

"Eros Turannos" was written, or revised into its final form, in the fall of 1913, when Robinson stayed at the Ledoux country home near Cornwall on the Hudson. The poem originated during a happy resurgence of poetic creativity, following an interval of several years when Robinson had been "floundering" in the writing of novels, and in what he himself called "the first and last infirmity of noble and ignoble minds — the writing of plays".[2]

We have little evidence regarding the growth of the poem. In his biography of Robinson (1965) Chard Powers Smith* tried to establish an emotional chronology of the love poems, according to which "Eros Turannos" must have been at least sketched in the mid to late 1890's, set aside for reasons of delicacy for at least fifteen years, and then "revamped" in 1913.[3] As discussed below, this chronology must be questionable. In any case the only existing manuscript of the poem, in the Lewis M. Isaac Collection in the New York Public Library, is inscribed "Cornwall 19 October, 1913". With different pencil, probably later and at the time of presentation, is added: "First draft.

E.A.R."[4] As is often the case with Robinson manuscripts, even this draft presents a poem that is almost finished. All the six stanzas as we know them, are there, in their final sequence, and four of them largely in their final form. I have not been able to trace other manuscript material, and probably it does not exist. The typed manuscript submitted to *Poetry*,[5] the first printed version there and in book form, and the numerous later printings, show only minor variations, albeit of considerable interest.

The final version appears in **CP** (1921 and following editions):

*Eros Turannos.*

She fears him, and will always ask
    What fated her to choose him;
She meets in his engaging mask
    All reasons to refuse him;
But what she meets and what she fears
Are less than are the downward years,
Drawn slowly to the foamless weirs
    Of age, were she to lose him.

Between a blurred sagacity
    That once had power to sound him,
And Love, that will not let him be
    The Judas that she found him,
Her pride assuages her almost,
As if it were alone the cost. —
He sees that he will not be lost,
    And waits and looks around him.

A sense of ocean and old trees
    Envelops and allures him;
Tradition, touching all he sees,
    Beguiles and reassures him;
And all her doubts of what he says
Are dimmed with what she knows of days —
Till even prejudice delays
    And fades, and she secures him.

The falling leaf inaugurates
    The reign of her confusion;
The pounding wave reverberates
    The dirge of her illusion;
And home, where passion lived and died,
Becomes a place where she can hide,
While all the town and harbor side
    Vibrate with her seclusion.

We tell you, tapping on our brows,
   The story as it should be, —
As if the story of a house
   Were told, or ever could be;
We'll have no kindly veil between
Her visions and those we have seen, —
As if we guessed what hers have been,
   Or what they are or would be.

Meanwhile we do no harm; for they
   That with a god have striven,
Not hearing much of what we say,
   Take what the god has given;
Though like waves breaking it may be,
Or like a changed familiar tree,
Or like a stairway to the sea
   Where down the blind are driven.

*Variants.*

   *Stanza 2*, 1. 4. The draft has the noun "Judas", the ms. and the printed version in *Poetry* "seeker", the final text again "Judas". The same ms. and printed version introduce a comma after "her" in 1. 5 and after "waits" in 1. 8, both being eliminated in the final version. In the draft, dashes end 1. 4 and 1. 6; both are dropped in the *Poetry* version, the latter is reintroduced later.

   *Stanza 3*. L. 6 ends with a dash in the draft; it is dropped in *Poetry* and reintroduced later. A dash after "fades" in 1. 8 is dropped in CP.

   *Stanza 4*. There is a tentative version of 1. 1—4 and 8:

      The legend of her love remains
         An epic of confusion,
      And through it, like a trumpet, reigns
         The crash of her illusion;
      — — —
      [*shake heads?*] at her seclusion.

   Then follows the final version almost as it stands now, but with a tentative line 3:

      the shattered [?] wave reverberates.

"Crash" is exchanged by "dirge" in CP.

   *Stanza 5* begins in the draft:

      We say it is enough to prove
         That she has found him master, —
      As if the story of her love
         Were told or her disaster.

Then comes the final version of these four lines. The second half of the stanza begins by tentative jottings:

> We'll have [*such* changed to *no?* followed by open space]
> That may have changed [*what we?*] have seen, —
> As if we guessed what hers have been
> Or might have been, or would be,

changed again into:

> No protest will avail between
> her silence [ ?] and what we have seen, —
> As if we guessed where hers have been
> Or where she is [ ?], or would be.

*Stanza 6* begins by two tentative opening lines:

> We say. . . No matter what we say,
> Or what she may have given.

The draft (and that alone) has in l. 5 the noun "tide" in stead of "waves".


## 2. *The Critical Reception.*

E. A Robinson himself apparently never commented upon the poem; but he hardly counted it among his most important achievements. When in 1917 he advised a friend what poems to recite from *The Man Against the Sky*, he did not include "Eros Turannos".[6] When in 1931 Bliss Perry brought out his good-sized selection of Robinson's work, his choice being approved in "many sessions" by the poet himself, one poem was added at Robinson's insistence, two because of Perry's preference, but "Eros Turannos" is not in the collection at all. Several times in the course of his life Robinson himself pointed out some of his poems as his "best", but "Eros Turannos" was never among them.[7]

The readers felt differently, however, from the very beginning. A noticeable exception was Harriet Monroe, who had an "aggressive distaste" for classical and medieval poetic subjects. When she printed the poem in *Poetry* (March, 1914), she did not given it any of the two positions of honor, at the beginning or at the end of the poetry section, in the issue where it appeared, Carl Sandburg and Padraic Colum being preferred. "Eros Turannos" did not receive any of the awards of the magazine for the year, not even "mention honorable", and Miss Monroe did not include it in her anthology *The New Poetry* (New York, 1917).[8] But Harriet Monroe was an exception. In the

19

very year of its publication the poem was reprinted in W. St. Braithwaite's *Anthology of Magazine Verse for 1914* (Cambridge, Mass.). In 1916 Robinson included it in *The Man Against the Sky*, the collection which established his literary fame and which he later was to place first among his *Collected Poems*. Among the fifteen reviews — most of them brief — that were devoted to the volume upon its appearance, only those by Padraic Colum,* Amy Lowell,* and L. Untermeyer* mentioned the poem explicitly. But they counted it among the masterpieces, in a book that contains some of Robinson's best work.

With the poet's rising fame in the 1920's "Eros Turannos" also gained further recognition. In 1922 Yvor Winters (*I) in his *Poetry* review of *Collected Poems*, "A Cool Master", praised "the compact, intensely contemplated statement of *Eros Turannos*, a poem that is, in forty-eight lines, as complete as a Lawrence novel". He even used it as a yardstick of the poet's power. In Robinson's latest book Winters found nothing to equal it. But there were "at least two or three poems as great as any save that one Mr. Robinson has written; and there is nothing ... to preclude the possibility of another *Eros Turannos*". In 1923, and again in 1934, Harriet Monroe now admitted it to the second and third editions of her anthology. The poem was occasionally referred to in the growing Robinson literature, and placed in a larger context in the first comprehensive analysis of the poet's work by Cestre* (1930).

The popularity of Robinson's medieval romances proved shortlived; and in the decade following the poet's death interest in him dropped. But in the new critical atmosphere after 1945 his mediumlength poems were increasingly appreciated, and "Eros Turannos" in particular. Soon the poem became mandatory in anthologies both for the schools and the general reading public. While it never belonged among the special favorites of the New Critics, research was increasingly devoted to the details of its style and structure, so thoroughly that even the present survey will have to content itself with a selection. Above all, a number of critics discussed the poem from more general points of view. These discussions demonstrate both the representative character of "Eros Turannos" and the difficulties involved in placing the poem and its author convincingly within America's literary development.

To the left-wing critics of the 1930's Robinson's limitations with regard to subject weighed heavily. Some of the critics found him to be socially unaware, and concentrating on cases of personal maladjustment within an abstract world of his own creation (a criticism that was also levelled against Henry James): his poetry is distant from "the only problems we really know ... those that are posed by our own age". This artificial distance may give his work firmness, precision and poise, but also makes much of it cold and remote. Other critics saw his poetry as socially significant, but filled with "unending gloom" over the passing of an individualistic culture. The "fine dignity" of his best things, including the "subtlety" of a poem such as "Eros Turannos", does not quite compensate for his isolation from general humanity.[9]

Such criticism pointed out factual limitations in Robinson's work, but over-emphasized externalities and said little of the poem as a poem. Much more interesting were the efforts to place it within a strictly literary context, balancing its weakness against its value in terms of art.

Long before the appearance of "Eros Turannos" critics stressed the classical character of Robinson's work. As early as 1905 he was called "more nearly a Greek than any singer of note we have with us today".[10] In a review in 1912, which was much appreciated by the poet himself, Joyce Kilmer pointed to "the almost Greek lucidity of his work", combined with "a surprising lack of classical allusion and scholarly decoration".[11] From the 1920's onward general statements in the same vein multiplied, beginning with Carl van Doren's words about Robinson's "peculiar combination of Greek dignity and Yankee ease". And the direct parallels were gradually elaborated.[12]

Some critics extolled this classical tendency by contrasting it with its opposites, above all romanticism. This was done most pointedly in 1946 by Yvor Winters (*III) in his book on Robinson, with "Eros Turannos" as one of the prime examples. Winters admitted that Robinson "adopts a few current notions of a romantic nature", particularly in his weak, later work. But essentially he is a counter-romantic: "the fact that he writes verse is incidental". His great, shorter poems are marked by a classicism which makes them rational, clear, and almost void of sense imagery. They are free from the romantic narrowness and acquire an "impersonal greatness of style" that has seldom been achieved in our century. To Winters "Eros Turannos" is at the very apex of this art, "one of the greatest short poems in the language". Exception made for a certain "provincial cleverness", the poem is to him a universal tragedy in a Maine setting, created with an extraordinary power of generalization. Its brevity is not brought about by poverty: it has "the substance of a short novel or of a tragic drama", and its marvellous concentration is made possible by a writing "beyond praise".

Other critics saw a more dubious value in Robinson's classicism. In 1936 H. C. Robbins similarly summed up a number of general classical traits in his poems (without referring explicitly to "Eros Turannos"): their timelessness and serenity, their detachment and restraint, their symmetry and sense of proportion, and the stoic submission to fate, traits that are close to Greek tragedy and far from both Christian and romantic attitudes. But from these premises Robbins partly joined force with the left-wingers in their criticism: "To the extent that we are not ourselves classicists we resent the completeness of this detachment". The poet is too imperturbable, tearless and Olympian. Many of Robinson's figures remain unreal abstractions. Much of his poetry suffers, not in its artistic perfection, but in its power to arouse emotion.[13]

Others justly recognized a much more basic trend of romanticism in Robinson's work; and H. W. Wells saw the poet's real grandeur in his ability to balance these contrasts. Robinson's poetry "steers shrewdly between the Scylla and Charybdis of romantic exultation and despair". His "instinctive", "unpedantic and spiritual" classicism "harmonized ... naturally with his inherited romanticism".[14] But other critics saw the contrasts as much more profound and less easily reconciled. Early intimations in that direction are found in Allen Tate.[15] In his often reprinted review of *Talifer* (1933) he initially paid his respect to Robinson's early verse, "some of the finest lyrics of modern times". He later explicitly included "Eros Turannos" in this homage, a poem where "his genius was at its height"; Tate's immediate aim in 1933 was only to explain the failure of Robinson's later poems. But in its implications his criticism also touched upon a more general weakness in the attitudes of the poet.

Tate saw in Robinson's longer narratives a survival of romantic egotism and a lack of general standards. The greatest dramatic literature always has depended upon "a pattern of well understood behavior ... a seasoned code". Robinson's ideas lack this "compulsion of absolute truth"; they are only "the personal forms of some egoistic thrust of the will". With the loss of epic, myth and code as "terminal points of human conduct" our age has also lost "the power to depict action that is both single and complete". Consequently, Robinson's dramatic genius is "held to short flights": the dramatic lyric is "a fragment of a total action which the poet lacks the means to sustain". The ageing Robinson "goes over the same ground, again and again, writing a poem that will not be written", because he is confined to the romantic ego. He writes "less from the tragic vision than from the tragic sentiment; and the result is the pathetic tale of obscure ambition or thwarted passion, not tragedy".

To Allen Tate, then, Robinson's failures are due to the persistence of a romanticism turned sterile. With R. P. Adams* (1961) the explanation was reversed.

To Adams, Robinson is "potentially a great *romantic* poet". The core of romantic poetry, and implicitly of all great poetry, is to Adams a devotion to change, "a powerfully intense poetic conviction"; and such was the natural inclination of Robinson's mind. The tragedy of his poetic career was, that except on a few occasions he was "bluffed out of greatness ... by the inordinate popular prestige in his time of mechanistic materialism". He rarely managed to free himself from his static pessimism. He had no strong positive belief; his poetic morale was weak, and his creation largely remained half-hearted.

Only in "Eros Turannos" and a handful of other poems did Robinson manage to free himself from his dualism. Instead, the released powers here gave his poetical creations an "almost unbelievable beauty". In this part of his work there is for once a "balance between good and evil": Robinson "confounds the materialists and justifies his too often wavering faith in the qualities of life", proving himself a great poet in the truly romantic tradition.

In his discussion from 1954 — the most detailed analysis devoted to the poem so far — L. O. Coxe* rearranged the same qualities within the framework of a third literary tradition.

Like Winters, Coxe saw Robinson's main strength in his directness and closeness to reality: he is no romanticist, but "a poet with a prose in view". But no more is he a dramatist "in any sense of the word commonly accepted". And even less is he a classicist: he is a naturalist of the 19th century kind. If Coxe admires "Eros Turannos" as the very archetype of Robinson's best poetry, it is because of his ability in this poem to give a few stanzas "the scope of a long naturalistic novel" — "this naturalistic case-history, this story of a Maine Emma Bovary".

The unwillingness of some critics to accept Robinson therefore, in Coxe's view, springs from their reaction against the naturalistic sternness of his view of life. Robinson's only idea as a poet was "to come to a naked vision of the human condition without lusting after schemes of revision", seeing life as "a desperate business but essentially, immutably unalterable". This has led modern critics of "the liberal-romantic stock" to overlook the vision, maturity, and pathos of his themes, and his deeper independence of the "romantic ego". His best poems, on the contrary, center upon "the single, crucial failure of a man or woman to commit that destruction of the beloved self ... which alone and finally leaves the individual free". Such is the depth and grandeur of Robinson at his best, as in "Eros Turannos". It leaves him *"the* major American poet of our era, with only T. S. Eliot as a peer".

In his general discussion of the internal growth of American poetry R. H. Pearce* (1961) took "Eros Turannos" as his example of the art of "the great Robinson", and tried to strike a middle road between these contrasts.

To Pearce the poet seemed to have his starting point in the romantic tradition, which — with Emerson and R. W. B. Lewis — Pearce defined as the egocentric or Adamic mode: he exalted "the simple, genuine self against the whole world". But Robinson clearly saw that this world no longer existed, that the old community was broken, leaving the individual in isolation and failure. Robinson's honesty as a poet made him reject the old illusions and describe in his poetry "the exhaustion, perhaps the bankruptcy, of the simple, separate person". (Here the views of the left-wing critics of the 1930's are restated in a larger context). Robinson's poetic form shows the same honesty. Pearce too sees Robinson as a *romancier manqué*. But what he managed to write, was somewhat prosaic, antipoetic poems about isolated souls unable to communicate directly, works more dramatic than lyrical, compressed and controlled, with a conclusive, clear-cut objectivity. Even in their form his poems "record, with a frigid passion, the limitations of the expressivism cultivated by the major American poets before him".

"Eros Turannos" shows Robinson at his best; for this was the only kind of poem he really could write. When he froze in his lonely world, when he shied from that esthetic distance and that "complex of self-discovery and self-deceit" that is typical of "Eros Turannos", when he longed for "something more than stoic objectivity" and turned to myth and full-blown allegory, he failed, because there was no longer a community to sustain him. He remains a great poet within his real limits. But he is great only to the degree that he presents slices of life, "narrow and constrained, quickly exhausted of their potentiality for freedom and joy". Even "Eros Turannos" ends "magnificently, yet rather marmoreally".

### 3. *The Classical Background.*

The contrasts confronting each other in these judgments are not ironed out by a marshalling of literary isms. But in Robinson's case, the relative strength of the factors which constitute his literary background indicates realities that are essential to the understanding even of this one individual poem.

He was a thoroughly composite figure, transitional in almost all respects. And contrary to the ideas of some critics, this epithet should carry no sting. As a man and a poet he was suspended between contrasts which the previous generations had reconciled by simplifying or ignoring them, and which the next generation was to use squarely as contrasts; Robinson was constitutionally unable to do either. It was his innate conviction that life was "very much worth while",[16] as evidenced by the bare fact that he survived. But his vague metaphysical hopes struggled against a permanent feeling of life's elementary senselessness, which to him was not an axiom of philosophic fashion, but sprang from his deepest experience: the devil "isn't almighty, but he's pretty near it".[17]

Behind this attitude was not only his sad life story, but doubtless a low general vitality. He really *was* what R. P. Adams* calls halfhearted, but in a much more literal sense. There is about Robinson a diffidence and an apologetic evasiveness which sometimes make the reading of his letters almost unbearable, and — even worse in a literary man — an infectious weariness. In the early words of J. Middleton Murry: "He is not embittered, he is not angry; he is simply tired".[18] What he himself stubbornly called his optimism and denial of "materialism", was a lifelong whistling in the dark; and this metaphor should not be given the slightly derogatory note with which it is sometimes endowed. His position was basically complicated. He was unable to sustain any positive attitude or present any simple answer.

In choosing his literary subjects he faced the same dilemmas. He shared much of the high-strung idealism of the great romantics, who appealed to some of his deepest urges. But he hated all sentimentalism, partly because he had a good slice of it in himself. The material he could really work on, was much more close to that of the naturalists with their bitter truthfulness and their psychological disillusion. It was not for nothing that he called Zola "the greatest worker in the objective that the world has ever seen". What attracts me as a poet, he wrote in his early youth, is "natural things . . . of a more prosy connotation than those generally admitted into the domain of metre".[19]

This discrepancy raised artistic problems even with regard to form. In spite of Yvor Winters' verdict Robinson was essentially a poet, — "somehow prose is not my natural form of expression".[20] But at the time when his ideas were formulated, poetry still meant very definite things. In attitude he antedated his contemporaries by several decades, but not in taste. "You will come in time to realize", he wrote Mabel Dodge Luhan, "that I am not so infernally modern after all". In one of the longest speeches L. Untermeyer could remember having heard from him, Robinson around 1920 expressed his low regard for the exponents of the "new poetry": "they don't know what poetry is supposed to be or to do". He explicitly mentioned Carl Sandburg, Amy Lowell and Vachel Lindsay as examples, and pointed in stead to Kipling and Housman: "your young poets are for the very young. Thank God I'm not one of them".[21] The old forms did not quite suit his chosen material, but neither was he the man to create completely new ones. The resulting ambiguity of style confused and antagonized his contemporaries, conservatives and modernists alike.

This intermediate position partly explains his intense preoccupation with literary tradition, as demonstrated in 1954 in impressive breadth by E. S. Fussell.* The range of Robinson's literary sympathies was amazing, and sometimes appalling. He approached the most varied literary works with respectful interest, including some pure trash: they appealed to different sides of himself. And he needed support in the difficult thing he was trying to do. He experimented in metres from many periods and literatures. He applied his probing psychologizing to legends, myths, and historical figures. He tried to make the Arthurian world add its venerable patina to his modern conflicts. And he filled his poetry with continuous allusions to a usable past, not in the way of Eliot and Pound, but traditionally, sometimes in curious contrast to his real endeavors.

Among these literary traditions, that from the Classics has been underrated, and quite surprisingly so when it comes to this particular poem.

Robinson's lifelong attachment to ancient literature is well documented, more superficially by Fairclough,* thoroughly and brilliantly by Fussell.* Admittedly Robinson knew little Latin and only "a few scraps" of Greek.[22] But his absorption in the texts as he knew them, was intense, from his teen age onwards. He read the ancients widely and thoroughly. He translated verse and prose from both languages, and even began re-reading Greek after 1900. He toyed with classical verse, and wrote a number of poems on Greek and Roman themes. The many classical quotations, overt references and hidden allusions in his work are probably his most important single means of creating poetic distance, dimension and perspective.

Behind this attachment there was a kinship in spirit. Toward the end of his life Robinson characterized himself as "essentially a classicist in poetic composition". Fussell well sums up the general classical traits of his poetry which were strengthened or made more conscious by his direct contact with Greek and Roman literature: his "emphasis on moderation and control, on self-knowledge and the acceptance of limitation, on the social effects of human behavior, on retribution for moral blindness or outrage of the moral law", forming a part of the "rich and subtle" ethical foundation of his poetry. Also in trends of Robinson's style Fussell points to a direct heritage from the ancients, noticeable in the hardness, precision, restraint and elevated nobility of his language, the use of intellectual or abstract diction, the sense of decorum, formality, balance and unity.[23]

But Robinson's devotion was even more personal and profound. If his attachment to the Classics was different in kind from that of the professed "classical revivalists" among his contemporaries, it was because to him the ancients in a deeper way reflected his own basic problem as a poet. In an early letter (1894) Robinson called his own attitude "Hellenic", and then qualified the statement by saying that while he lacked some of the "serene and childlike joy of life" in the Greeks, he felt in him "the spirit of wise moderation and love of classical completeness which, I suppose, is more marked in the later poets of Pericles' time than in the Homeric period".[24] This completeness in the rendering and interpretation of life, including even its "prosy connotation", he was bound to find in much classical writing. Behind the polished serenity of the conventional image he must have sensed the "modern" awareness of complication and tragedy, brought to expression without breaking the balance of artistic mastery.

To what extent the spirit and technique of such models have helped the poet Robinson find his way through his own material would deserve a thorough investigation. In particular this holds good of his relation to the Greek Anthology. He has himself written ten "Variations of Greek Themes" (published in the second edition of *Captain Craig*, 1915), and a good many other poems in the style of the epigram. There may be a direct connection between such efforts and the vignettes of tragic destinies in Tilbury Town in which, from the 1890's onward, Robinson first found his own voice as a poet, several years before Edgar Lee Masters learnt from the Anthology to write his epitaphs of human happiness and failure along Spoon River.

But in most of these poems there is a dramatic trend which points to an even more important source. Robinson's definition in 1894 of his own classicism sprang from his studies in Sophocles. Six months later he advised a friend to read the Greek dramatists in order to "solidify" his literary character, and he continued that "a year's study of the three masters will make a complete transformation in your whole mental and moral outlook".[25]

This was no academic advice on Robinson's part. In the 1890's he himself worked for three years on a translation of Sophocles' *Antigone*, based on a prose version prepared by a friend. Robinson did not regard this translation very highly in his later years. But at the time he allegedly considered it to be "the cornerstone of his career", and before *Captain Craig* it was actually his most ambitious piece of work. He read, and read about, and referred to the other Greek dramatists as well. And they did not only encourage his absorb-ing interest in the dramatic portrayal of human psychology: more strongly than any other ancient writers they must have brought home to him his own twisted and tragic sense of life. For good reasons he drafted in the margin of his translation of *Antigone* a poem beginning: "There is no happiness for any man".[26] How deeply Robinson felt this connection is demonstrated by the "Chorus of Old Men in *Aegeus*" (first printed 1896), the earliest of his verse to go into CP without a single verbal alteration. This magnificent recreation of a chorus on "man's agony" from the lost Aegeus tragedies of Sophocles and Euripides shows how thoroughly he was able to identify himself both with the style of Greek drama and its spirit.[27]

Above all, Euripides must have had a direct appeal to him. Not only did Robinson borrow motives from the dramatist in several of his poems: in his last years he could mention "three or four plays" by Euripides as a source of inspiration on a par with the work of

Shakespeare, the single writer who probably meant most to him.[28] He must have recognized in the Greek playwright a poetic and human situation strikingly akin to his own.

Like Robinson, Euripides was torn between idealistic longing and critical skepticism, hope and pessimistic disillusion. His scattered and contradictory philosophical remarks show a deep uncertainty about life's ultimate meaning, which reflects the "modern" breakdown of accepted standards in the dramatist's own time. He tried to believe in absolute truths and a God reigning the world in justice — but who is he? We know him "only from hearsay". God appears as "unfathomable"; is he just an expression of natural necessity, human reason, or mere chance? When in an early letter Robinson wonders "whether the invisible powers are a fortuitous issue of unguided cosmos, or the cosmos itself", when in his early sonnet "Kosmos" he asks whether God is a jester, he speaks with Euripides' voice, and quite possibly is aware of it.[29]

Euripides saw the same confusing riddles in man's actions and his real motives: deep in his heart the poet harbored faith in God's providence, but when he saw the tangled fate of men he "didn't know what to think". His protagonists are no longer traditional heroes in black and white, but earthly men and women, not least women, confronted with situations of hopeless ambiguity, rended by maddening and illogical passions, by Love "whose name is senselessness", and analyzed with a cynical psychological naturalism which often leaves scant space for Euripides' basic ethical pathos.[30] And at the same time Robinson saw his Greek predecessor accept life's condition with that stoic resignation which is typical of him and which Robinson himself shared, and solve again and again, with unflinching patience, Robinson's own artistic problem: how to force an all-too-human hesitancy and despair into the relieving forms of universal beauty.

This attachment to classical drama is only one of the many factors in Robinson's poetic work. But in "Eros Turannos" it came to play a decisive part in one of his most personal creations. In his early poems he used his classical allusions quite indiscriminately, and sometimes tritely. By 1913 this habit was wearing off with the poet's increasing maturity. In *The Man Against the Sky* little classical raw material was left, and it was soon to be replaced by Biblical and medieval themes. But in "Eros Turannos" the influence went much deeper than theme and allusions, and became connected with the motive powers both of idea and form. And even without manuscript evidence we can guess, at least in outline, how the impact played upon the poet's imagination.

The "story" in "Eros Turannos" came to Robinson from his own New England background, and has numerous parallels in his production. He intended to present to his readers another of his isolated and frustrated individuals, pictured in the framework of an upper class marriage, based on miscalculation and ending in failure. But this particular material had a special and personal meaning for him. In his Robinson biography C. P. Smith* has connected the plot of the poem with the fact (well concealed by earlier biographers) that the poet all through his life was hopelessly infatuated with a lady in Gardiner, Emma Loehen Shepherd. She was married young to the poet's older, dashing and externally successful brother Herman, a man who swiftly deteriorated, and disappointed his wife in several ways, until he finally died; their marriage had then long since disintegrated. Smith tries to prove that not only "Eros Turannos", but many other Robinson poems about love and marriage represent a "running record" in ever new disguises of this erotic triangle which involved the poet himself so deeply. As mentioned above, Smith also tries to establish a chronological sequence of the poems, based on Robinson's changing emotions toward the couple: he began by despising him and pitying her, and ended by commiserating with them both, realizing through it all that her love had proved unbreakable even in adversity.[31]

This profound frustration doubtless offers an important background both to Robinson's poetry and to his attitude toward life. But Smith often overlooks that in Robinson's writing the particulars of this relation to his sister-in-law are not used as a recording of private facts, but as a material for poems, a qualification doubly important in an artist as careful and wary of his effects as was Robinson. In every single instance — at least in his successful work — the esthetic whole was his main concern. And this is especially true of "Eros Turannos".

In actual fact we do not know when and from what source the "story" of the poem came to him, — from tradition and gossip, from observation in- our out-side his family, or from both. In any case his personal relationship doubtless added emotional coloring both to the drawing of the poetic characters and of their background. But important traits in the psychological and social picture obviously are not based on personal experience. And everything is made to serve a new purpose, the composition of a poem, which by its very idea presented Robinson with his artistic dilemma. He intended to tell this marriage story in its everyday, "prosy" sordidness and with its psychological tangle of motivation as if it were a modern novel (he had just spent years trying to write a novel himself). He would make the story express his own deep uncertainty about life, even when it came to grasping and understanding the reality of human relation-ships, a confusion which he must have felt painfully with regard to his own harassed family. But this time he would not content himself with a vignette or an ironic anecdote, a naturalistic sketch of character and circumstance. He saw in the material a possibility of lifting the local and all-too-human onto the level of tragedy, giving the lyrical poem that dramatic poignancy which he had been unable to create in his own recent attempts at playwriting, bringing out the emotional grandeur of the subject and making it monumental and poetically representative as an example of human endurance in suffering, the only solution to life's problem he personally was completely sure of. In this complex and ambitious task he found inspiration and support in the Greeks throughout.

The title is the only overt classical reference in the poem. But it is more conscious than has been noticed. Indirectly, to literate readers, it gains some of its ominous emphasis from its resemblance to the title of the Greek tragedy above all tragedies about love and disaster under the doom of fate, Sophocles' *Oidipus tyrannos*. The idea itself, of Eros as the ruthless master, is found in several Greek sources. It is hardly probable that Robinson ever read in Hesiod's *Theogony* the pertinent description of Eros who "subdues the hearts of all gods and all men and overwhelms sensible consideration". But during his long work on *Antigone* he studied carefully, and almost certainly translated himself, the famous chorus (781 ff.) about *Eros aniketos*, "the Victor", who captures and forces mortals and immortals alike, fools and con-fuses their senses, and "leads the purest of human souls astray, to shame and ill fame".[32]

The Greek form used in Robinson's title allows us to be even more specific. No corresponding expression exists in Latin literature. In Greek the combination *Eros tyrannos* is found only in two authors, in a minor erotic poet (Nicetas Eugenianus) whom Robinson in all probability had never read, and in Euripides — in one fragment (132) and in *Hippolytos* (525 ff.), the chorus describing the God of Love as "all men's lord". Here, as occasionally elsewhere, Robinson's title is a direct quotation; and as often was the case he overestimated his readers' ability to know and identify his allusions. The ostentatious grecism is emphasized by the spelling *turannos*, which in English dictionaries is an ordinary way of rendering the Greek ypsilon. Robinson later used the same transcription in another poem (*Musterion* — CP, 1937, p. 747).[33]

The general parallels are obvious between "Eros Turannos" and Euripides' *Hippolytos*, a tragedy describing the futile struggle of a queen against a senseless and corrupting love, which destroys both herself and a young and innocent royal prince, all in accordance with the directions of insulted Aphrodite, the goddess whose presence makes *Hippolytos* "a play of universal significance, as against a mere presentation of a particular passion in a particular individual".[34] We don't know what translation of Euripides Robinson used beside the Greek original, quite probably that in Loeb's Classical Library (1912), which has a parallel text in Greek. But he may also well have known the translation by Gilbert Murray (1911) to whom he later refers directly;[35] and the parallels are particularly striking in Murray's emphatic and Swinburnian version.

Some of the opening passages actually contain Robinson's poem *in nuce*. In Aphrodite's first speech about Hippolytos she describes how Phaedra once "Saw him, and, as she saw, her heart was torn/ With great love, by the working of my will/ ... She built a shrine, and named it *Love-at-home*/ ... And here that grievous and amazéd queen,/ Wounded and wondering, with ne'er a word/ Wastes slowly; and her secret none hath heard/ Nor dreamed". Phaedra's discussion with herself, her analysis of her own motives, her effort to hide her sickness, and then to fight it: "My third mind, when these two availed me naught/ To quell love, was to die", remind the reader of the introductory stanzas in "Eros Turannos". The speeches and choruses about the blinding Cypris and Eros, the "Master of Men", who spellbind and subdue everyone and "bend the pride/ Of the hearts of God and man", show similar parallels.[36]

Equally important is the general heroic setting, which adds grandeur to the scene, in *Hippolytos* as in other Greek plays: "'Twas in some great house, surely, that began/ This plague upon us"; then the baser kind followed, "blind and joyous!" Euripides also has others of the central symbols in the poem: "Could I wing me to my rest amid the roar/ Of the deep Adriatic on the shore". There is a hint of tragic reconciliation to fate in the reference to the great victims of love in the past, who are now dwelling among the Muses: "And fear not, fret not; for a thing too stern/ Hath met and crushed them!"[37] Amid this, Phaedra herself fills the stage, as does Robinson's heroine and so many of those of Euripides, with the dimensions of pitiable and magnificent humanity.

These parallels of course do not imply that "Eros Turannos" all comes out of Euripides. But obviously the Greek element in the poem is much more than a "classical title-tag" to be compensated for by the modernity of thought, as suggested by Untermeyer (*I). During the period when the motif lived and grew in Robinson's mind, before the largely finished first draft, the Greek models doubtless were present to him, clarifying his aims, influencing his material, and pushing him in their direction as the subject moved into form. There are parallels in particular techniques, as pointed out below. There are less palpable similarities, as intimated in a general way by Conrad Aiken, "an element suggestive of the rapid lyrical summary, cryptically explanatory, a little subdued and brooding, as under a gigantic shadow — of the choruses in the tragedies of Æschylus and Sophocles".[38] But most important is the blending of all these elements in the dramatic *ethos*.

This impact may have been strengthened indirectly through later poets in the classical tradition, not least Swinburne. But the most obvious parallel influence came from one of Euripides' modern disciples, Ibsen, whom Robinson greatly admired, and who has meant much in bringing out the dramatic trend in his own writing.[39] There is a more than general resemblance between a poem like "Eros Turannos" and a number of Ibsen's modern plays of marriage, from *A Doll's House* and *The Wild Duck* to *Hedda Gabler* and *When We Dead Awaken*, monumental tragedies of disappointed women realizing and reacting to their mistaken choice of partner. Above all, *Ghosts*, Ibsen's most Euripidean drama, comes close to Robinson's poem, in its sombre setting and action and in the figure of the betrayed Mrs. Alving, a victim of her social heritage and the rottenness of her lover, discovering his meanness too late, and living on in terrible loneliness with her rake of a husband in the manor house overlooking the fjord, trying to cover up his excesses against the eyes of the "town and harbor side". In its entire atmosphere "Eros Turannos" worthily holds its place in the line between Ibsen's masterpiece from 1881 and O'Neill's *Mourning Becomes Electra* fifty years later.

What must have struck Robinson in particular in *Ghosts* at this junction must have been the way in which Ibsen was able to create the necessary poetic distance in spite of the down-to-earth naturalism and psychological relativism of the story that was told, and to give his limited and not too edifying fable a universal grandeur by dramatic methods that to Robinson must have betrayed their close affinity with the Greeks. In his own handling of similar material Robinson struck a similar course. And while the parallels cannot always be pointed out in detail, Robinson, unlike Ibsen, demonstrated his awareness of the relationship by referring directly to his Greek master (*sat sapienti*) in the very title, but only there, warning the initiated readers before the play begins that whatever the plot, we are going to attend a performance on the highest level.

### 4. *Interpretation.*

The poem is technically a narrative. Only one voice is speaking. As is usual in Robinson, practically everything takes place on the psychological level. There is hardly any action in the ordinary sense. What there is, is left largely to the reader's imagination, as an "off-stage affair".[40]

But although the poem is no "play", it has strong connections with drama, — not only, in T. S. Eliot's words, by grasping character "through the relations of two or more persons to each other",[41] but also by its arrangement. The poet of course knows all the time what he is aiming at, and what is finally going to "happen". But everything evolves objectively, that is: as events occur, and only as far as, and in the sequence in which, they would naturally appear to the spectator-narrator, a man of Tilbury Town ("a casual though fairly sympathetic observer", R. P. Adams*). The poem is kept largely in the present tense, and in the first two thirds there is no direct reference to a narrator: we are just presented with facts. In Euripides, only the drama as a whole reveals to us the twisted mind of Phaedra or the flatness of Jason. Similarly, in Robinson's poem, we shall only know at the end how to regard the heroine, and there is a long way to go.

The movement in detail within this compass can also be described appropriately in terms of classical drama. Half of the six stanzas give the exposition, a kind of first act presenting the two protagonists, the history of their past relationship, the built-in shortcoming (*hamartia*) of the heroine and her equally Aristotelian misjudgment of the situation, all told in the disguised dialogue of the couple. Then follows the sudden change of fate (*peripetia*), and the "discovery" (anagnorisis) or "recognition" in the classical sense, the "change from ignorance to knowledge". The remaining three stanzas describe the result of the tragic downfall, a *stasis* of complication (Coxe*), expressed in the conflicting voices of the chorus, and a concluding climax with the ultimate revelation of character and interpretation of the entire action.

These are, however, formal categories, that may serve diverse aims. The narrative itself "plunges us into the middle" (Barnard*) with a Browning-like suddenness that is natural in the opening words of a drama, but hardly appeared as very "classical" to the poetry readers of Robinson's time. And the action which follows, displays a highly complicated pattern.

In the first three stanzas Robinson manages, with a minimum of words, to present setting, persons and plot with amazing realism. As is customary in his poetry, the social background is seen only through the minds of the two protagonists, but it leaves nothing to be desired in clarity. The heroine is placed in one of the New England "manor houses" on the hill of which there was a grey-stone Tudor example even in the Gardiner of Robinson's childhood, — these aristocratic mansions left behind by time, often in a state of decacy, their isolated inhabitants retreating into their "eloquent silences" of "tragic intensity", milieus described strikingly by the poet's fellow New Englanders Amy Lowell, Robert Frost and R. P. Tristram Coffin.[42] And the poem explains the process of attrition by which a lady in this milieu and of this standing may come to accept as suitor a rogue who does not love her.

This is a prosaic story. And it is made no less so by the qualities of her prospective mate, about which we are left in no doubt. For once, Robinson clearly takes sides in the delineation of his characters. The social position of the suitor is not stated unambiguously; he *may* himself belong to the upper class. But the details are more fully explained if he is regarded as a *parvenu*, with a moral depravity and a touch of the vulgar which also reflect his background. It is surprising that Coxe* can see in the prospective husband a "worthless", but relatively innocuous type, who "finds a solace and security in the love of his wife and in her solid place in the community". *She* from the very beginning "fears" him (this shocking overture to a love poem), and with the intellectual part of herself knows him to be dangerous. She has "sounded" his suspicious depths and realized that his oily charm with its ambiguously "engaging" qualities is the "mask" of a liar and adventurer who — having nothing to offer but himself — is after her money and social position, not her fading beauty (if she ever had any). Originally in the draft Robinson called him a "seeker". Finally he named him a "Judas", after the man who also wore a mask, was also willing to sell love for money (Perrine*) and betrayed his love with a kiss.[43] And while the narrator later comes to realize that his judgment may be wrong about the heroine, no such concession is made about her partner.

After this reflected image, which suggests his slippery character even by its indirection, the lover needs only to be sketched with a few additional, direct touches. As is often the case in Robinson, the eyes are used as an indicator, together with the dubious character of "what he says". In two words we are given a sketch of the development of his calculations. Initially he is "beguiled" (misled) about his chances by the aristocratic note of her surroundings.[44] Then he is "*re*assured" by a better understanding of her psychology: "He sees that he will not be lost". He needs only to wait confidentially for the seed to grow and things to take their course, "looking around him" at the world that is going to be his.

What actually fills the first three stanzas, then, between the verbs "fears him" and "secures him", is the long drawn-out dialogue in *style indirect libre* during which the heroine vanquishes her social instincts and her better judgment and gradually deceives and persuades herself to disregard the warnings in her own mind. This analysis is carried through as an "obviously scientific diagnosis" (Untermeyer, *II) or, equally appropriate, as an example of that tireless dialectic play which Euripides adopted from the Sophists. A brief, but exhaustive paraphrase of the main points was early given by Perrine.* The problem is put concisely in the first stanza, where the opening chiasma (fears — meets — meets — fears) summarizes her hesitations. In the concluding lines of stanza 1 and 3 we are confronted with the main argument, that is even more decisive than her attraction to the man: her fear of approaching old age, an idea that is also very familiar to the Greeks. (Possibly, social decay and isolation have already made other suitors rare.) The dominant note is one of painful and half-hearted indecision, a twisted game of pros and cons, which makes the reader *feel* the tension and duration of the struggle, although the description fills only 24 lines.

A supreme touch is the fact that even the social pride of the lady gradually turns against her better interests and "assuages" her further into illusion, in a perverted mixture of rationalization and social bad conscience, and that the final defense mechanism, her simple "prejudice" (mentioned by its blunt name) reacts too slowly and finally "fades", unable to prevent the catastrophe.[45] The detail rounds off the social picture of an aristocracy that is no longer certain of its own standards, nor is able to judge those of others, and is itself inefficiently "fading" away.

Some features of the language underline this seamy side of the picture. In general Winters criticizes the "dryness" of the poem; but in these stanzas, at least, this quality makes part of their conscious effect. The vacillation in the heroine's own mind is reflected in the many brief and weightless words in the first two stanzas and the second half of the third, and in similar rhymes, all but three ending in monosyllables. The bickering is no less brilliantly expressed in the analytic and prosy, discursive tone of these stanzas. There is little of poetic grandeur in "always asked" questions with an undertone of cold evaluation, in dryly calculating expressions like "all reasons", "sagacity", "sound", "found", "almost", "as if", "doubts", "what she knows". In the second stanza two commas in the draft, that were later eliminated, further emphasized this prosaic quality by forcing pauses of cogitation and stopping the even flow of verse.[46] In the 2. and 3. stanzas the more complicated syntax ("between ... the cost", "and all her doubts ... secures him") reflects the dilemma, in contrast to the simple and swift-moving sentences that have reference to *him*, and which correspond to his carefree and justified assurance in "looking around him".

The involved use of time serves the same purpose. The first three stanzas of course present some of the lasting elements of the erotic relationship, leading up to the conclusion. But the events told in these stanzas all refer to the period before the marriage, a fact which has been overlooked by some critics. During the winter and spring of final decision the narrative repeatedly moves back and forth between various stages of her development, by direct reference ("once"), and by a telescoped expression like the "blurred sagacity", everything pressing inexorably toward *one* solution.

There are parallel features in the metric form. After the opening quatrains with their stated arguments the three pondering new rhymes in these stanzas indicate the wary elaboration of thought, searching and hesitant. The ambivalent circling around *one* center of attention (in both actors) is made directly audible in the flat and soundless feminine rhymes in lines 2, 4, and 8, all ending in *him*, as does the thought (choose him — refuse him — lose him; sound him — found him — around him; allures him — reassures him — secures him). And the reiteration has a cumulative effect that finally seems to make "him" inevitable. In the fourth stanza the result is reached, and the rhyme disappears with the lover himself.

What Robinson thus manages to build up, in these first three stanzas, is a background of sad and almost trite banality that is contemporary both with Euripides and Zola: such are the facts of life as the observer-narrator sees them and has to present them. But he has also different and equally important things in mind. For this purpose other elements are brought in, less palpable, but no less real.

In the first place these are elements of pure form. More important than the general similarity between "Eros Turannos" and a Greek drama is the simplicity and clarity of the poem, and its touch of timelessness. There is little concrete information; the protagonists are just "she" and "he". The poem is objective; the poet-observer makes us "outsiders with him" (Pearce*), and has everything under complete artistic control. There is a strict unity of place, of action, and (within reasonable limits) of time. The disposition is logical and pellucid in the Greek tradition; the poem opens with the clear distribution of roles or dramatic "parts" in the first act (8 + 6 + 6 + 4 lines), and the material is equally well balanced in the following acts. The movement of thought is perfectly natural, and often strictly symmetrical. As R. P. Adams* points out, the structure is the same in each stanza and in the poem as a whole: "a building up of tension as we learn the story, then a held pause as the speaker shifts his ground, then the conclusion, which returns us to the story with a greatly heightened awareness of its meaning and importance".[47]

The language is handled with strict economy of means. It shows a tense precision, and has a strong intellectual note, abstract, without sensory detail. Pearce* observes that many of the packed lines in "Eros Turannos" function "almost as proverbs and epigrams; we learn lessons", listening to a master-rhetorician who gives the whole a "memorializing" effect. The final stanza of the poem makes us understand why Robinson spoke of himself as "an incurable preacher" (Barnard*). That to some extent, at least, the restraint is conscious, is indicated by Robinson himself when he later wrote that in his Arthurian poems he was able to use his idiom more freely because of "the romantic framework".[48]

This character of rational and solemn clarity is emphasized by the verse. Occasionally the metrical form may serve other aims, as pointed out above, and may suggest and support almost everything by its very sense of masterly control. But the general effect is one of almost majestic clarity and force. In the stanzaic structure each of the first couplets normally is a unit, always ending in comma or semicolon, and carrying great and conclusive weight. Their suspension and "held-breath quality" is heightened by the following triplet, which also builds up the stanza toward its final "climax of action or emotion". The same effect is strengthened by the fact that in most of the stanzas there is at the end of the sixth line a pause and turn of thought which reinforces both the stretching of the triplet rhyme and the heavily conclusive final rhyme (R. P. Adams,* Barnard*).

Of course, there is no line-to-line correspondence between idea and verse. But often the interplay is obvious, with an "astonishing range of effects". At the same time the rhythmic soberness and clarity do not destroy the musical expressiveness and the "poetic" quality of the verse. The feminine rhymes "ease the epigrammatic bite" in soft transitions. In the third stanza, *s* and *l* sounds build up "a liquid sibilance, punctuated by a few stopped consonants, particularly the *t*'s in lines one and three and the *d*'s in the last four lines". This close interrelation of structure, language and verse makes for a "subtle grace", "an impression of elegance, economy and precision seldom matched in English" (R. P. Adams,* Barnard,* Pearce*).[49]

Style and verse form can only support or underline, however. Decisive in creating atmosphere is the introduction of poetic symbols, which can add depth to the conflict and prepare for things to come.

In the use of these symbols Pearce* sees the same trend which is typical of the language. He finds that the symbols often are so restricted and controlled as to operate more like similes: they are not sympathetically expressive of the emotions of the protagonists, they are only used in order to clarify *our* understanding and direct *our* attention. This may hold good about some of the symbols, but certainly not about others; some of them clearly have *both* functions. And in any case their clarity does not make them narrow or emotionally poor. Coxe* well defines how these images "control and provide a center for the meanings possible to the poem" in accordance with the general technique of Robinson's symbolism. From the beginning they serve as motifs only, with latent power and meaning; statement and symbol support and constitute a gloss upon each other. Then, without actually acquiring new material, they are repeated and expanded as the poem opens up into more elaborate and definite suggestion.

These motifs have a double aspect, a "calculated ambiguity" which adds to the feeling of suspense and fatality (Coxe*). A warning is sounded as early as the second line of the poem, with the introduction of the classical idea of fate. In the context the word is used as a verb, quite colloquially and without much weight. From the very beginning, however, it hints at the merciless character of the erotic urge and the hidden gravity of the crisis. It is tied by alliteration to her "fears", and points toward the inexorable march of time ("age", "days") that is soon to be expanded in the nature images.

A more palpable symbol — not mentioned directly in these first stanzas, but felt as a background all the time — is the house, a frequent element in Robinson's imagery. Like the royal mansion in Greek tragedy it stands for tradition, pomp and power, and implicitly also for a more superficial happiness, the object of that mean covetousness and the background of that pride and prejudice which are discussed soberly enough in these stanzas. But much more the "house" is gradually going to appear as the symbol of spiritual values, closely attached to Robinson's own aristocratic attitude: that accumulated refinement, that perception and integrity and that drama of great contrasts which make for a life in the deeper sense, and are unfathomable to the masses in the vulgar dwellings belov.

This symbol is again related to those of nature, and with a similar import. Around the house stretches the park, with its "old trees". Here as elsewhere in Robinson's poetic landscapes the words imply "the importance of roots, the dependence of the present upon the past".[50] And through the park runs the river to the sea.

Negatively, in the first stanza, the water gliding smoothly and "foamlessly" over the weirs symbolize in marvellously compressed form a life that is no real life, that isn't lived to the full. And Barnard* points out how Robinson here makes the accumulated consonants slow up the movement of the final four lines by their very sound, making palpable the "intolerable distances" of that lonely future which the heroine envisages.

Positively, the image calls forth its counterimage, the open, foamy and storm-struck seas of passion. The ocean is a frequent symbol in Robinson's poetry as well as in his poetic tradition, involving "the inevitable course of an existence which is unchanged by human will or human aspiration". It is blind like fate, and no less cruel. But it has dimension. It suggests that "life has an inevitable movement and a grand scope extending far beyond the restricted vision and limited aspiration of the individual".[51] In its restless march against the "harbor side" the ocean thus hints at the deeper values in the existence of those who have the passion and daring to live in the grand style, not only socially. And as the poem evolves, these symbols are gradually linked, even physically. The stair-like descent of the water over the weirs points toward the stairs that in the concluding stanza, in the style of a palace, run through the park and down into the sea, connecting the house with the elements.

These symbolic values are emphasized by the fact that they are presented to us, not as observed through the mind of the heroine (to whom they are matter-of-course), but reflected in the eyes of the intruder. The manor in its park, overlooking the sea and "touched by tradition" in everything, is to him little but a part of his calculation. *He* has no hesitations at having his life glide foamlessly over the weirs. Thus, by his sly observation, even *he* inadvertently points to the possibility of a nobler heritage, a depth of sentiment and an openness to life that is denied to him, and which is the hallmark of "those on the hill".

Even the final, slowly developing symbols of blindness ("mask", "blurred", "sound", "dimmed", "fades", "illusion", "veil") which are pointed out by Coxe,* — that foible which leads her astray in the everyday sense and finally throws her into his arms — also, from a different point of view, may be regarded as the prerogative of those who have a deeper vision, different from the short-range astuteness of the plebeian.

This background prepares us for the appearance of a heroine. And like Euripides, Robinson gives grandeur even to her shortcomings by focussing the exposition almost exclusively on her alone. Hippolyt is pallid beside Phaedra, Jason beside Medea; in "Eros Turannos" the "seeker" is not only morally depraved, but basically insignificant, also because of his lack of deeper involvement. He is of interest largely as a catalyst of *her* thoughts and emotions. Until the end of the second stanza he is only seen through her eyes, and is not admitted onto the stage until her role is established. The spotlight soon returns to her; after the crisis he does not directly reappear. It is *her* decision which gives him what importance he may have, both in happiness and disaster.

Thus, both in style and content these three first stanzas clearly bring out the dichotomy in the material itself as presented by Robinson. But if they are regarded in isolation from the following stanzas — as they should be, — the symbolic hints of a larger dimension still remain hints only. They are ambiguous. And they are partly used negatively, supporting the not too kind description of both actors. The dominant impression left on the reader is that of prosaic vacillation; and the naturalistic note makes the heroine neither impressive nor attractive. There is much of calculation even on her part, cool decisions and revisions with an eye to the last chance. Also, it is unavoidable that the sordidness of the object of her inclination taints even her. Above all, if we consider what is to follow about her disillusionment, little is done to make us believe in the depth of her love. Directly, that feeling is mentioned only once in these three stanzas. Her endless hesitation cannot add much conviction to it. Neither can the spelling of the word with a capital L, whether or not it directly refers to God Eros in the title of the poem.

The consistency of the description is underlined by the cold verbs "choose", "lose", "refuse", "reassures him" and "secures him". Winters* admires the "hard and subdued irony of the last lines of the second and third stanzas" which doesn't seem to intrude into foreign surroundings. They may carry a double meaning (security is exactly the thing her decision does *not* give her, — Coxe*). They may also have a note of the almost cynical resignation of a woman worn out by long indecision. But most of all their slightly vulgar ring indicates the way in which the lady's story is still bound to appear to those looking at it from the outside.

All that has thus been built up, changes abruptly and completely during the events of the summer of her wedding. They occur between stanza 3 and 4 and are seen only through their results as summarized in the latter. Not only *her* life is changed, but even more the picture of herself in the reader, — a technique well known to the Greeks.

There is some difference of opinion regarding the exact nature of these events. Contrary to other critics Barnard* believes that "the story is brought to a climax by the husband's desertion of the wife". He is "beguiled" into accepting marriage and respectability; but "after the novelty has worn off, [he] becomes bored and moves on". To Barnard, only some such "dramatic" happening would make the town seeth with excited gossip.

The point is not too important. But the suitor's fascination in stanza 2 with the aristocratic milieu of the heroine makes it improbable that he should — almost right away — voluntarily relinquish his newly-won position as lord of the manor, however "footloose" he may be. (The freshness of her love has hardly entered into the picture at all.) And the poem does not demand this interpretation. Her full under-standing of his depravity, her realization that she has only been used for a purpose, and the consequent death of the kind of love she has felt, would account sufficiently for her "seclusion", — from her own frustrated dreams, from her husband, with whom she has no longer an emotional fellowship, and from the outside world. She does not need to be "alone" (Barnard*) to be thus secluded. Her "hiding" is rather more terrifying if it is physically shared with him, as Mrs. Alving and her husband in Ibsen's *Ghosts* live on together in the same house. And even this situation may be realized, or at least guessed at, by the townspeople.[52]

The purpose of the stanza, however, is not to emphasize the com-monplace character of the events. On the contrary, it changes the trite existence of Emma Bovary into great drama. Her earlier position, as seen by the reader, is re-evaluated, in the light of new evidence presented as facts in the stanza itself. The violence of her reaction, her visible despair, make it obvious that previous opinion about her must have been wrong, that her experience in the affair must have been much more shattering than was assumed, and consequently takes on a new meaning.

The completeness of the turn-about is evidenced by the change of tone in stanza four: suddenly, gates are thrown wide open to emotion, without any qualifications whatsoever. Diction becomes as grave, definite and majestic as it was shifty and ambiguous before. The style has a new tension. Language and verse take a note of finality, concentrated in the heavy and expressive nouns arranged in the time sequence of catastrophe (confusion — illusion — seclusion), and in the powerful and resounding verbs (inaugurates, reverberates), most of them in rhyming position. But above all, the change is brought about, and made convincing, by the new and conscious use on a different level of a set of symbols that earlier were only hinted at.

It is interesting to note, that this technique was not from the beginning clear to Robinson himself. In the draft version of the fourth stanza, as printed above, the first line ("The legend of her love remains / an epic of confusion") tied the new stanza to the three

previous ones; the final version makes the transition sharp, her confusion being the result of his deceit. More important, in the draft
version Robinson introduces in this stanza a wholly new set of symbols
(legend, epic, trumpet, crash) which is not only much weaker in its
expressive power, but might rather draw the imagination away from
the classical atmosphere in the opening to a world of more vaguely
traditional romance. The final version instead confines itself strictly
to what has already been built up or hinted at, but with a new impact.

The "falling leaf" in the old park now indicates both the loveliness
of the past summer and its brevity, the merciless change to autumn,
and the cruel alteration in the heroine's own life, with the same ring
of fate and finality: the period of decay in nature "inaugurates" the
lasting "reign" of her grief. So does the steadily "pounding" wave
of the ocean (more than would the draft version, "shattered", which
is not so clearly reiterative). The image is further strengthened by
another auditive simile: instead of the "crash" (which is dropped
only in CP) comes the "reverberation" of the solemn and conclusive
"dirge", an image which Robinson had already used before with
tremendous weight and in classical context in "The Chorus of Old
Men in *Aegeus*". And the air filled with the roar of the breakers
resounds again in the "vibration" of the final line, made audible by
the "plucking, sounding" quality of the word itself (Coxe*).[53]

But all is centered around the house, behind ocean and park. And
what can now be seen by all eyes, is stated clearly in a new word:
"*passion*" must have been there, as behoves high places. The observer
measures it pitifully by the depth of her helpless "confusion" and
"illusion". The entire story with its new interpretation of evidence is
compressed into the logical chiasma of "home — lived — died —
hide", which has in it both the warmth she had hoped for, and the
icy cold which became her fate in stead. Her husband now is out of
the picture, wherever he may be: she is majestically alone with herself
and her loss. How conscious is the effect can again be seen from the
draft version. Originally, in the concluding lines of the fourth stanza,
Robinson let town and harbor side "shake heads at her seclusion".
In the final version he removes the discussion of popular opinion to
the fifth stanza, and concentrates the fourth around *her* emotions, to
which her surroundings are only a sounding board.

The impact of this stanza is immense. But in itself it would hardly,
within the length of the poem, be quite sufficient to change the picture
that was built up so carefully through the first half. With audacious

art Robinson therefore continues the re-evaluation in the fifth stanza, which is completely different in tone, but nevertheless serves the same purpose. At the end of stanza 4 he has vaguely confronted the heroine in her seclusion with the "town and harbor side"; but hitherto, the citizens of this community have only been present invisibly. In the fifth stanza they suddenly fill the air with their whispering comment, thus making *her* loneliness appear as even more complete. They occupy the entire stage like the Greek chorus, summing up our common experience and lifting it toward its conclusion.

In his general praise of the poem Winters* criticizes this "commonplace" stanza severely: while its paraphrasable substance is necessary, he finds the statement to be undistinguished. Even to Coxe* it is "prosaic and bare". But this criticism is slightly beside the mark. As the manuscript demonstrates, the stanza is the one that caused Robinson himself most trouble, and in the draft we can again follow a gradual tightening of expression. The poet removes the vague image of "finding him master", which is equally inappropriate whether it refers to the lover or (more probably) to Eros. With it go the flat and overexplicit noun "disaster" and the bad rhymes "prove — love". And there is a similar tightening of the image of the "veil". But in the main, these corrections tend to bring out more clearly those qualities that correspond to Robinson's intentions, and to the role of the stanza in the poem.

What Robinson likes to drive home in the first place, is the unavoidable human uncertainty of judgment about our fellow beings, since their motives will for ever remain hidden from our eyes. The stories we so much like to tell about our neighbors, describing them as they "should be" in our opinion, *are* just "stories" (Coxe*), reconstruction and guesswork based on scant material, — what Robinson himself once called "the lash of a tongue-weary town" with its "inch-ruling of the infinite" (CP, pp. 516, 975). The stanza presents us with "the complication of events and motives and themes ... of attitudes and views" (Coxe*), even with regard to the heroine. And again, *our* groping uncertainty is expressed in diction and form, as *hers* was in the first three stanzas: in the prosaic, discursive language with its alternatives ("as if — as if", "or — or"), in the many short and dry words, in the play of possibilities implied in the tenses of the verbs, and in the return of the same form of vague and questioning rhyme reflecting the futile speculation and focussed on the center of the problem (should be — could be — would be).

But this interlude does not now break the back of the poem, dissolving it into relativism or scepticism. It serves as a warning against cheap sentimentality: we are looking for facts and truth, as far as they are available. The stanza, as it stands, also serves as an emotional pause, relieving the tension after the highstrung previous stanza and before the final build-up. But the main result is different, due to the fine balance that is maintained between the qualifications and the purpose they serve.

The stanza is a kind of dialogue. Lines 1—2 and 5—6 both end in dashes which, as the corrections show, are used with much care by Robinson. In these four lines an impersonal group of observers ("we") is talking to its fellow-citizens ("you"), including the reader. In the other lines the group is answered by the poet-observer, in a position corresponding to that of the leader of the chorus in Greek drama. He partly feels himself to belong to the community, as does the Greek leader, and the poet's description of the group through their remarks is not at all unfriendly. But he is not completely identified with it. This distinction is brought out in the first line in the slightly vulgar expression "tapping on our brows", indicating the eternal popular explanation of unusual behavior that the exceptional person is just crazy. The line is censured by Winters.* But obviously it refers to observers more rash and narrowminded than the narrator himself.

In retrospect, the distinction between leader and group is also borne out by the analysis itself in the three first stanzas with their subtle and complex psychological interpretation and their involved symbols: this is not the talk of the town, but the conclusions of a more finely organized observer. And he does not, in stanza five, flatly reject his earlier views as "superficial", as R. P. Adams* will have it: many of them still stand, together with the facts on which they were based. But he makes us realize that there is more behind the facts, and that the general picture has changed before our eyes.[54]

In order to bring out the hidden quality of the emotions in the heroine, on which the poem now hinges, Robinson does not in this stanza refer again to all the earlier symbols. Their impact has to be saved for the end. But like mountains rising above the plain they are now placed in convincing relief by the low-brow ponderings of the chorus. In a similar way the lover served as the heroine's foil in the first act; but now the contrast is much more striking. The nature of her feelings is compressed into one central image, that appears for the last time and now with its full impact:

> As if the story of a house
> Were told, or ever could be.

The same idea is served by the image of the "veil". Winters* calls it "especially unfortunate", and in fact the metaphor is not completely pellucid. But in R. P. Adams'* reading the import, at least, is beyond doubt, and Robinson's own tentative first versions confirm it. *She* is for ever silent about herself. *She* will never protest our theories. Thus we can freely persist in our conviction that we see the naked reality in her case, not allowing it to be falsified by any screen of kindliness. But in fact, *we* have now proved to be the blind; and what *we* miss, is stated in the word *"visions"*. With its rich connotations it involves all those dreams and hopes, and that overpowering passion, which "we" are for ever unable to grasp, even in vague adumbration.

Thus we are ready for the final stanza. And again the line of the poem is drawn with superb power of balance.

The chorus has performed its service, and in the first three lines of stanza 6 quietly fades out of the picture. We have realized that the innocuous ponderings of the crowd (including ourselves) are not only doubtful, but in the larger context irrelevant. The events of the poem recede into the irrevocable past, as expressed in the tense of the triple rhyming verbs. Instead, through the opening with its consciously soft-spoken note ("meanwhile", "not much") the heroine, who in the previous stanza was the unknowing and uncaring object of our discussion, now moves back onto the scene in lonely and distant majesty. Her position is stated, no more through a report of observation and gossip, but as a fact; and it is even emphasized by our ignored presence: she is "not hearing much of what we say". At the same time she is somehow further de-personalized. As the central figure of the poem she is lifted onto the symbolic stage. "She" disappears in the timeless, heroic group of "they", the great sufferers of mankind, among whom she belongs, as Euripides places the fate-stricken Phaedra beside Semele and Eos (*Hippolytos*, 451 ff.).

But now there is also a question of more than suffering. It is pointed out by Coxe* that by packing the poem with "words that suggest descent, depth and removal from sight" Robinson gives the poem as a whole a descending line, an accumulation of sorrow that is reflected in the imagery. This is completely true: up to the end of the fourth stanza there is hardly any relief from the growing oppression of man by fate, and it carries on forcefully as the main motif to the very end.

But in the fifth stanza the possibility of a different movement is hinted at. And in the final stanza this contrasting force is clearly felt.

Its character was already indicated by Cestre* (p. 15) when he wrote about the deeper values suggested in Robinson's frustrated heroes and heroines, and by Harriet Monroe,* when she called the poem one of Robinson's "beautiful brevities [in which] a spiritual triumph is wrung out of meagre and reluctant destinies". R. P. Adams* offers a full definition. In one sense the defeat of the heroine is complete: she has preferred "to be overcome by an ecstacy of passion rather than by mere attrition", and she has lost thereby everything she *can* lose. But she has one compensation: she has *lived*, — which her externally triumphant marriage partner has not. In the sum of things her life has "counted" (Barnard*). In the terms of tradition, she has rejected the flat Greek ideal of *sofrosyne*, in the favor of a more profound ideal that was also Greek. She has paid the price that life demands, and gained what will never even be understood by those who never dared to try.

In the opening lines of the last stanza this deepening of the motif is made emphatic by the re-introduction of the mythological figure who gave the poem its title. Earlier, Eros largely loomed in the background, the wilful and cruel manipulator of man's destinies, as he is in Euripides. And that line is followed through to the bitter end, where the doomed are driven down to death like slaves (Perrine*). But now he also emerges in a different light, freed of anthropomorphic traits, with the grandeur of a god in *our* sense, the majestic representative of Fate as pictured by Schiller:

> das grosse, gigantische Schicksal,
> welches den Menschen erhebt, wenn es den Menschen zermalmt.[55]

His gifts are destructive. But only by accepting them is life made worth living.

And the heroine is changed accordingly. From what we now know, she is no longer a slightly banal figure, torn between everyday considerations in all their meanness. She may suffer "dumbly and incomprehendingly", as Barnard* would have it. But whether she knows herself or not, she belongs to that group elect that "with a god have striven", in a battle where the supreme and universal values of life are at stake. And in her defeat she has not totally lost: taking up the challenge is a victory in itself. In his tentative draft version of the stanza Robinson still placed emphasis on the heroine's sacrifice:

"what *she* may have given". In the definite version some gain on her part is also implied. The rhyme itself widens our idea of the fate of those that have striven: they also take "what the *god* has given".

The conclusion follows, and raises the final artistic problem. What the poem had of drama in the external sense is past. There is nothing more to "tell", no further events, in the actors or around them, just an acceptance of fate without action. The only possible climax, then, is that of our own feelings toward the heroine. Robinson succeeds, by bringing together for the last time, in three successive lines with conclusive, monosyllabic rhymes, his set symbols; and his careful preparation gives him the force he needs. He pours into them our deepened insight, they acquire their full range of meaning. And they give the heroine her real dimensions, surrounding her with "sudden, lavish beauty" (Zabel*).

There is no dilution of the tragic note. In the poem as in life, existence remains senseless and desperate, without any Emersonian assurance of compensation or retribution on either side of death. But it is life in its fullness that thus obeys its own laws. The eternal rise and breaking of the waves of passion, the familiar tree of tradition or love mangled by the wanton destructiveness of the powers, are no more the backdrop of the passive suffering of one pathetic woman, but the setting of a life accepted and lived on its own terms. When in the last image *she* joins the procession of *them*, the blinded lovers, who, touched by the wand of their god, are driven by him down the stairs from the house and into the sea, she is no longer an individual, but a symbol of the unfathomable forces of existence, moving to the conclusion with the "finality of fate itself".[56]

The above interpretation is corroborated indirectly by the artistic power of the last stanza. The three weighty feminine rhymes (striven — given — driven) draw the conclusion of the entire poem, with emphasis finally balanced as it should be. The triplet rhymes give the accumulation of imagery the same effect. As Barnard* points out, there is an extremely effective use of language sound, the assonance in the long *a* and the hammering recurrence of *d* in the last line. But there is also "a steady acceleration. Line 5 must be read slowly, for all but two of the syllables contain long vowels, and the consonant combinations in 'like waves breaking' compel deliberation; line 6 moves faster because of the short vowels, but 'changed' still slows the pace; whereas in line 7 there is nothing to stop the rush of words, until in the last line they pause to measure the heavy footfalls of Fate."[57]

R. P. Adams* suggests a somewhat different interpretation of the conclusion, based on his contrasting of rationalist materialism and romantic faith. He sees the former represented by the shallow lover and by Tilbury Town, and expressed in the symbols of the "endless, unprofitable tomorrow and tomorrow", the foamless weirs, the monotonous movements of the sea, and the trees in the cheap dreams of the adventurer. He makes the "pounding waves" in stanza four a part of the superficial towns-people's speculations about the lady. Consequently, he considers the last four "tough-minded" lines of the poem "as being probably ironic, as again referring at least partly to the town's point of view, which is explicitly said to be inadequate, rather than to the truer view the speaker hints at". He even implies that the narrator will thus dissociate himself from a certain sentimentality in the heroine.

Such ideas demonstrate how rich the poem is in possible implication, but they are hardly convincing. There is certainly irony in the poem, and Robinson was aware of such possibilities.[58] But the interpretation should not be allowed to break that clear line of rising emotion that, in my reading, runs through the poem from the fourth stanza onward and unceasingly to the end, with a consistent artistic purpose. A slightly ambiguous note in the four concluding lines would disturb that new and deeper meaning which the symbols have acquired, *beyond* the ideas of the townspeople. It would leave the reader with little to support the climax emotionally, except the barren statement about "what the god has given".

The interpretation of the conclusion hinges on the eternal question of the "dramatic" character of the poem. One does not need to apply to "Eros Turannos" what one critic states generally about much of Robinson's work, that he masters "tragedy in the purely Aristotelian sense".[59] It suffices to ask whether the poem shows a controlled development toward crisis and climax and leaves in the reader a unified effect comparable to that created by Greek drama.

Coxe,* in accordance with his views, used Henry James in order to clarify his disagreement with Allen Tate on this point. Apart from a tendency to "unfold a scene" there is to him nothing dramatic in Robinson's poems: "the excitement they convey is of a muted sort, akin to that which James himself generates". L. Untermeyer unknowingly answered this assertion by the pertinent observation that the closing effect of "Eros Turannos" is "muted, but sustained" (*III). And Allen Tate himself recently, without reference to Coxe, has referred to James differently in the same context, in a way that does not necessarily contradict the reading in this paper. "Eros Turannos" is to Tate "a great meditative, dramatic lyric". But it is "written from a personal point of view, not unlike James' "Trapped Spectator"; it is not in any sense an objective narrative. The "I" (or "we") who tells the action merely adumbrates it, speculates upon a situation which he has *observed*. The conflicts inherent in human love are concentrated in the last two stanzas, in which the limited knowledge of the observer is an element of mystery in the drama, which is not resolved but, in James' sense, *rendered*".[60]

## 5. *Conclusion.*

This juxtaposition of materials and opinion does not present a picture that is radically new, either of the poem or of its author. But perhaps the analysis may throw into relief some neglected aspects, and thus contribute to that fresh discussion of Robinson and his work that has recently been asked for.[61]

The unevenness of Robinson's poetry, surprising in a writer of his stature, springs from that very motleyness of his gifts which was reflected in his homelessness as an author, and which as a whole had in it more of weakness than of strength. In much of his poetry the conflicting trends worked at cross purposes. He could not wholly embrace the philosophies or adopt the literary tenets of any school. His disillusioned image of man and his sense of cosmic frustration had not yet found their adequate form. The result often was halfway solutions and outright failures. His attempts at traditional styles, classical or romantic, often turned out to be just traditional, without a sustaining conviction, and not really good enough, melodramatic or slightly sentimental, loose in texture and flabby in thought. The lengthy efforts of his later years in the great romantic style emphasized these shortcomings. No more successful were his dry "naturalistic" verse novels, marred by his idea that modernism meant over-complication, involution and intellectual surprise, an endless hide-and-seek around problems of dubious importance, "tragedies at a fourth remove".[62]

He succeeded as a poet when through this "complex blend of rebellion, conservatism, and reaction" (Fussell*) he managed to make the contrasts serve his own literary personality. These successes did not spring from one source any more than his failures did. But it is the aim of this paper to re-emphasize the importance of his classicism

21

in this respect, a classicism derived not only from more recent tradition, but from the originals themselves, and not only as an ideal of form, but as a model expression of Robinson's own sense of life. This subterranean stream of poetic support comes to the surface in his "naturalistic" brief sketches, whenever they succeed. It gives coherence to his medium-sized portraits, from "Eben Flood's Party" to "The Poor Relation", where the poet has not yet lost his grip. The indirect impact is no less palpable in his shorter poems in the great romantic vein, above all "Luke Havergal", where the upsurge of emotion is still rigidly controlled in a cool and impersonal balance. In "Eros Turannos" for once all these elements are consummately fused.

The poem is typical of Robinson to an almost amazing extent. If one reads through his work with "Eros Turannos" in mind, one is struck by the recurrence of the setting and the motifs, the type of his men and women, the character of their problems, and the attitude of the author towards his material. What is hardly paralleled anywhere, is the way in which in this poem his entire world is brought into *one* completely convincing creation. And on one point after another Robinson here comes close to, and probably consciously conforms to, poetic ideals adopted from the ancient sources. Emotion is strong, but severely disciplined. The plot is naturalistically striking, but not trite. Psychology is interesting, but the analysis not intricate beyond the demands of the subject. Idea and structure show an almost flawless unity of purpose: without being a drama the short poem has the impact of one. There is perfect equilibrium between reality, brought out in its essential earthiness, and impersonal and general poetic conclusions.

This formal compactness is a reflection of deeper harmonies. As emphasized by R. P. Adams,* the effect of the poem rests on a rare balance of struggling elements even in its attitude toward life. But this harmony does not smother the contrasts in superficial conciliation. On the contrary, it brings them out clearly, also the shortcomings that were long ago pointed out by the critics.

Doubtless the poem reflects a lack of supporting fellowship and shared standards, an isolation and despair which is typical of Robinson's world, and which the Greeks did not really know before Euripides. *His* chorus often carried no message of comforting verities, and his contemporaries hated him for it. In language and approach the poem has a coldness which stems both from its classical monumentality, its New England tightlippedness, and its modern cynicism towards psychology. These qualities together create an air of distance and abstraction which makes the reader understand why Robinson increasingly longed to "break into" his own work, and also the reasons why he often did not succeed without breaking the poem itself.

There *is* something static and limited in his classical world. The deepest trend in Robinson's anti-romanticism is expressed by Pearce,* in terms which would have appealed to Worringer and Wölfflin contrasting classical art with Gothic, Baroque and Romanticism: he calls Robinson's typical work "an end in itself, not a beginning toward something else". Winters* had a similar deficiency in mind when he complained about the intellectual dryness in Robinson, his distrust of the suggestive power of language, which made Winters write almost reluctantly (and to some extent he even included "Eros Turannos") that you may admire the poem and recognize its greatness, "and yet feel, however fallaciously, that one has more or less exhausted its interest after a few readings".

But these truths about the poem are only true in part. Its limitations are the corollary of its strength. Its classicism is the constraining shell around something else and more.

This does not mean that the poem should be read as a tract about the failure of romantic individualism. Even less should it be interpreted as a reversal to "real", that is, more hopefully romantic ideas about life and death. The power of the poem comes from its supreme expression of Robinson's own somber code, that lonely "optimistic desperation" which is his personal note in literature.[63] Only the tragic acceptance of human fate brings out what little life may have of intrinsic value; in Ibsen's words, "our loss is our single eternal gain". Certainly this is no gospel of edification. But the poet's depth of conviction gives the objective poem an unworded message, and fills it with an emotion which vibrates beneath the hammered surface and is no less deeply felt because it is subdued. Behind the individual fate described sounds that warning against life unlived which fills James' "The Beast in the Jungle" with nameless terror. But there is also a warmth of human compassion, which needs only to be expressed through the symbols, rising monumentally against their background of shallow ouside observation.

The reasons why Robinson apparently did not fully appreciate the importance of the poem (above, p. 289) must remain a matter of conjecture. Perhaps one could not expect the poet himself to grasp that representative inclusiveness that to *us* makes "Eros Turannos" involve

21*

his basic experience of life. This experience is presented in terrifying concentration, in one narrow and immediate, local and special sample of human defeat and degradation. But this time the dramatic flight is not short, as is often the case in Robinson's poems. As "Eros Turannos" grows towards its conclusion the central figure in its frayed and twisted frailty takes on a mythical grandeur. It expresses an eternal verity that reverberates in the modern reader's mind without needing the sustenance of the community of a positive creed. This general significance comes from Robinson's own personality. But it also has a link through inheritance back to those ancient masters who long before him knew how to give general relevance to no less violent discords, and to let even all-too-human tragedy create in the spectator not just tragic and pathetic sentiment, but catharsis.

But here, general agreement is for ever impossible. We are faced with eternal pairs of contrast, between psychological types, ideals of art, and attitudes toward life itself, where arguments take us nowhere. It is wiser to accept what the god has given, as Robinson expressed it on his own behalf, in his own dry voice: "I know that those things I have done are my own (to use the world's nonsense) and that they have to be done in my way".[64]

## BIBLIOGRAPHY

The bibliography lists all references to "Eros Turannos" which the author has run into, however brief, if they express a judgment. Inclusion of the poem in anthologies is not paid attention to. In text and notes references to the bibliography are marked by an asterisk and as a rule without reference to page.

Adams, Léonie, "The Ledoux Collection of E. A. Robinson Manuscripts", *The Library of Congress Quarterly Journal of Current Acquisitions*, VII (1949), No. 1, 12.
Adams, Richard P., "The Failure of E. A. Robinson", *Tulane Studies in English*, XI (1961), 97—151.
Anderson, Charles R., ed., *American Literary Masters*, II (New York, 1965), 511 f.
Arns, K., "E. A. Robinson", *Germanisch-romanische Monatsschrift*, XII (1924), 230.
Barnard, Ellsworth, *E. A. Robinson. A Critical Study* (New York, 1952); see Index + p. 49.
Cestre, Charles, *An Introduction to E. A. Robinson* (New York, 1930), p. 14.
Colum, Padraic, Review of *The Man Against the Sky*, *The Poetry Review of America*, I (1916), 15 f.
Coxe, Louis O., I: "E. A. Robinson: The Lost Tradition", *Sewanee Review*, LXII (1954), 247—266.
— II: *E. A. Robinson*. University of Minnesota Pamphlets on American Writers, 17 (Minneapolis, Minn., 1962), passim, and particularly pp. 18, 22, 24—33. Largely a reprint of I.

Cunliffe, Marcus, *The Literature of the United States*. Pelican Books A 289 (London, 1954), p. 243.

Davis, Charles T., "E. A. Robinson: Paradox and Beyond" (*Abstracts of Papers Read at the Meeting of the American Literature Group [of the MLA] in Washington, D. C., December 26, 1962* (1963, mimeographed).

Eble, Kenneth, "A Forgotten Novel: Kate Chopin's *The Awakening*", *Western Humanities Review*, X (1955—56), 268.

Fairclough, H. R., *The Classics and Our Twentieth-Century Poets*. Stanford University Publications, Language and Literature, II, 2 (Stanford University, 1927), 14—27 passim.

Fussell, Edwin S., *E. A. Robinson. The Literary Background of a Traditional Poet* (Berkeley, Los Angeles, 1954), p. 43.

Gorman, Herbert S., *The Procession of Masks* (Boston, 1923), p. 19.

Grigson, Geoffrey, ed., *The Concise Encyclopædia of Modern World Literature* (London, 1963), p. 374.

Herzberg, Max J., ed., *The Reader's Encyclopedia of American Literature* (London, 1963), p. 966.

Hicks, Granville, *The Great Tradition. An Interpretation of American Literature Since the Civil War*, rev. ed. (New York, 1935), p. 244. Compare Hicks' own comment upon the passage, *Saturday Review*, 1965, April 10, p. 31.

Hoffman, Fr. J., *A College Book of American Literature*, 3. ed., rev. (New York, 1965), p. 872.

Howard, Leon, *Literature and the American Tradition* (New York, 1960), p. 253.

Kreymborg, A., *Our Singing Strength. An Outline of American Poetry (1620—1930)* (New York, 1929), p. 307.

Lerner, Max, *America as a Civilization* (New York, 1957), p. 929.

Lowe, Robert L., "E. A. Robinson to H. Monroe: Some Unpublished Letters", *Modern Philology*, LX (1962—63), 32.

Lowell, Amy, Review of *The Man Against the Sky*, *The New Republic*, VII (1916), 96 f.; reprinted in her *Tendencies in Modern American Poetry* (Boston, New York, 1921), p. 63.

Lüdeke, H., *Geschichte der amerikanischen Literatur* (Bern, 1952), p. 470; 2. neubearbeitete und erweiterte Aufl. (Bern, 1963), p. 375.

Monroe, Harriet, "Robinson as Man and Poet", *Poetry*, XLVI (1935), 155.

Morris, Lloyd, *The Poetry of E. A. Robinson* (New York, 1923), pp. 24 ff.

Neff, Emory, *E. A. Robinson* (New York, 1948; The American Men of Letters Series); see Index.

Pearce, Roy Harvey, *The Continuity of American Poetry* (Princeton, N. J., 1961), pp. 256—269.

Perrine, Laurence, "Robinson's 'Eros Turannos'", *Explicator*, VIII, No. 3 (Dec. 1949), comment 20.

Redman, Ben Ray, *E. A. Robinson*, 2. printing (New York, 1928; Modern American Writers, 6), p. 69.

Roth, Samuel, "A Bookshop Night's Adventure", *The Bookman*, LVIII (1923-24), 142.

Smith, Chard Powers, *Where the Light Falls. A Portrait of E. A. Robinson* (New York, London, 1965); see Index + p. 393.

Stovall, Floyd, "The Optimism Behind Robinson's Tragedies", *American Literature*, X (1938—39), 12.

Straumann, Heinrich, *American Literature in the Twentieth Century* (London, 1951), p. 140; revised ed. (London, 1962), p. 178.

Untermeyer, L., I: Review of *The Man Against the Sky*, *Chicago Evening Post*, 1916, March 10.

— , II: *American Poetry Since 1900* (New York, 1923), p. 57.

— , III: *Modern American Poetry. A Critical Anthology*, 5. rev. ed. (New York, 1936), p. 140.

— , IV: *E. A. Robinson. A Reappraisal* (Washington, D.C., 1963), p. 21.

Williams, Stanley T., *Literary History of the United States*, ed. R. E. Spiller e. a., II (New York, 1948), 1161.

Winters, Yvor, I: "A Cool Master", *Poetry*, XIX (1921—22), 285 f.

— , II: "Religious and Social Ideas in the Didactic Work of E. A. Robinson", *Arizona Quarterly*, I, Spring (1945), 76.

— , III: *E. A. Robinson* (Norfolk, Conn., 1946; The Makers of Modern Literature); see Index.

— , IV: *In Defense of Reason. Primitivism and Decadence: A Study of American Experimental Poetry* (New York, 1947), p. 37.

Zabel, M. D., "Robinson in America", *Poetry*, XLVI (1935), 161; reprinted in his *Literary Opinion in America* (New York, 1937), pp. 397—406.

## NOTES

[1] For the general background, see the bibliographies listed in LHUS, and particularly that of C. B. Hogan (New Haven, Conn., 1936), that is *not* listed there. Abbreviations used in the present article are CP (*Collected Poems*, stereotyped edition), SL (*Selected Letters*, New York, 1940), and US (*Untriangulated Stars*, Cambridge, Mass., 1947). Names marked with an asterisk refer to the Bibliography above.

The text of the poem is reprinted with the permission of the Macmillan Co., which holds the copyright. The manuscript material is used with the permission of the New York Public Library. Photostat material was provided by Springfield Library and Museums Association (Springfield, Mass.) and Illinois State Historical Society (Springfield, Ill.).

In 1962 the poem was set as a subject in examinations in English at the University of Oslo; a number of suggestions from the papers are used in the present article. Cand. philol. Orm Øverland and Per E. Seyersted, M. A., have assisted in looking up material in American libraries. Professors Curtis Dahl, Otto Reinert and Henry H. Wasser have read the article in manuscript, and it owes much to their critical acumen.

[2] SL, p. 78 f.; letter to Harriet Monroe January 14, 1913, Lowe,* p. 32. The poem was not written in the summer, as stated by Neff,* p. 168, and repeated by Smith,* p. 240.

[3] C. P. Smith,* passim, particularly pp. 64, 88 ff., 198, 200, 204, 228, 240.

[4] Compare similar inscriptions of "First Draft" in manuscripts for the same volume in the Library of Congress (L. Adams,* 10).

[5] Facsimile in *Poetry*, CI (1962), 147.

[6] SL, p. 104.

[7] *Poems*. Selected, with a Preface by B. Perry (New York, 1931), Preface. C. P. Smith,* pp. 339 f.

[8] Lowe,* pp. 32—34.

[9] Granville Hicks.* The view is much more positive in V. F. Calverton, *The Liberation of American Literature* (New York, 1932), pp. 415 f.

[10] J. L. French, quoted from Neff,* p. 144.

[11] J. Kilmer, "A Classic Poet", *New York Times Book Review*, 1912, Sept. 8, p. 487; Robinson's thank-you-letter in L. Untermeyer, *IV, p. 34.

[12] Carl van Doren in *The Nation*, CXIII, (1921), 570 f., reprinted in his *A Roving Critic* (New York, 1923), p. 236; Conrad Aiken in *The Freeman*, IV, No. 80 (Sept. 21, 1921), 44; John Drinkwater in *Yale Review*, XI (1922), 471, reprinted in his *The Muse in Council* (Boston, 1925); Fairclough* (1927 — "something Sophoclean"); L. Beebe, *Aspects of the Poetry of E. A. Robinson* (Cambridge, Mass., 1928), pp. 24 f., 30–32; C. Cestre,* p. 5; Fussell* (1954); Ch. R. Anderson* (Greek tragedy).

[13] H. C. Robbins, "The Classicism of E. A. Robinson", *The Congregational Quarterly*, XIV (London, 1936), 166—171.

[14] H. W. Wells, *New Poets from Old* (New York, 1940), pp. 316—319.

[15] Allen Tate, "Again, O Ye Laurels", *The New Republic*, LXXVI (1933), 312 f., reprinted in his *Reactionary Essays on Poetry and Ideas* (New York, 1936), pp. 193–201; quoted here from his *Collected Essays* (Denver, 1959), pp. 358–364; compare his *Sixty American Poets, 1896–1944*, rev. ed. (Washington, D.C., 1954), p. 107. The second quotation from a letter to the author of the present article, July 19, 1965.

[16] Barnard,* p. 204.

[17] SL, p. 85.

[18] *The Nation and the Athenaeum*, XXXII (1922–23), 286 f.

[19] US, p. 282; SL, p. 13.

[20] SL, p. 90.

[21] M. D. Luhan, *Movers and Shakers* (New York, 1936), p. 138; *Saturday Review*, April 10, 1965, p. 33.

[22] SL, p. 129 (1922).

[23] Fussell,* pp. 137 f.; for the rest, compare his entire chapter 5.

[24] US, p. 141.

[25] Fussell,* p. 143. Compare Robinson's words from 1902 about getting "some Greek lymph" into his system, Neff,* p. 113.

[26] See Robinson's letters, passim; Fussell,* p. 139; and *New England Quarterly*, XVII (1944), 604 f. Robinson (ibid.) in 1930 called the translation "juvenile experiments" and ordered that it should never be printed.

[27] Neff,* p. 56. Compare ibid., p. 132 f.: "With the world so beautiful and life itself so hideous, I don't wonder the closing choruses of the Greek tragedies were all alike" (1903).

[28] Fussell,* p. 57 and 63. That Robinson saw life "much as Euripides saw life", was also pointed out by A. E. Romig, "Tilbury Town and Camelot", *The University of Colorado Studies*, XIX (1931–32), 307.

[29] Euripides in the lost play *Melanippe* (quoted in Plutarch, *Moralia*); *The Trojan Women*, 884–886; *Hecuba*, 488–491; Robinson's letter (from 1891): US, p. 24; his sonnet "Kosmos" (not in CP) quoted from Barnard,* p. 196.

[30] *Hippolytos*, 1102–1110; *The Women of Troy*, 989.

[31] C. P. Smith,* passim; compare note 3 above.

[32] Neff* and Perrine* refer in general terms to the Greek idea of "tragic madness", but only with reference to a modern source on the *Allegory of Love*. For details about Robinson's translation of *Antigone*, see his letters passim; in *Captain Craig* (CP, pp. 117 f., 140) he quotes the chorus in *Antigone*, 332 ff. Robinson's reference

(US, p. 232) to a *hyporchema* in Antigone must build on a misunderstanding of the Greek word; there is
no such thing in the play.

[33] For the Latin and Greek material, see
I. B. Carter's and C. F. H. Bruch-
mann's books on *Epitheta deorum*
(Lips., 1902 and 1893), and Pauly-
Wissowa's *Real-Encyclopädie* s.v. Eros.
Robinson refers to Hippolyt as a
figure in one of his earliest published
letters (SL, p. 4, 1890).

[34] G. M. A. Grube, *The Drama of Euripides* (London, 1941), p. 197.

[35] SL, p. 98 (1916); Fussell,* p. 37
(1931). In the draft version Robinson
uses the word "master", probably
about Eros. That's also the Murray
translation of *Eros tyrannos* ("Master
of Men").

[36] Euripides, *The Plays*, transl. G. Murray, I (London, 1919), pp. 4 (*Hipp.*
26 ff.), 23 (391 ff.); 25 (438 ff.), 26 f.
(476 f.), 29 f. (525 ff.); 65 (1268 ff.).
As mentioned above, the first edition
of Murray's version of *Hippolytos* was
published in 1911.

[37] Euripides, ibid., pp. 24 (409 ff.), 39
(733 ff.), 26 (451 ff.).

[38] C. Aiken, l.c.

[39] See for Robinson's interest in Ibsen,
for instance, Neff,* p. 58 (from the
1890's), Coxe, *II, p. 19 (from around
1914), SL, p. 82 (quotation from
*Hedda Gabler* 1914), and E. W. Bates,
*E. A. Robinson and his Manuscripts*
(Colby College Monographs, No. 11;
Waterville, Maine, 1944), p. 30 (from
the late 1920's); generally, Fussell,*
pp. 130–133. For Ibsen and Euripides,
see H. Steiger, "Euripides, ein antiker
Ibsen?", *Philologus*, LXXX (1925),
113–135, and his book *Euripides* (Das
Erbe der Alten, 5; Leipzig, 1912).

[40] C. Aiken, l. c.

[41] Fussell,* p. 43, about Hawthorne and
James; used by Fussell about "Eros
Turannos".

[42] See Amy Lowell (*Tendencies in Modern
American Poetry*),* pp. 11 ff., and R. P.
Tristram Coffin, *New Poetry of New
England: Frost and Robinson* (Balti-
more, 1938), pp. 33, 77 et. al. Amy
Lowell writes that "I know of no
place in America so English in atmosphere as Gardiner". The Robinson family lived in a relatively modest
surburban villa, the family of the poet's
love Emma Shepherd in an adjoining
village in "an older, larger and finer
house. . . . a Greek revival mansion
looking down its terraces through trees
to the great river" (Smith*, p. 88,
with a picture of the Robinson home).
The setting in the poem is, of course,
even more grand.

[43] "Seeker" was probably changed in
order to avoid an unintended pun
with "found".

[44] Compare "beguiled and foiled" (CP,
p. 4). Coxe (*I, p. 255) suggests that
the word may have an undertone of
irony: she is not the only one to be
misled.

[45] Compare similar expressions in CP:
"a music ... that assuages and
redeems" (p. 44), "With no illusion
to assuage / The lonely changelessness
of dying" (p. 47), "such balm /
Assuaged him only for another
onslaught" (p. 981).

[46] Compare his similar alteration of the
punctuation in successive printings
of "Luke Havergal" in order to secure
exact timing (Neff,* p. 72).

[47] When Winters (*III, p. 147 f.) writes
about "a slightly unneccessary sub-
division and restatement of matter,
a slight lack of concentration" in
Robinson, and finds traces of it even
in "Eros Turannos", it is difficult
to follow him.

[48] *The Bookman*, LXXV (1932), 676.

[49] R. P. Adams* also finds that the
rhyme scheme formally divides the
poem into two equal parts in accor-

dance with its general plan, tying stanzas 2, 3, 5, and 6 slightly together. It is difficult to discover any such link.

[50] Charles T. Davis, "Image Patterns in the Poetry of E. A. Robinson", *College English*, XXII (1960–61), 383.

[51] Charles T. Davis, op. cit., 385 f.

[52] Several critics interpret other details inaccurately, or without sufficient attention to the time sequence. Fairclough* maintains that the heroine's "love for her husband fades away through fear", Cestre* that "an ill-mated woman, full of resentment for the missed happiness, reflects that it will be a lesser evil for her to nurse the feeble gleam of affection she still feels, than moodily to break off the marriage tie", Neff* that she "holds to her Judas husband out of pride and out of fear of lonely old age." Lüdeke* even calls the couple "ein Paar, das sich liebt, aber nicht mehr jung ist". Barnard* criticizes the ideas of Cestre and Neff, but himself makes the surprising statement that in keeping with Robinson's optimism "the cheated partner in "Eros Turannos"... may conceivably form a new attachment to a more worthy person".

[53] Compare for the imagery the third chorus in Sophocles' *Antigone* (transl. Lewis Campbell, *The Seven Plays in English Verse*, New ed., rev., London, 1909, p. 20): "As when the briny surge / That Thrace-born tempests urge / (The big wave ever gathering more and more) / Runs o'er the darkness of the deep, / And with far-reaching sweep / Uprolls the storm-heap'd tangle on the shore, / While cliff to beaten cliff resounds with sullen roar".

[54] Compare Barnard,* p. 173: "the Town's opinion is not merely the shadow that makes the truth shine brighter; we know how the popular mind works, and therefore its judg-ment of a person gives us, when we have made the proper allowances, a measure of positive insight into that person's character".

[55] Schiller in the poem "Shakespeare's Schatten".

[56] Barnard,* p. 71. — The image "tide" was replaced by "waves" in the final version, making the same word recur that is used earlier in the poem. For the tree image, compare in a Robinson poem from the same period: "Like once-remembered mighty trees go down / To ruin" and no trace can now be found of them (CP, p. 64), and similarly at the end of "Tasker Norcross": "I knew him — as a man may know a tree — / For twenty years" (CP, p. 508).

The comparison with Emma Bovary might suggest that the poem ends in suicide; Coxe (*II, p. 22) uses the word "destruction". This conclusion would, however, break the line of the poem. The heroine is no psychological riddle like Richard Cory; and the poet's careful analysis definitely points toward the resigned acceptance of what the god has taken and given.

[57] Untermeyer (*IV, 1963) finds that the final verse of the poem is an example of Robinson's falling "so much in love with the suggestion of a phrase that he let it run into mere sonority, a rich but sometimes hollow rhetoric recalling Swinburne". This statement can hardly be said to take into account the consistent rise of the poem from its own foundations, as analyzed above. Moreover, Untermeyer's view in the matter has been vacillating. Earlier (*III, 1936) he praised the same conclusion of the poem (quoted above, p. 320), only adding that it "might have been composed by a more controlled Swinburne".

[58] Compare SL, p. 93 (1916), and several instances pointed out by Coxe.*

[59] Romig, l. c.

[60] Letter to the author of this article July 19, 1965 (quoted by permission). Léonie Adams* may have a similar idea in mind when to the vindication and "direct exfoliation" of passion in *Tristram* she prefers "the mystery obliquely arrived at in the last stanza of "Eros Turannos" and there fixed in such solid irony of context and perspective".

[61] Davis.*

[62] L. Bogan, *Poetry*, XXXVII (1930–31), 220.

[63] US, p. 246.

[64] SL, p. 64.

# THE NEW DEAL AND AMERICAN LITERATURE

## By Henry H. Wasser

Far from having the narrow, violent thrust of an ideology or a systematic philosophy, the New Deal was concerned with restoring democratic vistas and solving crises pragmatically. We can, therefore, discover a literary spokesman for this political change, but not a literary ideologue.

Archibald MacLeish in his "Preface to an American Manifesto" (1934) is a leading candidate for this rôle of spokesman. He sought to account for the hold Roosevelt the pragmatist had upon the minds of Americans; to him Roosevelt represented hope that the conclusions of rigid economic laws, whether understood by bankers or by revolutionaries, would not obtain in American society. Whether Roosevelt would succeed in breaking America out of the iron cage of economic necessity was not so important as the attempt, for "it is only to the free, inventive gestures of the human soul that men wholly and believingly respond. They will, in a crisis, rise against arrogance. They may for a time fight from hatred. But only to hope will they give themselves entirely. And only writers writing out of hope can lead them to anything more permanent than the barricades."[1]

MacLeish epitomized his views, which he thought consistent with these of the New Deal, by writing that in Marxist theory economics comes first; in fascist practice politics comes first; and in democratic theory man comes first. Later MacLeish was to argue that the enormous potential strength of democracy had not been fully realized and that in 1939 it could only be realized by aggressive pro-democratic action. Urging America's help for the Allies and later, entrance into World War II, he declared that the promises of America remain for those who reach for them: "The promises are theirs who take them."[2]

While the poet MacLeish busied himself with New Deal manifestoes which were shrill and oversimplified, the novelist James T. Farrell

studied the cultural climate of the New Deal program. Farrell opened
his essay, not sufficiently esteemed by critics and scholars, by quoting
President Roosevelt: "Always the heart and soul of our country will
be the heart and soul of the common man — men and women — who
have never ceased to love their families, their homes, and their country... the faith of America is the faith of the common man."[3] Apparently accepting this credo, Farrell contended that unfortunately its
cultural climate produced a pseudo-populist literature of the common
man, exemplified by many motion pictures and radio plays of the time.
He would have preferred to relate the literature of the New Deal to
the authentic tradition of populism and progressivism, just as ultimately the New Deal could be related to that of genuine populism
and progressivism. The weakness of the neo-populist art and literature
was that it emphasized the concept of Americanism as a means of
unifying all races, creeds, and classes. This goal was impossible to
realize, and the literature of the concept became mere romanticizing.
Instead of penetratingly describing class differences and pointing out
the conditions of life that frustrate the boy and girl of plebeian origin
in struggling for success and growth, as Dreiser had done, this literature
sentimentalized the theme that the common man is human and that
all men are the common man.

However, social programs do not create a Dreiser, and what was
significant was that for the first time and partly under the influence
of the New Deal, the lower classes in the 1930's were central figures
in American fiction. The racial background of the writers themselves
changed; the orphan asylum, the streets of the city, poolrooms, lower
class homes and family life, the backward sections of America such
as parts of Georgia and the decaying sections of New England were
brought into the novel and the short story from the inside, not the
outside. First and second generation Americans of different racial
and national backgrounds became major characters in American
fiction. Social snobbery, so often a theme of literature, was revealed
in the lower classes as ugly racial prejudice. Tension and violence
were inherent in this fiction because they were the modes by which
the lower classes express their frustration.

This "bottom dog" literature (a term Farrell probably derives from
Edward Dahlberg's 1930 novel *Bottom Dogs*) related the quality of
life among "one third of the nation." While depicting human misery,
it wrote of the plebeian classes on a more human level. Conditions of
life among the lower classes in New Deal America were described, and

characters were made aware of their dilemma by authors writing from within, not from without. Social problems were presented with an almost total sense of the immediacy of life. To be sure, one may note that the "bottom dog" literature of the Thirties dealt with those major crises and aspects of life that in the Sixties are the main concern of sociologists, social workers, psychiatrists, and criminologists. And further, as Farrell commented, ". . . it is easy to confuse such writings with neo-populist works on the 'common man' that sentimentalize poverty and point up an editorialized national unity and a verbally formalized affirmation of democracy that exudes snobbery . . ."[4] But to make men better, a prime objective of the literature of the New Deal period, one must first tell them what they are really like, as did the authentic populist literature of the time. Pseudo-populist literature falsely idealized the common man and relied for conviction on the author's editorializing.

Among the works growing out of the New Deal cultural environment which presented life in America on the level of newspaper editorials, oversimplifying character and situation, Farrell placed Steinbeck's enormously successful *The Grapes of Wrath*. One can accept Farrell's unstated implication that his own *Studs Lonigan* bridges the gap between documentation and artistic excellence, becoming an authentic "populist" work, and yet one can still with good reason hold the view that Steinbeck's novel was part of the main drive of American literature during the 1930's in which the mood of social evangelism among writers and critics was strong. An intimate sense of the way in which economic and social forces worked together to bring tragedy to innocent people was demonstrated in *The Grapes of Wrath*. Sympathizing deeply with his characters Steinbeck was nevertheless quite willing to reveal them in all their ignorance, their casual carnality, and their inability to understand their own plight. Despite the depressed conditions of life, he conveyed an awareness of the promise of America, its exciting challenge to the artist and sociologist alike. He endeavored to arouse an indifferent public by showing the worst in poverty and cruelty that America had tolerated, and to stimulate a mood of inquiry into the background and traditions of a nation which could get itself into a depression.

Many of the once-indifferent public came to believe that the New Deal had restored the faith of the American people in their capacity to control their own destiny, in their form of government, and in their future. In his novel Steinbeck has his Joads represent this faith in life.

They had the life-instinct, the will to live, the vital persistence of the common people. Ma said, "Easy. You got to have patience. Why, Tom — us people will go on livin' when all of them people is gone. Why, Tom, we're the people that live. They ain't gonna wipe us out. Why we're the people — we go on."[5]

*The Grapes of Wrath* reminded Americans that since their economic system involved not a few instances of injustice and hardship, it needed constant control and adjustment by the conscience and authority of the people. Believing that the community was responsible for the man without work, home, or food, Steinbeck held that what cannot be cured by individual effort must be met by collective measures, the attitude also of the New Deal. People, he thought, must be made aware of the social problems which remain to be solved within the system which had been beneficial to most.

This was also the tone of Carl Sandburg in *The People, Yes*, in which the poet asserts the persistence and the final triumph of the plain people, avowing that while the "tycoons, big shots and dictators" loom momentarily against the sky, the people, although often baffled and cheated, remain always the builders of the earth and the final source of wisdom.[6]

To a greater extent than poetry, however, the theatre is often a direct and naked expression of a *Zeitgeist*. Certainly the plays of the Thirties, unlike those of the Twenties, emphasized the social, economic, and political background of individual psychologies. Also, in accord with another emphasis of the New Deal, the attitude of such dramatists as S. N. Behrman, Robert Sherwood, and Clifford Odets was more moral than political. Even in Odets' *Awake and Sing* Jacob says to Ralph, "Make your life something good ... life shouldn't be printed on dollar bills."[7]

The theatre rediscovered an America beyond its own narrow world, an America which covered the whole continent and which went back into history. It began to echo the general awakening interest in the American heritage so characteristic of President Roosevelt and the New Deal. Paul Green's *The Lost Colony* (1937) was an example of inquiry into the earliest beginnings of the nation. The broader horizons of the New Deal landscape were reflected in Steinbeck's play *Of Mice and Men* (1937). Although its themes are loneliness and hunger for brotherhood, it observes the state of the nation broadly conceived, by concentrating on the unemployed of the farm lands and the itinerant and ranch workers, and by its allusions to bus and truck drivers who travel throughout the country. Plays were set in the South, Southwest, Midwest, and West as well as in the East. Along with the widely ranging settings came the suggestion that America's under-privileged would never reach the home they desired until they gained greater consciousness of themselves and their society, as instanced in the theme of Steinbeck's play. The theatre of the Thirties even attempted to make the stage an instrument of public education through a passionate involvement with the national scene. In *Both Your Houses* (1933) Maxwell Anderson uses as his major conflict the collision be-tween idealism and hardboiled politics behind the scenes of the New Deal.

Some of the passions and interests of the New Deal may have been reflected in the theatre, but, perhaps more important, a change of direction, of perspective, in literature occurred. In the Thirties America replaced Europe as the object of the affections of American writers. Thomas Wolfe writes in his last letter to Foxhall Edwards in *You Can't Go Home Again*: "... I think that the true discovery of America is before us. I think the true fulfillment of our spirit, of our people, of our mighty and immortal land is yet to come. I think the true discovery of our democracy is still before us."[8]

This national self-discovery gave birth to a new kind of literature called by some a sub-literature, by others a preparation for literature, whose subject matter was the American scene and whose drive was to know America in its details and to master its essence. Reacting against the skepticism and frivolity of the Twenties, this literature created a new folklore out of the newly found past, documented with extraordinary self-scrutiny the underprivileged in American life, and wrote W. P. A. guides to states and roads. It started by reporting the agonies and humiliations of the depression and ended by confidently and buoyantly reporting on the national heritage.

In the Thirties W. P. A. writers, documentary reporters, folklorists, cameramen, biographers and historians assembled a great number of facts on life in America. Perhaps this literature of fact grew out of a realization that American writing previously had rarely confronted, in direct fashion, the country itself. Since American society did not seem to know its own fundamental impulses and motives, writers had to discover and then to impart the details. Consequently they did not usually attempt art or imaginative truth, but explored and described, often with great brilliance and heightened sensibility. Even the impressionistic criticism of Van Wyck Brooks in the *Flowering of New England* was a collection of data concerning a flourishing period of American literary history, a rediscovery of American national literary inheritance, rather than an attempt to bring the art of criticism to New England writers.

In addition to being inspired by the New Deal, this documentary literature was like the New Deal in opening many new fields of investigation. Just as the New Deal demonstrated the various adjustments of crisis government, it approached in different ways the problem of the survival of democracy. Also lacking centrality of direction and belief, but marking off all America for its subject, it became a seismograph of the social tremors of the period. In Alfred Kazin's phrase, this was a crisis literature in which the sense of search, of imminent discovery, was more exciting than the idea of the ends toward which it moved.

This intimate responsiveness to social currents was best phrased in H. G. Wells' famous characterization of Franklin Delano Roosevelt as "... a ganglion for reception, expression, transmission, combination and realization."[9] Wells' words can be applied generally to an era that found perhaps its most apt expression in a literature of responsive social description. The pattern of development of this literature in the years of the New Deal seemed to begin with national self-scrutiny, continue its design in national consciousness, and finish its web in national self-celebration. Such writings as Carl Sandburg's *Abraham Lincoln*, Carl Van Doren's *Benjamin Franklin*, Henry Commager's *Theodore Parker*, Allan Nevins' *John D. Rockefeller* and John Dos Passos' *The Ground We stand On* well illustrate the new nationalism.

The contours of New Deal America, people more than places, are clearly seen in those works synthesizing text and photograph like Erskine Caldwell and Margaret Bourke-White's *Say, Is This the U.S.A.?* and *You Have Seen Their Faces*, and especially in that remarkable book, James Agee and Walker Evans' *Let Us Now Praise Famous Men* (1941). Raised to an art, the documentary films as developed particularly by Pare Lorentz in the *Plow That Broke the Plains* (1936) — the disintegration of the wheat country by annual droughts — and *The River* (1938) — the land impoverished as a result of erosion caused by Missisippi Valley floods — are incisive and dramatic comments on New Deal measures for preventing further damage, and for rehabilitating the land.

Furnishing more than philosophical underpinning, the New Deal subsidized documentary literature and pseudo-populist writing. At one time employing over 6,000 writers and researchers, the Federal Writers Project had on its roster such authors as Conrad Aiken, Vardis Fisher, Maxwell Bodenheim, Richard Wright, and John Steinbeck. The Federal Theatre Project (1935—39) introduced the technical innovation of the "living newspaper" — a blend of radio-play methods and the movie newsreel. In *Triple A Plowed Under* it showed the farmers' plight; in *Power* it dramatized the search for cheap utilities and the discovery of the TVA — ultimately the enduring symbol of the New Deal; in *One Third of a Nation* it highlighted the slum problem; and in *It Can't Happen Here* it turned into a play Sinclair Lewis' novel warning of the perils to New Deal America. American subjects in music and art were also rediscovered under New Deal subsidy.

The newly awakened self-assertion of the American people can be detected in H. L. Mencken's monumental *The American Language*. Edmund Wilson in his review of the 1936 edition noted that ". . . one is made to feel throughout *The American Language* the movement and pressure of the American people, vindicating their independence, filling out their enormous country, attracting and consolidating with themselves the peoples of older nations, inseminating that older world itself with their habits of thought and their speech."[10]

Although Mencken's contributions to the *American Mercury* at the time were often scornful of the New Deal economic and political projects, his scholarly work asserting the independence and perhaps even the triumph of the American language over traditional literary English reflected the new national self-confidence developed by the New Deal. In the first edition in arguing for American, Mencken wrote mainly in orthodox British English, but in later editions he succeeded in adapting the American idiom to the requirements of philological exposition. This Whitmanesque love of the spoken word also lay behind the colloquial style of Dos Passos in *U.S.A.* (1938). Like Whitman Dos Passos tried to include all America in his work. In his trilogy he, as did the New Deal, looked for the return of health to his sick country, not to the dictatorship of the proletariat but to a restoration of the democratic vista and to a rebuilding of a democratic society. In a Camera Eye sequence the "I" ponders what leverage "might bring back (I too Walt Whitman) our storybook democracy."[11]

Thus the impact of the New Deal on the writer was both direct and diffuse. Direct in that the exposure of the roots of the American heritage and the reawakening of national self-confidence by the New Deal inspired an extraordinarily rich documentary literature. Diffuse in that its influence on artistic literature was far more intangible. Still it may be discerned in a deepening of the authentically populist aspect of literature in such writers as Farrell, Dos Passos, and Steinbeck, in an increasing emphasis on the American scene as the primary subject for literary art, and in a greater inside concern for the "bottom dog" in fiction of power.

## NOTES

[1] Archibald MacLeish, "Preface to an American Manifesto" (1934), *A Time to Speak* (Boston, 1941), p. 24.

[2] Archibald MacLeish, "America Was Promises", *Collected Poems 1917—1952* (Boston, 1952), p. 340.

[3] James T. Farrell, "Social Themes in American Realism", *Literature and Morality* (New York, 1947), p. 16.

[4] Ibid. p. 24.

[5] John Steinbeck, *The Grapes of Wrath* (New York, 1939), p. 383.

[6] Carl Sandburg, *The People, Yes* (New York, 1936), p. 55.

[7] Clifford Odets, "Awake and Sing", *Three Plays* (New York, 1935), p. 33.

[8] Thomas Wolfe, *You Can't Go Home Again* (New York, 1940), p. 741.

[9] Quoted in Alfred Kazin, *On Native Grounds* (New York, 1956), p. 384.

[10] Edmund Wilson, *The Shores of Light* (New York, 1952), p. 631.

[11] John Dos Passos, "The Big Money", *U.S.A.* (New York, 1942), p. 150.

# ABOUT THE AUTHORS

EINAR BOYESEN, b. 1888. Educated at Oslo (dr. philos.). Lektor and Rektor at secondary schools and teachers' colleges; 1938—58 Permanent Undersecretary to the Norwegian Ministry of Education. Active in many Government commissions and educational organizations, Norwegian and international. Published numerous articles and books on Education and History, among others the biography of *Hartvig Nissen* (2 vols., 1947—48) and the history of *J. W. Cappelen Publishing House* (1953).

JOHANNES KJØRVEN, b. 1934. Educated at Bowdoin and Oslo (cand. philol.). British Council Fellow 1964. Since 1960 Lektor at the Teachers' College and the University College, Trondheim.

OTTO REINERT, b. 1923. Educated at Oslo and Yale (Ph. D.). Taught at Wheaton College and the University of Washington, Seattle, where he is now Associate Professor; 1961—64 Lektor at the University of Oslo. Has published articles on Finn Carling, Dryden, Hemingway, drama and dramatists (Ibsen, Shaw, Wilde), three anthologies (*Working with Prose*, 1959, *Drama*, 1961 and 1964, *Modern Drama*, 1962 and 1966), and a translation with introduction of Ibsen's *Hedda Gabler* (1962). Forthcoming is a critical edition of J. Addison's poems.

PER E. SEYERSTED, b. 1921. In business until 1956. Educated at the universities of Besançon, Boston, California (Berkeley), and Harvard (M. A.). ACLS Fellow 1964—66. Taught at the University of Oslo. Has published articles on Bjørnstjerne Bjørnson, H. H. Boyesen, Kate Chopin, W. D. Howells, A. L. Kielland, and Turgenev. Is finishing a biography of Kate Chopin and an anthology of her work.

SIGMUND SKARD, b. 1903. Educated at the Sorbonne and Oslo (dr. philos.), where he taught Comparative Literature 1933—1938. In American Government service in Washington, D.C. 1941—45; since 1946 Professor of American Literature at Oslo. Lectured at many European and American universities. Published in Norwegian numerous articles (some of which are collected in *Dåd og dikt*, 1963), *Amerikanske problem* (1949), volumes of poetry, and translations, incl. the Goliards, Dante, Petrarch, and an anthology of American poetry in own translation (1960); in English i.a. *The Voice of Norway* (with Halvdan Koht, 1944), *The Use of Color in Literature* (1946), *American Studies in Europe* (2 vols., 1958) and *The American Myth and the European Mind* (1960).

PETTER CHRISTIAN STEENSTRUP, b. 1920. Educated at Oslo (cand. philol.). Since 1952 Lektor at the secondary school of Tønsberg.

PER SVEINO, b. 1925. Educated at Oslo (cand. philol.). Fulbright—Smith/Mundt Fellow at Harvard 1952—53, Storm Fellow at the Sorbonne 1954. Lektor at secondary schools in Trondheim and Halden, since 1956 in Ålesund. Is working on a book on Orestes Brownson.

HENRY H. WASSER, b. 1919. Educated at Ohio State University and Columbia (Ph. D.). Taught at George Washington University, University of Akron, New York University and at the City College, City University of New York where he has been Associate Professor since 1961. Fulbright Visiting Professor at the University of Salonika, Greece (1955—56) and the University of Oslo (1962—64). Published articles on Henry Adams, W. Blake, A. de Tocqueville, the methods of American Studies, contemporary American intellectual history, and a book on *The Scientific Thought of Henry Adams* (1956).

ORM ØVERLAND, b. 1935. Educated at Yale and Oslo (cand. philol.). Research Assistant in Oslo 1962—63, ASF Fellow 1963—64, ACLS Fellow 1965—66, and since 1966 Universitetsstipendiat (Assistant Professor) at Oslo. Taught at Texas Southern University. Published articles on Louis I. Kahn and Ezra Pound. Is working on a book on J. F. Cooper: *The Prairie*.

## PUBLICATIONS OF
## THE AMERICAN INSTITUTE
### UNIVERSITY OF OSLO

*Americana Norvegica. Norwegian Contributions to American Studies.*
Vol. I. Editors: Sigmund Skard and Henry H. Wasser. (1966.) 340 pp.

Einar Haugen: *The Norwegian Language in America. A Study in Bilingual Behavior.* (1953.) Out of print.
Vol. I: The Bilingual Community. XIV, 317 pp.
Vol. II: The American Dialects of Norwegian. VII, 377 pp.

Halvdan Koht: *The American Spirit in Europe. A Survey of Transatlantic Influences.* (1949.) IX, 289 pp. Out of print.

Sigmund Skard: *American Studies in Europe. Their History and Present Organization.* (1958.)
Vol. I: The General Background, The United Kingdom, France, and Germany. Pp. 1–358.
Vol. II: The Smaller Western Countries, The Scandinavian Countries, The Mediterranean Nations, Eastern Europe, International Organization, and Conclusion. Pp. 359–736.

## UNIVERSITY OF PENNSYLVANIA PRESS
### PHILADELPHIA, PA.